DAVID BUSCH'S
CANON® EOS® 7D

GUIDE TO DIGITAL SLR PHOTOGRAPHY

David D. Busch

Course Technology PTR

A part of Cengage Learning

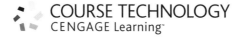

COURSE TECHNOLOGY
CENGAGE Learning™

Australia, Brazil, Japan, Korea, Mexico, Singapore, Spain, United Kingdom, United States

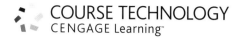

COURSE TECHNOLOGY
CENGAGE Learning™

David Busch's Canon® EOS® 7D Guide to Digital SLR Photography
David D. Busch

Publisher and General Manager, Course Technology PTR:
Stacy L. Hiquet

Associate Director of Marketing:
Sarah Panella

Manager of Editorial Services:
Heather Talbot

Marketing Manager:
Jordan Castellani

Executive Editor:
Kevin Harreld

Project Editor:
Jenny Davidson

Technical Reviewer:
Michael D. Sullivan

Interior Layout Tech:
Bill Hartman

Cover Designer:
Mike Tanamachi

Indexer:
Katherine Stimson

Proofreader:
Sandi Wilson

For product information and technology assistance, contact us at
Cengage Learning Customer & Sales Support, 1-800-354-9706.

For permission to use material from this text or product,
submit all requests online at **cengage.com/permissions**.
Further permissions questions can be e-mailed to
permissionrequest@cengage.com.

Canon and EOS are registered trademarks of Canon Inc. in the United States and other countries.

All other trademarks are the property of their respective owners.

All images © David D. Busch unless otherwise noted.

Library of Congress Control Number: 2009942400

ISBN-13: 978-1-4354-5691-4

ISBN-10: 1-4354-5691-2

Course Technology, a part of Cengage Learning
20 Channel Center Street
Boston, MA 02210
USA

Cengage Learning is a leading provider of customized learning solutions with office locations around the globe, including Singapore, the United Kingdom, Australia, Mexico, Brazil, and Japan. Locate your local office at: **international.cengage.com/region**.

Cengage Learning products are represented in Canada by Nelson Education, Ltd.

For your lifelong learning solutions, visit **courseptr.com**.

Visit our corporate Web site at **cengage.com**.

Printed in the United States of America
2 3 4 5 6 7 12 11 10

Acknowledgments

Once again thanks to the folks at Course Technology PTR, who have pioneered publishing digital imaging books in full color at a price anyone can afford. Special thanks to executive editor Kevin Harreld, who always gives me the freedom to let my imagination run free with a topic, as well as my veteran production team including project editor Jenny Davidson and technical editor Mike Sullivan. Also thanks to Bill Hartman, layout; Katherine Stimson, indexing; Sandi Wilson, proofreading; Mike Tanamachi, cover design; and my agent, Carole Jelen, who has the amazing ability to keep both publishers and authors happy. I'd also like to thank the Continent of Europe, without which this book would have a lot of blank spaces where illustrations are supposed to go.

Special thanks go to my associate, photographer and author Dan Simon, who helped me wend through the mysteries of the EOS 7D's new wireless capabilities. Dan did all the groundwork and testing, then crafted a chapter that made using this complex feature seem simple.

About the Author

With more than a million books in print, **David D. Busch** is one of the bestselling authors of books on digital photography and imaging technology, and the originator of popular series like *David Busch's Pro Secrets* and *David Busch's Quick Snap Guides.* He has written seven hugely successful guidebooks for Canon digital SLR models, including the all-time #1 bestseller for the Canon EOS 40D, additional user guides for other camera models, as well as many popular books devoted to dSLRs, including *Mastering Digital SLR Photography, Second Edition* and *Digital SLR Pro Secrets.* As a roving photojournalist for more than 20 years, he illustrated his books, magazine articles, and newspaper reports with award-winning images. He's operated his own commercial studio, suffocated in formal dress while shooting weddings-for-hire, and shot sports for a daily newspaper and upstate New York college. His photos and articles have been published in *Popular Photography & Imaging, The Rangefinder, The Professional Photographer,* and hundreds of other publications. He's also reviewed dozens of digital cameras for CNet and *Computer Shopper.*

When About.com named its top five books on Beginning Digital Photography, debuting at the #1 and #2 slots were Busch's *Digital Photography All-In-One Desk Reference for Dummies* and *Mastering Digital Photography.* During the past year, he's had as many as five of his books listed in the Top 20 of Amazon.com's Digital Photography Bestseller list—simultaneously! Busch's 100-plus other books published since 1983 include bestsellers like *David Busch's Quick Snap Guide to Using Digital SLR Lenses.* His advice has been featured on National Public Radio's *All Tech Considered.*

Busch is a member of the Cleveland Photographic Society (www.clevelandphoto.org), which has operated continuously since 1887.

Visit his website at http://www.dslrguides.com/blog.

Contents

PART I
GETTING STARTED WITH YOUR CANON EOS 7D

Chapter 1
Canon EOS 7D: Thinking Outside of the Box   5

Chapter 2
Canon EOS 7D Quick Start   27

Chapter 3
Canon EOS 7D Roadmap 43

PART II
BEYOND THE BASICS

Chapter 4
Understanding Exposure 71

Chapter 5
Mastering the Mysteries of Autofocus 107

Chapter 6
Advanced Shooting, Live View, and Movies 135

PART III
ADVANCED TOOLS

Chapter 7
Customizing with the Shooting and
Playback Menus   171

Chapter 8
Customizing with Set-up, Custom Functions, and My Menus 227

Chapter 9
Working with Lenses   275

Chapter 10
Working with Light   307

Chapter 11
Using the EOS 7D's Wireless Flash Controller   353

PART IV
ENHANCING YOUR EXPERIENCE

Chapter 12
Downloading, Editing, and Printing Your Images   385

Chapter 13
Canon EOS 7D: Troubleshooting and Prevention   407

Glossary   433

Index   445

Preface

You don't want good pictures from your new Canon EOS 7D—you demand *outstanding* photos. After all, the 7D is the most advanced mid-level camera that Canon has ever introduced. It boasts an astounding 18 megapixels of resolution, blazing fast automatic focus, and cool features like the real-time preview system called Live View, full high-definition movie shooting, and an amazing new wireless flash capability. But your gateway to pixel proficiency is dragged down by the slim little book included in the box as a manual. You know everything you need to know is in there, somewhere, but you don't know where to start. In addition, the camera manual doesn't offer much information on photography or digital photography. Nor are you interested in spending hours or days studying a comprehensive book on digital SLR photography that doesn't necessarily apply directly to your 7D.

What you need is a guide that explains the purpose and function of the 7D's basic controls, how you should use them, and *why*. Ideally, there should be information about file formats, resolution, aperture/priority exposure, and special autofocus modes available, but you'd prefer to read about those topics only after you've had the chance to go out and take a few hundred great pictures with your new camera. Why isn't there a book that summarizes the most important information in its first two or three chapters, with lots of illustrations showing what your results will look like when you use this setting or that?

Now there is such a book. If you want a quick introduction to the 7D's focus controls, wireless flash synchronization options, how to choose lenses, or which exposure modes are best, this book is for you. If you can't decide on what basic settings to use with your camera because you can't figure out how changing ISO or white balance or focus defaults will affect your pictures, you need this guide.

Introduction

Canon has done it again! It's packaged up most of the most alluring features of its advanced digital SLRs and stuffed them into a compact, highly affordable semi-professional body called the EOS 7D. Your new 18-megapixel camera is loaded with capabilities that few would have expected to find in a sub-$2,000 dSLR. Indeed, the 7D retains the ease of use that smoothes the transition for those new to digital photography. For those just dipping their toes into the digital pond, the experience is warm and inviting.

Nor will you easily outgrow this camera. It's got resolution that's more than 85 percent of what you get with the 21-megapixel Canon EOS 5D Mark II "pro" camera, improved autofocus, and lots of customization options. Its new wireless flash capabilities, which allow the camera's built-in electronic flash to control off-camera flash units remotely, were incorporated first in the 7D. Canon must love serious photographers, because it seems to work extra hard to give them incredible value for their money.

But once you've confirmed that you made a wise purchase decision, the question comes up, *how do I use this thing?* All those cool features can be mind-numbing to learn, if all you have as a guide is the manual furnished with the camera. Help is on the way. I sincerely believe that this book is your best bet for learning how to use your new camera, and for learning how to use it well.

If you're a Canon EOS 7D owner who's looking to learn more about how to use this great camera, you've probably already explored your options. There are DVDs and online tutorials—but who can learn how to use a camera by sitting in front of a television or computer screen? Do you want to watch a movie or click on HTML links, or do you want to go out and take photos with your camera? Videos are fun, but not the best answer.

There's always the manual furnished with the 7D. It's compact and filled with information, but there's really very little about *why* you should use particular settings or features, and its organization may make it difficult to find what you need. Multiple cross-references may send you flipping back and forth between two or three sections of the book to find what you want to know. The basic manual is also hobbled by black-and-white line drawings and tiny monochrome pictures that aren't very good examples of what you can do.

Also available are third-party guides to the 7D, like this one. I haven't been happy with some of these guidebooks, which is why I wrote this one. The existing books range from skimpy and illustrated by black-and-white photos to lushly illustrated in full color but too generic to do much good. Photography instruction is useful, but it needs to be related directly to the Canon EOS 7D as much as possible.

I've tried to make *David Busch's Canon EOS 7D Guide to Digital SLR Photography* different from your other 7D learn-up options. The roadmap sections use larger, color pictures to show you where all the buttons and dials are, and the explanations of what they do are longer and more comprehensive. I've tried to avoid overly general advice, including the two-page checklists on how to take a "sports picture" or a "portrait picture" or a "travel picture." Instead, you'll find tips and techniques for using all the features of your Canon EOS 7D to take *any kind of picture* you want. If you want to know where you should stand to take a picture of a quarterback dropping back to unleash a pass, there are plenty of books that will tell you that. This one concentrates on teaching you how to select the best autofocus mode, shutter speed, f/stop, or flash capability to take, say, a great sports picture under any conditions.

David Busch's Canon EOS 7D Guide to Digital SLR Photography is aimed at both Canon and dSLR veterans as well as newcomers to digital photography and digital SLRs. Both groups can be overwhelmed by the options the 7D offers, while underwhelmed by the explanations they receive in their user's manual. The manuals are great if you already know what you don't know, and you can find an answer somewhere in a booklet arranged by menu listings and written by a camera vendor employee who last threw together instructions on how to operate a camcorder.

Of course, once you've read this book and are ready to learn more, you might want to pick up one of my other guides to digital SLR photography. I'm listing them here not to hawk my other books, but because a large percentage of the e-mails I get are from readers who want to know if I've got a book on this topic or that. In the chapters that follow, I also may mention another one of my books that covers a particular subject in more depth than is possible in a camera-specific guide. Again, that's only for the benefit of those who want to delve more deeply into a topic. *Most* of what you need to know to use and enjoy your 7D is contained right here in this book. My other guides offered by Course Technology PTR include:

Quick Snap Guide to Digital SLR Photography

Consider this a prequel to the book you're holding in your hands. It might make a good gift for a spouse or friend who may be using your 7D, but who lacks even basic knowledge about digital photography, digital SLR photography, and Canon EOS photography. It serves as an introduction that summarizes the basic features of digital SLR cameras in general (not just the 7D), and what settings to use and when, such as continuous autofocus/single autofocus, aperture/shutter priority, EV settings, and so forth.

The guide also includes recipes for shooting the most common kinds of pictures, with step-by-step instructions for capturing effective sports photos, portraits, landscapes, and other types of images.

David Busch's Quick Snap Guide to Using Digital SLR Lenses

A bit overwhelmed by the features and controls of digital SLR lenses, and not quite sure when to use each type? This book explains lenses, their use, and lens technology in easy-to-access two- and four-page spreads, each devoted to a different topic, such as depth-of-field, lens aberrations, or using zoom lenses. If you have a friend or significant other who is less versed in photography, but who wants to borrow and use your Canon EOS 7D from time to time, this book can save you a ton of explanation.

David Busch's Quick Snap Guide to Lighting

This book tells you everything you need to know about using light to create the kind of images you'll be proud of. It's not Canon-specific, and it doesn't include any details on using any of the Canon-dedicated flash units, but the information you'll find applies to any digital SLR photography.

Mastering Digital SLR Photography, Second Edition

This book is an introduction to digital SLR photography, with nuts-and-bolts explanations of the technology, more in-depth coverage of settings, and whole chapters on the most common types of photography. While not specific to the 7D, this book can show you how to get more from its capabilities.

Digital SLR Pro Secrets

This is my more advanced guide to dSLR photography with greater depth and detail about the topics you're most interested in. If you've already mastered the basics in *Mastering Digital SLR Photography*, this book will take you to the next level.

Why the Canon EOS 7D Needs Special Coverage

There are many general digital photography books on the market. Why do I concentrate on books about specific digital SLRs like the 7D? One reason is that I feel dSLRs are the wave of the future for serious photographers, and those who join the ranks of digital photographers with single lens reflex cameras deserve books tailored to their equipment.

When I started writing digital photography books in 1995, digital SLRs cost $30,000 and few people other than certain professionals could justify them. Most of my readers a dozen years ago were stuck using the point-and-shoot, low-resolution digital cameras of the time—even if they were advanced photographers. I myself took countless digital pictures with an Epson digital camera with 1024×768 (less than 1 megapixel!) resolution, and which cost $500.

As recently as 2003 (before the original Digital Rebel was introduced), the lowest-cost dSLRs were priced at $3,000 or more. Today, anyone with around $600 can afford one of those basic cameras, and not much more than $1,700 buys you a sophisticated model like the Canon EOS 7D (with lens). The digital SLR is no longer the exclusive baili-wick of the professional, the wealthy, or the serious photography addict willing to scrimp and save to acquire a dream camera. Digital SLRs have become the favored camera for anyone who wants to go beyond point-and-shoot capabilities. And Canon cameras have enjoyed a dominating position among digital SLRs because of Canon's innovation in introducing affordable cameras with interesting features and outstanding performance (particularly in the area of high ISO image quality). It doesn't hurt that Canon also pro-vides both full-frame and smaller format digital cameras and a clear migration path between them (if you stick to the Canon EF lenses that are compatible with both).

You've selected your camera of choice, and you belong in the Canon camp if you fall into one of the following categories:

- Individuals who want to get better pictures, or perhaps transform their growing interest in photography into a full-fledged hobby or artistic outlet with a Canon 7D and advanced techniques.

- Those who want to produce more professional-looking images for their personal or business website, and feel that the 7D will give them more control and capabilities.

- Small business owners with more advanced graphics capabilities who want to use the 7D to document or promote their business.

- Corporate workers who may or may not have photographic skills in their job descriptions, but who work regularly with graphics and need to learn how to use digital images taken with a Canon EOS 7D for reports, presentations, or other applications.

- Professional webmasters with strong skills in programming (including Java, JavaScript, HTML, Perl, etc.) but little background in photography, but who real-ize that the 7D can be used for sophisticated photography.

- Graphic artists and others who already may be adept in image editing with Photoshop or another program, and who may already be using a film SLR (Canon or otherwise), but who need to learn more about digital photography and the spe-cial capabilities of the 7D dSLR.

Who Am I?

After spending years as the world's most successful unknown author, I've become slightly less obscure in the past few years, thanks to a horde of camera guidebooks and other photographically oriented tomes. You may have seen my photography articles in *Popular Photography & Imaging* magazine. I've also written about 2,000 articles for magazines like *Petersen's PhotoGraphic* (which is now defunct through no fault of my own), plus *The Rangefinder, Professional Photographer*, and dozens of other photographic publications. But, first, and foremost, I'm a photojournalist and made my living in the field until I began devoting most of my time to writing books.

Although I love writing, I'm happiest when I'm out taking pictures, which is why I invariably spend several days each week photographing landscapes, people, close-up subjects, and other things. I spend a month or two each year traveling to events, such as Native American "powwows," Civil War re-enactments, county fairs, ballet, and sports (baseball, basketball, football, and soccer are favorites). A few months ago, I took 14 days for a solo visit to Europe, strictly to shoot photographs of the people, landscapes, and monuments that I've grown to love. I can offer you my personal advice on how to take photos under a variety of conditions because I've had to meet those challenges myself on an ongoing basis.

Like all my digital photography books, this one was written by someone with an incurable photography bug. My first Canon SLR was a Pellix back in the 1960s, and I've used a variety of newer models since then. I've worked as a sports photographer for an Ohio newspaper and for an upstate New York college. I've operated my own commercial studio and photo lab, cranking out product shots on demand and then printing a few hundred glossy 8 × 10s on a tight deadline for a press kit. I've served as a photo-posing instructor for a modeling agency. People have actually paid me to shoot their weddings and immortalize them with portraits. I even prepared press kits and articles on photography as a PR consultant for a large Rochester, N.Y., company, which shall remain nameless. My trials and travails with imaging and computer technology have made their way into print in book form an alarming number of times, including a few dozen on scanners and photography.

Like you, I love photography for its own merits, and I view technology as just another tool to help me get the images I see in my mind's eye. But, also like you, I had to master this technology before I could apply it to my work. This book is the result of what I've learned, and I hope it will help you master your 7D digital SLR, too.

As I write this, I'm currently in the throes of upgrading my website, which you can find at www.dslrguides.com/blog, adding tutorials and information about my other books.

There's a lot of information about several Canon models right now, but I'll be adding more tips and recommendations (including a list of equipment and accessories that I can't live without) in the next few months. I've also set up a wish list of Canon cameras, lenses, and accessories on Amazon.com for those who want to begin shopping now. I hope you'll stop by for a visit to http://astore.amazon.com/canonphoto-20.

Part I

Getting Started with Your Canon EOS 7D

This first part of the book, consisting of just three short chapters, is designed to familiarize you with the basics of your Canon EOS 7D as quickly as possible, even though I have no doubt that you've already been out shooting a few hundred (or thousand) photographs with your pride and joy.

After all, inserting a memory card, mounting a lens, stuffing a charged battery into the base, and removing the lens cap to fire off a shot or two isn't rocket science. Even the rawest neophyte can rotate the Mode Dial (located at top left on the camera body) until a P (Program auto) indicator appears at lower right in the monochrome LCD on top. Point the 7D at something interesting and press the shutter release. Presto! A pretty good picture will pop up on the color LCD on the back of the camera. It's easy!

But in digital photography, there is such a thing as *too* easy. If you bought a 7D, you certainly had no intention of using the camera as a point-and-shoot snapshooter. After all, the 7D is a tool suitable for the most advanced photographic pursuits, with an extensive array of customization possibilities. As such, you don't want the camera's operation to be brainless; you want *access* to the advanced features to be easy.

You get that easy access with the Canon 7D. However, you'll still need to take the time to learn how to use these features, and I'm going to provide everything you need to know in these first three chapters to begin shooting:

- **Chapter 1:** This is a "Meet Your 7D" introduction, where you'll find information about what came in the box with your camera and, more importantly, what *didn't* come with the camera that you seriously should consider adding to your arsenal. I'll also cover some things you might not have known about charging the 7D's battery, choosing a memory card, setting the time and date, and a few other pre-flight tasks. This is basic stuff, and if you're a Canon veteran you can skim over it quickly. A lot of this first chapter is intended for EOS newbies, and even if you personally don't find it essential, you'll probably agree that there was some point during your photographic development (so to speak) that you would have wished this information was spelled out for you. There's no extra charge!

- **Chapter 2:** Here, you'll find a Quick Start aimed at those who may not be old hands with Canon cameras having this level of sophistication. The 7D has some interesting new features, including one of the most advanced autofocus systems ever seen in a sub-$2,000 camera body (and which deserves an entire chapter of its own later in this book). But even with all the goodies to play with and learning curve still to climb, you'll find that Chapter 2 will get you shooting quickly with a minimum of fuss.

■ **Chapter 3:** This is a Streetsmart Roadmap to the Canon EOS 7D. Confused by the tiny little diagrams and multiple cross-references for each and every control that send you scurrying around looking for information you know is buried somewhere in the small and inadequate manual stuffed in the box? This chapter uses multiple large full-color pictures that show every dial, knob, and button, and explain the basics of using each in clear, easy-to-understand language. I'll give you the basics up front, and, even if I have to send you deeper into the book for a full discussion of a complex topic, you'll have what you need to use a control right away.

Once you've finished (or skimmed through) these three chapters, you'll be ready for Part II, which explains how to use the most important basic features, such as the 7D's exposure controls, nifty new autofocus system, and the related tools that put Live View and movie-making tools at your fingertips. Then, you can visit Part III, the advanced tools section, which explains all the dozens of set-up options that can be used to modify the capabilities you've learned to use so far, how to choose and use lenses, and introduces the EOS 7D's built-in flash and external flash capabilities. I'll wind up this book with Part IV, which covers image software, printing, and transfer options and includes some troubleshooting that may help you when good cameras (or film cards) go bad.

1

Canon EOS 7D: Thinking Outside of the Box

Whether you subscribe to the "my camera is just a tool" theory, or belong to the "an exquisite camera adds new capabilities to my shooting arsenal" camp, picking up a new Canon EOS 7D is a special experience. Those who simply wield tools will find this camera as comforting as an old friend, a solid piece of fine machinery ready and able to do their bidding as part of the creative process.

Other photographers see the low-light capabilities (up to ISO 12800), the rapid-fire 8 frames-per-second continuous shooting, anvil-like ruggedness, and ultra high 18-megapixel resolution of the 7D, and gain a sense of empowerment. *Here* is a camera with fewer limitations and more capabilities for exercising renewed creative vision. In either case, using less mawkish terms, the 7D is one of the coolest cameras Canon has ever offered. Whether you're upgrading from another brand, from another Canon model (like the 50D), or (O brave one!) your 7D is your first digital camera and/or SLR, welcome to the club.

But, now that you've unwrapped and recharged the beast, mounted a lens, and fueled it with a memory card, what do you *do* with it? That's where this chapter—and the chapters that follow—should come in handy. Like many of you, I am a Canon user of long standing. And, like other members of our club, I had to learn at least some aspects of my newest EOS camera for the very first time at some point. Experienced pro, or Canon newbie, you bought this book because you wanted to get the most from a very powerful tool, and I'm here to help.

Depending on your path to the camera, the Canon EOS 7D is either the company's most ambitious amateur camera, or most affordable entry-level "pro" camera, which are both distinctions that I find almost meaningless in the greater scheme of things. I know consummate professionals who produce amazing images with an original Digital Rebel; experienced wedding photographers who evoke the most romantic photos from a Canon 30D. The EOS 7D is a professional camera in most of the traditional senses: built like a tank with a magnesium body, reliable for hundreds of thousands of exposures, capable of lightning-fast autofocusing and superb image quality, whether you're shooting in a studio or drenched in driving rain. But whether your *images* are of professional quality, both technically and inspirationally, depends on what's between your ears, and how you apply it. The goal of this book is to provide you with the information you need to put your brain cells and your Canon's electro-mechanical components to work productively.

There's a lot to learn, but you don't have to master every detail all at once. Some of the other camera guides I've seen winnow this information down to about one-third as many pages. Indeed, I find it odd that those guidebooks use the same basic template for the 7D cameras as for a resolutely amateur-level model like the Rebel XS. A professional/semi-professional camera like the 7D has a lot more depth than that, and deserves the in-depth coverage you'll find here.

Whether you've already taken a dozen or twelve hundred photos with your new camera, now that you've got that initial creative burst out of your system, you'll want to take a more considered approach to operating the camera. This chapter and the next are designed to get your camera fired up and ready for shooting as quickly as possible. After all, the 7D is not a point-and-shoot camera. Unlike the Rebel models, there are no "Basic Zone" options with icons on a handy dial representing a person (for portraits), flower (close-ups), mountain scene (landscapes), or runner (sports activity). Instead, there are only the dials and buttons and settings that you might expect to find on a top-tier camera like this one. So I'm going to provide a basic pre-flight checklist that you need to complete before you really spread your wings and take off. You won't find a lot of detail in these first two chapters. Indeed, I'm going to tell you just what you absolutely *must* understand, accompanied by some interesting tidbits that will help you become acclimated to your 7D. I'll go into more depth and even repeat some of what I explain here in later chapters, so you don't have to memorize everything you see. Just relax, follow a few easy steps, and then go out and begin taking your best shots—ever.

Even if you're a long-time Canon shooter, I hope you won't be tempted to skip this chapter or the next one. I realize that you probably didn't purchase this book the same day you bought your camera and that, even if you did, the urge to go out and take a few hundred—or thousand—photos with your new camera is enticing. As valuable as a book like this one is, nobody can suppress their excitement long enough to read the instructions before initiating play with a new toy.

No matter how extensive your experience level is, you don't need to fret about wading through a manual to find out what you must know to take those first few tentative snaps. I'm going to help you hit the ground running with this chapter, which will help you set up your camera and begin shooting in minutes. I'll go into more depth and even repeat some of what I explain here in later chapters, so you don't have to memorize everything you see. Because I realize that some of you may already have experience with Canon cameras similar to the 7D, each of the major sections in this chapter will begin with a brief description of what is covered in that section, so you can easily jump ahead to the next if you are in a hurry to get started.

First Things First

This section helps get you oriented with all the things that come in the box with your Canon EOS 7D, including what they do. I'll also describe some optional equipment you might want to have. If you want to get started immediately, skim through this section and jump ahead to "Initial Set-up" later in the chapter.

The Canon EOS 7D comes in an impressive gray-and-red box filled with stuff, including connecting cords, booklets, CDs, and lots of paperwork. The most important components are the camera and lens (if you purchased your 7D with a lens), battery, battery charger, and, if you're the nervous type, the neck strap. You'll also need a Compact Flash memory card, as one is not included. If you purchased your EOS 7D from a camera shop, as I did, the store personnel probably attached the neck strap for you, ran through some basic operational advice that you've already forgotten, tried to sell you another Compact Flash card, and then, after they'd given you all the help you could absorb, sent you on your way with a handshake.

Perhaps you purchased your 7D from one of those mass merchandisers that also sell washing machines and vacuum cleaners. In that case, you might have been sent on your way with only the handshake, or, maybe, not even that if you resisted the efforts to sell you an extended warranty. You save a few bucks, but don't get the personal service a professional photo retailer provides. It's your choice. There's a third alternative, of course. You might have purchased your camera from a mail order or Internet source, and your 7D arrived in a big brown (or purple/red) truck. Your only interaction when you took possession of your camera was to scrawl your signature on an electronic clipboard.

In all three cases, the first thing to do is carefully unpack the camera and double-check the contents with the checklist on one end of the box, helpfully designated with a CONTENTS heading. At a minimum, the box should include a Digital Camera EOS 7D, Wide Strap EW-EOS7D, Battery Pack LP-E6, Battery Charger LC-E6/LC-E6E, Stereo AV Cable AVC-DC400ST, Interface Cable IFC-200U, Wide Strap EW-EOS7D Neck strap, and two software CD-ROMs, all described in more detail on the pages that follow. You also got an instruction manual, a quick start pocket guide, and a leaflet introducing the included software. It's possible that the camera was accompanied by a lens, as well, and that the contents I've listed will vary slightly depending on when and where you bought the camera.

While this level of set-up detail may seem as superfluous as the instructions on a bottle of shampoo, checking the contents *first* is always a good idea. No matter who sells a camera, it's common to open boxes, use a particular camera for a demonstration, and then repack the box without replacing all the pieces and parts afterwards. Someone might actually have helpfully checked out your camera on your behalf—and then mispacked the box. It's better to know *now* that something is missing so you can seek redress immediately, rather than discover two months from now that the video cable you thought you'd never use (but now *must* have) was never in the box.

At a minimum, the box should have the following:

- **Canon EOS 7D digital camera.** It almost goes without saying that you should check out the camera immediately, making sure the color LCD on the back isn't scratched or cracked, the memory card and battery doors open properly, and, when a charged battery is inserted and lens mounted, the camera powers up and reports for duty. Out-of-the-box defects like these are rare, but they can happen. It's probably more common that your dealer played with the camera or, perhaps, it was a customer return. That's why it's best to buy your 7D from a retailer you trust to supply a factory-fresh camera.

- **Battery Pack LP-E6.** You'll need to charge this 7.4V, 1800mAh (milliampere hour) battery before using it. I'll offer instructions later in this chapter. It should be furnished with a protective cover, which should always be mounted on the battery when it is not inside the camera, to avoid shorting out the contacts.

- **Battery Charger LC-E6/LC-E6E.** One of these chargers is required to vitalize the LP-E6 battery.

- **Stereo AV Cable AVC-DC400ST.** Use this cable to connect your 7D to a standard definition (analog) television through the set's yellow RCA video jack and red/white RCA audio jacks when you want to view and hear the camera's output on a larger screen monitor. It plugs into the same connector as the USB cable described next; you can't use both at the same time.

- **Interface Cable IFC-200U.** You can use this USB cable to transfer photos from the camera to your computer (I don't recommend that because direct transfer uses a lot of battery power), to upload and download settings between the camera and your computer (highly recommended), and to operate your camera remotely using the software included on CD-ROM.

■ **Wide Strap EW-EOS7D Neck strap.** Canon provides you with a "steal me" neck strap emblazoned with your camera model. It's not very adjustable, and, while useful for showing off to your friends exactly which nifty new camera you bought, I never attach the Canon strap to my cameras, and instead opt for a more serviceable strap from UPstrap (www.upstrap-pro.com) or Op-Tech (www.optechusa.com). If you carry your camera over one shoulder, as many do, I particularly recommend UPstrap (shown in Figure 1.1). It has a patented non-slip pad that offers reassuring traction and eliminates the contortions we sometimes go through to keep the camera from slipping off. I know several photographers who refuse to use anything else. If you do purchase an UPstrap, be sure to mention that I sent you hence. You won't get a discount, but I like to let photographer-inventor Al Stegmeyer know I'm maintaining my faith in his remarkable straps.

Figure 1.1
Third-party neck straps, like this UPstrap model, are often preferable to the Canon-supplied strap.

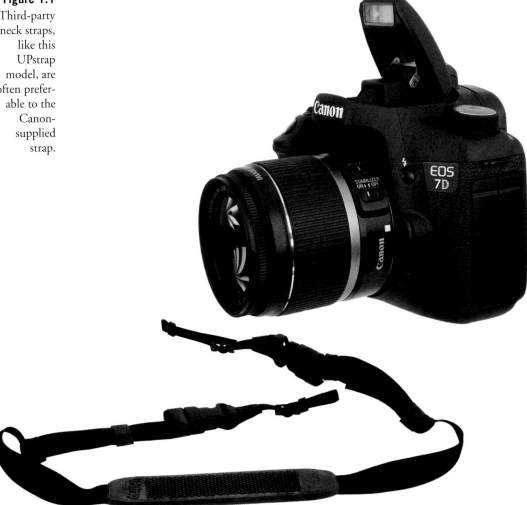

- **Body cap/rear lens cap.** The body cap keeps dust from infiltrating your camera when a lens is not mounted. Always carry a body cap (and rear lens cap, also supplied with the 7D) in your camera bag for those times when you need to have the camera bare of optics for more than a minute or two. (That usually happens when repacking a bag efficiently for transport, or when you are carrying an extra body or two for backup.) The body cap/rear lens cap nest together for compact storage.

- **User's manuals.** Even if you have this book, you'll probably want to check the printed user's guide that Canon provides, if only to check the actual nomenclature for some obscure accessory, or to double-check an error code. Google "Canon 7D manual PDF" to find a downloadable, non-printable version that you can store on your laptop, a CD-ROM, or other media in case you want to access this reference when the paper version isn't handy. If you have an old Compact Flash card that's too small to be usable on a modern dSLR (I still have some 128MB and 256MB cards), you can store the PDF on that. But an even better choice is to put the manual on a low-capacity USB "thumb" drive, which you can buy for less than $10. You'll then be able to access the reference anywhere you are, because you can always find someone with a computer that has a USB port and Adobe Acrobat Reader available. You might not be lucky enough to locate a computer with a Compact Flash card reader.

- **Pocket guide.** This little booklet tucked away in the camera's paperwork offers a reasonable summary of the Canon 7D's basic commands and settings, and can be stowed in your camera bag more easily than a "field guide" or even this book.

- **CD-ROMs.** You'll find the Canon Digital Solution Disk with software applications (described in Chapter 9), and a Software Instruction manual (in PDF form) on the pair of CD-ROMs packaged with the camera.

- **Warranty and registration card.** Don't lose these! You can register your Canon 7D by mail, although you don't really need to in order to keep your warranty in force, but you may need the information in this paperwork (plus the purchase receipt/invoice from your retailer) should you require Canon service support.

Don't bother rooting around in the box for anything beyond what I've listed previously. There are a few things Canon classifies as optional accessories, even though you (and I) might consider some of them essential. Here's a list of what you *don't* get in the box, but might want to think about as an impending purchase. I'll list them roughly in the order of importance:

- **Compact Flash card.** First-time digital camera buyers are sometimes shocked that their new tool doesn't come with a memory card. Why should it? The manufacturer doesn't have the slightest idea of how much storage you require, or whether you want a slow/inexpensive card or one that's faster/more expensive, so why should they pack one in the box and charge you for it? For an 18-megapixel camera, you really need one that's a minimum of 8GB in size.

- **Extra LP-E6 battery.** Even though you might get 500 to more than 1,000 shots from a single battery, it's easy to exceed that figure in a few hours of shooting sports at 8 fps. Batteries can unexpectedly fail, too, or simply lose their charge from sitting around unused for a week or two. Buy an extra (I own four, in total), keep it charged, and free your mind from worry. This is the same battery used in the EOS 5D Mark II.

- **Add-on Speedlite.** One of the best uses for your Canon 7D's built-in electronic flash is as a remote trigger for an off-camera Speedlite such as the Canon 580EX II, which was designed especially for cameras in this class. Your built-in flash can function as the main illumination for your photo, or softened and used to fill in shadows. If you do much flash photography at all, consider an add-on Speedlite as an important accessory.

- **AC Adapter Kit ACK-E6.** This device is used with a *DC coupler* that replaces the LP-E6 battery and powers the Canon 7D from AC current. There are several typical situations where this capability can come in handy: when you're cleaning the sensor manually and want to totally eliminate the possibility that a lack of juice will cause the fragile shutter and mirror to spring to life during the process; when indoors shooting tabletop photos, portraits, class pictures, and so forth for hours on end; when using your 7D for remote shooting as well as time-lapse photography; for extensive review of images on your television; or for file transfer to your computer. These all use prodigious amounts of power, which can be provided by this AC adapter. (Beware of power outages and blackouts when cleaning your sensor, however!)

- **Angle Finder C right angle viewer.** This handy accessory fastens in place of the standard rubber eyecup and provides a 90-degree view for framing and composing your image at right angles to the original viewfinder, useful for low-level (or high-level) shooting. (Or, maybe, shooting around corners!)

- **HDMI cable HTC-100.** You'll need this optional cable if you want to connect your camera directly to an HDTV for viewing your images. Not everyone owns a high-def television, and Canon saved the holdouts a few bucks by not including one (or charging for it).

Initial Set-up

This section helps you become familiar with the three important controls most used to make adjustments: the multi-controller and the Main and Quick Control Dials. You'll also find information on charging the battery, setting the clock, mounting a lens, and making diopter vision adjustments. If you're comfortable with all these things, skim through and skip ahead to "Activating Your EOS 7D" in the next section.

The initial set-up of your Canon EOS 7D is fast and easy. Basically, you just need to charge the battery, attach a lens, and insert a Compact Flash card. I'll address each of these steps separately, but if you already feel you can manage these set-up tasks without further instructions, feel free to skip this section entirely. You should at least skim its contents, however, because I'm going to list a few options that you might not be aware of.

Battery Included

Your Canon EOS 7D is a sophisticated hunk of machinery and electronics, but it needs a charged battery to function, so rejuvenating the LP-E6 lithium-ion battery pack furnished with the camera should be your first step. A fully charged power source should be good for approximately 800 shots, based on standard tests defined by the Camera & Imaging Products Association (CIPA) document DC-002.

A BATTERY AND A SPARE

My experience is that the CIPA figures are often a little optimistic, so it's probably a good idea to have a spare battery on hand. I always recommend purchasing Canon brand batteries (for less than $50) over less-expensive third-party packs. My reasoning is that it doesn't make sense to save $20 on a component for an $1,800-plus camera, especially since batteries (from Canon as well as other sources) have been known to fail in potentially harmful ways. Canon, at least, will stand behind its products, issue a recall if necessary, and supply a replacement if a Canon-brand battery is truly defective. A third-party battery supplier that sells under a half-dozen or more different product labels and brands may not even have an easy way to get the word out that a recall has been issued.

If your pictures are important to you, always have at least one spare battery available, and make sure it is an authentic Canon product.

All rechargeable batteries undergo some degree of self-discharge just sitting idle in the camera or in the original packaging. Lithium-ion power packs of this type typically lose a small amount of their charge every day, even when the camera isn't turned on. The small amount of juice used to provide the "skeleton" outline on the top-panel monochrome LCD when the 7D is turned off isn't the culprit; Li-ion cells lose their power through a chemical reaction that continues when the camera is switched off. So, it's very likely that the battery purchased with your camera is at least partially pooped out, and you'll want to revive it before going out for some serious shooting.

There are many situations in which you'll be glad you have that spare battery:

- **Remote locales.** If you like to backpack and will often be far from a source of electricity, rechargeable cells won't be convenient. They tend to lose some charge over time, even if not used, and will quickly become depleted as you use them. You'll have no way to recharge the cells, lacking a solar-powered charger that might not be a top priority for your backpacking kit.

- **Unexpected needs.** Perhaps you planned to shoot landscapes one weekend, and then are given free front-row tickets to a Major League Soccer game. Instead of a few dozen pictures of trees and lakes, you find yourself shooting hundreds of images of David Beckham and company, which may be beyond the capacity of the single battery you own. If you have a spare battery, you're in good shape.

- **Unexpected failures.** I've charged up batteries and then discovered that they didn't work when called upon, usually because the rechargeable cells had past their useful life, the charger didn't work, or because of human error. (I *thought*, I'd charged them!) That's one reason why I always carry three times as many batteries as I think I will need.

- **Long shooting session.** Perhaps your niece is getting married, and you want to photograph the ceremony, receiving line, and reception. Several extra batteries will see you through the longest shooting session.

Power Options

Several battery chargers are available for the Canon EOS 7D. The compact LC-E6, shown in Figure 1.2, is furnished with the camera, and so is the charger that most 7D owners end up using. Purchasing one of the optional charging devices offers more than

Figure 1.2
The flashing status light indicates that the battery is being charged.

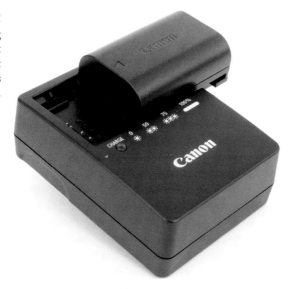

some additional features: You gain a spare that can keep your camera running until you can replace your primary power rejuvenator. Here's a list of your power options:

- **LC-E6.** The standard charger for the 7D (and also compatible with earlier cameras that use the same batteries), this one is the most convenient, because of its compact size and built-in wall plug prongs that connect directly into your power strip or wall socket and requires no cord.

- **LC-E6E.** This is similar to the LC-E6, and also charges a single battery, but requires a cord. That can be advantageous in certain situations. For example, if your power outlet is behind a desk or in some other semi-inaccessible location, the cord can be plugged in and routed so the charger itself sits on your desk or another more convenient spot. The cord is standard and works with many different chargers and devices (including the power supply for my laptop), so I purchased several of them and leave them plugged into the wall in various locations. I can connect my 7D's charger, my laptop computer's charger, and several other electronic components to one of these cords without needing to crawl around behind the furniture. The cord draws no power when it's *not plugged into a charger*. Unhook the charger from the cord when you're not actively rejuvenating your batteries.

- **Car Battery Cable CBC-E6.** It includes the Car Battery Cable CB-570 (plug into your vehicle's lighter or accessory socket). The vehicle battery option allows you to keep shooting when in remote locations that lack AC power.

- **Battery Grip BG-E7.** This accessory holds one or two LC-E6 batteries (or six AA cells with the BGM-E6 battery holder). You can potentially double your shooting capacity, while adding an additional shutter release, Main Dial, AE lock/FE lock, and AF point selection controls for vertically oriented shooting.

- **AC Adapter Kit ACK-E6.** As I mentioned earlier, this device allows you to operate your EOS 7D directly from AC power, with no battery required. Studio photographers need this capability because they often snap off hundreds of pictures for hours on end and want constant, reliable power. The camera is probably plugged into a flash sync cord (or radio device), and the studio flash are plugged into power packs or AC power, so the extra tether to this adapter is no big deal in that environment. You also might want to use the AC adapter when viewing images on a TV connected to your 7D, or when shooting remote or time-lapse photos.

Charging the Battery

When the battery is inserted into the CG-580 charger properly (it's impossible to insert it incorrectly), a Charge light begins flashing. It flashes on and off until the battery reaches a 50 percent charge, then blinks in two-flash cycles between 50-75 percent charged, and in a three-flash sequence until the battery is 90 percent charged, usually within about 90 minutes. You should allow the charger to continue for about 60 minutes more, until the status lamp glows green steadily, to ensure a full charge.

When the battery is charged, flip the lever on the bottom of the camera and slide in the battery (see Figure 1.3). To remove the battery from the camera, press the white retaining lever.

Figure 1.3
Insert the battery in the camera; it only fits one way.

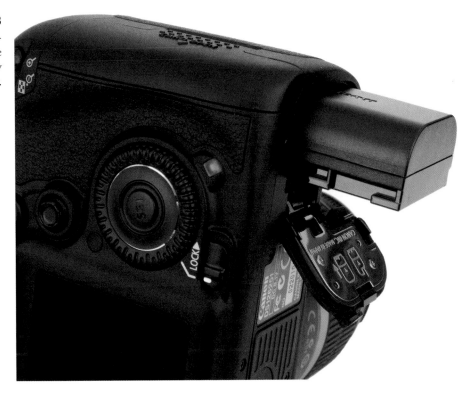

Final Steps

Your Canon EOS 7D is almost ready to fire up and shoot. You'll need to select and mount a lens, adjust the viewfinder for your vision, and insert a Compact Flash card. Each of these steps is easy, and if you've used an EOS 50D, 40D, 30D, or 20D (or one of the digital Rebels), you already know exactly what to do. I'm going to provide a little extra detail for those of you who are new to the Canon or digital SLR worlds.

Mounting the Lens

As you'll see, my recommended lens mounting procedure emphasizes protecting your equipment from accidental damage, and minimizing the intrusion of dust. If your 7D has no lens attached, select the lens you want to use and loosen (but do not remove) the rear lens cap. I generally place the lens I am planning to mount vertically in a slot in my camera bag, where it's protected from mishaps, but ready to pick up quickly. By loosening the rear lens cap, you'll be able to lift it off the back of the lens at the last instant, so the rear element of the lens is covered until then.

After that, remove the body cap by rotating the cap towards the shutter release button. You should always mount the body cap when there is no lens on the camera, because it helps keep dust out of the interior of the camera, where it can settle on the mirror, focusing screen, the interior mirror box, and potentially find its way past the shutter onto the sensor. (While the 7D's sensor cleaning mechanism works fine, the less dust it has to contend with, the better.) The body cap also protects the vulnerable mirror from damage caused by intruding objects (including your fingers, if you're not cautious).

Once the body cap has been removed, remove the rear lens cap from the lens, set it aside, and then mount the lens on the camera by matching the alignment indicator on the lens barrel (red for EF lenses and white for EF-S lenses) with the red or white dot on the camera's lens mount (see Figure 1.4). Rotate the lens away from the shutter release until it seats securely. (You can find out more about the difference between EF and EF-S lenses in Chapter 7.) Set the focus mode switch on the lens to AF (autofocus). If the lens hood is bayoneted on the lens in the reversed position (which makes the lens/hood combination more compact for transport), twist it off and remount with the edge facing outward (see Figure 1.5). A lens hood protects the front of the lens from accidental bumps, stray fingerprints, and reduces flare caused by extraneous light arriving at the front element of the lens from outside the picture area.

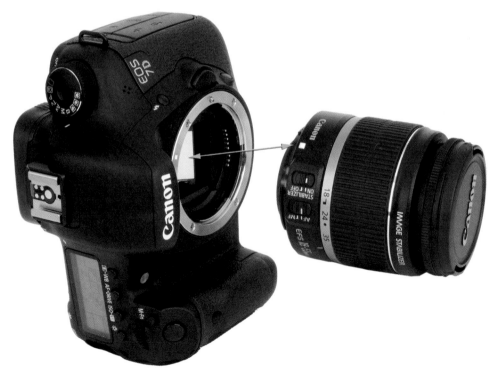

Figure 1.4
Match the white dot on EF-S lenses with the white dot on the camera mount to properly align the lens with the bayonet mount. For EF lenses, use the red dots.

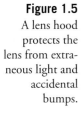

Figure 1.5
A lens hood protects the lens from extraneous light and accidental bumps.

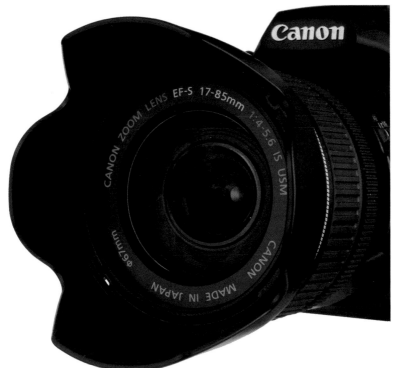

Adjusting Diopter Correction

Those of us with less than perfect eyesight can often benefit from a little optical correction in the viewfinder. Your contact lenses or glasses may provide all the correction you need, but if you are a glasses wearer and want to use the EOS 7D without your glasses, you can take advantage of the camera's built-in diopter adjustment, which can be varied from −3 to +1 correction. Press the shutter release halfway to illuminate the indicators in the viewfinder, then rotate the diopter adjustment wheel next to the viewfinder (see Figure 1.6) while looking through the viewfinder until the indicators appear sharp.

If the available correction is insufficient, Canon offers 10 different Dioptric Adjustment Lens Series E correction lenses for the viewfinder window. If more than one person uses your 7D, and each requires a different diopter setting, you can save a little time by noting the number of clicks and direction (clockwise to increase the diopter power; counterclockwise to decrease the diopter value) required to change from one user to the other. There are 18 detents in all.

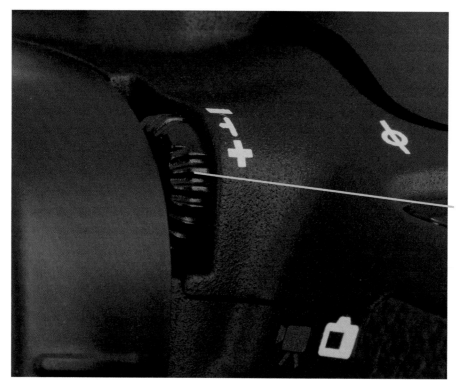

Figure 1.6
Viewfinder diopter correction from –3 to +1 can be dialed in.

Diopter adjustment wheel

Inserting a Compact Flash Card

You can't take photos without a Compact Flash card inserted in your EOS 7D (although there is a Release shutter without card entry in Shooting 1 menu that enables/disables shutter release functions when a memory card is absent—learn about that in Chapter 7). So, your final step will be to insert a Compact Flash card. Slide the door on the right side of the body toward the back of the camera to release the cover, and then open it. (You should only remove the memory card when the camera is switched off, but the 7D will remind you if the door is opened while the camera is still writing photos to the Compact Flash card.)

Insert the memory card with the label facing the back of the camera, as shown in Figure 1.7, oriented so the edge with the double row of tiny holes goes into the slot first. Close the door, and your preflight checklist is done! (I'm going to assume you remember to remove the lens cap when you're ready to take a picture!) When you want to remove the memory card later, press the gray button (shown at the bottom of Figure 1.8) to make the Compact Flash card pop out.

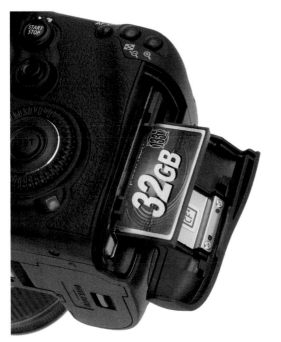

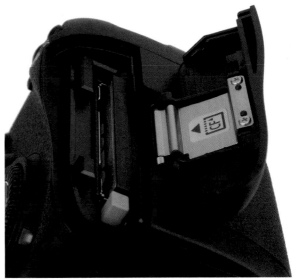

Figure 1.7 Insert the Compact Flash in the slot with the label facing the back of the camera.

Figure 1.8 To remove the memory card, press the gray button at the bottom. The card will pop out.

Formatting a Memory Card

There are three ways to create a blank Compact Flash card for your 7D, and two of them are at least partially wrong. Here are your options, both correct and incorrect:

- **Transfer (move) files to your computer.** When you transfer (rather than copy) all the image files to your computer from the Compact Flash card (either using a direct cable transfer or with a card reader, as described later in this chapter), the old image files are erased from the card, leaving the card blank. Theoretically. This method does *not* remove files that you've labeled as Protected (choosing the Protect Images function in the Playback menu) nor does it identify and lock out parts of your memory card that have become corrupted or unusable since the last time you formatted the card. Therefore, I recommend always formatting the card, rather than simply moving the image files, each time you want to make a blank card. The only exception is when you *want* to leave the protected/unerased images on the card for awhile longer, say, to share with friends, family, and colleagues.

- **(Don't) Format in your computer.** With the Compact Flash card inserted in a card reader or card slot in your computer, you can use Windows or Mac OS to reformat the memory card. Don't! The operating system won't necessarily arrange the structure of the card the way the 7D likes to see it (in computer terms, an incorrect *file system* may be installed). The only way to ensure that the card has been properly formatted for your camera is to perform the format in the camera itself. The only exception to this rule is when you have a seriously corrupted memory card that your camera refuses to format. Sometimes it is possible to revive such a corrupted card by allowing the operating system to reformat it first, then trying again in the camera.

- **Set-up menu format.** To use the recommended method to format a memory card, press the Menu button, rotate the Main Dial (located on top of the camera, just behind the shutter release button), choose the Set-up 1 menu (which is represented by a wrench icon with a single dot next to it), use the Quick Control Dial (that round wheel to the right of the LCD) to navigate to the Format entry and press the Set button in the center of the dial to access the Format screen. Rotate the Quick Control Dial again to select OK and press the Set button one final time to begin the format process.

How Many Shots Left? Guess!

If the EOS 7D has a serious flaw, my nomination is the camera's apparent inability to tell you how many shots you have left. Of course, you know you have a great camera when the counter that keeps track of the number of shots remaining is its most annoying defect. What's the deal? The counter on the monochrome LCD tops out at a measly 999 shots, which is a ridiculously low number given the capacity of modern Compact Flash cards. With an 18-megapixel camera like the 7D, a 4GB Compact Flash card is rather small. (I've standardized on 32GB for my own work. Read about the "eggs/basket" myth in Chapter 13.) If you use a modestly sized 4GB or 8GB card, it's almost inevitable that the counter will indicate no more than 999 shots remaining if you're shooting JPEG Fine or JPEG Standard—even though you may actually have much more capacity than that remaining.

Fortunately, there is a workaround. The Quick Control screen (which I'll explain in more detail in Chapter 3) has a counter that can tally up to 9999 shots. Just press the Q button until the Quick Control screen appears, and presto, your true number of shots remaining appears in the lower-left corner. It's not as convenient as having the picture count appear on the monochrome status LCD, but the display is better than being left totally in the dark.

MANY FORMATS COMPLICATE THE COUNT

As I'll explain in Chapter 3, the EOS 7D is able to shoot in many different file size and resolution formats, including JPEG Fine (best image quality), JPEG Standard (good image quality), and three pixel dimensions for each of the two JPEG choices (Large: 5184 × 3456—18 megapixels; Medium: 3456 × 2304 pixels—8 megapixels; Small: 2592 × 1728 pixels—4.5 megapixels.) To make things more interesting, any of those six quality/resolution combinations can be combined with one of three different RAW ("unprocessed," although you'll learn that isn't precisely true) formats. And the three RAW settings (RAW, MRAW, and SRAW—the RAW formats in full, medium, and small resolution) can be used alone. There are 27 different formats to choose from. (I'll tell you how to choose one in Chapter 3.)

Unfortunately, each of those 27 format combinations uses up a slightly different amount of memory card space, so the format you choose partially determines how many images you'll be able to fit on the card. (When using any of the JPEG choices, the compressibility, or "squeezability" of a particular image also comes into play.) Table 1.1 provides the basic information.

To understand how your 7D's counter can overflow so easily, consider that an 8GB card can hold about 1,186 JPEG Fine shots in full resolution (Large) format, but the counter shows just 999 pictures remaining (as it also will for full resolution JPEG Standard). If you're using a "small"-sized 4GB card, the counter overflows at 999 exposures when you shoot at JPEG Standard (the actual capacity is about 1,232 exposures). Even puny 2GB cards can cause the counter to falter if you elect to use Medium or Small resolution settings.

So, ironically, if you choose a size-friendly file format in order to squeeze more images onto your memory card, the 7D won't tell you just how many more pictures remain, until the count dips below 999. Some other camera brands insert a K (for kilo, or thousands) in the counter (as in 1.4K) to show large numbers of exposures remaining. The 7D does not.

There's not much excuse for this, because 8GB and 4GB cards have become so prevalent, and it's a real pain for someone like me who uses 32GB memory cards to avoid swapping when traveling on long trips. I get 1,240 RAW shots on a single 32GB card, but I don't really know how many I have left until I've taken almost 300!

Table 1.1 shows the typical number of shots you can expect using a modestly sized 4GB Compact Flash memory card (although I expect 8GB and 16GB cards to be the most popular size card among 7D users as prices continue to plummet during the life of this book). All figures are by actual count with my own 4GB Compact Flash card (and so may differ from Canon's published figures). Double them if you prefer 8GB cards.

Table 1.1 File Format Comparisons

File Format	Large	Medium	Small
JPEG Fine	583	1113	1743
JPEG Standard	1164	2190	3373
RAW	156	N/A	N/A
MRAW	231	N/A	N/A
SRAW	347	N/A	N/A
RAW+JPEG Fine	122	137	143
RAW+JPEG Standard	137	146	149
MRAW+JPEG Fine	164	191	203
MRAW+JPEG Standard	192	208	216
SRAW+JPEG Fine	216	264	289
SRAW+JPEG Standard	266	299	314

Activating Your EOS 7D

This section helps you turn your 7D on, set the time and date, and choose shooting, metering, and autofocus modes.

Powering up your EOS 7D for the first time couldn't be easier: there's an Off/On switch located on the left side of the top panel, below the Mode Dial. Flip it towards the right and the camera is turned on. Nothing complicated about that.

You'll also want to position the Quick Control Dial switch either to the left to enable the QCD (the position most EOS 7D photographers default to), or to the right, to lock it out. The QCD has a number of functions. You can use it to set the lens opening (aperture) when using Manual or Bulb exposure settings. It can also be used to add or subtract exposure from the basic setting ("exposure compensation," as described in Chapter 3). If you've set an aperture or exposure compensation value and want to make sure it isn't accidentally changed, switch the lever to the Lock position. (See Figure 1.9.)

Figure 1.9
The Lock position disables the Quick Control Dial.

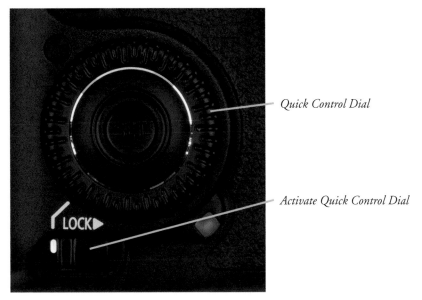

Quick Control Dial

Activate Quick Control Dial

EARLIER MODEL CONFUSION ELIMINATED

If you're coming to the 7D from the EOS 50D, 40D, or earlier xxD camera, the simple Off/On switch is a major improvement. With those previous models, the On switch was "embedded" in the Quick Control Dial (the large dial located to the right of the LCD), and it had, (seemingly), *two* "On" positions. The rotating lever had an Off setting, one marked On, and a third setting marked with a symbol that looks like an uppercase L tipped over on its side. That's actually a marker "pointing" at the Quick Control Dial. Both the On and the L positions turn on the 50D and similar cameras.

The first position powered up the camera and disabled the Quick Control Dial (QCD), and the second position turned on the camera and enabled the QCD. With the 7D, the power switch and QCD enable/disable switch have been separated.

WATCH THAT QCD POSITION!

While I was writing this book, I hosted a lighting seminar for neophyte photographers using cameras of all breeds, and out of 30 photographers in two sessions, no fewer than four Canon shooters were having trouble setting the aperture when using the Manual exposure mode I was having them use while working with studio flash units. (Each of them rarely used Manual.) All four had accidentally set the QCD switch to Lock (if they were 7D owners) or to the On (only) position (if they were 50D or 40D users), disabling the Quick Control Dial. I expect that this happens more frequently than I suspected, so I'm calling it to your attention once more in these two sidebars.

Setting the Time and Date

The first time you use the Canon EOS 7D, it may ask you to enter the time and date. (This information may have been set by someone checking out your camera on your behalf prior to sale.) Just follow these steps:

1. Press the Menu button, located in the upper-left corner of the back of the 7D.

2. Rotate the Main Dial (near the shutter release button on top of the camera) until the Set-up 2 menu is highlighted. It's marked by a wrench with two dots next to it, as shown in Figure 1.10.

3. Rotate the Quick Control Dial (QCD) to move the highlighting down to the Date/Time entry.

4. Press the Set button in the center of the QCD to access the Date/Time setting screen, shown in Figure 1.11.

5. Rotate the QCD to select the value you want to change. When the gold box highlights the month, day, year, hour, minute, second, or year format you want to adjust, press the Set button to activate that value. A pair of up/down pointing triangles appears above the value.

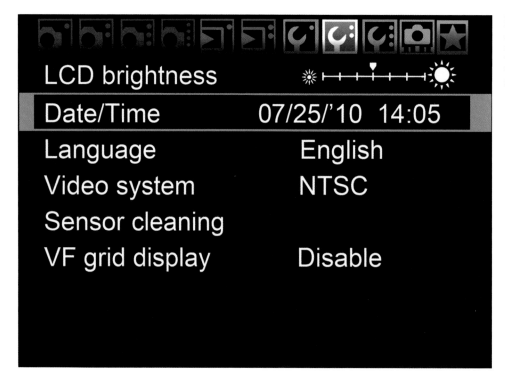

Figure 1.10
Choose the Date/Time entry from the Set-up 2 menu.

Figure 1.11
Adjust the
date and
time format.

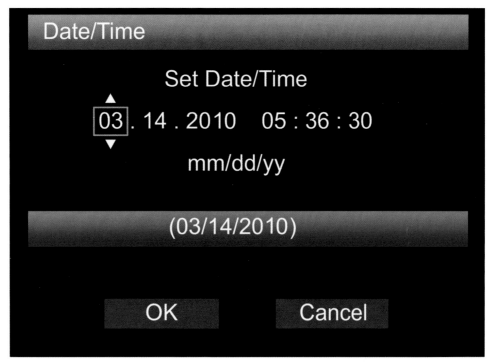

6. Rotate the Quick Control Dial to adjust the value up or down. Press the Set button to confirm the value you've entered.

7. Repeat steps 5 and 6 for each of the other values you want to change. The date format can be switched from the default mm/dd/yy to yy/mm/dd or dd/mm/yy.

8. When finished, rotate the QCD to select either OK (if you're satisfied with your changes) or Cancel (if you'd like to return to the Set-up 2 menu screen without making any changes). Press Set to confirm your choice.

9. When finished setting the date and time, press the Menu button to exit.

Your Canon EOS 7D is ready to go. If you need a quick start for its basic operation, jump ahead to Chapter 2.

2

Canon EOS 7D Quick Start

Now it's time to fire up your EOS 7D and take some photos. The easy part is turning on the power—that OFF-ON switch on the left side, just aft of the Mode Dial. Turn on the camera, make sure that the Quick Control Dial switch is set at the white line, and, if you mounted a lens and inserted a fresh battery and Compact Flash card—as I prompted you in the last chapter—you're ready to begin. You'll need to select a shooting mode, metering mode, focus mode, and, if need be, elevate the 7D's built-in flash.

Selecting a Shooting Mode

The following sections show you how to choose semi-automatic or automatic shooting, or exposure modes; select a metering mode (which tells the camera what portions of the frame to evaluate for exposure) and set the basic autofocus functions. If you understand how to do these things, you can skip ahead to "Other Functions."

You can choose a shooting method from the Mode Dial located on the top-left edge of the Canon EOS 7D. The camera has two modes that Canon calls *fully automatic*—Creative Auto and Full Auto, which make virtually all the decisions for you (except when to press the shutter). There are also five *semi-automatic/manual* modes (what Canon calls Creative Zone on the Rebel and xxD model), including Program, Shutter-priority, Aperture-priority, Manual, and Bulb, which allow you to provide input over the exposure and settings the camera uses. There are also three Camera User Settings that can be used to store specific groups of camera settings, which you can then recall quickly by spinning the Mode Dial to C1, C2, or C3. You'll find a complete description of fully automatic and semi-automatic/manual modes, as well as Camera User Settings in Chapter 4.

Turn your camera on by flipping the power switch to ON, and make sure the Quick Control Dial lock is all the way to the left. Next, you need to select which shooting mode to use. If you're very new to digital photography, you might want to set the camera to Full Auto (the green frame on the Mode Dial), Creative Auto (CA), or P (Program mode) and start snapping away. (See Figure 2.1.) These modes will make all the appropriate settings for you for many shooting situations. Your choices are as follows:

- **Full Auto.** In this mode, the EOS 7D makes all the exposure decisions for you, and will pop up the flash if necessary under low-light conditions.

- **CA.** This Creative Auto mode is basically the same as the Full Auto option described next, but allows you to change the brightness and other parameters of the image. The 7D still makes most of the decisions for you, but you can make some simple adjustments using the Creative Auto setting screen that appears when this mode is selected. (See Figure 2.2.) You can find instructions for using this mode and the other shooting modes in Chapter 4.

- **P (Program).** This semi-automatic mode allows the 7D to select the basic exposure settings, but you can still override the camera's choices to fine-tune your image. The flash does not pop up automatically in this mode or any of the other semi-automatic/manual modes, but if you want to use it, you can elevate the flash manually by pressing the Flash Up button located above the lens release button on the left side of the camera.

- **Tv (Shutter-priority).** This mode (Tv stands for *time value*) is useful when you want to use a particular shutter speed to stop action or produce creative blur effects. The 7D will select the appropriate f/stop for you.

- **Av (Aperture-priority).** Choose when you want to use a particular lens opening, especially to control sharpness or how much of your image is in focus. The 7D will select the appropriate shutter speed for you. Av stands for *aperture value*.

- **M (Manual).** Select when you want full control over the shutter speed and lens opening, either for creative effects or because you are using a studio flash or other flash unit not compatible with the 7D's automatic flash metering.

- **B (Bulb).** Choose this mode and the shutter will remain open as long as you hold down the release button. It is useful for making exposures of indeterminate length (say, you want to capture some fireworks, and leave the shutter open until a burst appears, then release the shutter after a few seconds when the light trails have been captured). The B setting can also be used to produce exposures longer than the 30 seconds (maximum) the 7D can take automatically.

Figure 2.1
The Mode Dial includes both automatic and semi-automatic/manual settings.

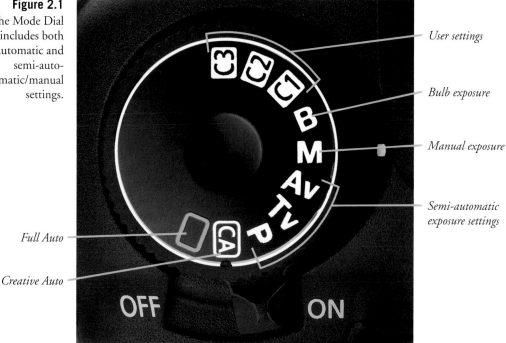

User settings

Bulb exposure

Manual exposure

Semi-automatic exposure settings

Full Auto

Creative Auto

Figure 2.2
You can tweak the settings of the Creative Auto mode using this screen of options.

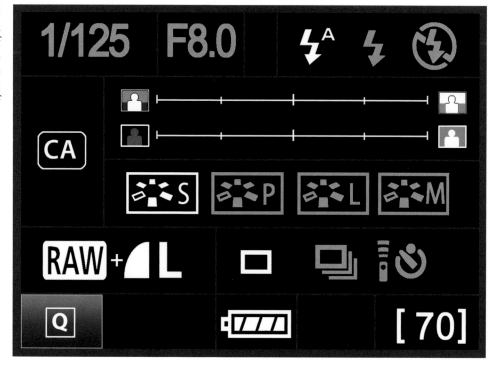

Choosing a Metering Mode

You might want to select a particular metering mode for your first shots, although the default evaluative metering is probably the best choice as you get to know your camera. To change metering modes, press the Metering/WB button (shown in Figure 2.3) and spin the Main Dial to cycle among the choices shown in Figure 2.4:

- **Evaluative metering.** The standard metering mode; the 7D attempts to intelligently classify your image and choose the best exposure based on readings from 63 different zones in the frame, with emphasis on the autofocus points.

- **Partial metering.** Exposure is based on a central spot, roughly nine percent of the image area.

- **Spot metering.** Exposure is calculated from a smaller central spot, about 2.3 percent of the image area.

- **Center-weighted averaging metering.** The 7D meters the entire scene, but gives the most emphasis to the central area of the frame.

You'll find a detailed description of each of these modes in Chapter 4.

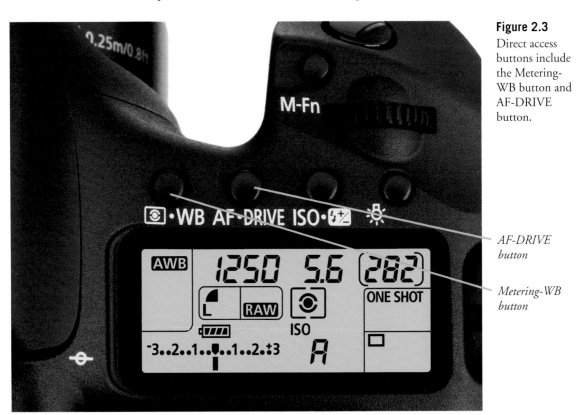

Figure 2.3
Direct access buttons include the Metering-WB button and AF-DRIVE button.

AF-DRIVE button

Metering-WB button

Figure 2.4
Metering
modes (left to
right, top third
of the screen):
evaluative,
partial, spot,
center-
weighted.

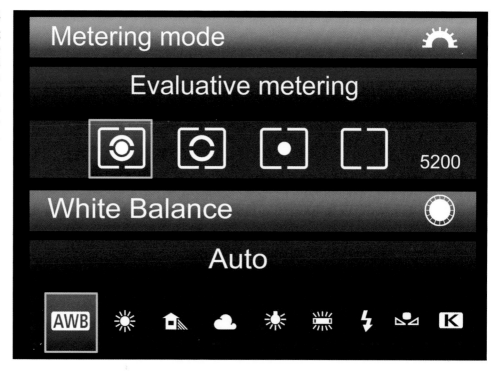

BUTTON, BUTTON

Each top-panel button has two functions. To set the left function of each pair (that is AF
with the AF-DRIVE button), hold the button and rotate the Main Dial. To set the right
function of each pair, rotate the Quick Control Dial. Each pair of choices appears in a
single pop-up screen with Main Dial and QCD icons to remind you which dial sets
which function.

Choosing a Focus Mode

You can easily switch between automatic and manual focus by moving the AF/MF
switch on the lens mounted on your camera. However, if you're using a semi-automatic
shooting mode, you'll still need to choose an appropriate focus mode. (You can read
more on selecting focus parameters in Chapter 5.)

To set the focus mode, press the AF-DRIVE button on the top panel of the camera (see
Figure 2.3, shown earlier), and spin the Main Dial until the mode you want appears in
the LCD. (See Figure 2.5.)

The three choices are as follows:

- **One-Shot.** This mode, sometimes called *Single Autofocus*, locks in a focus point when the shutter button is pressed down halfway, and the focus confirmation light glows in the viewfinder. The focus will remain locked until you release the button or take the picture. If the camera is unable to achieve sharp focus, the focus confirmation light will blink. This mode is best when your subject is relatively motionless.

- **AI Focus.** In this mode, the 7D switches between One-Shot and AI Servo as appropriate. That is, it locks in a focus point when you partially depress the shutter button (One-Shot mode), but switches automatically to AI Servo if the subject begins to move. This mode is handy when photographing a subject, such as a child at quiet play, which might move unexpectedly.

- **AI Servo.** This mode, sometimes called *Continuous Autofocus*, sets focus when you partially depress the shutter button, but continues to monitor the frame and refocuses if the camera or subject is moved. This is a useful mode for photographing sports and moving subjects.

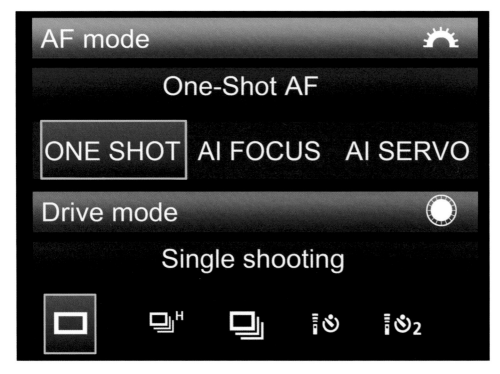

Figure 2.5

Set autofocus mode.

Selecting a Focus Point

The Canon EOS 7D can use 19 different focus points to calculate correct focus, and provides an amazing number of ways to select which of these zones is selected. You can direct the camera to choose a focus point for you, specify that only certain *groups* of zones are used, and select between spot or extended focus zones. You can memorize different preferred focus zones and return to them at a press of a button, and even select different zones for horizontal and vertical operation. The Custom Functions menu (which I'll explain in Chapter 8) has 12 different options relating to autofocus alone. Indeed, use of autofocus deserves an entire chapter of its own, and I'm going to provide it for you in Chapter 5.

For this easy quick-start chapter, I recommend you leave the autofocus setting at the Auto select: 19 point AF option and allow the EOS 7D to select an autofocus point for you automatically. If you've played with your camera and changed the AF options, here's how to switch back to the auto selection mode:

1. Press the AF point selection button once for several seconds, then press down the multi-function (M-Fn) button. (Both are shown in Figure 2.6.)

2. Press the M-Fn button repeatedly until the Auto select: 19 point AF choice is highlighted on either the LCD or in the viewfinder, as you can see in Figures 2.7 and 2.8.

3. Tap the shutter release button to return to the normal display when the setting is made.

Figure 2.6
Press the AF point selection button, then the multi-function (M-Fn) button until automatic point selection is chosen.

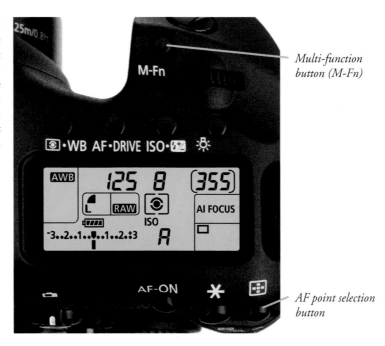

Multi-function button (M-Fn)

AF point selection button

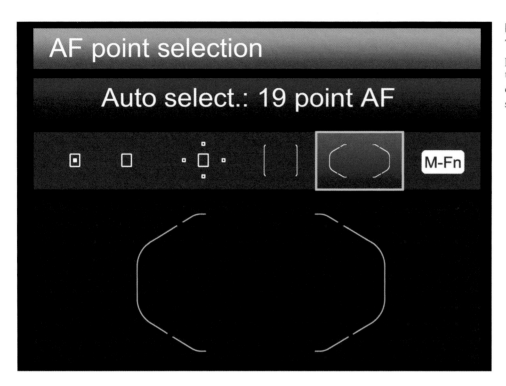

Figure 2.7
The LCD display looks like this when choosing point selection mode.

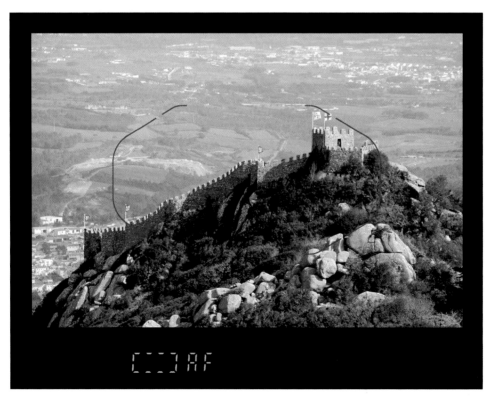

Figure 2.8
When choosing point selection mode, the viewfinder window shows this display.

Other Settings

There are a few other options, such as white balance, using the self-timer, or working with flash. You can use these right away if you're feeling ambitious, but don't feel ashamed if you postpone using these features until you've racked up a little more experience with your EOS 7D.

Adjusting White Balance and ISO

If you like, you can custom-tailor your white balance (color balance) and ISO sensitivity settings. To start out, it's best to set white balance (WB) to Auto, and ISO to ISO 100 or ISO 200 for daylight photos, and ISO 400 for pictures in dimmer light. You'll find complete recommendations for both these settings in Chapter 4. You can adjust either one now by pressing the Metering-WB button (for white balance) and rotating the Quick Control Dial, or by pressing ISO-Flash exposure compensation button (for ISO sensitivity) and rotating the Main Dial until the setting you want appears on the status LCD. Both buttons were shown earlier in Figure 2.3.

If you've been playing with your camera's settings, or your 7D has been used by someone else, you can restore the factory defaults by selecting Clear settings from the Set-up 3 menu, and/or Clear all Custom Func, from the Custom Functions main menu. I'll show you exactly how to do this in Chapter 8.

Using the Self-Timer

If you want to set a short delay before your picture is taken, you can use the self-timer. Press the AF-DRIVE button (the screen shown earlier in Figure 2.6 will appear) and rotate the Quick Control Dial until the self-timer icon (for a 10-second delay) or the self-timer icon accompanied by the numeral 2 (for a 2-second delay) appear on the status LCD. Canon supplies a rubber eyepiece cover, which attaches to your camera strap and can be slid over the eyepiece in place of the rubber eyecup. This prevents light from entering through the eyepiece, which can confuse the exposure meter. I've found that extraneous light is seldom a problem unless a bright light source is coming from directly behind the camera, in which case I use my hand to shield the viewfinder.

Press the shutter release to lock focus and start the timer. The self-timer lamp will blink and the beeper will sound (unless you've silenced it in the menus) until the final two seconds, when the lamp remains on and the beeper beeps more rapidly.

Using the Built-in Flash

Working with the EOS 7D's built-in flash (as well as external flash units like the Canon 580EX II) deserves at least a chapter of its own, and I'm providing two (see Chapters 10 and 11). But the built-in flash is easy enough to work with that you can begin using it right away, either to provide the main lighting of a scene or as supplementary illumination to fill in the shadows. The 7D will automatically balance the amount of light emitted from the flash so that it illuminates the shadows nicely, without overwhelming the highlights and producing a glaring "flash" look. (Think *Baywatch* when they're using too many reflectors on the lifeguards!)

The 7D's flash has a power rating of 12/39 (meters/feet) at ISO 100, using the GN (guide number) system that dates back to the film era and before electronic flash units had any sort of automatic features. I'll explain guide numbers (which can be a little confusing) in more detail in Chapter 10, but in plain terms, the flash's rating means that the unit is powerful enough to properly illuminate a subject that's 10 feet away at f/4 at the *lowest* ISO (sensitivity) setting of your camera. Boost the ISO (or use a wider f/stop) and you can shoot subjects that are located at a great distance. For example, at ISO 800, the 7D's flash is good enough for a subject at 20 feet using f/5.6 or, alternatively, you can expose that scene at the original 10 feet distance at f/11. Ordinarily, the 7D takes care of all these calculations for you. If you need a bigger blast of light, you can add one of the Canon external flash units, described in Chapter 10.

To pop up the flash, just press the flash button (shown in Figure 2.9). When using these modes, the flash functions in the following way:

- **P (Program mode).** The 7D selects a shutter speed from 1/60th to 1/250th second and appropriate aperture automatically.

- **Tv (Shutter-priority mode).** You choose a shutter speed from 30 seconds to 1/250th second, and the 7D chooses the lens opening for you, while adjusting the flash output to provide the correct exposure.

- **Av (Aperture-priority mode).** You select the aperture you want to use, and the camera will select a shutter speed from 30 seconds to 1/250th second, and adjust the flash output to provide the correct exposure. In low light levels, the 7D may select a very slow shutter speed to allow the flash and background illumination to balance out, so you should use a tripod. (You can disable this behavior using Custom Function I-07 Flash sync. speed in Av mode, as described in Chapter 8.)

- **M (Manual mode).** You choose both shutter speed and aperture, and the camera will adjust the flash output to produce a good exposure based on the aperture you've selected.

You can read about flash exposure compensation, red-eye reduction options, and other built-in flash features in Chapter 10.

Figure 2.9

The pop-up electronic flash can be used as the main light source, or for supplemental illumination.

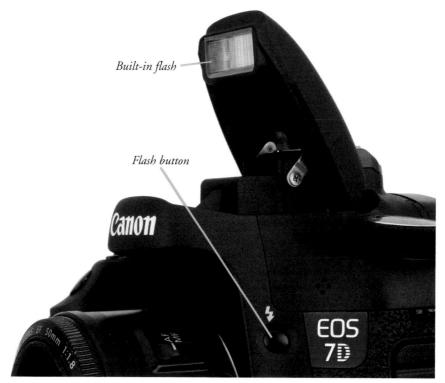

Built-in flash

Flash button

Taking a Picture

This final section of the chapter guides you through taking your first pictures, reviewing them on the LCD, and transferring your shots to your computer.

Just press the shutter release button halfway to lock in focus at the selected autofocus point for about four seconds. When the shutter button is in the half-depressed position, the exposure, calculated using the shooting mode you've selected, is also locked.

Press the button the rest of the way down to take a picture. At that instant, the mirror flips up out of the light path to the optical viewfinder (assuming you're not using Live View mode, discussed in Chapter 6), the shutter opens, the electronic flash (if enabled) fires, and your 7D's sensor absorbs a burst of light to capture an exposure. In fractions of a moment, the shutter closes, the mirror flips back down restoring your view, and the image you've taken is escorted off the CMOS sensor chip very quickly into an in-camera store of memory called a buffer, and the EOS 7D is ready to take another photo. The buffer continues dumping your image onto the Compact Flash card as you keep snapping pictures without pause (at least until the buffer fills and you must wait for it to get ahead of your continuous shooting, or your memory card fills completely).

Reviewing the Images You've Taken

The Canon EOS 7D has a broad range of playback and image review options. Here are the basics, as shown in Figure 2.10:

- **Display image.** Press the Playback button (marked with a blue right-pointing triangle at the lower-left edge of the back of the 7D just above the Trash button) to display the most recent image on the LCD in full-screen single image mode. If you last viewed your images using the thumbnail mode (described later in this list), the Index display appears instead.

- **View additional images.** Rotate the Quick Control Dial to review additional images, one at a time. Turn it counterclockwise to review images from most recent to oldest, or clockwise to start with the first image on the Compact Flash card and cycle forward to the newest.

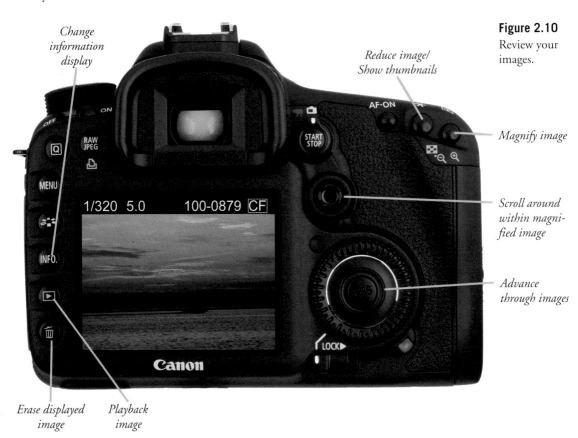

Change information display

Reduce image/ Show thumbnails

Figure 2.10
Review your images.

Magnify image

Scroll around within magnified image

Advance through images

Erase displayed image

Playback image

■ **Jump ahead or back.** If you want to zip through your shots more quickly to find a specific image, rotate the Main Dial to leap ahead or back 10 or 100 images, depending on the increment you've set using the last entry in the Playback 2 menu. I find the 7D's use of the Main Dial is faster. You can also jump ahead by screens of images, by date, or by folder. I'll show you how to select these options in the discussion of the Playback menu in Chapter 8.

■ **View image information.** Press the Info button repeatedly to cycle among overlays of basic image information, detailed shooting information, or no information at all.

■ **Zoom in on an image.** When an image is displayed full-screen on your LCD, press the Magnify/Enlarge button repeatedly to zoom in. The Magnify/Enlarge button is located in the upper-left corner of the back of the camera, marked with a blue magnifying glass with a plus sign in it. The Reduce Image button, located to the left of the Magnify/Enlarge button, zooms back out. Press the Playback button to exit magnified display.

■ **Scroll around in a magnified image.** Press the Magnify/Enlarge button, then use the multi-controller (the joystick-like knob to the upper right of the color LCD) to scroll around within a magnified image.

■ **View thumbnail images.** You can also rapidly move among a large number of images using the Index mode described in the section that follows this list.

Cruising through Index Views

You can navigate quickly among thumbnails representing a series of images using the 7D's Index mode. Here are your options:

■ **Display thumbnails.** Press the Playback button to display an image on the color LCD. If you last viewed your images using Index mode, an Index array of four or nine reduced-size images appears automatically (see Figure 2.11). If an image pops up full-screen in single image mode, press the Reduce Image button once to view four thumbnails, or twice to view nine thumbnails. You can switch between four, nine, and single images by pressing the Reduce Image button to see more/smaller versions of your images, and the Magnify/Enlarge button to see fewer/larger versions of your images.

■ **Navigate within a screen of index images.** In Index mode, use the QCD or multi-controller joystick to move the blue highlight box around within the current Index display screen.

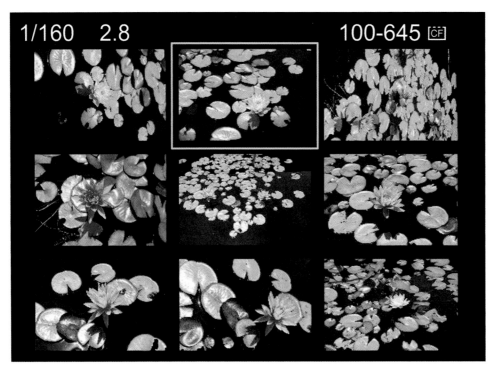

Figure 2.11
Review thumb-
nails of four or
nine images
using Index
review.

- **View more Index pages.** To view additional Index pages, rotate the Main Dial. The display will leap ahead or back by the Jump increment you've set in the Playback 2 menu (as described in Chapter 7), either 10 or 100 images, by index page, by date, folder, movies, or still images.

- **Check image.** When an image you want to examine more closely is highlighted, press the Magnify/Enlarge button until the single image version appears full-screen on your LCD.

Transferring Photos to Your Computer

The final step in your picture-taking session will be to transfer the photos you've taken to your computer for printing, further review, or image editing. Your 7D allows you to print directly to PictBridge-compatible printers and to create print orders right in the camera.

For now, you'll probably want to transfer your images either by using a cable transfer from the camera to the computer or by removing the Compact Flash card from the 7D and transferring the images with a card reader. The latter option is generally the best, because it's usually much faster and doesn't deplete the battery of your camera. However, you can use a cable transfer when you have the cable and a computer, but no card reader (perhaps you're using the computer of a friend or colleague, or at an Internet café). You'll find more information on image transfer and the software you can use to perform this function in Chapter 12.

To transfer images from the camera to a Mac or PC computer using the USB cable:

1. Turn off the camera.

2. Pry back the rubber cover that protects the EOS 7D's USB port, and plug the USB cable furnished with the camera into the USB port. (See Figure 2.12.)

3. Connect the other end of the USB cable to a USB port on your computer.

4. Turn on the camera. Your installed software usually detects the camera and offers to transfer the pictures, or the camera appears on your desktop as a mass storage device, enabling you to drag and drop the files to your computer.

Figure 2.12
Images can be transferred to your computer using a USB cable.

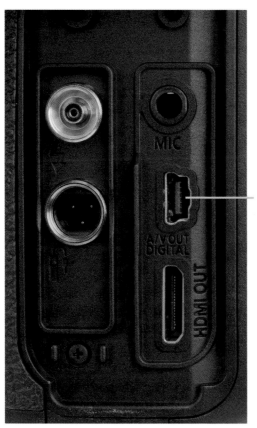

USB/AV connector

To transfer images from a Compact Flash card to the computer using a card reader, as shown in Figure 2.13:

1. Turn off the camera.

2. Slide open the Compact Flash card door, and press the gray button, which ejects the card.

3. Insert the Compact Flash card into your memory card reader. Your installed software detects the files on the card and offers to transfer them. The card can also appear as a mass storage device on your desktop, which you can open and then drag and drop the files to your computer.

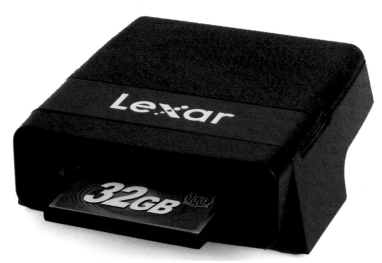

Figure 2.13
A card reader is the fastest way to transfer photos.

3

Canon EOS 7D Roadmap

Most of the Canon EOS 7D's key functions and settings that are changed frequently can be accessed directly using the array of dials and buttons and knobs that populate the camera's surface. With so many dedicated controls available, you'll find that the bulk of your shooting won't be slowed down by a visit to the vast thicket of text options called Menu-land. That's a distinct paradigm shift from early point-and-shoot cameras, which had only four or five buttons, and relied on menus to control virtually every setting you might want to make. With the 7D, you can press specific buttons dedicated to image quality, white balance, ISO sensitivity, shooting mode, exposure compensation, and playback options, and then spin a command dial or make adjustments using the multi-controller.

While it might take some time to learn the position and function of each of these controls, once you've mastered them the 7D camera is remarkably easy to use. That's because dedicated buttons with only one or two functions each are much faster to access than the alternative—a maze of menus that must be navigated every time you want to use a feature. The advantage of menu systems—dating back to early computer user interfaces of the 1980s—is that they are easy to *learn*. The ironic disadvantage of menus is that they are clumsy to *use*.

Imagine that you are familiar with digital SLRs in general, but know virtually nothing about the Canon EOS 7D. You've decided that you want to format the memory card. A-ha! There's a big ol' MENU button on the left side of the camera. Press it, and you'll see a series of different menu icons, which, when you scroll through them, have entries for shooting options, playback, camera set-up, and customized functions. In the case of the 7D, none of the menu screens you see scroll; all the choices available for that screen are shown each time the menu tab appears. So, with a couple clicks of the Main Dial, you spy a Set-up menu with the command Format as its third entry. Scroll down to

Format using the other dial (the Quick Control Dial), press the SET ("enter") button, and there you are, looking at the Format screen. A couple more button presses, and you've successfully formatted your memory card.

You didn't really need instructions—the menu system itself led you to the right command. If you don't format another card for weeks and weeks, you can come back to the menus and discover how to perform the task all over again. The main cost to you was the time required to negotiate through all the menus to carry out the function; while menus are easy to learn, the multiple steps they call for (10 or more dial twirls or button presses may be required) can be cumbersome to use.

Direct access command buttons are the exact opposite: you have to teach yourself how to use them, and then remember what you've learned over time, but, once learned, buttons are much faster to use. For example, to change the autofocus mode with the 7D, all you need to do is press the AF-DRIVE button on top of the camera and rotate the Main Dial until the autofocus mode you want to use is indicated on the top-panel LCD. To switch from single exposure to continuous shooting, self-timer, or other "drive" modes, hold down the same button and rotate the Quick Command Dial. No menus required—but you have to learn the location of the particular button you need to use.

Or, if you need to change the ISO setting on your 7D, would you rather press the ISO button and spin the Main Dial until the desired value appears on the LCD—or would you prefer tapping a menu button, using cursor keys to locate the ISO setting submenu, pressing a button to select the ISO menu, navigating to the ISO value you want, and then pressing an OK button to confirm your choice? Yet, that's the procedure mandated by countless point-and-shoot digital cameras and more than a few digital SLRs. The Canon dedicated button approach (also used by other digital SLR vendors) is a much better design.

So, if you want to operate your 7D efficiently, you'll need to learn the location, function, and application of all these controls. What you really need is a street-level roadmap that shows where everything is, and how it's used. But what Canon gives you in the user's manual is akin to a world globe with an overall view and many cross-references to the pages that will tell you what you really need to know. Check out the Nomenclature pages of the Canon 7D manual (pages 16 and 17), which offer two tiny black-and-white line drawings of the camera body that show front, back, two sides, and the top and bottom of the 7D. There are more than dozens of callouts pointing to various buttons and dials. If you can find the control you want in this cramped layout, you'll still need to flip back and forth among multiple pages (individual buttons can have several different cross-references!) to locate the information.

Most other third-party books follow this format, featuring black-and-white photos or line drawings of front, back, and top views, and many labels. I originated the up-close-and-personal full-color, street-level roadmap (rather than a satellite view) that I use in this book and my previous camera guidebooks. I provide you with many different views and lots of explanation accompanying each zone of the camera, so that by the time you finish this chapter, you'll have a basic understanding of every control and what it does. I'm not going to delve into menu functions here—you'll find a discussion of your Set-up, Shooting, and Playback menu options in Chapters 7 and 8. Everything here is devoted to the button pusher and dial twirler in you.

You'll also find this "roadmap" chapter a good guide to the rest of the book, as well. I'll try to provide as much detail here about the use of the main controls as I can, but some topics (such as autofocus and exposure) are too complex to address in depth right away. So, I'll point you to the relevant chapters that discuss things like set-up options, exposure, use of electronic flash, and working with lenses with the occasional cross-reference.

Canon EOS 7D: Front View

The front of the 7D (see Figure 3.1) is the face seen by your victims as you snap away. For the photographer, though, the front is the surface your fingers curl around as you hold the camera, and there are really only three buttons to press, all within easy reach of the fingers of your left hand, plus the shutter button and Main Dial, which are on

Figure 3.1

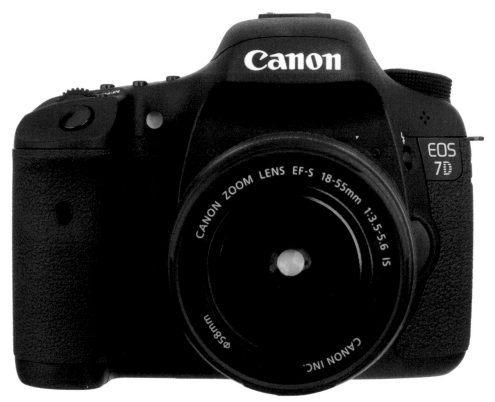

the top/front of the handgrip. There are additional controls on the lens itself. You'll need to look at several different views to see everything.

Figure 3.2 shows a three-quarters view of the left side of the EOS 7D (when viewed from the front). You can see the flash hot shoe on top and the door for the Compact Flash card at the left edge. The other components you need to know about are as follows:

■ **Shutter release button.** Angled on top of the handgrip is the shutter release button. Press this button down halfway to lock exposure and focus (in One-Shot mode and AI Focus with non-moving subjects).

■ **Main Dial.** This dial is used to change shooting settings. When settings are available in pairs (such as shutter speed/aperture), this dial will be used to make one type of setting, such as shutter speed, while the Quick Control Dial (on the back of the camera) will be used to make the other, such as aperture setting.

■ **Remote control sensor.** This infrared sensor detects the invisible flash of a Canon remote control, like the RC-5.

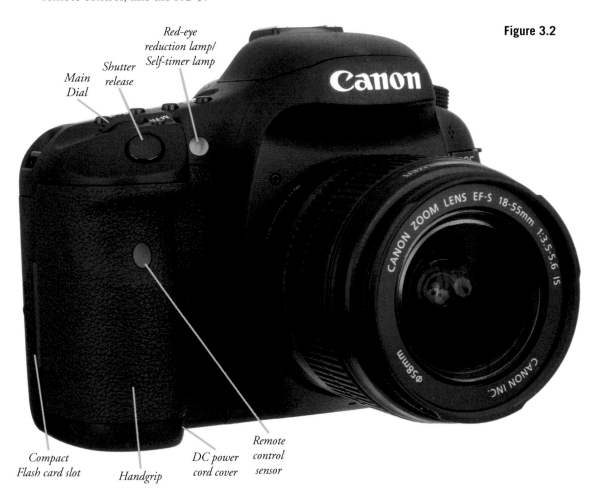

Figure 3.2

Red-eye
reduction lamp/
Self-timer lamp

Shutter
release

Main
Dial

Compact
Flash card slot

Handgrip

DC power
cord cover

Remote
control
sensor

- **Red-eye reduction/self-timer lamp.** This LED provides a blip of light shortly before a flash exposure to cause the subjects' pupils to close down, reducing the effect of red-eye reflections off their retinas. When using the self-timer, this lamp also flashes to mark the countdown until the photo is taken. (You can turn off the lamp if you don't want it.)

- **DC power cord cover.** (Not visible.) This cover, on the inside edge of the handgrip, opens to allow the DC power cable to connect to the 7D through the battery compartment.

- **Handgrip.** This provides a comfortable handhold, and also contains the 7D's battery.

- **Compact Flash card slot.** Slide the door over this slot towards the back of the camera to provide access to the Compact Flash memory card.

You'll find more controls on the other side of the 7D, shown in Figure 3.3. In the illustration, you can see the Mode Dial on top, and the rubber cover on the side that protects the camera's USB, TV, HDMI, external flash, and remote control ports.

Figure 3.3

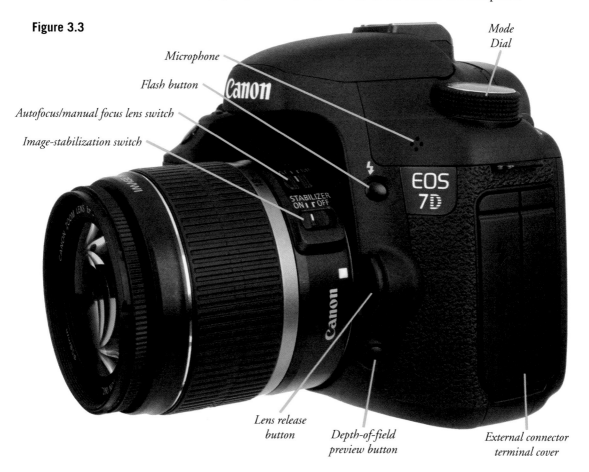

Mode Dial

Microphone

Flash button

Autofocus/manual focus lens switch

Image-stabilization switch

Lens release button

Depth-of-field preview button

External connector terminal cover

The main buttons shown include:

- **Flash button.** This button, shown in Figure 3.3, releases the built-in flash so it can flip up (see Figure 3.4) and start the charging process. If you decide you do not want to use the flash, you can turn it off by pressing the flash head back down.

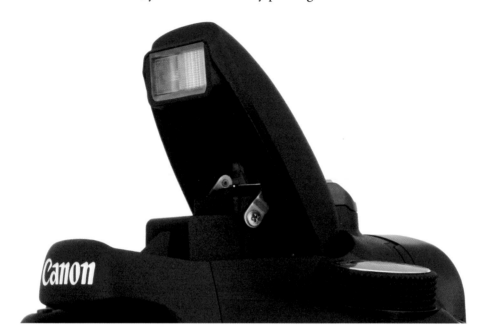

Figure 3.4
When the flash pops up, the charging process begins. The flash will pop up when needed auto-matically in Full Auto and Creative Auto modes.

- **Lens release button.** Press and hold this button to unlock the lens so you can rotate the lens to remove it from the camera.

- **Depth-of-field preview button.** This button, adjacent to the lens mount, stops down the lens to the taking aperture so you can see in the viewfinder how much of the image is in focus. The view grows dimmer as the aperture is reduced.

- **Lens switches.** Canon autofocus lenses have a switch to allow changing between automatic focus and manual focus, and, in the case of IS lenses, another switch to turn image stabilization on and off.

The main feature on this side of the EOS 7D is two rubber covers (see Figure 3.5) that protect the five connector ports underneath from dust and moisture. The five connec-tors, shown in Figure 3.6, are as follows:

- **USB port.** Plug the USB cable furnished with your EOS 7D into this digital terminal and connect the other end to a USB port in your computer to transfer photos.

- **Video port.** You can link this connector with a television to view your photos on a large screen.

Figure 3.5

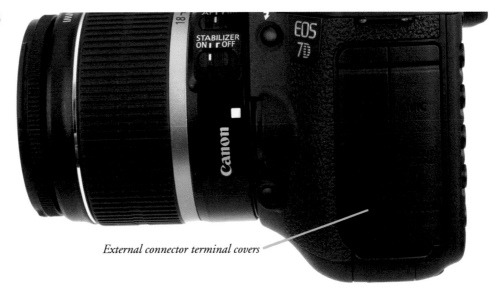

External connector terminal covers

■ **PC terminal.** This connector is for a non-dedicated electronic flash unit, including studio flash.

■ **Remote control terminal.** You can plug various Canon remote release switches, timers, and wireless controllers into this connector.

■ **HDMI port.** You need to buy an accessory cable to connect your 7D to an HDTV, as one to fit this port is not provided with the camera. If you have a high-resolution television, it's worth the expenditure to be able to view your camera's output in all its glory.

Figure 3.6

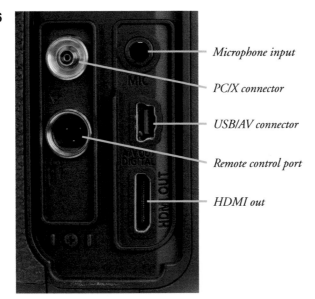

Microphone input

PC/X connector

USB/AV connector

Remote control port

HDMI out

The Canon EOS 7D's Business End

The back panel of the EOS 7D (see Figure 3.7) bristles with more than a dozen different controls, buttons, and knobs. That might seem like a lot of controls to learn, but you'll find, as I noted earlier, that it's a lot easier to press a dedicated button and spin a dial than to jump to a menu every time you want to change a setting.

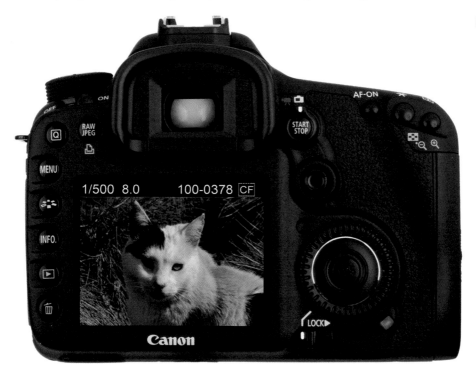

Figure 3.7

You can see the controls clustered on the left side of the 7D in Figure 3.8. The key buttons and components and their functions are as follows:

- **Quick Control button.** Pressing this button produces the Quick Control screen, which displays the current shooting settings on the rear color LCD monitor. You can use the multi-controller to select one of the displayed functions, and rotate the Main Dial or Quick Control Dial to change the highlighted setting. (See the sidebar, "Using the Quick Control Screen" which follows this list.)

- **Viewfinder eyepiece.** You can frame your composition by peering into the viewfinder. It's surrounded by a soft rubber frame that seals out extraneous light when pressing your eye tightly up to the viewfinder, and it also protects your eyeglass lenses (if worn) from scratching. It can be removed and replaced by the cap attached to your neck strap when you use the camera on a tripod, to ensure that light coming from the back of the camera doesn't venture inside and possibly affect the exposure reading.

■ **One-touch RAW+JPEG/Direct print button.** In shooting mode, this useful button allows you to switch to RAW+JPEG mode for One-Shot if you have set your camera's current recording quality to either JPEG (only) or RAW (only). (If the camera is already set to RAW+JPEG, the button has no effect.) (See the section, "One-touch RAW+JPEG" which follows this list.) In Playback mode, this button activates the Direct printing function, as described in Chapter 12.

■ **Speaker.** When you play back movie clips, the sound emanates from this small speaker located to the left of the viewfinder window.

■ **MENU button.** Summons/exits the menu displayed on the rear LCD of the 7D. When you're working with submenus, this button also serves to exit a submenu and return to the main menu.

■ **Picture Styles.** This button pops up the Picture Styles menu on the LCD, so you can select a given style or modify an existing style. You'll find more about Picture Styles in Chapter 7.

Figure 3.8

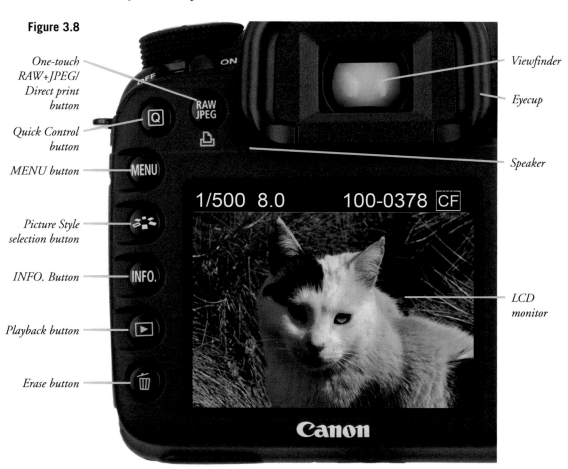

One-touch RAW+JPEG/ Direct print button

Quick Control button

MENU button

Picture Style selection button

INFO. Button

Playback button

Erase button

Viewfinder

Eyecup

Speaker

LCD monitor

■ **INFO. button (shooting mode).** Changes the amount of picture information displayed. In shooting mode, pressing the INFO. button will display a plain screen (with just the image, and no other data overlaid on top), or up to three additional screens. I'll show you how to choose which of the three other screens are displayed, using the Shooting 3 menu INFO. button display options choice, in Chapter 8. (You can choose none, any two, or all three, if you like.) The three additional screens that can be shown in a cycle when the INFO. button is pressed repeatedly are as follows:

■ **Camera settings.** Shows a list of basic settings for the camera, including color space, white balance information, noise reduction status, and the actual number of free shots remaining on your memory card. (The counter on the top-panel LCD can display no more than 999 shots remaining.) (See Figure 3.9.)

■ **Electronic level.** Displays the current degree of tilt of the camera, both rotation around the lens axis, and forward/back tilt. This capability is especially handy when you're mounting the camera on a tripod that does not have a built-in bubble level, and you want to square up the camera. (See Figure 3.10.)

Shooting mode for C1, C2, and C3 user settings

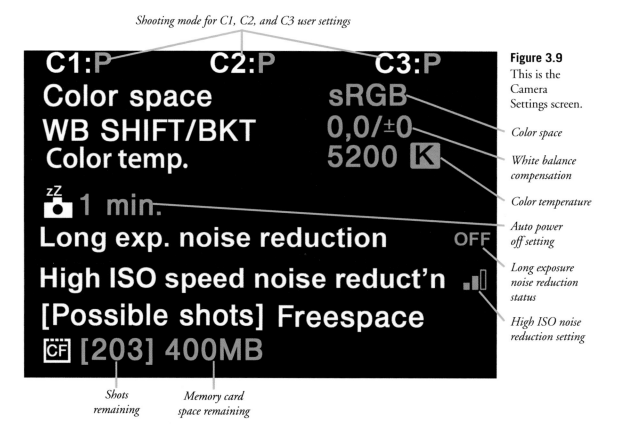

Figure 3.9
This is the Camera Settings screen.

Color space

White balance compensation

Color temperature

Auto power off setting

Long exposure noise reduction status

High ISO noise reduction setting

Shots remaining   *Memory card space remaining*

■ **Shooting functions.** Displays the current shooting settings of the camera, including shutter speed, aperture, ISO sensitivity, autofocus modes, battery status, and image quality settings. Press the Q button at the upper-left corner of the back of the camera, and you can adjust any of these that are user-selectable, as described in the sidebar that follows. (See Figure 3.11.)

■ **INFO. button (Live View/Movie mode).** When pressed repeatedly while using Live View or Movie mode, the INFO. button cycles among a slightly different set of informational screens. I'll show you those screens, and how to use them, in Chapter 6, which shows you how to use Live View mode and shoot video clips with your EOS 7D.

■ **INFO. button (other modes).** In playback mode, while reviewing images, pressing the INFO. button cycles among basic display of the image; a detailed display with a thumbnail of the image, shooting parameters, and a brightness histogram; and a display with less detail but with separate histograms for brightness, red, green, and blue channels. When setting Picture Styles, the INFO. button is used to select a highlighted Picture Style for modification. When trimming an image, the INFO. button selects the orientation. I'll describe all these different informational screens in Chapter 7.

Figure 3.10
The electronic
level can be
used to square
up the camera.

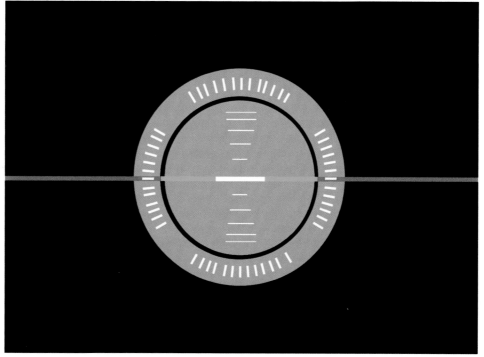

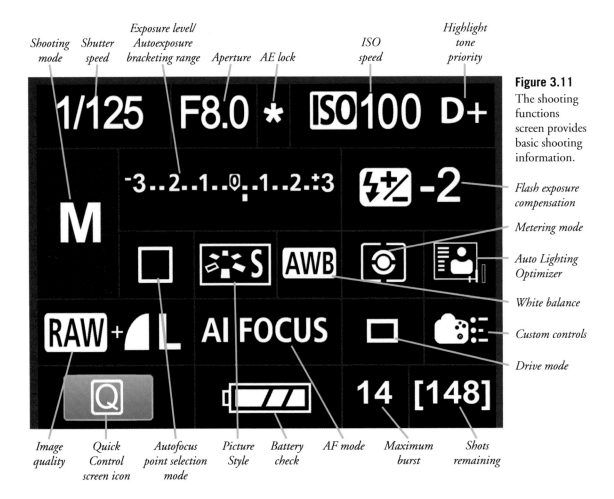

Figure 3.11
The shooting functions screen provides basic shooting information.

Shooting mode · *Shutter speed* · *Exposure level/ Autoexposure bracketing range* · *Aperture* · *AE lock* · *ISO speed* · *Highlight tone priority*

Flash exposure compensation
Metering mode
Auto Lighting Optimizer
White balance
Custom controls
Drive mode

Image quality · *Quick Control screen icon* · *Autofocus point selection mode* · *Picture Style* · *Battery check* · *AF mode* · *Maximum burst* · *Shots remaining*

- **Playback button.** Displays the last picture taken. Thereafter, you can move back and forth among the available images by rotating the Quick Control Dial, to advance or reverse one image at a time, or the Main Dial, to jump forward or back using the jump method described in the discussion of the Playback menu in Chapter 7. To quit playback, press this button again. The 7D also exits playback mode automatically when you press the shutter button (so you'll never be prevented from taking a picture on the spur of the moment because you happened to be viewing an image).

- **Erase button.** Press to erase the image shown on the LCD. A menu will pop up displaying Cancel and Erase choices. Rotate the Main Dial or the Quick Control Dial to select one of these actions, then press the SET button to activate your choice.

- **LCD.** View your images and navigate through the menus on this screen, which has a glorious 920,000 dots. It's big, it's bright, and it shows enough detail that you can zoom in and examine focus, grain, and sharpness.

USING THE QUICK CONTROL SCREEN

You can activate the Quick Control screen (shown in Figure 3.12) by pressing the Q button, located at the upper-left corner of the 7D's back panel. Then, use the multi-controller joystick (located just to the right of the upper edge of the color LCD; I'll explain this control in the next section) to highlight one of the settings in the screen.

You can't change the exposure mode; instead rotate the Mode Dial to Bulb, Manual, Av (Aperture-priority), Tv (Shutter-priority), P (Program), or CA (Creative Auto). The choices you can select change, depending on the position of the Mode Dial.

Once you've highlighted a setting, you can change it by rotating either the Main Dial or Quick Control Dial. You can then move the highlighting to a different setting using the multi-controller, if you want to make multiple changes. Press the Q button a second time to lock in the settings and exit the Quick Control screen.

Figure 3.12
Use the multi-controller button to select settings to modify in the Quick Control screen.

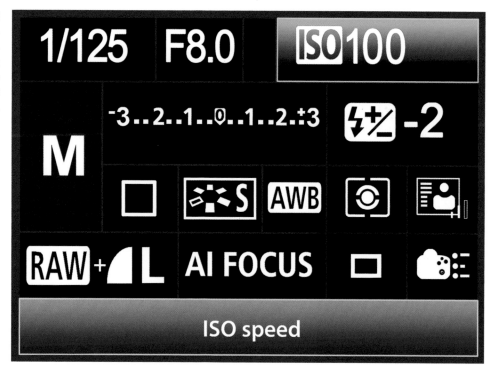

Using the One-Touch RAW+JPEG Button

This button lets you capture a RAW or JPEG version of the next shot you take, even if you've selected the "other" file format as your default for your current shooting session. As I'll explain in more detail in Chapter 7, you can choose to shoot three types of RAW files: standard RAW (RAW), Medium RAW (MRAW), or Small RAW (SRAW), either alone or simultaneously with any of six different types of JPEG files (Large, Medium, and Small, each in Fine or Standard image quality). Or, you can elect to shoot using one of the six JPEG settings, with no RAW files. But what do you do when you've selected a RAW (only) or JPEG (only) and decide you'd like the other type of image file, too, for your next shot?

That's where the handy One-touch RAW+JPEG button comes into play. If you've chosen to shoot only RAW or only JPEG you can press this button and capture the other format, *using a quality setting you define ahead of time.* That's the cool part of using this button: you can tell the EOS 7D to capture a Small RAW (SRAW) image when pressed while you're shooting JPEG only, or to capture, say, a Medium JPEG Standard file when you're shooting RAW and decide you need a reduced-resolution JPEG version of a shot. Not only can you grab the alternate format on an ad hoc basis, you can specify the quality level of your other shot. Just follow these steps:

1. **Define alternate formats.** First, you must tell the 7D the quality level you'd like for your alternate format images, when not using an automatic mode. Press the MENU button, and rotate the Main Dial (located just aft of the shutter release) until the Shooting 3 menu is highlighted. (It's the red-coded choice marked by a camera icon with three dots to the right of the icon.)

2. **Select One-touch RAW+JPEG.** Rotate the Quick Control Dial or use the multi-controller joystick to highlight the One-touch RAW+JPEG choice and press SET. The screen shown in Figure 3.13 appears.

3. **Choose RAW and JPEG quality.** Highlight either Simultaneous RAW or Simultaneous JPEG using the Quick Control Dial or multi-controller and press SET. In the screen that appears, choose the default simultaneous quality setting you want to use by rotating the QCD, then press SET to confirm. Specify both RAW and JPEG settings.

4. **Exit settings.** Press the MENU button twice, or tap the shutter release to exit when finished.

5. **Use One-touch RAW+JPEG button.** Thereafter, each time you press the button when shooting RAW or JPEG (only), the next shot (only) will be taken using the alternate setting at the quality level you've just defined. The simultaneous shooting is cancelled after that one shot is taken: you must keep pressing the One-touch RAW+JPEG button to use it for multiple shots. The button has no effect if you're already using a RAW+JPEG quality setting (as described in more detail in Chapter 7).

Figure 3.13
Use this screen
to set the
quality level
for your
simultaneous
RAW or JPEG
shots.

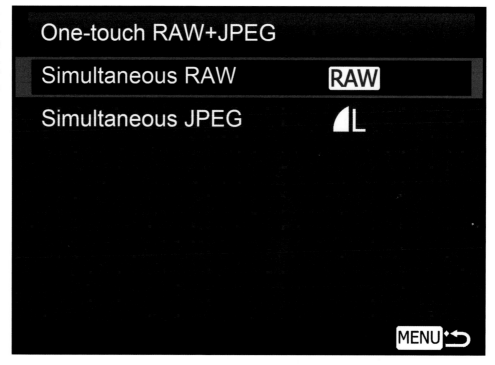

One-touch RAW+JPEG

Simultaneous RAW   RAW

Simultaneous JPEG   ◢L

MENU ↰

Figure 3.13
Use this screen to set the quality level for your simultaneous RAW or JPEG shots.

Right Side Controls

More buttons reside on the right side of the back panel, as shown in Figure 3.14. The key controls and their functions are as follows:

■ **Diopter adjustment knob.** Rotate this knob to adjust the diopter correction for your eyesight.

■ **Live View/Movie switch.** Flip to the left to enable movie shooting, and to the right to enable Live View viewing.

■ **Start/stop button.** Press to start or stop Live View or movie shooting.

■ **Multi-controller knob.** This joystick-like button can be shifted up, down, side to side, and diagonally for a total of eight directions, or pressed. It can be used for several functions, including AF point selection, scrolling around a magnified image, trimming a photo, or setting white balance correction.

■ **AF-ON.** Press this button to activate the autofocus system without needing to partially depress the shutter release. This control, used with other buttons, allows you to lock exposure and focus separately. Lock exposure by pressing the shutter release halfway, or by pressing the AE lock button; autofocus by pressing the shutter release halfway, or by pressing the AF-ON button. Functions of this button will be explained in more detail in Chapter 5.

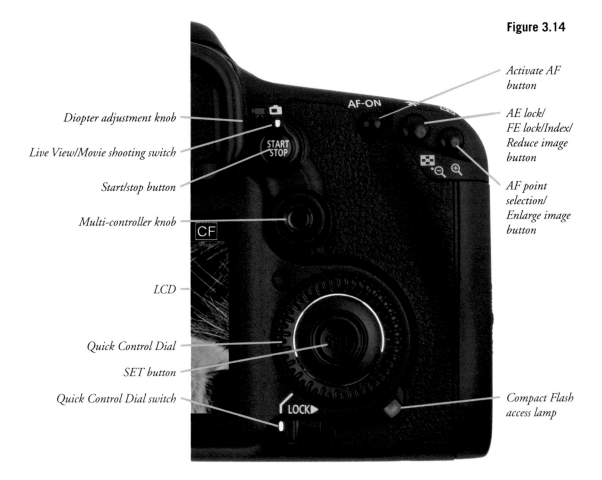

Figure 3.14

Diopter adjustment knob

Live View/Movie shooting switch

Start/stop button

Multi-controller knob

LCD

Quick Control Dial

SET button

Quick Control Dial switch

Activate AF button

AE lock/ FE lock/Index/ Reduce image button

AF point selection/ Enlarge image button

Compact Flash access lamp

■ **AE/FE (autoexposure/flash exposure) lock/Thumbnail/Zoom Out button.** This button has several functions, which differ depending on the AF point and metering mode. You can find more about these variations in Chapter 5.

In shooting mode, it locks the exposure or flash exposure that the camera sets when you partially depress the shutter button. The exposure lock indication (*) appears in the viewfinder. If you want to recalculate exposure with the shutter button still partially depressed, press the * button again. The exposure will be unlocked when you release the shutter button or take the picture. To retain the exposure lock for subsequent photos, keep the * button pressed while shooting.

When using flash, pressing the * button fires an extra preflash when you partially depress the shutter button; that allows the unit to calculate and lock exposure prior to taking the picture.

In playback mode, press this button to switch from single-image display to nine-image thumbnail index. Move among the thumbnails with the Quick Control Dial. When an image is zoomed in, press this button to zoom out.

- **AF point selection/Zoom In button.** In shooting mode, this button activates autofocus point selection. (See Chapter 5 for information on setting autofocus/exposure point selection.) In playback mode, this button zooms in on the image that's displayed, or the highlighted thumbnail index image.

- **Access lamp.** When lit or blinking, this lamp indicates that the Compact Flash card is being accessed.

- **Quick Control Dial.** Used to select shooting options, such as f/stop or exposure compensation value, or to navigate through menus. It also serves as an alternate controller for some functions set with other controls, such as AF point.

- **SET button.** Selects a highlighted setting or menu option.

- **Quick Control Dial switch position.** Slide to the left to activate the Quick Control Dial, or to the right to deactivate the optional features of the Quick Control Dial. (Which some users prefer for simplicity or to avoid accidentally changing the aperture in manual or aperture-priority exposure modes; most don't bother with this.)

REDUCING DIAL CONFUSION

The Canon EOS 7D makes efficient use of both the Main Dial and Quick Control Dial in many menus (as you'll learn in Chapters 7 and 8, which explains each menu and option). When both dials can be used, icons in the menus show you the settings that can be made with each. For example, when adjusting image quality in the Shooting 1 menu, the RAW format choices are displayed in a single row with an icon of the Main Dial above them. The JPEG options are presented in the next row, with an icon of the Quick Control Dial above them. You can tell at a glance that the Main Dial is used to switch from one RAW format to another, and the QCD is used to cycle among the JPEG choices. As I mentioned in Chapter 1, if you unexpectedly find that certain functions that you expected to activate with the Quick Control Dial don't work, check to make sure the ON/OFF switch is set to the full "ON" or "L"-shaped position rather than OFF.

Going Topside

The top surface of the Canon EOS 7D has its own set of frequently accessed controls. The three of them just forward of the status LCD panel have dual functions and are marked with hyphenated labels. Press the relevant button (you don't need to hold it down) and then rotate the Main Dial to choose the left function of the pair, such as metering mode, autofocus, or ISO, and the Quick Control Dial to select the right function, such as white balance, drive mode, or flash exposure compensation. The settings you make will be indicated in the LCD status panel, which is described in the section that follows this one.

The key controls, shown in Figure 3.15, are as follows:

- **Shutter release button.** Partially depress this button to lock in exposure and focus. Press all the way to take the picture. Tapping the shutter release when the camera has turned off the auto exposure and autofocus mechanisms reactivates both. When a review image is displayed on the back-panel color LCD, tapping this button removes the image from the display and reactivates the autoexposure and autofocus mechanisms.

- **Mode Dial.** Rotate this dial to switch among exposure modes, and to choose one of the Camera User Settings (C1, C2, or C3). You'll find these modes and options described in more detail in Chapter 8 (where I show you how to register your settings in the C1/C2/C3 "slots", ...)

- **Sensor focal plane.** Precision macro and scientific photography sometimes requires knowing exactly where the focal plane of the sensor is. The symbol on the side of the pentaprism marks that plane.

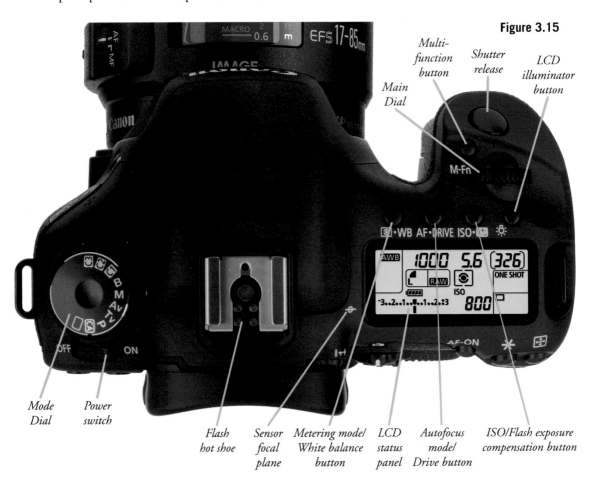

Figure 3.15

■ **Flash hot shoe.** Slide an electronic flash into this mount when you need a more powerful Speedlite. A dedicated flash unit, like those from Canon, can use the multiple contact points shown to communicate exposure, zoom setting, white balance information, and other data between the flash and the camera. There's more on using electronic flash in Chapters 10 and 11.

■ **LCD illuminator button.** Press this button to turn on the amber LCD panel lamp that backlights the LCD status panel for about six seconds, or to turn it off if illuminated. The lamp will remain lit beyond the six-second period if you are using the Mode Dial or other shooting control.

■ **Metering mode/WB button.** This button has two functions. Rotate the Main Dial after pressing this button to change between evaluative, partial, spot, or center-weighted metering. Rotate the Quick Control Dial to cycle among AWB (Automatic White Balance), Daylight, Shade, Cloudy/Twilight/Sunset, Tungsten, White Fluorescent, Flash, Custom, and Color Temperature. You'll find more information about customizing white balance in Chapter 7.

■ **AF-DRIVE button.** Press once and then rotate the Main Dial to change between One-Shot, AI Focus, and AI Servo autofocus modes (you'll find more about those modes in Chapter 5). Drive mode settings include single shooting, high-speed continuous (up to 8 fps), low-speed continuous (up to 3 fps), and 10- or 2-second self-timer/remote control, selected by holding down the button and rotating the Quick Control Dial.

■ **ISO/Flash exposure compensation button.** Press and rotate the Main Dial to choose an ISO setting; use the Quick Control Dial to change electronic flash exposure compensation. You'll find more about ISO options in Chapter 4, and flash EV settings in Chapter 10.

■ **Monochrome LCD status panel.** This LCD readout provides information about the status of your camera and its settings, including exposure mode, number of pictures remaining, battery status, and many other settings. I'll illustrate all these in the next section.

■ **Main Dial.** This dial is used to make many shooting settings. When settings come in pairs (such as shutter speed/aperture in manual shooting mode), the Main Dial is used for one (for example, shutter speed), while the Quick Control Dial is used for the other (aperture). When an image is on the screen during playback, this dial also specifies the leaps that skip a particular number of images during playback of the shots you've already taken. Jumps can be either 1 image, 10 images, 100 images, jump by date, or jump by screen (that is, by screens of thumbnails when using index mode), date, or folder. (Jump method is selected in the Playback 2 menu, as described in Chapter 7.) This dial is also used to move among tabs when the MENU button has been pressed, and is used within some menus (in conjunction with the Quick Control Dial) to change pairs of settings.

Table 3.1 Control Button Functions		
Button	**Main Dial**	**Quick Control Dial**
Meter/WB	Evaluative/Partial/Spot/ Center-weighted average metering modes	Auto/Daylight/Shade/Cloudy/ Tungsten/White Fluorescent/ Flash/Custom/Kelvin color temperatures
AF-DRIVE	One-Shot/AI Focus/ AI Servo autofocus modes	Single shooting/Continuous high 8 fps/Continuous 3 fps/ Self-timer 2 seconds/Self-timer 10 seconds/Remote
ISO-Flash EV	ISO Auto/ISO 100-6,400/ H (12,800)*	Flash compensation (+ or – up to 3 stops)

*When ISO Expansion is turned on with Custom Function (C.Fn I-3)

LCD Panel Readouts

The top panel of the EOS 7D (see Figure 3.16) contains an amber-colored (when back-lit) monochrome LCD readout that displays status information about most of the shooting settings. All of the information segments available are shown in Figure 3.17. I've color-coded the display to make it easier to differentiate them; the information does *not* appear in color on the actual 7D. Many of the information items are mutually exclusive (that is, in the white balance area at upper left, only one of the possible settings illustrated will appear).

Figure 3.16

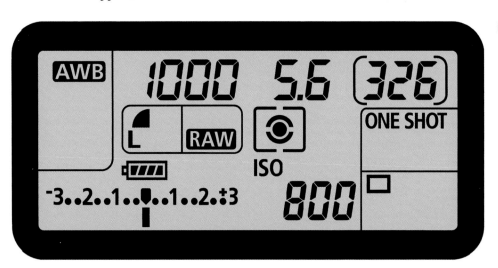

Figure 3.17

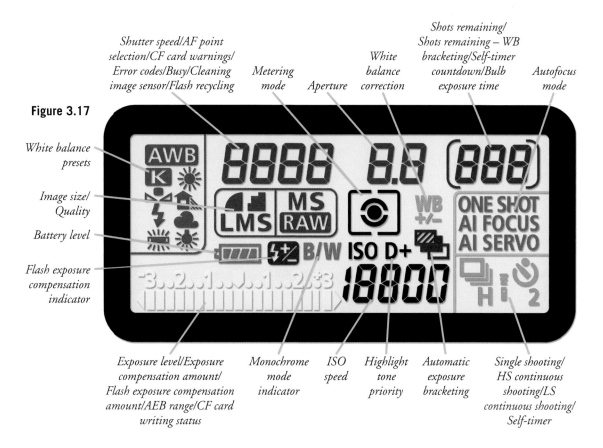

Shutter speed/AF point selection/CF card warnings/Error codes/Busy/Cleaning image sensor/Flash recycling

Metering mode

Aperture

White balance correction

Shots remaining/Shots remaining – WB bracketing/Self-timer countdown/Bulb exposure time

Autofocus mode

White balance presets

Image size/Quality

Battery level

Flash exposure compensation indicator

Exposure level/Exposure compensation amount/Flash exposure compensation amount/AEB range/CF card writing status

Monochrome mode indicator

ISO speed

Highlight tone priority

Automatic exposure bracketing

Single shooting/HS continuous shooting/LS continuous shooting/Self-timer

Some of the items on the status LCD also appear in the viewfinder, such as the shutter speed and aperture (pictured at top in blue in the figure), and the exposure level (in yellow at the bottom).

Lens Components

The typical lens, like the one shown in Figures 3.18 and 3.19, has seven or eight common features:

- **Filter thread.** Lenses have a thread on the front for attaching filters and other add-ons. Some also use this thread for attaching a lens hood (you screw on the filter first, and then attach the hood to the screw thread on the front of the filter).

- **Lens hood bayonet.** This is used to mount the lens hood for lenses that don't use screw-mount hoods (the majority).

- **Zoom ring.** Turn this ring to change the zoom setting.

Figure 3.18

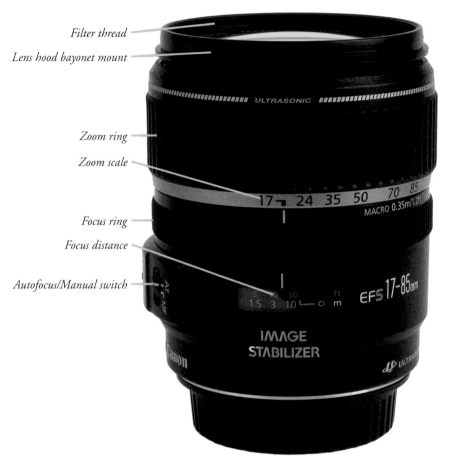

Filter thread

Lens hood bayonet mount

Zoom ring

Zoom scale

Focus ring

Focus distance

Autofocus/Manual switch

Figure 3.19

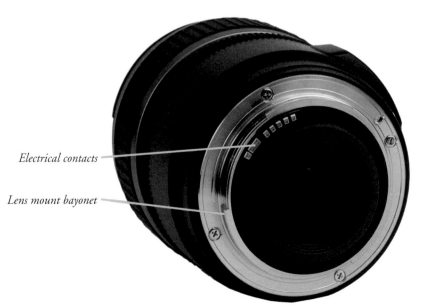

Electrical contacts

Lens mount bayonet

- **Zoom scale.** These markings on the lens show the current focal length selected.

- **Focus ring.** This is the ring you turn when you manually focus the lens.

- **Distance scale.** This is a readout that rotates in unison with the lens' focus mechanism to show the distance at which the lens has been focused. It's a useful indicator for double-checking autofocus, roughly evaluating depth-of-field, and for setting manual focus guesstimates.

- **Autofocus/Manual switch.** Allows you to change from automatic focus to manual focus.

- **Image stabilization switch (not shown).** Lenses with IS include a separate switch for adjusting the stabilization feature.

Looking Inside the Viewfinder

Much of the important shooting status information is shown inside the viewfinder of the EOS 7D. As with the status LCD up on top, not all of this information will be shown at any one time. Figure 3.20 shows what you can expect to see. These readouts include:

- **Spot metering reference circle.** Shows the circle that delineates the metered area when spot metering is activated.

- **Autofocus zones.** Shows the 19 areas used by the 7D to focus. The camera can select the appropriate focus zone for you, or you can manually select one or all of the zones, as described in Chapter 5.

- **Autoexposure lock.** Shows that exposure has been locked. This icon also appears when an automatic exposure bracketing sequence is in process.

- **Flash ready indicator.** This icon appears when the flash is fully charged. It also shows when the flash exposure lock has been applied for an inappropriate exposure value.

- **Flash status indicator.** Appears along with the flash ready indicator: the H is shown when high speed (focal plane) flash sync is being used. The * appears when flash exposure lock or a flash exposure bracketing sequence is underway.

- **Flash exposure compensation.** Appears when flash EV changes have been made.

- **Shutter speed/aperture readouts.** Most of the time, these readouts show the current shutter speed and aperture. This pair can also warn you of Compact Flash card conditions (full, error, or missing), ISO speed, flash exposure lock, and a buSY indicator when the camera is busy doing other things (including flash recycling).

- **Exposure level indicator.** This scale shows the current exposure level, with the bottom indicator centered when the exposure is correct as metered. The indicator may also move to the left or right to indicate under- or overexposure (respectively). The scale is also used to show the amount of EV and flash EV adjustments, the number of stops covered by the current automatic exposure bracketing range, and is used as a red-eye reduction lamp indicator.

- **ISO sensitivity.** This useful indicator shows the current ISO setting value. Those who have accidentally taken dozens of shots under bright sunlight at ISO 1600 because they forgot to change the setting back after some indoor shooting will treasure this addition.

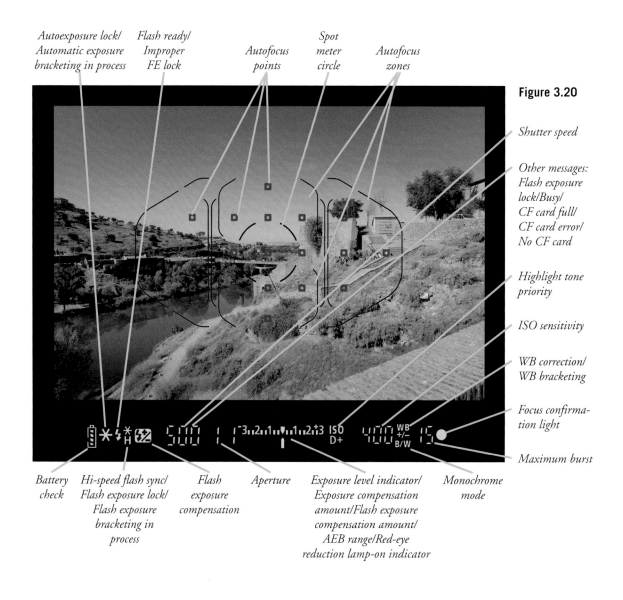

Figure 3.20

Autoexposure lock/
Automatic exposure
bracketing in process

Flash ready/
Improper
FE lock

Autofocus
points

Spot
meter
circle

Autofocus
zones

Shutter speed

Other messages:
Flash exposure
lock/Busy/
CF card full/
CF card error/
No CF card

Highlight tone
priority

ISO sensitivity

WB correction/
WB bracketing

Focus confirma-
tion light

Maximum burst

Battery
check

Hi-speed flash sync/
Flash exposure lock/
Flash exposure
bracketing in
process

Flash
exposure
compensation

Aperture

Exposure level indicator/
Exposure compensation
amount/Flash exposure
compensation amount/
AEB range/Red-eye
reduction lamp-on indicator

Monochrome
mode

- **B/W indicator.** Illuminates when the Monochrome Picture Style is being used. There's no way to restore color when you're shooting JPEGs without RAW, so this indicator is another valuable warning.

- **White balance correction.** Shows that white balance has been tweaked.

- **Maximum burst available.** Changes to a number to indicate the number of frames that can be taken in continuous mode using the current settings.

- **Focus confirmation.** This green dot appears when the subject covered by the active autofocus zone is in sharp focus.

Underneath Your EOS 7D

There's not a lot going on with the bottom panel of your EOS 7D. You'll find a tripod socket, which secures the camera to a tripod and is also used to lock on the optional BG-E7 battery grip, which provides more juice to run your camera to take more exposures with a single charge. It also adds a vertically oriented shutter release, Main Dial, AE lock/FE lock and AF point selection controls for easier vertical shooting. There's a terminal connector under a rubber cover to provide a connection between the 7D and accessories that fasten to the underside. To mount the grip, slide the battery door latch to open the door, then push down on the small pin that projects from the hinge. That will let you remove the battery door. Then slide the grip into the battery cavity, aligning the pin on the grip with the small hole on the other side of the tripod socket. Tighten the grip's tripod socket screw to lock the grip onto the bottom of your 7D. Figure 3.21

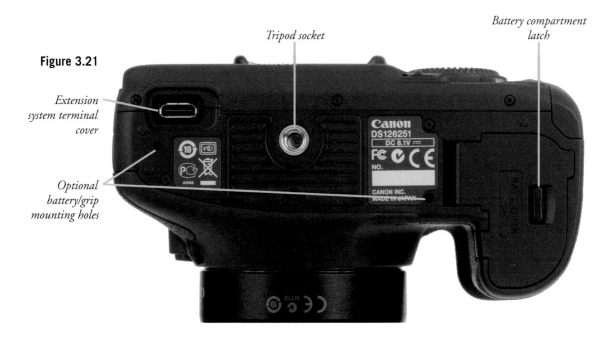

Figure 3.21

Tripod socket

Battery compartment latch

Extension system terminal cover

Optional battery/grip mounting holes

shows the underside view of the camera, and Figure 3.22 offers a close-up look at the accessory terminal connection. Note that the cover for the terminal is not "tethered" to the camera and can be easily misplaced. Take care!

Figure 3.22

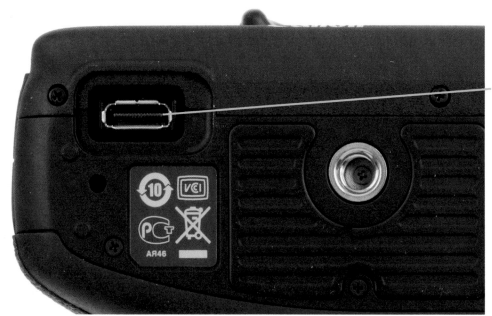

Extension system terminal connection

Part II

Beyond the Basics

When you bought your Canon EOS 7D, you probably thought your days of worrying about getting the correct exposure, achieving focus, and using its more advanced features, like Live View and movie making were over. To paraphrase an old Kodak tagline dating back to the 19th Century—the goal is, "you press the button, and the camera does the rest."

For the most part, that's a realistic objective. The 7D is one of the smartest cameras available when it comes to calculating the right exposure for most situations, locking in focus, and shooting video clips. For exposure, you can generally choose one of the automatic modes—either Auto or Creative Auto—or spin the Mode Dial to Program (P), Aperture-priority (Av), or Shutter-priority (Tv), and shoot away. Autofocus, too, is quick and easy. You can use One-Shot AF for stationary subjects, AI Servo AF for subjects that are in motion, or AI Focus to allow the 7D to decide which of the other two modes to use, depending on circumstances. Most of the other advanced features are also straightforward to use.

So, why do you need the three chapters in Part II: Beyond the Basics? I think you'll find that even if you've mastered the fundamentals and controls of the EOS 7D, there is lots of room to learn more and use the features of the camera to their fullest. Even if you're getting great exposures a high percentage of the time, you can fine-tune tonal values and use your shutter speed, aperture, and ISO controls creatively. Your camera's high performance autofocus system may zero in on your subject in most situations—but you still need to be able to tell the 7D *what* to focus on, and *when*. Other tools at your disposal let you freeze an instant of time, record a continuous series of instants as a movie, and improve your images in other imaginative ways. The chapters in Part II will help you move your photography to the next level by understanding exposure, mastering the mysteries of autofocus, and using the Canon EOS 7D's advanced features.

4

Understanding Exposure

As you learn to use your 7D creatively, you're going to find that the right settings—as determined by the camera's exposure meter and intelligence—need to be *adjusted* to account for your creative decisions or special situations.

For example, when you shoot with the main light source behind the subject, you end up with *backlighting*, which results in an overexposed background and/or an underexposed subject. The EOS 7D recognizes backlit situations nicely, and can properly base exposure on the main subject, producing a decent photo. Features like Highlight Tone Priority and the Auto Lighting Optimizer can fine-tune exposure to preserve detail in the highlights and shadows.

But what if you *want* to underexpose the subject, to produce a silhouette effect? Or, perhaps, you might want to flip up the 7D's built-in flash unit to fill in the shadows on your subject. The more you know about how to use your 7D, the more you'll run into situations where you want to creatively tweak the exposure to provide a different look than you'd get with a straight shot.

This chapter shows you the fundamentals of exposure, so you'll be better equipped to override the EOS 7D's default settings when you want to, or need to. After all, correct exposure is one of the foundations of good photography, along with accurate focus and sharpness, appropriate color balance, freedom from unwanted noise and excessive contrast, as well as pleasing composition.

The EOS 7D gives you a great deal of control over all of these, although composition is entirely up to you. You must still frame the photograph to create an interesting arrangement of subject matter, but all the other parameters are basic functions of the camera. You can let your 7D set them for you automatically, you can fine-tune how the camera applies its automatic settings, or you can make them yourself, manually. The amount of control you have over exposure, sensitivity (ISO settings), color balance, focus, and image parameters like sharpness and contrast make the 7D a versatile tool for creating images.

In the next few pages I'm going to give you a grounding in one of those foundations, and explain the basics of exposure, either as an introduction or as a refresher course, depending on your current level of expertise. When you finish this chapter, you'll understand most of what you need to know to take well-exposed photographs creatively in a broad range of situations.

Getting a Handle on Exposure

Exposure determines the look, feel, and tone of an image, in more ways than one. Incorrect exposure can impair even the best-composed image by cloaking important tones in darkness, or by washing them out so they become featureless to the eye. On the other hand, correct exposure brings out the detail in the areas you want to picture, and provides the range of tones and colors you need to create the desired image. However, getting the perfect exposure can be tricky, because digital sensors can't capture all the tones we are able to see. If the range of tones in an image is extensive, embracing both inky black shadows and bright highlights, the sensor may not be able to capture them all. Sometimes, we must settle for an exposure that renders most of those tones—but not all—in a way that best suits the photo we want to produce. You'll often need to make choices about which details are important, and which are not, so that you can grab the tones that truly matter in your image. That's part of the creativity you bring to bear in realizing your photographic vision.

For example, look at the two typical tourist snapshots presented side by side in Figure 4.1. The camera was mounted on a tripod for both, so the only way you can really see that they are two different images is by examining the differences in the way the water flows in the ice-free area of the foreground. However, the pair of pictures does vary in exposure. The version on the left was underexposed, which helps bring out detail in the snow and sky in the background, but makes the shadows of the building look murky and dark. The overexposed version on the right offers better exposure for the foreground area, but now the brightest areas of the building and sky are much too light.

With digital camera sensors, it's tricky to capture detail in both highlights and shadows in a single image, because the number of tones, the *dynamic range* of the sensor, is limited. The solution, in this particular case, was to resort to a technique called High Dynamic Range (HDR) photography, in which the two exposures from Figure 4.1 were combined in an image editor such as Photoshop, or a specialized HDR tool like Photomatix (about $100 from www.hdrsoft.com). The resulting shot is shown in Figure 4.2. I'll explain more about HDR photography later in this chapter. For now, though, I'm going to concentrate on showing you how to get the best exposures possible without resorting to such tools, using only the features of your Canon EOS 7D.

Figure 4.1
At left, the image is exposed for the background highlights, losing shadow detail. At right, the exposure captures detail in the shadows, but the background highlights are washed out.

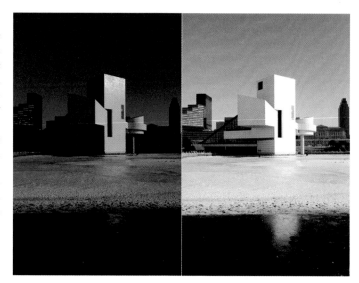

Figure 4.2
Combining the two exposures produces the best compromise image.

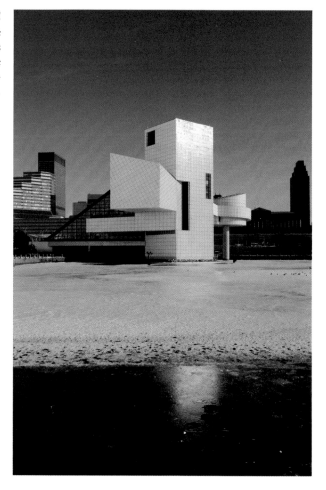

To understand exposure, you need to understand the six aspects of light that combine to produce an image. Start with a light source—the sun, an interior lamp, or the glow from a campfire—and trace its path to your camera, through the lens, and finally to the sensor that captures the illumination. Here's a brief review of the things within our control that affect exposure.

- **Light at its source.** Our eyes and our cameras—film or digital—are most sensitive to that portion of the electromagnetic spectrum we call *visible light.* That light has several important aspects that are relevant to photography, such as color and harshness (which is determined primarily by the apparent size of the light source as it illuminates a subject). But, in terms of exposure, the important attribute of a light source is its *intensity.* We may have direct control over intensity, which might be the case with an interior light that can be brightened or dimmed. Or, we might have only indirect control over intensity, as with sunlight, which can be made to appear dimmer by introducing translucent light-absorbing or reflective materials in its path.

- **Light's duration.** We tend to think of most light sources as continuous. But, as you'll learn in Chapter 10, the duration of light can change quickly enough to modify the exposure, as when the main illumination in a photograph comes from an intermittent source, such as an electronic flash.

- **Light reflected, transmitted, or emitted.** Once light is produced by its source, either continuously or in a brief burst, we are able to see and photograph objects by the light that is reflected from our subjects towards the camera lens; transmitted (say, from translucent objects that are lit from behind); or emitted (by a candle or television screen). When more or less light reaches the lens from the subject, we need to adjust the exposure. This part of the equation is under our control to the extent we can increase the amount of light falling on or passing through the subject (by adding extra light sources or using reflectors), or by pumping up the light that's emitted (by increasing the brightness of the glowing object).

- **Light passed by the lens.** Not all the illumination that reaches the front of the lens makes it all the way through. Filters can remove some of the light before it enters the lens. Inside the lens barrel is a variable-sized diaphragm called an *aperture* that dilates and contracts to control the amount of light that enters the lens. You, or the 7D's autoexposure system, can control exposure by varying the size of the aperture. The relative size of the aperture is called the *f/stop* (see Figure 4.3).

- **Light passing through the shutter.** Once light passes through the lens, the amount of time the sensor receives it is determined by the 7D's shutter, which can remain open for as long as 30 seconds (or even longer if you use the Bulb setting) or as briefly as 1/8,000th second.

■ **Light captured by the sensor.** Not all the light falling onto the sensor is captured. If the number of photons reaching a particular photosite doesn't pass a set threshold, no information is recorded. Similarly, if too much light illuminates a pixel in the sensor, then the excess isn't recorded or, worse, spills over to contaminate adjacent pixels. We can modify the minimum and maximum number of pixels that contribute to image detail by adjusting the ISO setting. At higher ISOs, the incoming light is amplified to boost the effective sensitivity of the sensor.

F/STOPS AND SHUTTER SPEEDS

If you're *really* new to more advanced cameras (and I realize that many soon-to-be-ambitious photographers do purchase the 7D as their first digital SLR), you might need to know that the lens aperture, or f/stop, is a ratio, much like a fraction, which is why f/2 is larger than f/4, just as 1/2 is larger than 1/4. However, f/2 is actually *four times* as large as f/4. (If you remember your high school geometry, you'll know that to double the area of a circle, you multiply its diameter by the square root of two: 1.4.)

Lenses are usually marked with intermediate f/stops that represent a size that's twice as much/half as much as the previous aperture. So, a lens might be marked f/2, f/2.8, f/4, f/5.6, f/8, f/11, f/16, f/22, with each larger number representing an aperture that admits half as much light as the one before, as shown in Figure 4.3.

Shutter speeds are actual fractions (of a second), but the numerator is omitted, so that 60, 125, 250, 500, 1,000, and so forth represent 1/60th, 1/125th, 1/250th, 1/500th, and 1/1,000th second. To avoid confusion, EOS uses quotation marks to signify longer exposures: 2", 2"5, 4", and so forth representing 2.0, 2.5, and 4.0-second exposures, respectively.

Figure 4.3
Top row
(left to right):
f/2, f/2.8, f/4;
bottom row,
f/5.6, f/8, f11.

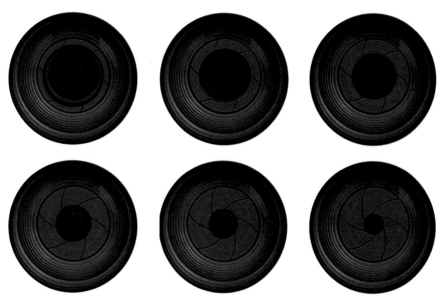

These factors—the quantity of light produced by the light source, the amount reflected or transmitted towards the camera, the light passed by the lens, the amount of time the shutter is open, and the sensitivity of the sensor—all work proportionately and reciprocally to produce an exposure. That is, if you double the amount of light that's available, increase the aperture by one stop, make the shutter speed twice as long, or boost the ISO setting 2X, you'll get twice as much exposure. Similarly, you can increase any of these factors while decreasing one of the others by a similar amount to keep the same exposure.

Most commonly, exposure settings are made using the aperture and shutter speed, followed by adjusting the ISO sensitivity if it's not possible to get the preferred exposure; that is, the one that uses the "best" f/stop or shutter speed for the depth-of-field (range of sharp focus) or action stopping we want (produced by short shutter speeds, as I'll explain later). Table 4.1 shows equivalent exposure settings using various shutter speeds and f/stops.

When the 7D is set for P (Program) mode, the metering system selects the correct exposure for you automatically, but you can change quickly to an equivalent exposure by holding down the shutter release button halfway ("locking" the current exposure), and then spinning the Main Dial until the desired *equivalent* exposure combination is displayed. You can use this standard Program Shift feature more easily if you remember that you need to rotate the dial towards the *left* when you want to increase the amount of depth-of-field or use a slower shutter speed; rotate to the *right* when you want to reduce the depth-of-field or use a faster shutter speed. The need for more/less DOF and slower/faster shutter speed are the primary reasons you'd want to use Program Shift. I'll explain Program mode exposure shifting options in more detail later in this chapter.

In Aperture-priority (Av) and Shutter-priority (Tv) modes, you can change to an equivalent exposure using a different combination of shutter speed and aperture, but only by either adjusting the aperture in Aperture-priority mode (the camera then chooses the shutter speed) or shutter speed in Shutter-priority mode (the camera then selects the aperture). I'll cover all these exposure modes and their differences later in the chapter. (See Figure 4.4.)

Table 4.1 Equivalent Exposures

Shutter Speed	f/stop	Shutter Speed	f/stop
1/30th second	f/22	1/1,000th second	f/4
1/60th second	f/16	1/2,000th second	f/2.8
1/125th second	f/11	1/4,000th second	f/2
1/250th second	f/8	1/8,000th second	f/1.4
1/500th second	f/5.6		

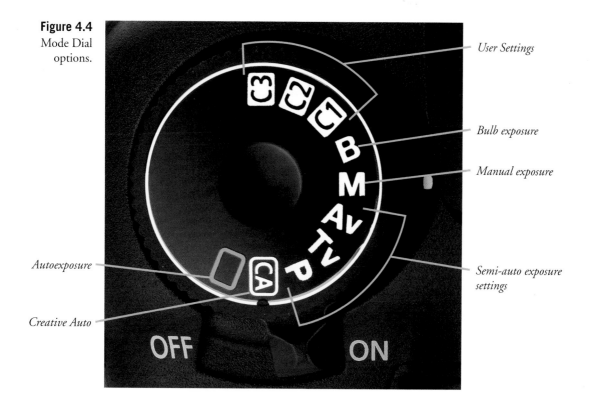

Figure 4.4
Mode Dial
options.

User Settings

Bulb exposure

Manual exposure

Autoexposure

Creative Auto

Semi-auto exposure
settings

OFF   ON

How the EOS 7D Calculates Exposure

Your Canon 7D calculates exposure by measuring the light that passes through the lens and is bounced up by the mirror to sensors located near the focusing surface, using a pattern you can select (more on that later) and based on the assumption that each area being measured reflects about the same amount of light as a neutral gray card that reflects a "middle" gray of about 12 to 18-percent reflectance. The photographic "gray cards" you buy at a camera store have an 18-percent gray tone; your camera is calibrated to interpret a somewhat darker 12-percent gray; I'll explain more about this later. That "average" 12-18-percent gray assumption is necessary, because different subjects reflect different amounts of light. In a photo containing, say, a white cat and a dark gray cat, the white cat might reflect five times as much light as the gray cat. An exposure based on the white cat will cause the gray cat to appear to be black, while an exposure based only on the gray cat will make the white cat washed out.

This is more easily understood if you look at some photos of subjects that are dark (they reflect little light), those that have predominantly middle tones, and subjects that are highly reflective. Figure 4.5 shows such an image of some actual cats (actually, the same cat rendered in black, gray, and white varieties through the magic of Photoshop), with each of the three strips exposed using a different cat for reference.

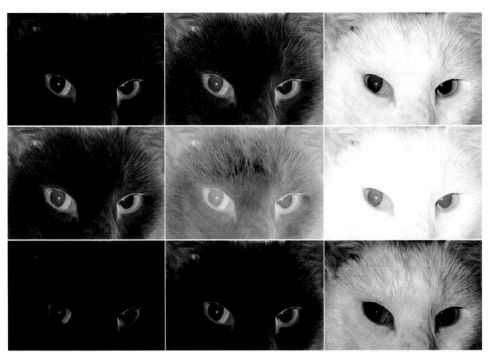

Figure 4.5

Exposure calculated by measuring the middle cat (top strip of three cats); by measuring the black cat at left (middle strip of three cats); and by measuring the white cat at right (bottom strip of three cats).

Here's what you are looking at:

- **Correctly exposed (top):** The top three pictures are shown as if the exposure were calculated by measuring the light reflecting from the middle, gray cat. That feline is rendered at its proper tonal value, and, because the resulting exposure is correct, the black cat at left and white cat at right are rendered properly as well.

- **Overexposed (middle):** The strip of three images in the middle of the figure show what would happen if the exposure were calculated by metering from the leftmost, black cat. The light meter sees less light reflecting from the black cat than it would see from a gray middle-tone subject, and so calls for more exposure. That brightens up the black cat, so it now appears to be gray. But the cat in the middle that was originally gray and the white cat at right are now overexposed.

- **Underexposed (bottom):** The strip of three images at the bottom of the figure illustrate what you'd get if the light meter measures the white cat. A lot of light is reflected by the white kitty, so the exposure is reduced, bringing that cat closer to a middle gray tone. The cats that were originally gray and black are now rendered too dark. Clearly, measuring the gray cat—or a substitute that reflects about the same amount of light, is the only way to ensure that the exposure is precisely correct.

If you want the most precise exposure calculations and you don't have a gray cat handy, the solution is to use a stand-in, such as the evenly illuminated gray card I mentioned earlier. But, because the standard Kodak gray card reflects 18 percent of the light that reaches it and, as I said, your camera is calibrated for a somewhat darker 12-percent tone, you would need to add about one-half stop *more* exposure than the value metered from the card.

Another substitute for a gray card is the palm of a human hand (the backside of the hand is too variable). But a human palm, regardless of ethnic group, is even brighter than a standard gray card, so instead of one-half stop more exposure, you need to add one additional stop. That is, if your meter reading is 1/500th of a second at f/11, use 1/500th second at f/8 or 1/250th second at f/11 instead. (Both exposures are equivalent.)

If you actually wanted to use a gray card, place it in your frame near your main subject, facing the camera, and with the exact same even illumination falling on it that is falling on your subject. Then, use the spot metering function (described in the next section) to calculate exposure. Of course, in most situations, it's not necessary to do this. Your camera's light meter will do a good job of calculating the right exposure, especially if you use the exposure tips in the next section. But, I felt that explaining exactly what is going on during exposure calculation would help you understand how your 7D's metering system works.

WHY THE GRAY CARD CONFUSION?

Why are so many photographers under the impression that cameras and meters are calibrated to the 18-percent "standard," rather than the true value, which may be 12 to 14 percent, depending on the vendor? The most common explanation is that during a revision of Kodak's instructions for its gray cards in the 1970s, the advice to open up an extra half stop was omitted, and a whole generation of shooters grew up thinking that a measurement off a gray card could be used as-is. The proviso returned to the instructions by 1987, it's said, but by then it was too late. Next to me is a ©2006 version of the instructions for KODAK Gray Cards, Publication R-27Q, and the current directions read (with a bit of paraphrasing from me in italics):

■ For subjects of normal reflectance increase the indicated exposure by 1/2 stop.

■ For light subjects use the indicated exposure; for very light subjects, decrease the exposure by 1/2 stop. (*That is, you're measuring a cat that's lighter than middle gray.*)

■ If the subject is dark to very dark, increase the indicated exposure by 1 to 1-1/2 stops. (*You're shooting a black cat.*)

Choosing a Metering Method

To calculate exposure automatically, you need to tell the 7D *where* in the frame to measure the light (this is called the *metering method*) and *what controls* should be used (aperture, shutter speed, or both) to set the exposure. That's called *exposure mode,* and includes

Program (P), Shutter-priority (Tv), Aperture-priority (Av), or Manual (M) options, plus Auto and Creative Auto. I'll explain all these next.

But first, I'm going to introduce you to the four metering methods, which can be selected by pressing the Metering mode/White balance selection button on the top panel, and using the Main Dial until the icon for the mode you want appears in the status LCD. Select any of the four if you're working with P, Tv, Av, or M exposure modes; if you're using Auto or Creative Auto, the first choice, evaluative metering, is selected automatically and cannot be changed.

- **Evaluative.** The 7D slices up the frame into 63 different zones, shown as yellow rectangles in Figure 4.6 (the top-panel status LCD icon is shown in the upper-left corner; it does not appear in the viewfinder). The zones used are linked to the autofocus system (the 19 autofocus zones are also shown in the figure). The camera evaluates the measurements, giving extra emphasis to the metering zones that indicate sharp focus to make an educated guess about what kind of picture you're taking, based on examination of thousands of different real-world photos. For example, if the top sections of a picture are much lighter than the bottom portions, the algorithm can assume that the scene is a landscape photo with lots of sky. This mode is the best all-purpose metering method for most pictures. I'll explain how to choose an autofocus/exposure zone in the section on autofocus operation later in this chapter.

- **Partial.** This is a *faux* spot mode, using roughly 9.4 percent of the image area to calculate exposure, which, as you can see in Figure 4.8, is a rather large spot, represented by a yellow disk. The status LCD icon is shown in the upper-left corner. Use this mode if the background is much brighter or darker than the subject.

- **Spot.** This mode confines the reading to a limited area in the center of the viewfinder, as shown in Figure 4.10, making up only 2.3 percent of the image. This mode is useful when you want to base exposure on a small area in the frame, such as a spotlight performer on stage, surrounded by a black background. If that area is in the center of the frame, so much the better. If not, you'll have to make your meter reading and then lock exposure by pressing the shutter release halfway, or by pressing the AE lock button.

- **Center-weighted.** In this mode, the exposure meter emphasizes a zone in the center of the frame to calculate exposure, as shown in Figure 4.12, on the theory that, for most pictures, the main subject will be located in the center. Center-weighting works best for portraits, architectural photos, and other pictures in which the most important subject is located in the middle of the frame. As the name suggests, the light reading is *weighted* towards the central portion, but information is also used from the rest of the frame. If your main subject is surrounded by very bright or very dark areas, the exposure might not be exactly right. However, this scheme works well in many situations if you don't want to use one of the other modes.

Figure 4.6
Evaluative
metering uses
63 zones
marked by blue
rectangles,
linked to the
autofocus
points shown
as red brackets.

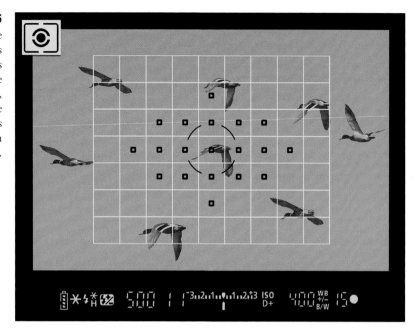

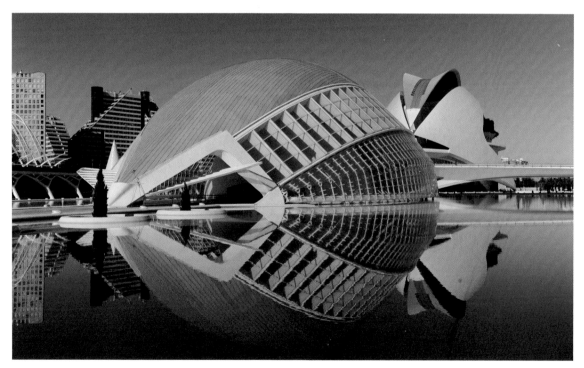

Figure 4.7 An evenly-lit scene like this one can be metered effectively using the evaluative metering setting.

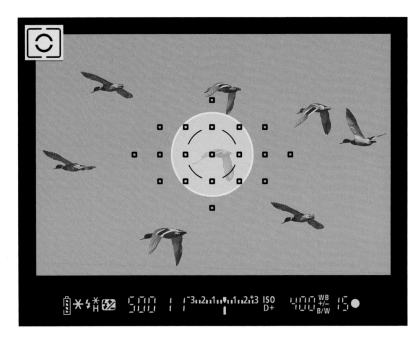

Figure 4.8
Partial metering uses a center spot that's roughly nine percent of the frame area.

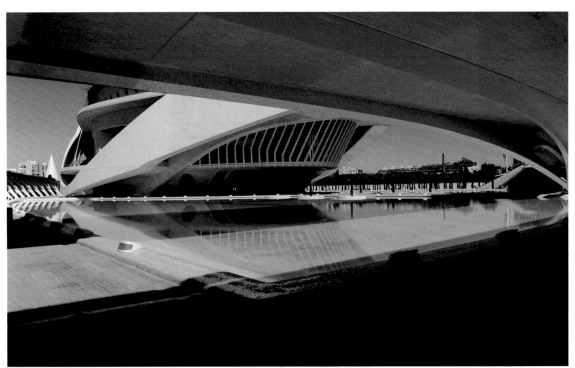

Figure 4.9 Partial metering allowed measuring exposure from the central area of the image, while ignoring the darker areas at top and bottom.

Figure 4.10
Spot metering calculates exposure based on a center spot that's only 3.8 percent of the image area.

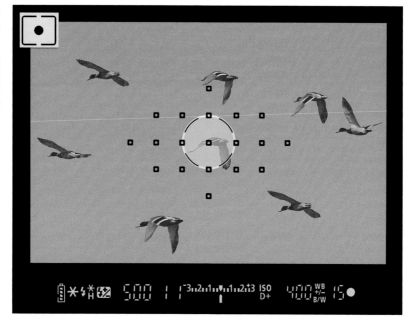

Figure 4.11
Spot metering allowed calculating exposure exclusively from the performer's face.

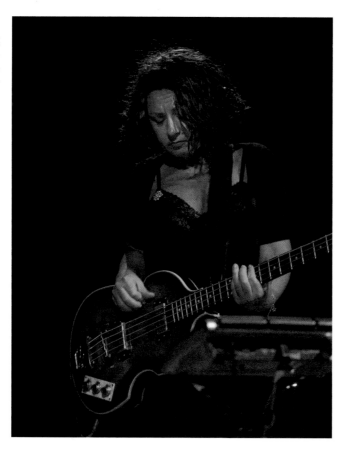

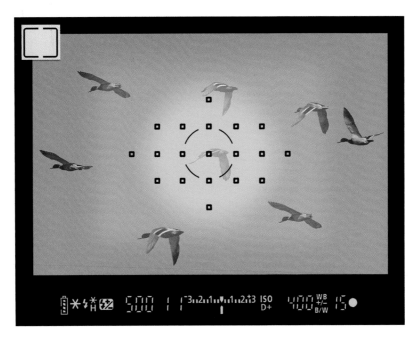

Figure 4.12
Center-weighted metering calculates exposure based on the full frame, but emphasizes the center area.

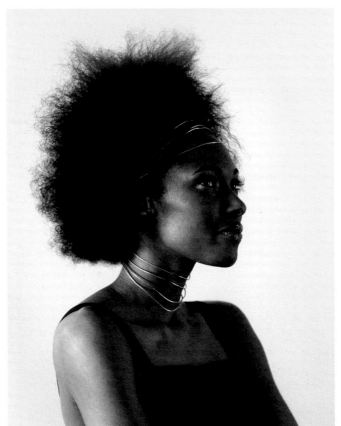

Figure 4.13
Center-weighted metering calculated the exposure for this shot from the large area in the center of the frame, with less emphasis on the bright, window-lit area behind the subject.

Choosing an Exposure Method

You'll find six methods for choosing the appropriate shutter speed and aperture: Full Auto, Creative Auto, Program (P), Shutter-priority (Tv), Aperture-priority (Av), and Manual (M). A seventh choice, Bulb, is not an exposure mode but, rather, just an option for allowing the shutter to remain open for long exposures as long as you keep the shutter release button pressed. To select one of these modes, just spin the Mode Dial (located at the top-left edge of the camera) to choose the method you want to use.

Your choice of which is best for a given shooting situation will depend on things like your need for lots of (or less) depth-of-field, a desire to freeze action or allow motion blur, or how much noise you find acceptable in an image. Each of the EOS 7D's exposure methods emphasizes one of those aspects of image capture or another. This section introduces you to all of them.

Full Auto

In this mode, the 7D sets evaluative metering for you, and chooses the shutter speed and aperture automatically. Indeed, you can't change any of the other shooting settings (other than image quality). In Auto mode, the 7D selects an appropriate ISO sensitivity setting, color (white) balance, Picture Style, color space, noise reduction features, and use of the Auto Lighting Optimizer. (All of these will be discussed in Chapter 7.) Use the Full Auto exposure mode when you hand your camera to a friend to take a picture (say, of you standing in front of the Eiffel Tower), and want to be sure they won't accidentally change any settings.

If you want completely automated operation, but would like to retain the ability to fine-tune some settings, use Creative Auto or Program modes, which I'll explain next.

Creative Auto

When you've selected this mode, the 7D makes most of the exposure decisions for you (just as in true Full Auto mode), but allows you to make some adjustments to other parameters, as described next. The camera will lock in ISO sensitivity, white balance, color space, noise reduction, and settings for the Auto Lighting Optimizer. But you can specify some other parameters, including selecting from three alternate Picture Styles in addition to Standard.

When you set the Mode Dial to the CA position, a screen resembling the one shown in Figure 4.14 appears (the currently set shutter speed and aperture appear only when the exposure meters are activated; turn them on by tapping the shutter release). The basic settings are the same as those produced by the Full Auto mode.

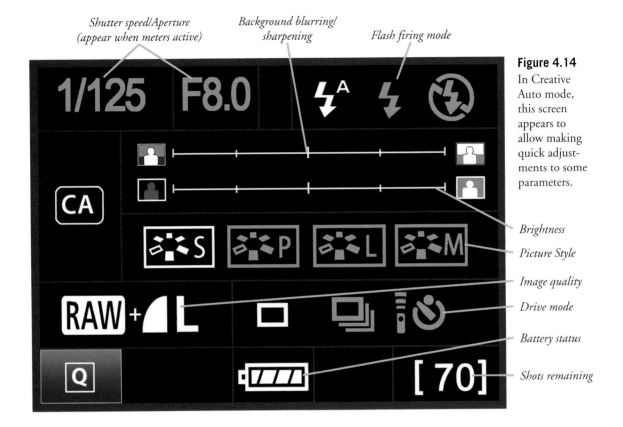

Shutter speed/Aperture (appear when meters active)

Background blurring/ sharpening

Flash firing mode

Figure 4.14
In Creative Auto mode, this screen appears to allow making quick adjustments to some parameters.

Brightness

Picture Style

Image quality

Drive mode

Battery status

Shots remaining

Just follow these steps:

1. **Change to settings screen.** Press the Q button to switch into shooting settings mode.

2. **Highlight setting to change.** Use the multi-selector to navigate to the setting you want to modify. A description of that setting appears at the bottom of the screen when that option is highlighted.

3. **Adjust the setting parameters.** Use the Main Dial to choose the options for the setting you selected.

4. **Confirm your choice.** Press the SET button to lock in your selection.

5. **Exit.** Tap the shutter release to exit the settings mode.

The settings you may adjust include:

- **Flash.** Auto Flash, Flash On, or Flash Off.

- **Blur/sharpen background.** Rotate the Main Dial to the left to blur the background (which causes the 7D to select a larger f/stop for the same exposure), or towards the right to sharpen the background (ending up with a smaller f/stop for the same exposure). This setting is not applied when the flash is used, and if the built-in flash is popped up, this setting is grayed out and cannot be changed.

- **Adjust image brightness.** Rotate the Main Dial to the left to reduce the overall exposure, making the image darker, or towards the right to increase exposure and make the image brighter.

- **Picture Style.** You can select Standard, Portrait, Landscape, or Monochrome Picture Styles, which, in the Creative Auto mode are equated to "standard images," "smooth skin tones," "vivid blues and greens," and "monochrome image." The actual name of the Picture Style is not shown, and the other preset styles, plus User Def styles (all of which I'll explain in Chapter 7) are not available from this screen in Creative Auto mode.

  Note that the Flash, Blur/sharpen, Image brightness, and Picture Style settings for Creative Auto will revert to their default values if you change from Creative Auto to another exposure mode, or turn off the camera.

- **Drive mode.** You can switch from single, continuous, or self-timer/remote drive modes. The self-timer/remote settings for Creative Auto are retained when you change modes or turn off the camera.

- **Image quality.** When you highlight this section, you can use the Main Dial to cycle among the various combinations of image size/JPEG quality/RAW options. Any changes you make in image quality here will be retained when you change modes or turn off the camera.

Aperture-Priority

In Av mode, you specify the lens opening used, and the 7D selects the shutter speed. Aperture-priority is especially good when you want to use a particular lens opening to achieve a desired effect. Perhaps you'd like to use the smallest f/stop possible to maximize depth-of-field in a close-up picture. Or, you might want to use a large f/stop to throw everything except your main subject out of focus, as in Figure 4.15. Maybe you'd just like to "lock in" a particular f/stop because it's the sharpest available aperture with that lens. Or, you might prefer to use, say, f/2.8 on a lens with a maximum aperture of f/1.4, because you want the best compromise between speed and sharpness.

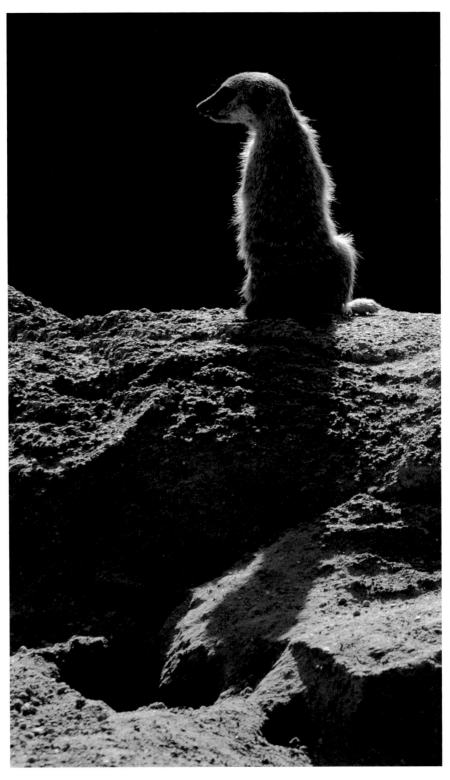

Figure 4.15
Use aperture-priority to "lock in" a large f/stop when you want to blur the background.

Aperture-priority can even be used to specify a *range* of shutter speeds you want to use under varying lighting conditions, which seems almost contradictory. But think about it. You're shooting a soccer game outdoors with a telephoto lens and want a relatively high shutter speed, but you don't care if the speed changes a little should the sun duck behind a cloud. Set your 7D to Av, and adjust the aperture until a shutter speed of, say, 1/1,000th second is selected at your current ISO setting. (In bright sunlight at ISO 400, that aperture is likely to be around f/11.) Then, go ahead and shoot, knowing that your 7D will maintain that f/11 aperture (for sufficient DOF as the soccer players move about the field), but will drop down to 1/750th or 1/500th second if necessary should the lighting change a little.

A blinking 30 or 8,000 shutter speed in the viewfinder indicates that the 7D is unable to select an appropriate shutter speed at the selected aperture and that over- and under-exposure will occur at the current ISO setting. That's the major pitfall of using Av: you might select an f/stop that is too small or too large to allow an optimal exposure with the available shutter speeds. For example, if you choose f/2.8 as your aperture and the illumination is quite bright (say, at the beach or in snow), even your camera's fastest shutter speed might not be able to cut down the amount of light reaching the sensor to provide the right exposure. Or, if you select f/8 in a dimly lit room, you might find your-self shooting with a very slow shutter speed that can cause blurring from subject move-ment or camera shake. Aperture-priority is best used by those with a bit of experience in choosing settings. Many seasoned photographers leave their 7D set on Av all the time.

Shutter-Priority

Shutter-priority (Tv) is the inverse of aperture-priority: you choose the shutter speed you'd like to use, and the camera's metering system selects the appropriate f/stop. Perhaps you're shooting action photos and you want to use the absolute fastest shutter speed available with your camera; in other cases, you might want to use a slow shutter speed to add some blur to a ballet photo that would be mundane if the action were completely frozen (see Figure 4.16). Shutter-priority mode gives you some control over how much action-freezing capability your digital camera brings to bear in a particular situation.

You'll also encounter the same problem as with aperture-priority when you select a shut-ter speed that's too long or too short for correct exposure under some conditions. I've shot outdoor soccer games on sunny Fall evenings and used shutter-priority mode to lock in a 1/1,000th second shutter speed, only to find my 7D refused to shoot when the sun dipped behind some trees and there was no longer enough light to shoot at that speed, even with the lens wide open.

Like Av mode, it's possible to choose an inappropriate shutter speed. If that's the case, the maximum aperture of your lens (to indicate underexposure) or the minimum aper-ture (to indicate overexposure) will blink.

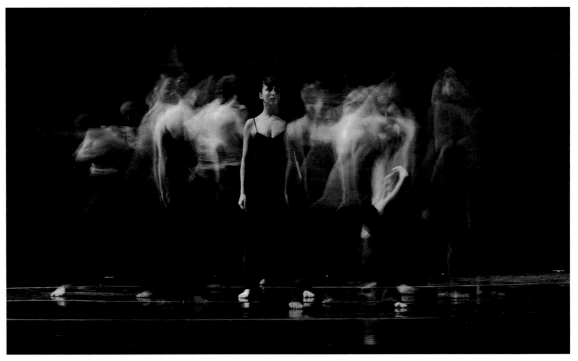

Figure 4.16 Lock the shutter at a slow speed to introduce blur into an action shot.

SAFETY SHIFT

The EOS 7D has a function called Safety Shift that operates in both shutter-priority and aperture-priority modes to help prevent bad exposures if the brightness of your subject changes abruptly so much that your selected shutter speed or f/stop no longer can be used to produce a good exposure. Perhaps you're photographing someone on stage and a spotlight is thrown on them at a critical moment, producing six or eight times as much illumination as you'd anticipated. Or, maybe the spotlight is turned off when you weren't expecting it. When Safety Shift is activated (through C.Fn I-06, explained in Chapter 8), the 7D will change your specified shutter speed (in Tv mode) or aperture (in Av mode) to compensate. It does not work when using other exposure modes.

Program Mode

Program mode (P) uses the 7D's built-in smarts to select the correct f/stop and shutter speed using a database of picture information that tells it which combination of shutter speed and aperture will work best for a particular photo. If the correct exposure cannot be achieved at the current ISO setting, the shutter speed indicator in the viewfinder will blink 30 or 8,000, indicating under- or overexposure (respectively). You can then boost or reduce the ISO to increase or decrease sensitivity.

The 7D's recommended exposure can be overridden if you want. Use the EV setting feature (described later, because it also applies to Tv and Av modes) to add or subtract exposure from the metered value. And, as I mentioned earlier in this chapter, you can change from the recommended setting to an equivalent setting (as shown in Table 4.1) that produces the same exposure, but using a different combination of f/stop and shutter speed. To accomplish this:

1. Press the shutter release halfway to lock in the current base exposure, or press the AE lock button (*) on the back of the camera (in which case the * indicator will illuminate in the viewfinder to show that the exposure has been locked).

2. Spin the Main Dial to change the shutter speed (the 7D will adjust the f/stop to match).

Your adjustment remains in force for a single exposure; if you want to change from the recommended settings for the next exposure, you'll need to repeat those steps.

Making EV Changes

Sometimes you'll want more or less exposure than indicated by the EOS 7D's metering system when using P, Tv, or Av exposure modes. Perhaps you want to underexpose to create a silhouette effect, or overexpose to produce a high key look. It's easy to use the 7D's exposure compensation system to override the exposure recommendations. There are two ways to make exposure value (EV) changes with the 7D. One method is fast and a bit clumsy to use, especially if your fingers aren't well coordinated. The other method takes a few seconds longer, but can be done smoothly by the most fumble-fingered among us.

Fast and Klutzy EV Changes

Just follow these steps with the 7D set for P, Tv, or Av:

1. Press the shutter release halfway or press the AE lock button (*).

2. Rotate the Quick Control Dial clockwise to add exposure, and counterclockwise to subtract exposure. Partially holding down the shutter release while spinning the QCD can be tricky, so I recommend pressing the * button instead. You don't need to hold down that button if you make your EV change within four seconds of depressing either button. But work fast! Otherwise, you'll have to go back to Step 1 and start over.

3. The exposure scale in the viewfinder and on the status LCD indicates the EV change you've made. (See Figure 4.17.) The EV change remains for the exposures that follow, until you manually zero out the EV setting with the Quick Control Dial. (As always, remember to activate the Quick Control Dial by sliding the Lock switch to the left.) EV changes are ignored when using other modes, including M (Manual exposure). Remember that the f/stop EV change applied may be limited by the apertures available with your lens.

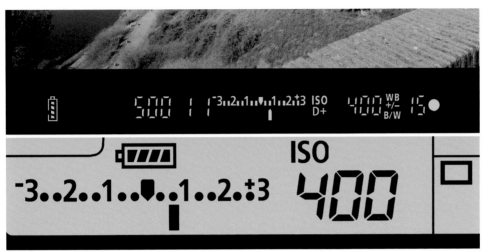

Figure 4.17
EV changes are displayed on the scale in the viewfinder (top) and the top-panel LCD screen (bottom).

Slower, Easier EV Changes

If you find yourself not turning the QCD quickly enough after you press the * button, try the second method for making EV changes with the 7D. It can be a little slower, but not if you follow the tip I offer in Step 1. Just press the Quick Control button and dial in the exposure change with the QCD (see Figure 4.18).

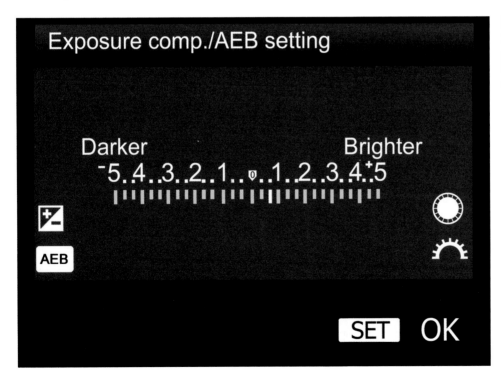

Figure 4.18
Exposure compensation can be set from this screen.

Manual Exposure

Part of being an experienced photographer comes from knowing when to rely on your EOS 7D's automation (including Full Auto, Creative Auto, or P mode), when to go semiautomatic (with Tv or Av), and when to set exposure manually (using M). Some photographers actually prefer to set their exposure manually, as the 7D will be happy to provide an indication of when its metering system judges your manual settings provide the proper exposure, using the analog exposure scale at the bottom of the viewfinder and on the status LCD.

Manual exposure can come in handy in some situations. You might be taking a silhouette photo and find that none of the exposure modes or EV correction features give you exactly the effect you want. Set the exposure manually to use the exact shutter speed and f/stop you need. Or, you might be working in a studio environment using multiple flash units. The additional flashes are triggered by slave devices (gadgets that set off the flash when they sense the light from another flash, or, perhaps from a radio or infrared remote control). Your camera's exposure meter doesn't compensate for the extra illumination, so you need to set the aperture manually.

Because, depending on your proclivities, you might not need to set exposure manually very often, you should still make sure you understand how it works. Fortunately, the EOS 7D makes setting exposure manually very easy. Just set the Mode Dial to M, turn the Main Dial to set the shutter speed, and the Quick Control Dial to adjust the aperture. (Assuming you've activated the QCD by moving the Lock lever to the left, as I've reminded you three times previously in this book!) Press the shutter release halfway or press the AE lock button, and the exposure scale in the viewfinder shows you how far your chosen setting diverges from the metered exposure.

Adjusting Exposure with ISO Settings

Another way of adjusting exposures is by changing the ISO sensitivity setting. Sometimes photographers forget about this option, because the common practice is to set the ISO once for a particular shooting session (say, at ISO 100 or 200 for bright sunlight outdoors, or ISO 800 when shooting indoors) and then forget about ISO. The reason for that is that ISOs higher than ISO 100 or 200 are seen as "bad" or "necessary evils." However, changing the ISO is a valid way of adjusting exposure settings, particularly with the Canon EOS 7D, which produces good results at ISO settings that create grainy, unusable pictures with some other camera models.

Indeed, I find myself using ISO adjustment as a convenient alternate way of adding or subtracting EV when shooting in manual mode, and as a quick way of choosing equivalent exposures when in automatic or semi-automatic modes. For example, I've selected a manual exposure with both f/stop and shutter speed suitable for my image using, say, ISO 200. I can change the exposure in 1/3-stop increments by tapping the ISO-Flash exposure compensation button and spinning the Main Dial one click at a time. The difference in image quality/noise at the base setting of ISO 200 is negligible if I dial in ISO 160 or 125 to reduce exposure a little, or change to ISO 250 or 320 to increase exposure. I keep my preferred f/stop and shutter speed, but still adjust the exposure.

Or, perhaps, I am using Tv mode and the metered exposure at ISO 200 is 1/500th second at f/11. If I decide on the spur of the moment I'd rather use 1/500th second at f/8, I can tap the ISO-Flash exposure compensation button and spin the Main Dial three clicks counterclockwise to switch to ISO 100. Of course, it's a good idea to monitor your ISO changes, so you don't end up at ISO 1600 (or higher, if ISO Expansion is enabled) accidentally.

ISO settings can, of course, also be used to boost or reduce sensitivity in particular shooting situations. The EOS 7D can use ISO settings from ISO 100 up to 6400 (or ISO 12800 if you've set C.Fn I-03 to 1).

The camera can adjust the ISO automatically as appropriate for various lighting conditions. When using the B setting or when using flash, automatic ISO settings are limited to ISO 400, except when using fill flash (ISO 100 or higher may be used if necessary to avoid overexposure), or when using bounce flash with an external Speedlite (ISO settings from ISO 400-1600 may be used). In all other exposure modes (Full Auto, Creative Auto, P, Tv, Av, and M), ISO settings from ISO 100-3200 are set automatically.

Exposure Bracketing

Bracketing is a method for shooting several consecutive exposures using different settings as a way of improving the odds that one will be exactly right. Before digital cameras took over the universe, it was common to bracket exposures, shooting, say, a series of three photos at 1/125th second, but varying the f/stop from f/8 to f/11 to f/16. In practice, smaller than whole-stop increments were used for greater precision. Plus, it was just as common to keep the same aperture and vary the shutter speed, although in the days before electronic shutters, film cameras often had only whole increment shutter speeds available.

Today, cameras like the EOS 7D can bracket exposures much more precisely, and bracket white balance as well. (See Figure 4.19.) While WB bracketing is sometimes used when getting color absolutely correct in the camera is important, Auto Exposure Bracketing (AEB) is used much more often. When this feature is activated, the 7D takes three consecutive photos: one at the metered "correct" exposure, one with less exposure, and one with more exposure, using an increment of your choice up to +3/–3 stops. (Choose between increments by setting Custom Function I-01 to 0 [1/3 stop] or 1 [1/2 stop].) In Av mode, the aperture is locked and the shutter speed will change, whereas in Tv mode, the shutter speed is locked and the aperture setting will change.

Figure 4.19
Your three bracketed shots will look like this.

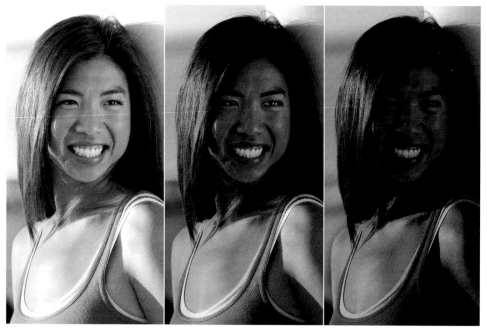

Using AEB is trickier than it needs to be, but Canon has made the feature more flexible, because you can now choose to bracket only overexposures or underexposures. Everything you really must know is here, but I'll show you exactly how to further customize bracketing in Chapter 8. For now, just follow these steps:

1. **Activate the EV/AEB screen.** Press the MENU button and use the Main Dial to select the Shooting 2 menu, and then rotate the Quick Control Dial to the AEB position and press the SET button. The dual Exposure comp./AEB setting screen shown earlier in Figure 4.18 will appear, with the exposure compensation scale displayed by default.

2. **Change to AEB settings.** Rotate the Main Dial and the display will change to the automatic exposure bracketing adjustment screen, shown in Figure 4.20. A second scale appears underneath the first with a cluster of three highlighted indicators that show the increment between bracketed shots, and the position on the main scale, which now indicates values from –8 to +8.

Tip

Note that while the numbering extends to a value of 8 in either direction, the scale itself extends only from –5 to +5. The middle indicator in the lower scale can be moved only between the –5/+5 limits, and the under-/overexposures on either side of it can cover an additional three stops, and align, if necessary, with the –8 to +8 values.

Number of stops to over/underexpose

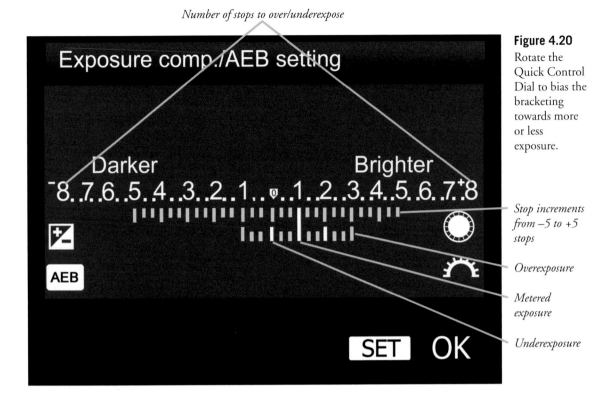

Figure 4.20
Rotate the Quick Control Dial to bias the bracketing towards more or less exposure.

Stop increments from –5 to +5 stops

Overexposure

Metered exposure

Underexposure

3. **Set the bracket range.** Continue to rotate the Main Dial to spread out or contract the three dots to include the desired range you want to cover. For example, with the dots clustered tightly together, the three bracketed exposures will be spread out over a single stop. Separating the cluster produces a wider range and larger exposure change between the three shots in the bracket set. In Figure 4.20, the three indicators are each separated by one full stop.

4. **Adjust zero point.** By default, the bracketing is zeroed around the center of the scale, which represents the correct exposure. But you might want to have your three bracketed shots all biased towards overexposure or underexposure. Perhaps you feel that the metered exposure will be too dark or too light, and you want the bracketed shots to lean in the other direction. Rotate the Quick Control Dial to move the bracket spread towards one end of the scale or the other. In Figure 4.20, the bracket set is adjusted so that the leftmost indicator is set for zero (the metered exposure); the middle indicator is set for one stop underexposure; and the right indicator for two stops underexposure. This bracket set will produce a set of three images at the metered exposure, plus additional shots with one and two shots less exposure.

5. **Confirm your choice.** Press the SET button to enter the settings.

6. **Take your three photos.** You can use single shooting mode to take the trio of pictures yourself, use the self-timer (which will expose all three pictures after the delay), or switch to continuous shooting mode to take the three pictures in a burst.

7. **Monitor your shots.** As the images are captured, three indicators will appear on the exposure scale in the viewfinder, with one of them flashing for each bracketed photo, showing when the base exposure, underexposure, and overexposure are taken.

8. **Turn off bracketing when done.** Bracketing remains in effect when the set is taken so you can continue shooting bracketed exposures until you turn off the camera, use the electronic flash, or return to the menu to cancel bracketing (or if Auto Cancel has been specified in the C.Fn I-04 setting).

Fine-Tuning Exposure Bracketing

You can use C.Fn I-05 to adjust the order in which bracketed shots are taken. Press the MENU button, use the Main Dial to choose the Custom Function tab, and select C.Fn I: Exposure. Scroll to Bracketing sequence with the Quick Command Dial and press the SET button. Choose C.Fn 05, and select one of the options described below. Press the SET button to activate your choice.

You can define the sequence in which both AEB and WB-BKT series are exposed. (I'll explain white balance bracketing in Chapter 8.) If your bias preference is set to blue/amber, the white balance sequence when option 0 is selected will be: current WB, more blue, more amber. If your bias preference is set to magenta/green, then the sequence for option 0 will be: current WB, more magenta, more green.

- **0:** Exposure sequence is metered exposure, decreased exposure, increased exposure (0, −, +). White balance sequence is current WB, more blue/more magenta (depending on how your bias is set), more amber/more green (ditto).

- **1:** The sequence is decreased exposure, metered exposure, increased exposure (−, 0, +). White balance sequence is more blue/more magenta, current WB, more amber/more green.

When automatic cancel is activated, bracketing remains in effect until you turn off the camera.

Bracketing and Merge to HDR

HDR (High Density Range) photography is, at the moment, an incredibly popular fad. There are even entire books that do nothing but tell you how to shoot HDR images. If you aren't familiar with the technique, HDR involves shooting two or three or more images at different bracketed exposures, giving you an "underexposed" version with lots of detail in highlights that would otherwise be washed out, an "overexposed" rendition that preserves detail in the shadows, and several intermediate shots. These are combined to produce a single image that has an amazing amount of detail throughout the scene's entire tonal range.

I call this technique a fad because the reason it exists in the first place is due to a (temporary, I hope) defect in current digital camera sensors. It's presently impossible to capture the full range of brightness that we perceive; digital cameras, including the EOS 7D, can't even grab the full range of brightness that *film* can see, as I showed you in Figures 4.1 and 4.2 at the beginning of this chapter.

But as the megapixel race slows down, sensor designers have already begun designing capture electronics that have larger density (dynamic) ranges, and I fully expect to see cameras within a few years that can produce images similar to what we're getting now with HDR manipulation in image editors.

HDR works like this: Suppose you wanted to photograph a dimly lit room that had a bright window showing an outdoors scene. Proper exposure for the room might be on the order of 1/60th second at f/2.8 at ISO 200, while the outdoors scene probably would require f/11 at 1/400th second. That's almost a 7 EV step difference (approximately 7 f/stops) and well beyond the dynamic range of any digital camera, including the EOS 7D.

When you're using Merge to HDR, a feature found in Adobe Photoshop (similar functions are available in other programs, including Photomatix [www.hdrsoft.com; free to try, $99 to buy]), you'd take several pictures. As I mentioned earlier, one would be exposed for the shadows, one for the highlights, and perhaps one for the midtones. Then, you'd use the Merge to HDR command (or the equivalent in other software) to combine all of the images into one HDR image that integrates the well-exposed sections of each version. You can use the EOS 7D's bracketing feature to produce those images.

The images should be as identical as possible, except for exposure. So, it's a good idea to mount the 7D on a tripod, use a remote release, and take all the exposures in one burst. Just follow these steps:

1. Mount the 7D on a tripod and connect the remote release cable.

2. Set the camera to shoot RAW images, as described in Chapter 3.

3. Set bracketing to a 2-stop increment, as described above and in Chapter 7.

4. Change bracketing order to –, 0,+, if necessary. This will give you a continuous bracketed set of underexposed, metered exposure, and overexposed images.

5. Manually focus or autofocus the 7D.

6. Set the camera to shutter priority and then trigger the shutter release to expose your set of three images.

7. Copy your images to your computer and continue in Photoshop with the Merge to HDR steps listed next.

The next steps show you how to combine the separate exposures into one merged high dynamic range image. The sample images shown in Figures 4.21, 4.22, and 4.24 show the results you can get from a two-shot bracketed sequence. I merged only two pictures for simplicity, because experience has shown that the differences between three or more bracketed exposures, even when taken at exposures that are 2 stops apart, can be too subtle to show up well on the printed page.

1. If you use an application to transfer the files to your computer, make sure it does not make any adjustments to brightness, contrast, or exposure. You want the real RAW information for Merge to HDR to work with. If you do everything correctly, you'll end up with at least two photos like the ones shown in Figures 4.21 and 4.22.

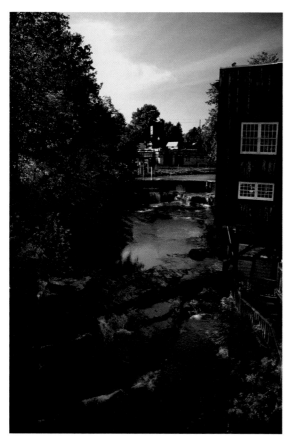

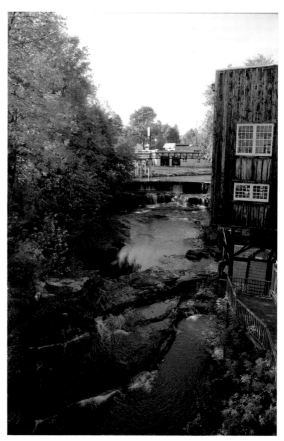

Figure 4.21 Make one exposure for the shadow areas.

Figure 4.22 Make a second exposure for the highlights, such as the sky.

2. Load the images into Photoshop using your preferred RAW converter.

3. Save as PSD files.

4. Activate Merge to HDR by choosing File > Automate > Merge to HDR.

5. Select the photos to be merged, as shown in Figure 4.23, where I have specified the two PSD files. You'll note a checkbox that can be used to automatically align the images if they were not taken with the 7D mounted on a rock-steady support.

6. Once HDR merge has done its thing, you must save in PSD to retain the file's full-color information, in case you want to work with the HDR image later. Otherwise, you can convert to a normal 24-bit file and save in any compatible format.

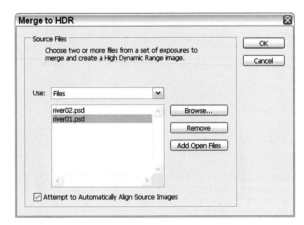

Figure 4.23
Use the Merge to HDR command to combine the two images.

If you do everything correctly, you'll end up with a photo like the one shown in Figure 4.24, which has the properly exposed foreground of the first shot, and the well-exposed sky of the second image. Note that, ideally, nothing should move between shots. In the example pictures, the river is moving, but the exposures were made so close together that, after the merger, you can't really tell.

What if you don't have the opportunity, inclination, or skills to create several images at different exposures, as described? If you shoot in RAW format, you can still use Merge to HDR, working with a *single* original image file. What you do is import the image into Photoshop several times, using Adobe Camera Raw to create multiple copies of the file at different exposure levels.

For example, you'd create one copy that's too dark, so the shadows lose detail, but the highlights are preserved. Create another copy with the shadows intact and allow the highlights to wash out. Then, you can use Merge to HDR to combine the two and end up with a finished image that has the extended dynamic range you're looking for.

Figure 4.24
You'll end up with an extended dynamic range photo like this one.

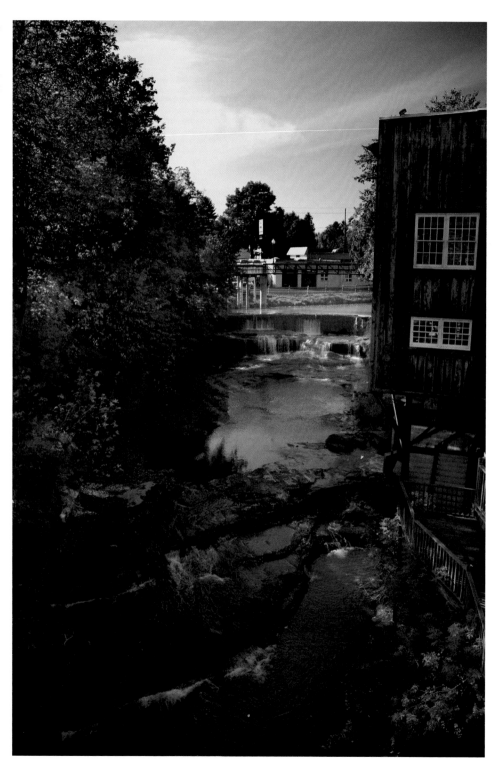

Dealing with Noise

Visual image noise is that random grainy effect that some like to use as a special effect, but which, most of the time, is objectionable because it robs your image of detail even as it adds that "interesting" texture. Noise is caused by two different phenomena: high ISO settings and long exposures.

High ISO noise commonly appears when you raise your camera's sensitivity setting above ISO 400. With Canon cameras, which are renown for their good ISO noise characteristics, noise may become visible at ISO 800, and is usually fairly noticeable at ISO 1600. At ISO 3200 noise is usually quite bothersome, which is why that lofty sensitivity rating is disabled by default and must be activated with ISO expansion using C.Fn I-03. This kind of noise appears as a result of the amplification needed to increase the sensitivity of the sensor. While higher ISOs do pull details out of dark areas, they also amplify non-signal information randomly, creating noise.

A similar noisy phenomenon occurs during long time exposures, which allow more photons to reach the sensor, increasing your ability to capture a picture under low-light conditions. However, the longer exposures also increase the likelihood that some pixels will register random phantom photons, often because the longer an imager is "hot," the warmer it gets, and that heat can be mistaken for photons. There's also a special kind of noise that CMOS sensors like the one used in the 7D are potentially susceptible to. With a CCD, the entire signal is conveyed off the chip and funneled through a single amplifier and analog-to-digital conversion circuit. Any noise introduced there is, at least, consistent. CMOS imagers, on the other hand, contain millions of individual amplifiers and A/D converters, all working in unison. Because all these circuits don't necessarily process in precisely the same way all the time, they can introduce something called fixed-pattern noise into the image data.

Fortunately, Canon's electronics geniuses have done an exceptional job minimizing noise from all causes in the 7D. Even so, you might still want to apply the optional long exposure noise reduction that can be activated using C.Fn II. This type of noise reduction involves the 7D taking a second, blank exposure, and comparing the random pixels in that image with the photograph you just took. Pixels that coincide in the two represent noise and can safely be suppressed. This noise reduction system, called *dark frame subtraction,* effectively doubles the amount of time required to take a picture, and is used only for exposures longer than one second. Noise reduction can reduce the amount of detail in your picture, as some image information may be removed along with the noise. So, you might want to use this feature with moderation.

To activate your 7D's long exposure noise reduction features, go to the Custom Function menu, choose C.Fn II: Image, and select either C.Fn II-01 (Long exposure noise reduction) or C.Fn II-02 (High ISO speed noise reduction) as explained further in Chapter 8.

You can also apply noise reduction to a lesser extent using Photoshop, and when converting RAW and sRAW files to some other format, using your favorite RAW converter, or an industrial-strength product like Noise Ninja (www.picturecode.com) to wipe out noise after you've already taken the picture.

Fixing Exposures with Histograms

While you can often recover poorly exposed photos in your image editor, your best bet is to arrive at the correct exposure in the camera, minimizing the tweaks that you have to make in post-processing. However, you can't always judge exposure just by viewing the image on your 7D's LCD after the shot is made. Nor can you get a 100-percent accurately exposed picture by using the 7D's Live View "exposure simulation" feature described in Chapter 6. Ambient light may make the LCD difficult to see, and the brightness level you've set can affect the appearance of the playback image.

Instead, you can use a histogram, which is a chart displayed on the EOS 7D's LCD that shows the number of tones being captured at each brightness level. You can use the information to provide correction for the next shot you take. The 7D offers two histogram variations: one that shows overall brightness levels for an image and an alternate version that separates the red, green, and blue channels of your image into separate histograms.

Both types are charts that include a representation of up to 256 vertical lines on a horizontal axis that show the number of pixels in the image at each brightness level, from 0 (black) on the left side to 255 (white) on the right. (The 3-inch LCD doesn't have enough pixels to show each and every one of the 256 lines, but, instead provides a representation of the shape of the curve formed.) The more pixels at a given level, the taller the bar at that position. If no bar appears at a particular position on the scale from left to right, there are no pixels at that particular brightness level.

DISPLAYING HISTOGRAMS

To view histograms on your screen, press the INFO. button while an image is shown on the LCD. Keep pressing the button until the histogram(s) are shown. The display will cycle between several levels of information, including flashing highlights and two screens that show histograms. (An explanation of all the information screens can be found in Chapter 7.) One histogram (Figure 4.25) shows overall brightness levels; the second one (Figure 4.26) shows tonal values for the red, green, and blue channels; while the third shows both types of histogram, but less information about your photo. During histogram display, you'll also see a thumbnail of your image at the top-left side of the screen. To change your default histogram type from Brightness to RGB, use the Histogram setting in the Playback 2 menu.

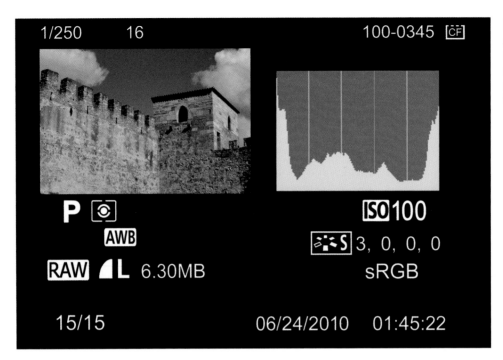

Figure 4.25
A histogram shows the relationship of tones in an image.

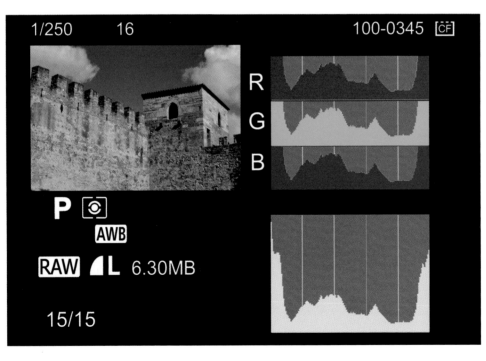

Figure 4.26
Color and brightness histograms.

A typical histogram produces a mountain-like shape, with most of the pixels bunched in the middle tones, with fewer pixels at the dark and light ends of the scale. Ideally, though, there will be at least some pixels at either extreme, so that your image has both a true black and a true white representing some details. Learn to spot histograms that represent over- and underexposure, and add or subtract exposure using an EV modification to compensate.

For example, Figure 4.27 shows the histogram for an image that is badly underexposed. You can guess from the shape of the histogram that many of the dark tones to the left of the graph have been clipped off. There's plenty of room on the right side for additional pixels to reside without having them become overexposed. Or, a histogram might look like Figure 4.28, which is overexposed. In either case, you can increase or decrease the exposure (either by changing the f/stop or shutter speed in manual mode or by adding or subtracting an EV value in autoexposure mode) to produce the corrected histogram shown in Figure 4.29, in which the tones "hug" the right side of the histogram to produce as many highlight details as possible. See "Making EV Changes," earlier in this chapter for information on dialing in exposure compensation.

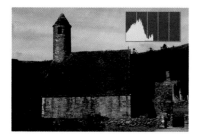

Figure 4.27 This histogram shows an underexposed image.

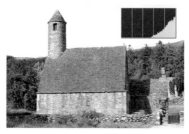

Figure 4.28 This histogram reveals that the image is overexposed.

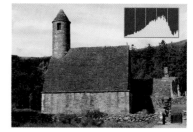

Figure 4.29 A histogram for a properly exposed image should look like this.

The histogram can also be used to aid in fixing the contrast of an image, although gauging incorrect contrast is more difficult. For example, if the histogram shows all the tones bunched up in one place in the image, the photo will be low in contrast. If the tones are spread out more or less evenly, the image is probably high in contrast. In either case, your best bet may be to switch to RAW (if you're not already using that format) so you can adjust contrast in post processing. However, you can also change to a user-defined Picture Style (User Def. 1, User Def. 2, or User Def. 3 in the Picture Style menu) with contrast set lower (–1 to –4) or higher (+1 to +4) as required.

5

Mastering the Mysteries of Autofocus

Getting the right exposure is one of the foundations of a great photograph, but a lot more goes into a compelling shot than good tonal values. A sharp image, proper white balance, good color, and other factors all can help elevate your image from good to exceptional. One of the most important and, sometimes, the most frustrating aspects of shooting with a highly automated—yet fully adjustable—camera like the 7D is achieving sharp focus. Your camera has lots of AF controls and options—some of them completely new to the Canon lineup—and new users and veterans alike can quickly become confused. In this chapter, I'm going to clear up the mysteries of autofocus and show you exactly how to use your 7D's AF features to their fullest. I'll even tell you when to abandon the autofocus system and turn to the ancient art of manual focus, too.

How Focus Works

Although Canon added autofocus capabilities in the 1980s, back in the day of film cameras, prior to that focusing was always done manually. Honest. Even though viewfinders were bigger and brighter than they are today, special focusing screens, magnifiers, and other gadgets were often used to help the photographer achieve correct focus. Imagine what it must have been like to focus manually under demanding, fast-moving conditions such as sports photography.

I don't have to imagine it. I did it for many years. I started my career as a sports photographer, and then traveled the country as a roving photojournalist for more years than I like to admit. (Okay, eighteen years. You forced it out of me.) Indeed, I was a holdout for manual focus right through the film era, even as AF lenses became the norm and

autofocus systems in cameras were (gradually) perfected. I purchased my first autofocus lens back in 2004, at the same time I switched from non-SLR digital cameras and
my film cameras to digital SLR models.

Manual focusing was problematic because our eyes and brains have poor memory for
correct focus, which is why your eye doctor must shift back and forth between sets of
lenses and ask "Does that look sharper—or was it sharper before?" in determining your
correct prescription. Similarly, manual focusing involves jogging the focus ring back and
forth as you go from almost in focus, to sharp focus, to almost focused again. The little clockwise and counterclockwise arcs decrease in size until you've zeroed in on the
point of correct focus. What you're looking for is the image with the most contrast
between the edges of elements in the image.

The camera also looks for these contrast differences among pixels to determine relative
sharpness. There are two ways that sharp focus is determined, phase detection and contrast detection.

Phase Detection

Like all digital SLRs that use an optical viewfinder and mirror system to preview an
image (that is, when not in Live View mode), the Canon EOS 7D calculates focus using
what is called a *passive phase detection* system. It's passive in the sense that the ambient
illumination in a scene (or that illumination augmented with a focus-assist beam) is
used to determine correct focus. (An *active* phase detection system might use a laser,
sonar, or other special signal.)

Parts of the image from two opposite sides of the lens are directed down to the floor of
the camera's mirror box, where an autofocus sensor array resides; the rest of the illumination from the lens bounces upwards towards the optical viewfinder system and the
autoexposure sensors. Figure 5.1 is a wildly over-simplified illustration that may help
you visualize what is happening.

SIMPLIFICATION MADE OVERLY SIMPLE

To reduce the complexity of the diagram, it doesn't show the actual path of the light passing through the lens, as it converges to the point of focus—on the viewfinder screen
when the mirror is down; and on the sensor plane when the mirror is flipped up and the
shutter has opened. Nor does it show the path of the light directed to the autoexposure
sensor. Only two of the 19 pairs of autofocus microlenses are shown, and greatly enlarged
so you can see their approximate position. All we're concerned about here is how light
reaches the autofocus sensor.

Figure 5.1

Part of the light is bounced downward to the autofocus sensor array, and split into two images, which are compared and aligned to create a sharply focused image.

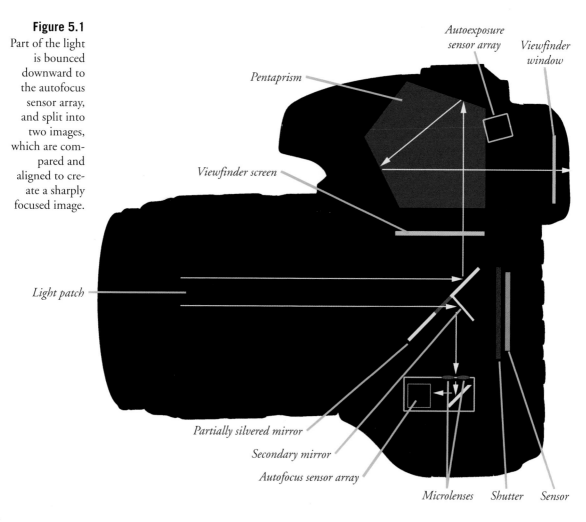

As light emerges from the rear element of the lens, most of it is reflected upwards towards the focusing screen, where the relative sharp focus (or lack of it) is displayed (and which can be used to evaluate manual focus). It then bounces off two more reflective surfaces in the pentaprism (in the 7D; other cameras may use a less expensive and less bright *pentamirror* system instead) emerging at the optical viewfinder correctly oriented left/right and up/down. (The image emerges from the lens reversed.) Some of the illumination is directed to the autoexposure sensor at the top of the pentaprism housing.

A small portion of the illumination passes through the partially silvered portion of the main mirror, and is directed downwards to the autofocus sensor array, which includes 19 separate autofocus "detectors." In the interests of arrow-clutter reduction (ACR), the diagram doesn't show that parts of the image from opposite sides of the lens surface are directed through separate microlenses, producing two half-images. These images are compared with each other, much like (actually, *exactly* like) a two-window rangefinder used in surveying, weaponry—and non-SLR cameras like the venerable Leica M film models.

When the image is out of focus—or out of phase—as in Figure 5.2, the two halves, each representing a slightly different view from opposite sides of the lens, don't line up. Sharp focus is achieved when the images are "in phase," and aligned, as in Figure 5.3. The two figures don't show exactly what happens, because all 19 AF sensors in the 7D are of the "cross" type, and the illustrations picture the simpler horizontal-only sensor. I'll explain cross-type sensors shortly, but, first, you needed to understand the basic phase detection process.

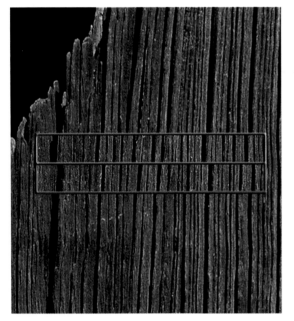

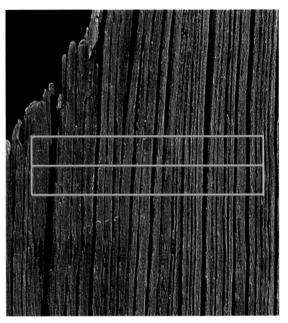

Figure 5.2 In phase detection, parts of an image are split in two and compared.

Figure 5.3 When the image is in focus, the two halves of the image align, as with a rangefinder.

As with any rangefinder-like function, accuracy is better when the "base length" between the two images is larger. (Think back to your high-school trigonometry; you could calculate a distance more accurately when the separation between the two points where the angles were measured was greater.) For that reason, phase detection autofocus is more accurate with larger (wider) lens openings than with smaller lens openings, and may not work at all when the f/stop is smaller than f/5.6. Obviously, the "opposite" edges of the lens opening are farther apart with a lens having an f/2.8 maximum aperture than with one that has a smaller, f/5.6 maximum f/stop, and the base line is much longer. The 7D is able to perform these comparisons and then move the lens elements directly to the point of correct focus very quickly, in milliseconds.

Unfortunately, while the 7D's focus system finds it easy to measure degrees of apparent focus at each of the focus points in the viewfinder, it doesn't really know with any certainty *which* object should be in sharpest focus. Is it the closest object? The subject in the center? Something lurking *behind* the closest subject? A person standing over at the side of the picture? Many of the techniques for using autofocus effectively involve telling the EOS 7D exactly what it should be focusing on, by choosing a focus zone or by allowing the camera to choose a focus zone for you. I'll address that topic shortly.

Cross-Type Focus Points

So far, we've only looked at focus sensors that calculate focus in a single direction. Figures 5.2 and 5.3 illustrate a horizontally oriented focus sensor evaluating a subject that is made up, predominantly, of vertical lines. But what does such a sensor do when it encounters a subject that isn't conveniently aligned at right-angles to the sensor array? You can see the problem in Figure 5.4, which pictures the same weather wood siding rotated 90 degrees. The horizontal grain of the wood isn't divided as neatly by the split image, so focusing using phase detection is more difficult.

In the past, the "solution" was to include a sprinkling of vertically oriented AF sensors in with the horizontally oriented sensors. The vertical sensors could detect differences in horizontal lines, while the horizontal sensors took care of the vertical lines. Both types were equally adept at handling *diagonal* lines, which crossed each type at a 45-degree angle. Today, however, Canon's entry-level digital SLRs use at least one "multi-function" sensor (in the center of the array) that has a cross-type arrangement. More advanced models have more cross sensors, including the 7D, in which all 19 focus sensors are of this cross type.

The value of cross-type focus sensors in phase detection is that such sensors can line up edges and interpret image contrast in both horizontal and vertical directions, as shown in Figure 5.5. The horizontal lines are still more difficult to interpret with the horizontal arm of the cross, but they stand out in sharp contrast in the vertical arms, and allow the camera to align the edges and snap the image into focus easily, as you can see at lower right. In lower light levels, with subjects that were moving, or with subjects that have no pattern and less contrast to begin with, the cross-type sensor not only works faster but can focus subjects that a horizontal- or vertical-only sensor can't handle at all. (Note that the actual horizontal, vertical, and cross-type sensors don't look like the illustrations—we're still in over-simplification mode.)

If things weren't interesting enough, you should know that the center focus spot in the EOS 7D is a kind of super-cross-type sensor—an X-shaped sensor, rotated from the traditional cross position, which is optimized for diagonal lines. (It detects horizontal and vertical lines, as well, with only slightly less aplomb.) However, this sensor requires a lens with an f/2.8 or larger maximum aperture.. The location of the sensors in the viewfinder is shown in Figure 5.6.

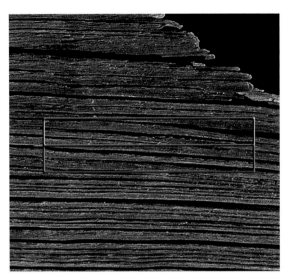

Figure 5.4 Horizontal focus sensors do a poor job of interpreting the alignment of horizontal lines; they work better with vertical lines or diagonals.

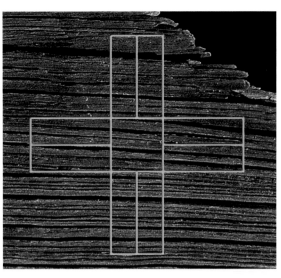

Figure 5.5 Cross-type sensors can achieve sharp focus with both horizontal and vertical lines.

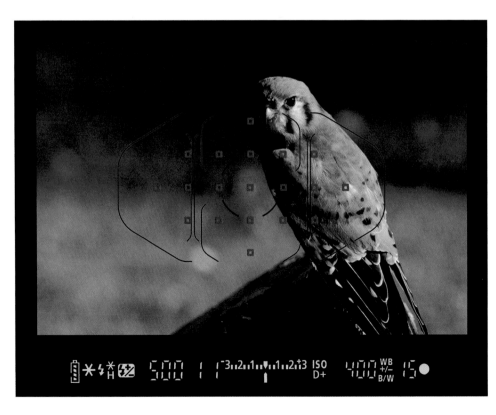

Figure 5.6 All 19 AF sensors in the 7D are of the cross type.

Contrast Detection

Contrast detection is a slower mode and used by the Canon 7D with Live View and Live Face Detection modes, because, to allow live viewing of the sensor image, the camera's mirror has to be flipped up out of the way so that the illumination from the lens can continue through the open shutter to the sensor. Your view through the viewfinder is obstructed, of course, and there is no partially silvered mirror to reflect some light down to the autofocus sensors. So, an alternate means of autofocus must be used, and that method is *contrast detection.* The 7D does have a Quick Mode feature that temporarily flips the mirror back down to allow phase detection autofocus, but unless you use that mode—which I'll discuss later, focus must be achieved either manually (with the color LCD live view as a focusing screen), or by contrast detection.

Contrast detection is a bit easier to understand and is illustrated by Figure 5.7. At top in the extreme enlargement of the wood siding, the transitions between pixels are soft and blurred. When the image is brought into focus (bottom), the transitions are sharp and clear. Although this example is a bit exaggerated so you can see the results on the printed page, it's easy to understand that when maximum contrast in a subject is achieved, it can be deemed to be in sharp focus.

Contrast detection is used in Live View mode, and may be the only focus mode possible with point-and-shoot cameras that don't offer a through-the-lens optical viewfinder as found in a digital SLR like the EOS 7D. Contrast detection works best with static subjects, because it is inherently slower and not well-suited for tracking moving objects.

Figure 5.7

Focus in contrast detection mode evaluates the increase in contrast in the edges of subjects, starting with a blurry image (top) and producing a sharp, contrasty image (bottom).

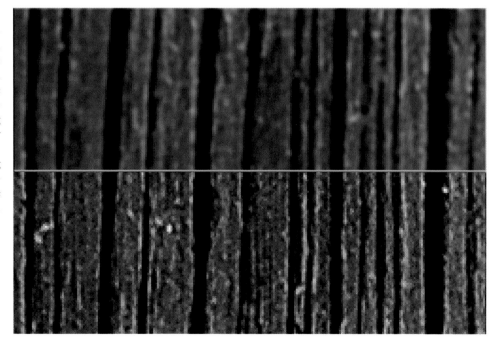

Contrast detection does not work as well as phase detection in dim light, because its accuracy is determined not by the length of the baseline of a rangefinder focus system, but by its ability to detect variations in brightness and contrast. You'll find that contrast detection works better with faster lenses, too, not as with phase detection,(which gains accuracy because the diameter of the lens is simply wider) but because larger lens openings admit more light that can be used by the sensor to measure contrast.

We'll look at contrast detection again when we explore Live View modes.

Focus Modes

Focus modes tell the camera *when* to evaluate and lock in focus. They don't determine *where* focus should be checked; that's the function of other autofocus features. Focus modes tell the camera whether to lock in focus once, say, when you press the shutter release halfway (or use some other control, such as the AF-ON button), or whether, once activated, the camera should continue tracking your subject and, if it's moving, adjust focus to follow it.

The 7D has three AF modes: One-Shot AF (also known as single autofocus), AI Servo (continuous autofocus), and AI Focus AF (which switches between the two as appropriate). I'll explain all of these in more detail later in this section. But first, some confusion…

MANUAL FOCUS

With manual focus activated by sliding the AF/MF switch on the lens, your 7D lets you set the focus yourself. There are some advantages and disadvantages to this approach. While your batteries will last longer in manual focus mode, it will take you longer to focus the camera for each photo, a process that can be difficult. Modern digital cameras, even dSLRs, depend so much on autofocus that the viewfinders of models that have less than full-frame-sized sensors are no longer designed for optimum manual focus. Pick up any film camera and you'll see a bigger, brighter viewfinder with a focusing screen that's a joy to focus on manually. Until the EOS 7D was introduced, you really needed to use a full-frame digital camera, like the Canon EOS 5D Mark II, to get such a bright view and easy manual focus. However, you can now swap the 7D's focus screen—great for viewing and autofocus—and use the EF-S Super Precision Matte screen, which is optimized for manual focus.

Adding Circles of Confusion

You know that increased depth-of-field brings more of your subject into focus. But more depth-of-field also makes autofocusing (or manual focusing) more difficult because the contrast is lower between objects at different distances. This is an added factor *beyond* the rangefinder aspects of lens opening size in phase detection. An image that's dimmer is more difficult to focus with any type of focus system, phase detection, contrast detection, or manual focus.

So, focus with a 200mm lens (or zoom setting) may be easier in some respects than at a 28mm focal length (or zoom setting) because the longer lens has less apparent depth-of-field. By the same token, a lens with a maximum aperture of f/1.8 will be easier to autofocus (or manually focus) than one of the same focal length with an f/4 maximum aperture, because the f/4 lens has more depth-of-field *and* a dimmer view. That's yet another reason why lenses with a maximum aperture smaller than f/5.6 can give your 7D's autofocus system fits—increased depth-of-field joins forces with a dimmer image that's more difficult to focus using phase detection.

To make things even more complicated, many subjects aren't polite enough to remain still. They move around in the frame, so that even if the 7D is sharply focused on your main subject, it may change position and require refocusing. An intervening subject may pop into the frame and pass between you and the subject you meant to photograph. You (or the 7D) have to decide whether to lock focus on this new subject, or remain focused on the original subject. Finally, there are some kinds of subjects that are difficult to bring into sharp focus because they lack enough contrast to allow the 7D's AF system (or our eyes) to lock in. Blank walls, a clear blue sky, or other subject matter may make focusing difficult.

If you find all these focus factors confusing, you're on the right track. Focus is, in fact, measured using something called a *circle of confusion.* An ideal image consists of zillions of tiny little points, which, like all points, theoretically have no height or width. There is perfect contrast between the point and its surroundings. You can think of each point as a pinpoint of light in a darkened room. When a given point is out of focus, its edges decrease in contrast and it changes from a perfect point to a tiny disc with blurry edges (remember, blur is the lack of contrast between boundaries in an image). (See Figure 5.8.)

If this blurry disc—the circle of confusion—is small enough, our eye still perceives it as a point. It's only when the disc grows large enough that we can see it as a blur rather than a sharp point that a given point is viewed as out of focus. You can see, then, that enlarging an image, either by displaying it larger on your computer monitor or by making a large print, also enlarges the size of each circle of confusion. Moving closer to the image does the same thing. So, parts of an image that may look perfectly sharp in a 5 × 7-inch print viewed at arm's length, might appear blurry when blown up to 11 × 14

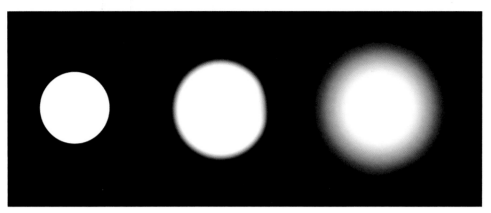

Figure 5.8
When a pin-point of light (left) goes out of focus, its blurry edges form a circle of confusion (center and right).

and examined at the same distance. Take a few steps back, however, and it may look sharp again.

To a lesser extent, the viewer also affects the apparent size of these circles of confusion. Some people see details better at a given distance and may perceive smaller circles of confusion than someone standing next to them. For the most part, however, such differences are small. Truly blurry images will look blurry to just about everyone under the same conditions.

Technically, there is just one plane within your picture area, parallel to the back of the camera (or sensor, in the case of a digital camera), that is in sharp focus. That's the plane in which the points of the image are rendered as precise points. At every other plane in front of or behind the focus plane, the points show up as discs that range from slightly blurry to extremely blurry until, as you can see in Figure 5.9, the out-of-focus areas become one large blur that de-emphasizes an unattractive textured white background.

In practice, the discs in many of these planes will still be so small that we see them as points, and that's where we get depth-of-field. Depth-of-field is just the range of planes that include discs that we perceive as points rather than blurred splotches. The size of this range increases as the aperture is reduced in size and is allocated roughly one-third in front of the plane of sharpest focus, and two-thirds behind it. The range of sharp focus is always greater behind your subject than in front of it.

Making Sense of Sensors

The number and type of autofocus sensors can affect how well the system operates. As I mentioned, the Canon EOS 7D has 19 AF points. Other EOS cameras may have from seven to nine AF points, or, high-end cameras like the 21MP Canon EOS-1Ds Mark III have a whopping 45 autofocus points. These focus sensors can consist of vertical or horizontal lines of pixels, cross-shapes, and often a mixture of these types within a single camera, although, as I mentioned, the EOS 7D includes cross-type sensors at all

Figure 5.9
The background is almost totally blurred, thanks to a wide f/stop.

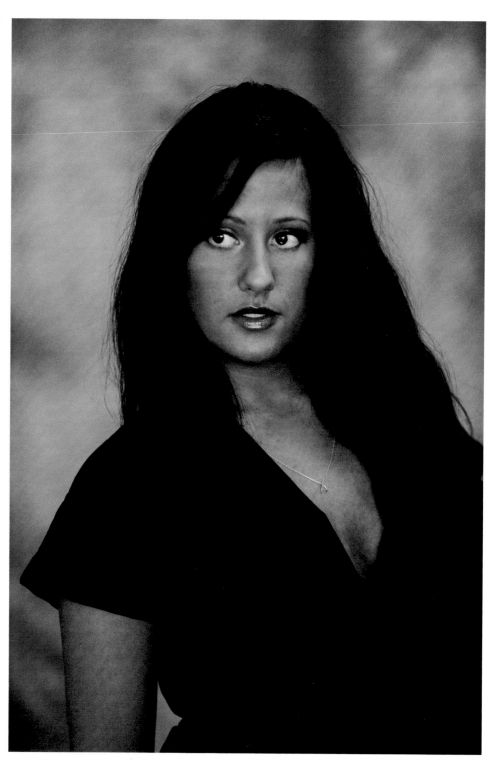

positions. The more AF points available, the more easily the camera can differentiate among areas of the frame, and the more precisely you can specify the area you want to be in focus if you're manually choosing a focus spot.

As the camera collects focus information from the sensors, it then evaluates it to determine whether the desired sharp focus has been achieved. The calculations may include whether the subject is moving, and whether the camera needs to "predict" where the subject will be when the shutter release button is fully depressed and the picture is taken. The speed with which the camera is able to evaluate focus and then move the lens elements into the proper position to achieve the sharpest focus determines how fast the autofocus mechanism is. Although your 7D will almost always focus more quickly than a human, there are types of shooting situations where that's not fast enough. For example, if you're having problems shooting sports because the 7D's autofocus system manically follows each moving subject, a better choice might be to switch autofocus modes or shift into manual and prefocus on a spot where you anticipate the action will be, such as a goal line or soccer net. At night football games, for example, when I am shooting with a telephoto lens almost wide open, I often focus manually on one of the referees who happens to be standing where I expect the action to be taking place (say, a halfback run or a pass reception). When I am less sure about what is going to happen, I may switch to AI Servo autofocus and let the camera decide.

Autofocus Modes

Choosing the right autofocus mode and the way in which focus points are selected is your key to success. Using the wrong mode for a particular type of photography can lead to a series of pictures that are all sharply focused—on the wrong subject. When I first started shooting sports with an autofocus SLR (back in the film camera days), I covered one game alternating between shots of base runners and outfielders with pictures of a promising young pitcher, all from a position next to the third base dugout. The base runner and outfielder photos were great, because their backgrounds didn't distract the autofocus mechanism. But all my photos of the pitcher had the focus tightly zeroed in on the fans in the stands behind him. Because I was shooting film instead of a digital camera, I didn't know about my gaffe until the film was developed. A simple change, such as locking in focus or focus zone manually, or even manually focusing, would have done the trick.

To save battery power, your 7D doesn't start to focus the lens until you partially depress the shutter release. But, autofocus isn't some mindless beast out there snapping your pictures in and out of focus with no feedback from you after you press that button. There are several settings you can modify that return at least a modicum of control to you. Your first decision should be whether you set the 7D to One-Shot, AI Servo AF, or AI Focus AF. With the camera set for one of the non-auto modes, press the AF-DRIVE button and spin the Main Dial until the choice you want is displayed on the rear color LCD and LCD status panel (see Figure 5.10). (The AF/M switch on the lens must be set to AF before you can change autofocus mode.)

One-Shot AF

In this mode, also called *single autofocus*, focus is set once and remains at that setting until the button is fully depressed, taking the picture, or until you release the shutter button without taking a shot. For non-action photography, this setting is usually your best choice, as it minimizes out-of-focus pictures (at the expense of spontaneity). The drawback here is that you might not be able to take a picture at all while the camera is seeking focus; you're locked out until the autofocus mechanism is happy with the current setting. One-Shot AF/single autofocus is sometimes referred to as *focus priority* for that reason. Because of the small delay while the camera zeroes in on correct focus, you might experience slightly more shutter lag. This mode uses less battery power than the other autofocus modes.

When sharp focus is achieved, the selected focus point will flash red in the viewfinder (or as black rectangles in bright light if you have set C.Fn III-08 to Auto), and the focus confirmation light at the lower right will flash green. If you're using evaluative metering, the exposure will be locked at the same time. By keeping the shutter button depressed halfway, you'll find you can reframe the image while retaining the focus (and exposure) that's been set.

Figure 5.10
Rotate the Main Dial until the AF choice you want becomes visible.

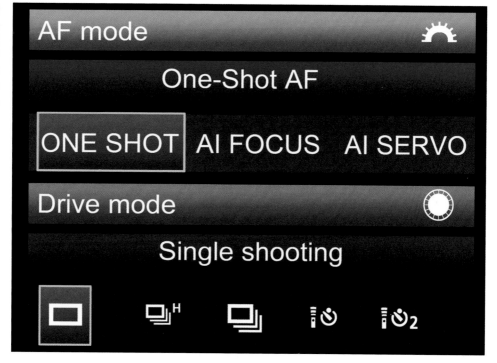

AI Servo AF

This mode, also known as *continuous autofocus* is the mode to use for sports and other fast-moving subjects. In this mode, once the shutter release is partially depressed, the camera sets the focus but continues to monitor the subject, so that if it moves or you move, the lens will be refocused to suit. Focus and exposure aren't really locked until you press the shutter release down all the way to take the picture. You'll often see continuous autofocus referred to as *release priority.* If you press the shutter release down all the way while the system is refining focus, the camera will go ahead and take a picture, even if the image is slightly out of focus. You'll find that AI Servo AF produces the least amount of shutter lag of any autofocus mode: press the button and the camera fires. It also uses the most battery power, because the autofocus system operates as long as the shutter release button is partially depressed.

AI Servo AF uses a technology called *predictive AF*, which allows the 7D to calculate the correct focus if the subject is moving toward or away from the camera at a constant rate. It uses either the automatically selected AF point or the point you select manually to set focus.

AI Focus AF

This setting is actually a combination of the first two. When selected, the camera focuses using One-Shot AF and locks in the focus setting. But, if the subject begins moving, it will switch automatically to AI Servo AF and change the focus to keep the subject sharp. AI Focus AF is a good choice when you're shooting a mixture of action pictures and less dynamic shots and want to use One-Shot AF when possible. The camera will default to that mode, yet switch automatically to AI Servo AF when it would be useful for subjects that might begin moving unexpectedly.

Autofocus Mode Options

Several options are available that affect your autofocus mode options. I'll describe all of them in detail in Chapter 8, but here are some that you might want to know about now. If you think you need to use one of them, you can skip ahead to the chapter and read more.

AI Servo AF Sensitivity

Custom Function C.Fn III-01 controls how the 7D's autofocus system in AI Servo AF operates when new subjects appear in the frame temporarily, perhaps passing in front of the subject you're shooting. You can specify a long delay, so that the new subject is ignored, a shorter delay, or specify that the 7D immediately refocuses when a new subject moves into the frame. You can select from a scale with Slow, Normal, and Fast reaction times, plus two intermediate points. See Chapter 8 for more information.

Focus Priority/Release Priority

Custom Function C. Fn III-02 allows you to specify whether the EOS 7D should take a picture immediately when the shutter release is pressed down all the way when using AI Servo AF (called release priority), or whether the camera should wait until sharpest focus is achieved before taking the picture (called focus priority). As I'll explain in Chapter 8, the choice boils down to whether you want a picture at any cost, even if it might be slightly out of focus, or whether you're willing to miss the decisive moment in order to achieve a sharper image.

Close Subject/Original Subject Priority

The Custom Function C.Fn III-03 option can be used to tell the 7D to switch to a closer subject that appears in the frame, or whether to ignore close subjects and continue tracking the original subject when using AI Servo AF mode. Use this with C.Fn III-01 to control the camera's behavior when unexpected (or even anticipated) subjects move into the frame.

Setting the AF Point

Once you've told the EOS 7D *when* to activate and lock autofocus, you need to help the camera decide *where* to focus, or, what part of the frame to lock in on. That's where things start to get really interesting, because the 7D has more options for setting the AF point than most cameras—even those in the Canon line.

Which of the 19 AF points are used to lock in focus is determined by the *AF area selection mode* you've chosen. There are five selection modes in all: four manual modes in which you choose the AF point yourself, and one automatic mode in which the 7D chooses the AF point for you. I'll show you how to switch among these five modes shortly. But first, you need to know what the modes are, and why you might want to use each of them.

Default AF Selection Modes

Three of the five modes are available by default; the other two can be activated or deactivated using Custom Function C. Fn III-6, as described later. The three default modes are as follows:

Single-Point AF

In this mode, you always select the focus point to be used, from the 19 available points. The currently selected point is highlighted, and covers approximately the area of the highlighted box. (See Figure 5.11.) To choose the AF point, press the AF point selection/Magnify button (located on the upper-left corner of the back of the camera). All 19 AF points will be displayed in the viewfinder. Use the multi-controller to move the

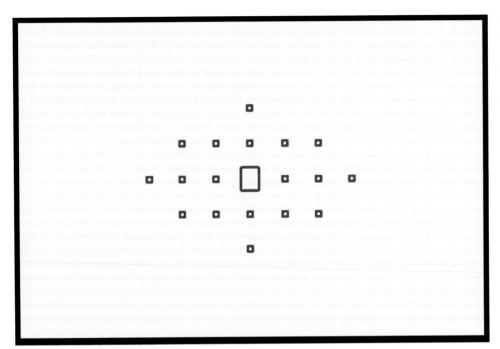

Figure 5.11
Manually select
any of the 19
focus points
using single-
point selection.

highlighting among the focus points until the one you want is selected. Press the multi-
controller center button to select the center AF point.

If you prefer, you can rotate the Main Dial to move the highlighting back and forth in
the horizontal direction, and the Quick Control Dial to move the AF point in the vertical direction. The dials are a quick way to switch from one AF point to another one
that's in the same row (or column, respectively).

This selection mode is good for general-purpose autofocus point selection when you
need moderately fine control over the position of the point. If you need more precise
control, activate the optional Spot AF mode using C.Fn III-06, as described in the next
section.

Zone AF

In this mode, you don't select the actual focus point; the camera does that. Instead, you
specify which of five possible zones should be used. The 7D then chooses the focus point
from among the four or nine points in the zone you've chosen.

This mode can be faster to use than any of the single-point selection modes, because
you're choosing a larger area (a zone) instead of an individual point. That makes it ideal
for moving objects, especially large objects that occupy most of a particular zone.
However, if your subject is *not* large and, in particular, is not likely to be the subject

closest to the camera, the zone system makes it more difficult to choose a specific object (use one of the single-point modes instead). Zone AF tends to lock onto the largest subject in the zone that is closest to the camera.

To use this point or mode (if Zone AF has been selected), press the AF point selection/Magnify button, and select the zone you want to use with the multi-controller or Main Dial and Quick Control Dial. Pressing the multi-controller center button highlights the center zone. The available zones are shown in Figure 5.12.

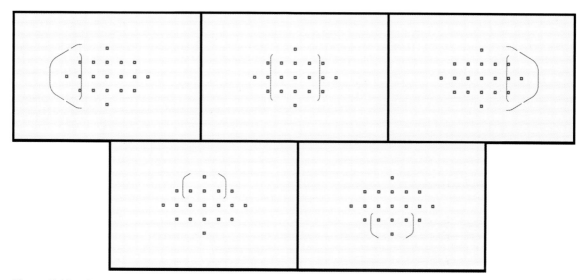

Figure 5.12 Choose one of five zones, and the camera will select an autofocus point within it.

Auto Select 19-point AF

In this mode, the EOS 7D chooses the AF point or points for you. It is always used when working in Full Auto or Creative Auto modes, and can be optionally used with any of the other exposure modes. When you press the shutter release halfway, the AF points chosen by the camera will be displayed. Because this mode tends to lock focus on the nearest subject, it works best for portraits, close-ups, and other scenes where the main subject is the nearest object to the camera. The display you see in the viewfinder is shown in Figure 5.13.

This mode operates slightly differently in One-Shot AF and AI Servo AF modes.

- **One-Shot AF mode.** When using this mode, when you press the shutter release halfway, the AF points used to achieve focus will be highlighted in the viewfinder.

- **AI Servo AF mode.** When using this mode, which is not available when working with Full Auto and Creative Auto settings, the manually selected focus point is used first, with the 7D switching to the other focus points if necessary.

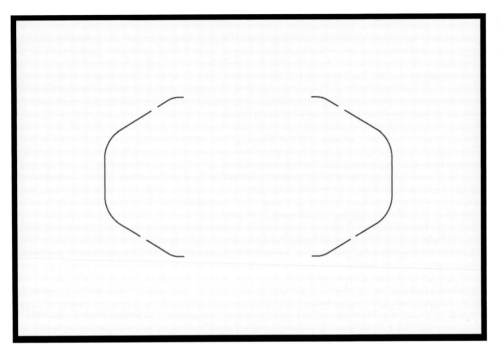

Figure 5.13
The 7D can
select any of
the zones
within this area
for you.

Additional AF Selection Modes

Two more AF selection modes can be added using Custom Function C. Fn III-6, as described later. The two additional modes are as follows:

Spot AF

This mode is basically exactly the same as Single-point AF, described earlier, but using a smaller, "spot" AF point. As with Single-point AF, you select the focus point to be used. The currently selected point is highlighted, but covers only the smaller point areas inside the highlighted box. (See Figure 5.14.) To choose the AF point, press the AF point selection/Magnify button, and use the multi-controller to move the highlighting among the focus points until the one you want is selected. Press the multi-controller center button to select the center AF point.

Or, you can rotate the Main Dial to move the highlighting back and forth in the horizontal direction, and the Quick Control Dial to move the AF point in the vertical direction to select a different point in the same row or column. This selection mode is best when you need to precisely select the position of the AF point.

Figure 5.14
The smaller
box inside the
larger area is
the actual focus
point.

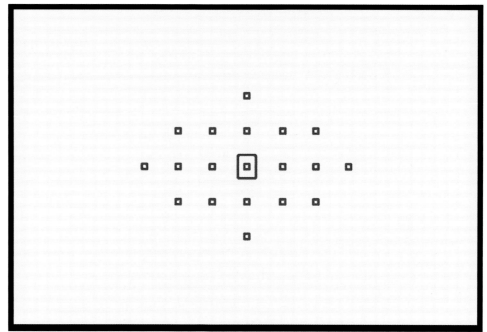

AF Point Expansion

This additional optional AF area selection mode is useful when you need to track moving objects, because the 7D will use the focus point you select manually, but also use information from the points immediately adjacent to it. So, if your subject moves, the camera will already have focus information available for use.

To choose the AF point (and the surrounding points that will also be used, as you can see in Figure 5.15), press the AF point selection/Magnify button, and use the multi-controller or Main Dial or Quick Control Dial to move the highlighting within the 19 points shown. As always, pressing the multi-controller center button moves the highlighting to the center AF point.

This mode operates slightly differently in AI Servo AF and One-Shot AF modes. When using AI Servo AF, the focus point you select manually will be used to track the moving object (the camera doesn't switch to the "expanded" points as the subject moves). In One-Shot AF, the 7D will switch to an expanded point if necessary, and highlight both the manually selected AF point and the expanded point in the viewfinder.

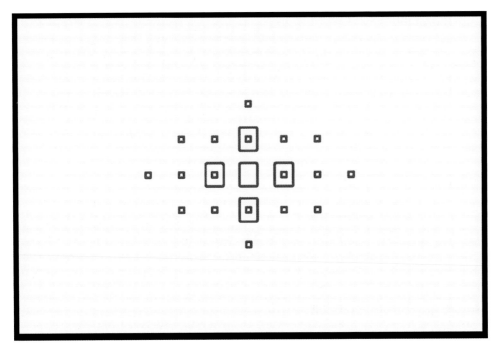

Figure 5.15
The 7D uses the manually selected focus zone (in this case, the center zone), and will track focus using information from the zones surrounding it.

Specifying the AF Area Selection Mode

To switch among the AF area selection modes I've just described, follow these steps:

1. Set the lens AF/MF switch to AF.

2. Press the AF point selection/Magnify button (located at the top-right corner of the back of the camera).

3. While looking through the viewfinder, press the M-Fn button (found just northwest of the Main Dial).

4. Each time you press the M-Fn button, the 7D will cycle to the next AF area selection mode.

5. By default, the modes selected will be Single-point AF, Zone AF, and 19-point AF.

6. If you want to add Spot AF and AF point expansion to the "rotation," visit C.Fn-III: Autofocus Drive 06 and enable those two modes, as described in Chapter 8.

Other AF Options

You'll find some additional interesting options in the Custom Function menu, as detailed in Chapter 8. Here are some quick summaries of the most important features. Skip ahead to the chapter if you'd like to implement them now.

Avoiding Endless Focus Hunting

If you frequently photograph subjects that don't have a lot of detail (which complicates focus) or use very long telephoto lenses (which may be difficult to autofocus because of their shallow depth-of-field and smaller maximum apertures), you may find the 7D constantly seeking focus unsuccessfully. C.Fn III-04 tells the 7D what to do when it is having difficulty focusing. You can tell it to keep trying (if that's what you really want), or instruct the 7D to give up when the autofocus system becomes "lost," giving you the opportunity to go ahead and focus manually.

Focus Point Selection Wrap

In the Custom Function menu at C.Fn III-07 you'll find Manual AF pt. Selec. Pattern, as described in Chapter 8, where you can instruct the 7D to stop moving the focus point highlighting when the selection reaches the edge of the AF 19-point array—or, it can continue, wrapping around to the opposite edge. Wrapping is purely a personal preference; it may be faster for those who are used to using the feature. I generally turn it off.

Show AF points/Grid in the Viewfinder

With C.Fn III-08 you can specify whether red highlighting is used for the AF points, the grid, and other elements are illuminated in the viewfinder in red under low light levels. Some people find the glowing red elements distracting and like to disable the function. You can select Auto (highlighting is used in low light levels), Enable (highlighting is used at all times), or Disable (red highlighting is never used).

Activate/Deactivate the Autofocus Assist Lamp

Use C.Fn III-11 to determine when the AF assist lamp or bursts from an electronic flash are used to emit a pulse of light that helps provide enough contrast for the EOS 7D to focus on a subject. You can select Enable to use the camera's built-in flash (when elevated) or an attached Canon Speedlite to produce a focus assist beam. Use Disable to turn this feature off if you find it distracting. You can also specify that only the focus assist beam from an attached dedicated strobe will be used.

Separate AF Area Selection for Horizontal/Vertical Scenes

One outstanding new feature of the EOS 7D is the ability to specify different AF area selection modes for horizontal and vertically oriented scenes. This ability is useful because the kinds of things we shoot in each orientation tend to be different. In horizontal mode, we may be shooting landscapes and other scenes where the emphasis is on the middle or lower half of the frame. With the camera rotated to vertical orientation (in my case for, say, basketball games, portraits, or fashion photography), we may prefer to concentrate focus on a different zone, such as the upper half of the frame.

C.Fn III-12 allows you to do that. You can elect to use the same AF area selection mode and manually selected AF point/zone for vertically and horizontally composed shots— or to select a different mode and point/zone for vertical and horizontal shots.

You can choose Same for both vertical/horizontal. The AF area selection mode and manually selected AF point or Zone (when using Zone AF) that you specify are used for any camera orientation. Or, you can choose a specific AF area selection mode and AF point/zone for each orientation. (See Figure 5.16.)

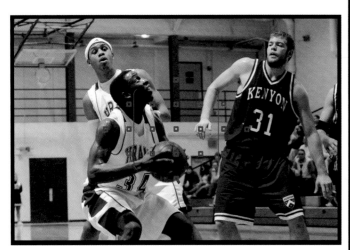
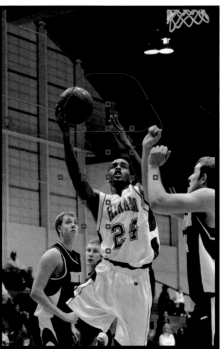

Figure 5.16 You might prefer to have the 7D use different focus zones for horizontally composed and vertically composed shots.

Fine-Tuning the Focus of Your Lenses

The Canon EOS 7D has a feature called AF Microadjustment, which I hope you never need to use, because it is applied only when you find that a particular lens is not focusing properly. If the lens happens to focus a bit ahead or a bit behind the actual point of sharp focus, and it does that consistently, you can use the adjustment feature, found in the Custom Function menu under C.Fn III-05 to "calibrate" the lens's focus.

Why is the focus "off" for some lenses in the first place? There are lots of factors, including the age of the lens (an older lens may focus slightly differently), temperature effects on certain types of glass, humidity, and tolerances built into a lens's design that all add up to a slight misadjustment, even though the components themselves are, strictly speaking, within specs. A very slight variation in your lens's mount can cause focus to vary slightly. With any luck (if you can call it that), a lens that doesn't focus exactly right will at least be consistent. If a lens always focuses a bit behind the subject, the symptom is *back focus.* If it focuses in front of the subject, it's called *front focus.*

You're almost always better off sending such a lens in to Canon to have them make it right. But that's not always possible. Perhaps you need your lens recalibrated right now, or you purchased a used lens that is long out of warranty. If you want to do it yourself, the first thing to do is determine whether your lens has a back focus or front focus problem.

For a quick-and-dirty diagnosis (*not* a calibration; you'll use a different target for that), lay down a piece of graph paper on a flat surface, and place an object on the line at the middle, which will represent the point of focus (we hope). Then, shoot the target at an angle using your lens's widest aperture and the autofocus mode you want to test. Mount the camera on a tripod so you can get accurate, repeatable results.

If your camera/lens combination doesn't suffer from front or back focus, the point of sharpest focus will be the center line of the chart, as you can see in Figure 5.17. If you do have a problem, one of the other lines will be sharply focused instead. Should you discover that your lens consistently front or back focuses, it needs to be recalibrated. Unfortunately, it's only possible to calibrate a lens for a single focusing distance. So, if you use a particular lens (such as a macro lens) for close focusing, calibrate for that. If you use a lens primarily for middle distances, calibrate for that. Close-to-middle distances are most likely to cause focus problems, anyway, because as you get closer to infinity, small changes in focus are less likely to have an effect.

Lens Tune-Up

The key tool you can use to fine-tune your lens is the AF Microadjustment entry in the Custom Function menu. You'll find the process easier to understand if you first run through this quick overview of the menu options:

- **0: Disable.** Deactivates autofocus micro adjustment.

- **1: Adjust all by same amount.** The same adjustment is applied to all your lenses. You'd use this if your camera, rather than just a lens or two, requires calibration. (In this case, I particularly recommend sending the camera back to Canon for repair.)

- **2: Adjust by lens.** You can set an adjustment individually for up to 20 different lenses. If you discover you don't care for the calibrations you make in certain situations (say, it works better for the lens you have mounted at middle distances, but is less successful at correcting close-up focus errors) you can deactivate the feature as you require. Adjustment values range from –20 to +20.

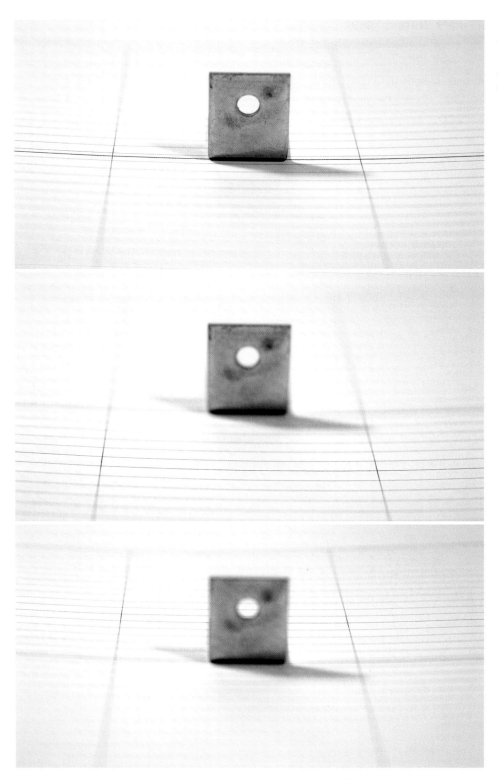

Figure 5.17
Correct focus (top), front focus (middle), and back focus (bottom).

Evaluate Current Focus

The first step is to capture a baseline image that represents how the lens you want to fine-tune autofocuses at a particular distance. You'll often see advice for photographing a test chart with millimeter markings from an angle, and the suggestion that you auto-focus on a particular point on the chart. Supposedly, the markings that actually *are* in focus will help you recalibrate your lens. The problem with this approach is that the information you get from photographing a test chart at an angle doesn't actually tell you what to do to make a precise correction. So, your lens back focuses three millimeters behind the target area on the chart. So what? Does that mean you change the value –3 increments? Or –15 increments? Angled targets are a "shortcut" that don't save you time.

Instead, you'll want to photograph a target that represents what you're actually trying to achieve: a plane of focus locked in by your lens that represents the actual plane of focus of your subject. For that, you'll need a flat target, mounted precisely perpendicular to the sensor plane of the camera. Then, you can take a photo, see if the plane of focus is correct, and if not, dial in a bit of fine-tuning in the AF Microadjustment menu, and shoot again. Lather, rinse, and repeat until the target is sharply focused.

You can use the focus target shown in Figure 5.18, or you can use a chart of your own, as long as it has contrasty areas that will be easily seen by the autofocus system, and without very small details that are likely to confuse the AF. Download your own copy of my chart from www.dslrguides.com/FocusChart.pdf. Then print out a copy on the largest paper your printer can handle. (I don't recommend just displaying the file on your monitor and focusing on that; it's unlikely you'll have the monitor screen lined up perfectly perpendicular to the camera sensor.) Then, follow these steps:

1. **Position the camera.** Place your camera on a sturdy tripod with a remote release attached, positioned at roughly eye-level at a distance from a wall that represents the distance you want to test for. Keep in mind that autofocus problems can be different at varying distances and lens focal lengths, and that you can enter only *one* correction value for a particular lens. So, choose a distance (close-up or mid-range) and zoom setting with your shooting habits in mind.

2. **Set the autofocus mode.** Choose the autofocus mode (One-Shot AF or AI Servo AF) you want to test. (Because AI Auto mode just alternates between the two, you don't need to test that mode.)

3. **Level the camera (in an ideal world).** If the wall happens to be perfectly perpendicular, you can use a bubble level, plumb bob, or other device of your choice to ensure that the camera is level to match. Many tripods and tripod heads have bubble levels built in. Avoid using the center column, if you can. When the camera is properly oriented, lock the legs and tripod head tightly.

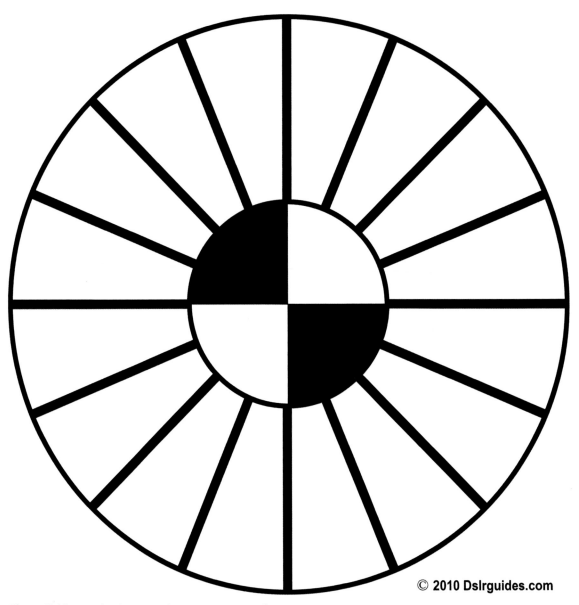

Figure 5.18 Use this focus test chart, or create one of your own.

4. **Level the camera (in the real world).** If your wall is not perfectly perpendicular, use this old trick. Tape a mirror to the wall, and then adjust the camera on the tripod so that when you look through the viewfinder at the mirror, you see directly into the reflection of the lens. Then, lock the tripod and remove the mirror.

5. **Mount the test chart.** Tape the test chart on the wall so it is centered in your camera's viewfinder.

6. **Photograph the test chart using AF.** Allow the camera to autofocus, and take a test photo, using the remote release to avoid shaking or moving the camera.

7. **Make an adjustment and rephotograph.** Make a fine-tuning adjustment (described next) and photograph the target again.

8. **Evaluate the image.** If you have the camera connected to your computer with a USB cable or through a WiFi connection, so much the better. You can view the image after it's transferred to your computer. Otherwise, *carefully* open the camera card door and slip the memory card out and copy the images to your computer.

9. **Evaluate focus.** Which image is sharpest? That's the setting you need to use for this lens. If your initial range doesn't provide the correction you need, repeat the steps between –20 and +20 until you find the best fine-tuning.

Make Adjustments

Making the adjustments is simple. From the Custom Function menu, select C.Fn III-05 AF Microadjustment, and choose either 1: Adjust all by the same amount or 2: Adjust by lens.

■ **Adjust all by same amount.** Highlight the entry and press the Set button. Then, press the INFO. button to produce a screen with a scale from –20 to +20. Use the Quick Control Dial to choose a value, and press SET to confirm.

■ **Adjust by lens.** Highlight the entry and press the SET button. Then, press the INFO. button to produce a screen with the name of the lens currently mounted on the camera, and a scale from –20 to +20. (See Figure 5.19.) Use the QCD to choose a value, and press SET to confirm. It will remember the setting you enter for that lens and restore it each time the lens is mounted on the camera. The 7D has enough memory to store values for 20 different lenses. If you want to register more than 20 lenses, select a lens with an adjustment that can be deleted, mount it on the camera, and reset its adjustment to 0. That will free up a slot for a different lens.

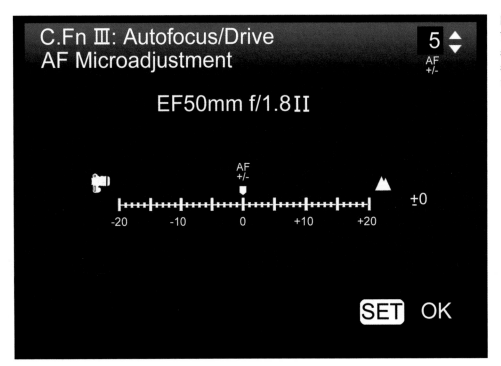

Figure 5.19

You can enter autofocus adjustments for up to 20 lenses.

6

Advanced Shooting, Live View, and Movies

You can happily spend your entire shooting career using the techniques and features already explained in this book. Great exposures, sharp pictures, and creative compositions are all you really need to produce great shot after great shot. But, those with enough interest in getting the most out of their Canon EOS 7D who buy this book probably will be interested in going beyond those basics to explore some of the more advanced techniques and capabilities of the camera. Capturing the briefest instant of time, transforming common scenes into the unusual with lengthy time exposures, and shooting movies to accompany still images are all tempting avenues for exploration.

So, in this chapter, I'm going to offer longer discussions of some of the more advanced techniques and capabilities that I like to put to work. Live View has been around long enough that it's becoming old hat for some, but, we have learned, it was really just a precursor to one of the 7D's real killer features—full HD video shooting. Indeed, the opening montages of Saturday Night Live were all shot using Canon cameras like the 7D and 5D Mark II, so you can see that movie shooting with your camera has a lot of potential. Because Live View is, in fact, so tightly integrated with movie shooting, we'll start with that.

Working with Live View

Live View is one of those features that experienced SLR users (especially those dating from the film era) sometimes think they don't need—until they try it. It's also one of those features (like truly "silent" shooting, without any shutter click) that point-and-shoot refugees are surprised that digital SLRs (until recently) have lacked. As I noted earlier, SLRs have actual, mechanical shutters that can't be completely silenced, as can be done with point-and-shoot cameras. I've fielded almost as many queries from those who want to know how to preview their images on the LCD—just as they did with their point-and-shoot cameras. Indeed, many point-and-shoot models don't even *have* optical viewfinders, engendering a whole generation of amateur photographers who think the only way to frame and compose an image is to hold the camera out at arm's length so the back-panel LCD can be viewed more easily.

While dSLR veterans didn't really miss what we've come to know as Live View, it was at least, in part, because they didn't have it and couldn't miss what they never had. After all, why would you eschew a big, bright, magnified through-the-lens optical view that showed depth-of-field fairly well, and which was easily visible under virtually all ambient light conditions? LCD displays, after all, were small, tended to wash out in bright light, and didn't really provide you with an accurate view of what your picture was going to look like.

There were technical problems, as well. Real-time previews theoretically disabled a dSLR's autofocus system, as focus was achieved by measuring contrast through the optical viewfinder, which is blocked when the mirror is flipped up for a live view. Extensive previewing had the same effect on the sensor as long exposures: the sensor heated up, producing excess noise. Pointing the camera at a bright light source when using a real-time view could damage the sensor. The list of potential problems goes on and on.

That was then. This is now.

The Canon EOS 7D has a gorgeous 3-inch LCD that can be viewed under a variety of lighting conditions and from wide-ranging angles, so you don't have to be exactly behind the display to see it clearly. (See Figure 6.1.) It offers a 100-percent view of the sensor's capture area (the optical viewfinder shows just 95 percent of the sensor's field of view). It's large enough to allow manual focusing—but if you want to use automatic focus, there's an option that allows briefly flipping the mirror back down for autofocusing, interrupting Live View, and then restoring the sensor preview image after focus is achieved. You still have to avoid pointing your 7D at bright light sources (especially the Sun) when using Live View, but the real-time preview can be used for fairly long periods without frying the sensor. (Image quality can degrade, but the camera issues a warning when the sensor starts to overheat.)

Unlike some of the previous attempts at a Live View-type mode by other sensors (and including Canon with its astrophotography model EOS 20Da), the 7D's Live View works. No beam-splitting prisms that divert some light to the sensor, no grainy black-and-white real-time preview, no need for a spare sensor to provide a simulated Live View. Canon's system works just like you'd want it to: the mirror flips up, the shutter opens, and what the sensor sees is displayed in full color on the LCD on the back of the camera. You can expect every new camera introduced by Canon and every other vendor to

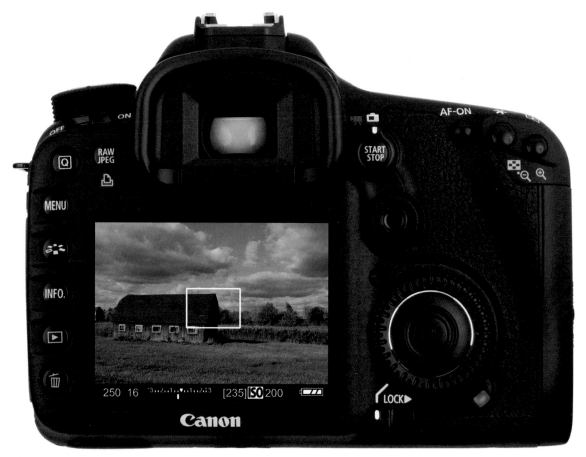

Figure 6.1 Live View really shines on the Canon EOS 7D's large 3-inch LCD.

include Live View features from now on. And, expect Live View to get better. Canon has made some significant improvements in its Live View implementation in the interim between its original introduction on the EOS 40D, and the unveiling of the upgraded version offered with the EOS 7D.

What You Can/Cannot Do with Live View

You may not have considered just what you can do with Live View, because the capability is so novel. But once you've played with it, you'll discover dozens of applications for this capability, as well as a few things that you can't do. Here's a list of Live View Do's/Don'ts/Cans/Can'ts.

■ **Preview your images on a TV.** Connect your EOS 7D to a television using the video cable, and you can preview your image on a large screen.

■ **Preview remotely.** Extend the cable between the camera and TV screen, and you can preview your images some distance away from the camera.

- **Shoot from your computer.** Canon gives you the software you need to control your camera from your computer, so you can preview images and take pictures without physically touching the EOS 7D.

- **Continuous shooting.** You can shoot bursts of images using Live View, but all shots will use the focus and exposure setting established for the first picture in the series.

- **Shoot from tripod or handheld.** Of course, holding the camera out at arm's length to preview an image is poor technique, and will introduce a lot of camera shake. If you want to use Live View for hand-held images, use an image-stabilized lens and/or a high shutter speed. A tripod is a better choice if you can use one.

- **Watch your power.** Live View uses a lot of juice and will deplete your battery rapidly. Canon estimates that you can get 130-170 shots per battery when using Live View, depending on the temperature. The optional AC adapter is a useful accessory.

Enabling Live View

You need to take some steps before using Live View. This workflow prevents you from accidentally using Live View when you don't mean to, thus potentially losing a shot, and it also helps ensure that you've made all the settings necessary to successfully use the feature efficiently. Here are the steps to follow:

1. **Choose a shooting mode.** Live View works with any exposure mode, including Full Auto and Creative Auto. You can even switch from one mode to another while Live View is activated (except that when you change from Full Auto or Creative Auto to one of the other modes while Live View is on, it will be deactivated and must be restarted).

2. **Enable Live View.** You'll need to activate Live View by choosing Live View shoot. setting from the Shooting 4 menu. Press SET and use the Quick Control Dial to select Enable and press the SET button again to exit. Note that even if you've disabled Live View, you can still set the Live View switch to Movie and shoot video.

3. **Choose other Live View functions.** Select from the other Live View functions in the Shooting 4 menu (described next), then press the MENU button to exit from the Live View function settings menu.

4. **Specify Movie or Live View shooting.** The Live View switch on the back of the camera (immediately to the right of the optical viewfinder window) can be toggled between the Movie and Live View settings.

5. **Activate Live View.** Press the Start/Stop button to begin or end Live View.

Several other optional functions can be set from the Live View function settings choices in the Shooting 4 menu (see Figure 6.2). They include:

- **Autofocus mode (Quick mode, Live mode, Live "face detection" mode).** This option, explained next, lets you choose between phase detection, contrast detection, and contrast detection with "face" recognition.

- **Grid display (Off, Grid 1, Grid 2).** Overlays Grid 1, a "rule of thirds" grid, on the screen to help you compose your image and align vertical and horizontal lines; or Grid 2, which consists of four rows of six boxes that allow finer control over placement of images in your frame.

- **Expo. simulation (Enable/Disable).** When disabled, the LCD will show the Live View image at standard brightness. Use this option when you want to be able to view the image easily, especially under reduced lighting conditions. Indeed, you can enhance the LCD image using the LCD brightness option in the Set-up 2 menu, as described in Chapter 8. Enable exposure simulation when you want the brightness of the LCD image to mimic the brightness level of the image you will capture. You can use this feature to roughly gauge whether the exposure is correct, without the need to reference a histogram. Exposure simulation is faster to use, but may not work as well under dim lighting.

Figure 6.2
Live View function settings can be found in the Shooting 4 menu.

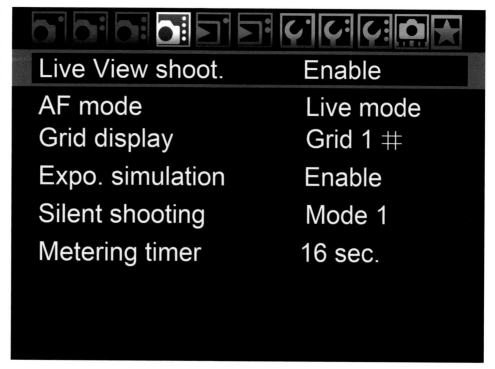

- **Silent shooting (Mode 1, Mode 2, Disable).** This option turns on or off optional quiet modes that reduce shutter noise. I'll explain your choices in more detail later.

- **Metering timer (4 sec. to 30 min).** This option allows you to specify how long the EOS 7D's metering system will remain active before switching off.

Activating Live View

Once you've enabled Live View, you can continue taking pictures normally through the 7D's viewfinder. When you're ready to activate Live View, press the Stop/Start button on the back of the camera, to the immediate right of the viewfinder window. The mirror will flip up, and the sensor image will appear on the LCD. Here are some things you should keep in mind when Live View is active:

- **Shooting functions don't interrupt.** You can change settings or review images normally when in Live View mode. Press the WB, AF-DRIVE, or ISO-Flash exposure compensation buttons on the top of the camera, or the Picture Control button to the left of the LCD, and an overlay appears superimposed on the Live View screen. You can use the Quick Control Dial and Main Dial to change those settings. You can also make adjustments to the Auto Lighting Optimizer and change Image quality by pressing the Q button on the left side of the camera. If you've chosen AF Quick autofocus mode, you can set the AF point and AF area selection mode, described in Chapter 5.

- **Live View continues.** When you press the shutter release, the 7D will take a photo, then display the image you just shot for review, as normal. When picture review is finished, the camera returns to Live View mode. You can take as many consecutive shots using Live View as you like, barring sensor overheating. To exit Live View entirely, press the Start/Stop button.

- **Metering mode cannot be changed.** Evaluative metering linked to the focus frame is used. You cannot change to partial, spot, or center-weighted metering when Live View is active.

- **Fixed continuous exposure.** If you shoot in continuous mode, the exposure determined for the first image will be used for all subsequent images in the series.

- **Press DOF button to check focus and exposure.** If you press the Depth-of-Field button while using Live View, the lens will stop down to the taking aperture and you'll see the effective focus range, as well as approximate image brightness.

- **Flash OK.** You can use flash when working with Live View, but the FE (flash exposure) lock, modeling flash, and test firing of the flash are not possible. In addition, to change the Speedlite's own custom functions, you'll need to use the camera's menus in the Flash Control section of the Shooting 1 menu. The flash's own Custom Function setting capability is disabled.

■ **Watch for overheating.** Leaving Live View on for extended periods increases the temperature of the sensor, potentially causing noise or odd colors in your image. If you want to take a long exposure, turn off Live View for several minutes before shooting to allow your sensor to cool. Live View will shut off automatically after 30 minutes, and a high temperature icon warns you when things start to heat up.

■ **Information display.** During Live View, useful information is shown on the screen, such as battery status, Picture Style, and most of the shooting information (shutter speed, f/stop, ISO setting, number of exposures remaining) you'd see through the viewfinder. Press the INFO. button to change the amount of information shown. (See Figure 6.3.)

Figure 6.3
Press the INFO. button to increase or decrease the amount of information shown on the LCD in Live View mode.

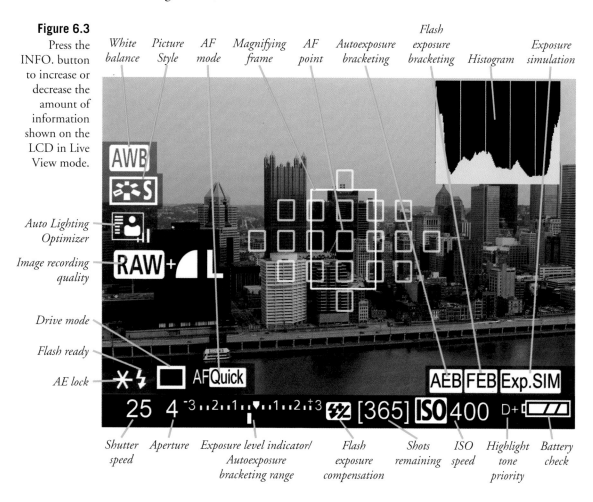

Focusing in Live View

Press the AF-ON button or press the shutter button halfway to activate autofocus using the currently set Live View autofocus mode. Those modes are Live mode, Live "face detection" mode, and Quick mode. You can also use manual focus. I'll describe each of these separately.

Live Mode

This mode uses contrast detection, using the relative sharpness of the image as it appears on the sensor to determine focus. This method is less precise, and usually takes longer than Quick mode. To autofocus using Live mode, follow these steps:

1. **Set lens to autofocus.** Make sure the focus switch on the lens is set to AF.

2. **Activate Live View.** Press the Start/Stop button.

3. **Choose AF point.** Use the multi-controller to move the AF point anywhere you like on the screen, except for the edges. Press the multi-controller button to return the AF point to the center of the screen.

4. **Select subject.** Compose the image on the LCD so the selected focus point is on the subject.

5. **Press and hold the shutter button halfway.** When focus is achieved, the AF point turns green, and you'll hear a beep if the sound has been turned on in the Shooting 1 menu. If the 7D is unable to focus, the AF point turns red instead.

6. **Take picture.** Press the shutter release all the way down to take the picture.

Live (Face Detection) Mode

This mode also uses contrast detection, using the relative sharpness of the image as it appears on the sensor to determine focus. The 7D will search the frame for a human face and attempt to focus on the face. Like Live mode, this method is less precise, and usually takes longer than Quick mode. To autofocus using Live (face detection) mode, follow these steps:

1. **Set lens to autofocus.** Make sure the focus switch on the lens is set to AF.

2. **Activate Live View.** Press the Start/Stop button.

3. **Face detection.** A frame will appear around a face found in the image. (See Figure 6.4.) (You can press the Zoom/* button on the upper-right back of the camera to magnify the area of the image inside the magnify frame.) If more than one face is found, a frame with notches that look like "ears" appears. In that case, use the multi-controller to move the frame to the face you want to use for focus. If no face is detected, the AF point will be displayed and focus will be locked into the center.

Figure 6.4
The 7D can detect faces during autofocus.

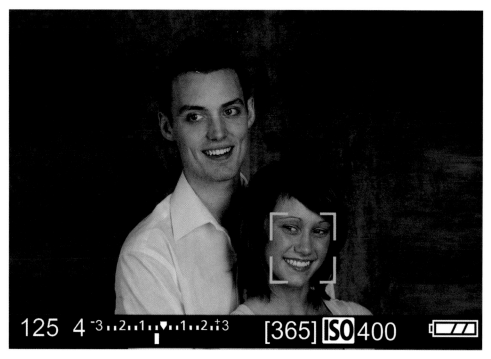

125   4 ⁻3··2··1··▼··1··2·⁺3   [365] **ISO** 400

4. **Troubleshoot (if necessary).** If you experience problems in Live (face detection) mode, press down on the multi-controller button to switch to from Live (face detection) mode to Live mode. Face detection is far from perfect. The AF system may fail to find a face if the person's visage is too large/small or light/dark in the frame, tilted, or located near an edge of the picture. It may classify a non-face as a face. If you switch to Live mode, you can always select another AF point and press the multi-controller button again to toggle back to Live (face detection) mode.

5. **Press and hold the shutter release halfway.** When focus is achieved, the AF point turns green, and you'll hear a beep. If the 7D is unable to focus, the AF point turns red instead.

6. **Take picture.** Press the shutter release all the way down to take the picture.

Quick Mode

This mode uses phase detection, as described earlier in the chapter. It temporarily interrupts Live View mode to allow the EOS 7D to focus the same AF sensor used when you focus through the viewfinder. Because the step takes a second or so, you may get better results using this autofocus mode when the camera is mounted on a tripod. If you hand-hold the 7D, you may displace the point of focus achieved by the autofocus system. It also simplifies the operation if you use One-Shot focus and center the focus point. You can use AI Servo and Automatic or Manual focus point selection, but if the focus point doesn't coincide with the subject you want to focus on, you'll end up with an out-of-focus image. Just follow these steps.

1. **Set lens to autofocus.** Make sure the focus switch on the lens is set to AF.

2. **Activate Live View.** Press the Start/Stop button.

3. **Choose AF point.** Press the AF-DRIVE button and use the multi-controller to choose which of the nine AF points to use.

4. **Select subject.** Compose the image on the LCD so the selected focus point is on the subject.

5. **Press and hold the shutter release halfway.** The LCD will blank as the mirror flips down, reflecting the view of the subject to the phase detection AF sensor.

6. **Wait for focus.** When the 7D is able to lock in focus using phase detection, a beep (if activated) will sound. If you are hand-holding the 7D, you may hear several beeps as the AF system focuses and refocuses with each camera movement. Then, the mirror will flip back up, and the Live View image reappears. The AF focus point will be highlighted in red on the LCD.

7. **Take picture.** Press the shutter release all the way down to take the picture. (You can't take a photo while Quick mode AF is in process, until the mirror flips back up.)

Manual Mode

Focusing manually on an LCD screen isn't as difficult as you might think, but Canon has made the process even easier by providing a magnified view. Just follow these steps to focus manually.

1. **Set lens to manual focus.** Make sure the focus switch on the lens is set to MF.

2. **Move magnifying frame.** Use the multi-controller to move the focus frame that's superimposed on the screen to the location where you want to focus. You can press the multi-controller to center the focus frame in the middle of the screen.

3. **Press the Zoom button.** The area of the image inside the focus frame will be magnified 5X. (See Figure 6.5.) Press the Zoom button again to increase the magnification to 10X. A third press will return you to the full-frame view. The enlarged area is artificially sharpened to make it easier for you to see the contrast changes and simplify focusing. When zoomed in, press the shutter release halfway and the current shutter speed and aperture are shown in orange. If no information at all appears, press the INFO. button.

4. **Focus manually.** Use the focus ring on the lens to focus the image. When you're satisfied, you can zoom back out by pressing the Zoom button.

Figure 6.5
You can manu-
ally focus the
center area,
which can be
zoomed in 5X
or 10X.

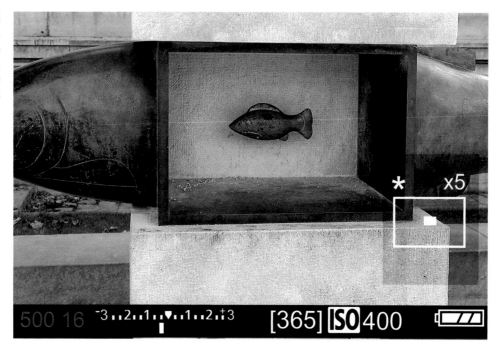

Using Simulated Exposure

If you've activated Exposure Simulation, the LCD won't maintain a constant brightness level under varying ambient lighting conditions but will instead brighten or dim to emulate the correct exposure or over/underexposure you'll get with the current settings.

Enabling this feature also activates the histogram, which you can use to judge exposure (as explained in Chapter 4). If the histogram is not visible on the Live View screen, press the INFO. button until it appears. The histogram may not display properly under very low or very high light levels, and is not available at all when you're using flash or exposures with the Bulb setting.

Silent Shooting

Although silent shooting is far from a stealth photography mode, it does produce a quieter shutter noise than what you get when not in Live View mode. That's because the mirror has already been flipped out of the way, so the sound produced primarily comes from the opening and closing of the shutter. You can activate silent shooting from the Live View function settings in the Shooting 4 menu. You have three choices:

■ **Mode 1.** This mode reduces the noise level of the shutter, but allows taking several shots in succession, including continuous shooting.

- **Mode 2.** This mode reduces the noise even further by delaying the action when you press the shutter release down (only a slight click is heard). When you let up slightly on the shutter release, the shot is taken, producing another soft click. Continuous shooting is not possible in Mode 2.

- **Disable.** Turns off the feature, producing the normal shutter noise sounds. This mode should be used if you're working with a tilt/shift lens, or an extension tube. Although you'll hear two clicks when using this mode, only one picture will be exposed. If you use flash, Mode 1 and Mode 2 are automatically disabled.

Shooting Movies

The Canon EOS 7D can shoot full HDTV movies with monaural sound (or stereo sound if you plug in an external microphone) at 1920 × 1080 resolution. In some ways, the camera's movie mode is closely related to the 7D's Live View still mode. In fact, the 7D uses Live View type imaging to show you the video clip on the LCD as it is captured. Many of the functions and setting options are the same, so the information in the previous sections will serve you well as you branch out into shooting movies with your camera.

You'll want to keep the following things in mind before you start:

- **Choose your resolution.** The 7D can capture movies in Full High Definition,1920 × 1080 pixel resolution, Standard High Definition, 640 × 480 resolution, and a 640 × 480 cropped resolution that provides a 7x telephoto effect. I'll show you how to specify resolution in the next section.

- **You can still shoot stills.** Press the shutter release all the way down at any time while filming movies in order to capture a still photo. The 7D will use the Image quality settings you specify in the Shooting 1 menu, and will operate only in single shooting drive mode (continuous shooting or self-timer delays are not possible). The flash is disabled. You can also extract a 2MP, 1MP, or .3MP image from your movie clips using ZoomBrowser. Still photos are stored as separate files.

- **Use the right card.** You'll want to use a fast memory card to store your clips; slower cards may not work properly. Chose a memory card with at least 4GB capacity (8GB or 16GB are even better). If the card you are working with is too slow, a five-level thermometer-like "buffer" indicator may appear at the right side of the LCD, showing the status of your camera's internal memory. If the indicator reaches the top level because the buffer is full, movie shooting will stop automatically.

- **Use a fully charged battery.** Canon says that a fresh battery will allow about one hour of filming at normal (non-Winter) temperatures.

- **Image stabilizer uses extra power.** If your lens has an image stabilizer, it will operate at all times (not just when the shutter button is pressed halfway, which is the case with still photography) and use a considerable amount of power, reducing battery life. You can switch the IS feature off to conserve power. Mount your camera on a tripod, and you don't need IS anyway.

- **Silent running.** You can connect your 7D to a television or video monitor while shooting movies, and see the video portion on the bigger screen as you shoot. However, the sound will not play—that's a good idea, because, otherwise, you could likely get a feedback loop of sound going. The sound will be recorded properly and will magically appear during playback once shooting has concluded.

MOVIE TIME

I've standardized on 16GB memory cards when I'm shooting movies; these cards will give you 49 minutes of recording at 1920 × 1080 Full HD resolution. (Figure 330MB per minute of capture.) A 4GB card, in contrast, offers just 12 minutes of shooting at the Full HD setting.

Movie Settings

The Movie Settings menu can be summoned by the MENU button only when the 7D has been set to Movie mode (rotate the Movie/Live View switch as far as it will go in the counter-clockwise direction). The six settings on the Movie menu (see Figure 6.6) include:

- **Autofocus mode (Quick mode, Live mode, Live "face detection" mode).** This option, explained earlier in the Live View section, lets you choose between phase detection, contrast detection, and contrast detection with "face" recognition. In movie modes, none of these autofocus modes will track a moving subject.

- **Grid display.** You can select Off, Grid #1, or Grid #2.

- **Movie rec. size.** Choose 1920 × 1080 (Full HD) at 30 or 24 fps; 1280 × 720 (HD) at 60 fps; or 640 × 480 pixel (Standard resolution) at 60 fps. The frame rates are for NTSC television mode; for the PAL system, the camera will substitute 50 fps for 60 fps, and 25 fps for 30 fps. (The motion picture standard, 24 fps, remains constant.)

- **Sound recording.** Set to On to record audio with your video clips using the 7D's built-in microphone; choose Off when you want to record silent movies (especially if you plan to add your own narration or music track(s) later on). Record stereo sound by plugging a stereo microphone into the camera's microphone jack. You have no control over sound levels, but the camera does a good job of adjusting them automatically. An external microphone is a good idea because the built-in microphone can easily pick up camera operation, such as the autofocus motor in a lens.

- **Silent shooting (Mode 1, Mode 2, Disable).** This option turns on or off optional quiet modes that reduce shutter noise when shooting still photos while in movie mode, as explained earlier in the Live View section.

- **Metering timer (4 sec. to 30 min).** This option allows you to specify how long the EOS 7D's metering system will remain active before switching off.

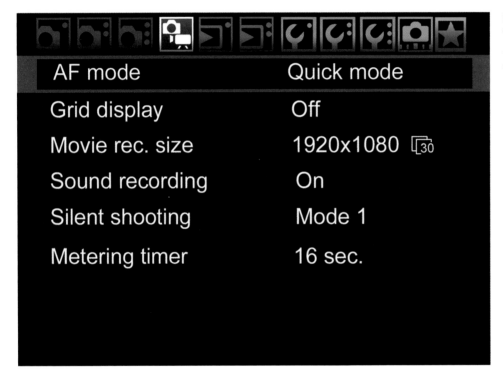

AF mode	Quick mode
Grid display	Off
Movie rec. size	1920x1080
Sound recording	On
Silent shooting	Mode 1
Metering timer	16 sec.

Figure 6.6
The Movie 1 menu has six entries.

Capturing Video/Sound

To shoot movies with your camera, just follow these steps:

1. **Change to Movie mode.** Set the Movie/Live View dial to the Movie setting (turn the switch as far as it will go in a counter-clockwise direction).

2. **Focus.** Use the autofocus or manual focus techniques described in the preceding sections to achieve focus on your subject.

3. **Begin filming.** Press the Start/Stop button to begin shooting. A red dot appears in the upper-right corner of the screen to show that video/sound are being captured. The access lamp also flashes during shooting.

4. **Changing shooting functions.** As with Live View, you can change settings or review images normally when shooting video. Press the WB, AF-DRIVE, or ISO-Flash compensation buttons on the top of the camera, or the Picture Control button to the left of the LCD, and an overlay appears superimposed on the Live View screen. You can use the Quick Control Dial and Main Dial to change those settings. You can also make adjustments to the Auto Lighting Optimizer and change Image quality by pressing the Q button on the left side of the camera. If you've chosen AF Quick autofocus mode, you can set the AF point and AF area selection mode, described in Chapter 5.

5. **Lock exposure.** You can lock in exposure by pressing the */Thumbnail/Zoom Out button on top of the 7D, located just aft of the Main Dial. Unlock exposure again by pressing the ISO button once more.

6. **Stop filming.** Press the Start/Stop button again to stop filming.

7. **View your clip.** Press the Playback button (located to the bottom left of the LCD). You will see a still frame with the clip timing and a symbol telling you to press the SET button to see the clip. A series of video controls appear at the bottom of the frame. Press SET again and the clip begins. A blue thermometer bar progresses in the upper-left corner as the timing counts down. Press SET to stop at any time.

GETTING INFO

The information display shown on the LCD screen when shooting movies is almost identical to the one displayed during Live View shooting. The settings icons in the left column show the same options, which can be changed in Movie mode, too, except that the drive mode choice is replaced by an indicator that shows the current movie resolution and time remaining on your memory card.

Tips for Shooting Better Video

Producing high-quality videos can be a real challenge for amateur photographers. After all, by comparison we're used to watching the best television and the movies can offer. Whether it's fair or not, our efforts are compared to what we're used to seeing produced by experts. While this chapter can't make you into a pro videographer, it can help you improve your efforts.

There are a number of different things to consider when planning a video shoot and, when possible, a shooting script and storyboard can help you produce a higher quality video.

Shooting Script/Storyboards

A shooting script is nothing more than a coordinated plan that covers both audio and video and provides order and structure for your video. A detailed script will cover what types of shots you're going after, what dialogue you're going to use, audio effects, transitions, and graphics.

A storyboard is a series of panels providing visuals of what each scene should look like. While the ones produced by Hollywood are generally of very high quality, there's nothing that says drawing skills are important for this step. Stick figures work just fine if that's the best you can do. The storyboard just helps you visualize locations, placement of actors/actresses, props and furniture, and also helps everyone involved get an idea of what you're trying to show. It also helps show how you want to frame or compose a shot.

Storytelling in Video

Today's audience is used to fast-paced, short scene storytelling. In order to produce interesting video for such viewers, it's important to view video storytelling as a kind of shorthand code for the more leisurely efforts print media offers. Audio and video should always be advancing the story. While it's okay to let the camera linger from time to time, it should only be for a compelling reason and only briefly.

It only takes a second or two for an establishing shot to impart the necessary information, and the same goes for a dramatic stare. Provide variety too. Change camera angles and perspectives often, never leave a static scene on the screen for a long period of time. (You can record a static scene for a reasonably long period and then edit in other shots that cut away and back to the longer scene with close-ups that show each person talking.)

Keep transitions basic! I can't stress this one enough. Watch a television program or movie. The action "jumps" from one scene or person to the next. Fancy transitions that involve exotic "wipes," dissolves, or cross fades take too long for the average viewer and make your video ponderous. Save dissolves to show the passage of time (it's a cinematic convention that viewers are used to and understand).

Composition

Just like in still photography, videography calls for careful composition, and, in the case of HD video, that composition must be framed by the 16:9 aspect ratio of the format. Unlike still photography, there's a lot more emphasis on using a series of images to build on each other to tell a story. Static shots where the camera is mounted on a tripod and everything's shot from the same distance are a recipe for dull videos. Watch a television program sometime and notice how often camera shots change distances and directions. Viewers are used to this variety and have come to expect it. Professional video productions are often done with multiple cameras shooting from different angles and positions.

Many professional productions though are shot with just one camera and careful planning, and you can do just fine with your EOS 7D. Here's a look at the different types of commonly used compositions:

- **Establishing shot.** Much like it sounds, this composition establishes the scene and tells the viewer where the action is taking place. Let's say you're shooting a video of your offspring's move to college; the establishing shot could be a wide shot of the campus with a sign welcoming you to the school in the foreground. Another example would be for a child's birthday party, the establishing shot could be the front of the house decorated with birthday signs and streamers or a shot of the dining room table decked out with party favors and candle covered birthday cake.

- **Medium shot.** This shot is composed from about waist to headroom (some space above the subject's head). It's useful for providing variety from a series of close-ups and also makes for a useful first look at a speaker.

- **Close-up.** The close-up, usually described as "from shirt pocket to head room," provides a good composition for someone talking directly to the camera.

- **Extreme close-up.** This shot has been described as the "big talking face" shot. Styles and tastes change over the years and now the big talking face is much more commonly used (maybe people are better looking these days?) and so this view may be appropriate. Just remember, the 7D is capable of shooting in high-definition video and you may be playing the video on a high-def TV, so be careful that you use this composition on a face that can stand up to high definition.

- **"Two" shot.** A two shot shows a pair of subjects in one frame. They can be side by side or one in the foreground and one in the background. Subjects can be standing or seated. A "three shot" is the same principle except that three people are in the frame.

- **Over the shoulder shot.** Long a tool of interview programs, the "Over the shoulder shot" uses the rear of one person's head and shoulder to serve as a frame for the other person. This puts the viewer's perspective as that of the person facing away from the camera.

Lighting for Video

Much like in still photography, how you handle light pretty much can make or break your videography. Lighting for video though can be more complicated than lighting for still photography, since both subject and camera movement is often part of the process. Lighting for video presents several concerns. First off, you want enough illumination to create a useable video. Beyond that, you want to use light to help tell your story or increase drama. Let's take a better look at both.

Illumination

You can significantly improve the quality of your video by increasing the light falling in the scene. This is true indoors or out by the way. While it may seem like sunlight is more than enough, it depends on how much contrast you're dealing with. If your subject is in shadow (which can help them from squinting) or wearing a ball cap, a video light can help make them look a lot better.

Lighting choices for amateur videographers are a lot better these days than they were a decade or two ago. An inexpensive shoe mount video light, which will easily fit in a camera bag, can be found for $15 or $20. You can even get a good quality LCD video light for less than $100. Work lights sold at many home improvement stores can also serve as video lights since you can set the camera's white balance to correct for any colorcasts.

Much of the challenge depends upon whether you're just trying to add some fill light on your subject versus trying to boost the light on an entire scene. A small video light in the camera's hot shoe mount or on a flash bracket will do just fine for the former. It won't handle the latter. Fortunately, the versatility of the 7D comes in quite handy here. Since the camera shoots video in Auto ISO mode, it can compensate for lower lighting levels and still produce a decent image. For best results though better lighting is necessary.

Creative Lighting

While ramping up the light intensity will produce better technical quality in your video, it won't necessarily improve the artistic quality of it. Whether we're outdoors or indoors, we're used to seeing light come from above. Videographers need to consider how they position their lights (often on tall light stands) to provide even illumination while up high enough to angle shadows down low and out of sight of the camera. Keep in mind that your subjects may be moving, too, so your lighting should accommodate non-static compositions.

When considering lighting for video, there are several considerations. One is the quality of the light. It can either be hard (direct) light or soft (diffused). Hard light is good for showing detail, but can also be very harsh and unforgiving. "Softening" the light, but diffusing it somehow, say, with an umbrella or white cardboard reflector, can reduce the intensity of the light but make for a kinder, gentler light as well.

While mixing light sources isn't always a good idea, one approach is to combine window light with supplemental lighting. Position your subject with the window to one side and bring in either a supplemental light or a reflector to the other side for reasonably even lighting.

Recording Audio

When it comes to making a successful video, audio quality is one of those things that separates the professionals from the amateurs. We're used to watching top-quality productions on television and in the movies, yet the average person has no idea of how much effort goes in to producing what seems to be "natural" sound. Much of the sound you hear in such productions is actually recorded on carefully controlled sound stages and "sweetened" with a variety of sound effects and other recordings of "natural" sound. Even when audio is recorded live on scene, high-quality microphones help deliver the best possible audio. Powerful directional ("shotgun") microphones pick up minimal background or stray noise, while windscreens minimize noise from the wind.

Your 7D has a good quality built-in microphone that can do a decent job of recording audio under carefully managed conditions. For best results, minimize extraneous noise (something that's harder to do than you might think). The human ear is good at filtering out many sounds that are not necessary for comprehension; the microphone is another story. It picks up every noticeable noise, something that quickly becomes bothersome when you're watching a video. You want some background sound for ambiance, but not enough to be distracting.

The camera strap's connector rings, if made of metal, may cause a noise that the camera's microphone picks up. You don't notice it when you're shooting, but you will when you play back the video. The answer is to either remove the strap when shooting video or use some Gaffer's tape to tape the noisy components in place (or wrap them in soft cloth or cushion with sponge rubber or any number of things to prevent them from banging against the camera). Another problem is that the built-in microphone also picks up the noise of the lens focusing or zooming so try to minimize these things while shooting. Of course, another option is to strip the audio out in a video editing program and replace it with sound recorded elsewhere. This can be a tricky proposition depending on what you're trying to show though.

Of course, if you have a high quality stereo microphone you can plug into the 7D, you'll get all-around better audio quality—and stereo sound to boot!

Tips for Better Audio

Since recording high quality audio is such a challenge, it's a good idea to do everything possible to maximize recording quality. Here are some ideas for improving the quality of the audio your 7D records:

■ **Get the camera and microphone close to the speaker.** The farther the microphone is from the audio source, the less effective it will be in picking up that sound. This means you'll have to boost volume in postproduction, which will also amplify any background noises. While having to position the camera and microphone closer to the subject affects your lens choices and lens perspective options, it will make the most of your audio source.

- **Turn off any sound makers you can.** Little things like fans and air handling units aren't obvious to the human ear, but will be picked up by the microphone. Try to turn off any machinery or devices that you can plus make sure cell phones are set to silent mode. Also, do what you can to minimize sounds such as wind, radio, television, or people talking in the background. Don't forget to close windows if you're inside to shut out noises from the outside.

- **Consider using an external microphone.** If making videos is important to you, think about buying a quality microphone. Even a good quality built-in microphone can pick up internal camera noises. Using an external microphone also means you can get the microphone closer to the subject while keeping the camera a little farther away. A shotgun (directional) microphone can also help isolate a speaker's audio from background noise.

- **Make sure to record some "natural" sound.** If you're shooting video at an event of some kind, make sure you get some background sound that you can add to your audio as desired in postproduction.

- **Consider recording audio separately.** Lip-syncing is probably beyond most of the people you're going to be shooting, but there's nothing that says you can't record narration separately and add it later. Any time the speaker is off camera, you can work with separately recorded narration, using a program like Adobe Premiere, rather than recording the speaker on camera. This can produce much cleaner sound.

Continuous Shooting

The Canon EOS 7D's pair of continuous shooting modes remind me how far digital photography has brought us. The first accessory I purchased when I worked as a sports photographer some years ago was a motor drive for my film SLR. It enabled me to snap off a series of shots in rapid succession, which came in very handy when a fullback broke through the line and headed for the end zone. Even a seasoned action photographer can miss the decisive instant when a crucial block is made, or a baseball superstar's bat shatters and pieces of cork fly out. Continuous shooting simplifies taking a series of pictures, either to ensure that one has more or less the exact moment you want to capture or to capture a sequence that is interesting as a collection of successive images.

The 7D's "motor drive" capabilities are, in many ways, much superior to what you get with a film camera. For one thing, a motor-driven film camera can eat up film at an incredible pace, which is why many of them are used with cassettes that hold hundreds of feet of film stock. At three frames per second (typical of film cameras), a short burst of a few seconds can burn up as much as half of an ordinary 36 exposure roll of film. Digital cameras, in contrast, have reusable "film," so if you waste a few dozen shots on non-decisive moments, you can erase them and shoot more. Save only the best shots, like the series shown in Figure 6.7.

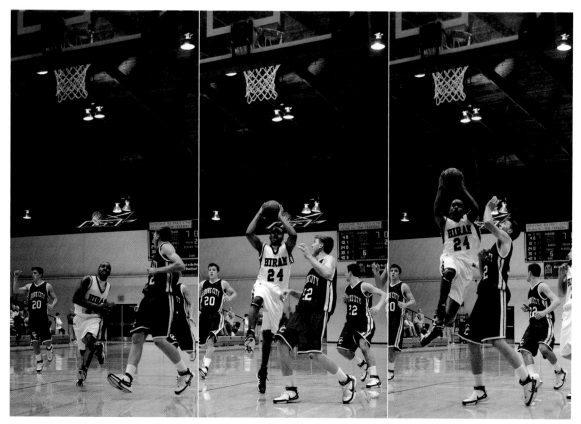

Figure 6.7 Continuous shooting allows you to capture an entire sequence of exciting moments as they unfold.

To use the 7D's continuous shooting modes, press the AF-DRIVE button. Spin the Quick Control Dial until either the high-speed continuous shooting (8 frames per second) or low-speed continuous shooting (3 fps) icons appear in the status LCD. (You can also use the Quick Control Screen.) When you partially depress the shutter button, the viewfinder will display a number representing the maximum number of shots you can take at the current quality settings. (If your battery is low, this figure will be lower.) The larger buffer in the 7D will generally allow you to take as many as 94 JPEG shots in a single burst, or 15 RAW photos.

To increase this number, reduce the image-quality setting by switching to JPEG only (from JPEG+RAW), to a lower JPEG quality setting, or by reducing the 7D's resolution from L to M or S. The reason the size of your bursts is limited is that continuous images are first shuttled into the 7D's internal memory buffer, then doled out to the Compact Flash card as quickly as they can be written to the card. Technically, the 7D takes the RAW data received from the digital image processor and converts it to the output format you've selected—either .jpg or .cr2 (raw) or both—and deposits it in the buffer ready to store on the card.

This internal "smart" buffer can suck up photos much more quickly than the CF card and, indeed, some memory cards are significantly faster or slower than others. Setting C.Fn II to "Strong" also limits the length of your continuous burst. When the buffer fills, you can't take any more continuous shots (a buSY indicator appears in the viewfinder and LCD status panel) until the 7D has written some of them to the card, making more room in the buffer. (You should keep in mind that faster CF cards write images more quickly, freeing up buffer space faster.)

More Exposure Options

In Chapter 4, you learned techniques for getting the *right* exposure, but I haven't explained all your exposure options just yet. You'll want to know about the *kind* of exposure settings that are available to you with the Canon EOS 7D. There are options that let you control when the exposure is made, or even how to make an exposure that's out of the ordinary in terms of length (time or bulb exposures). The sections that follow explain your camera's special exposure features, and even discuss a few it does not have (and why it doesn't).

A Tiny Slice of Time

Exposures that seem impossibly brief can reveal a world we didn't know existed. In the 1930s, Dr. Harold Edgerton, a professor of electrical engineering at MIT, pioneered high-speed photography using a repeating electronic flash unit he patented called the *stroboscope*. As the inventor of the electronic flash, he popularized its use to freeze objects in motion, and you've probably seen his photographs of bullets piercing balloons and drops of milk forming a coronet-shaped splash.

Electronic flash freezes action by virtue of its extremely short duration—as brief as 1/50,000th second or less. Although the EOS 7D's built-in flash unit can give you these ultra-quick glimpses of moving subjects, an external flash, such as one of the Canon Speedlites, offers even more versatility. You can read more about using electronic flash to stop action in Chapter 10.

Of course, the 7D is fully capable of immobilizing all but the fastest movement using only its shutter speeds, which range all the way up to 1/8,000th second. Indeed, you'll rarely have need for such a brief shutter speed in ordinary shooting. If you wanted to use an aperture of f/1.8 at ISO 100 outdoors in bright sunlight, for some reason, a shutter speed of 1/8,000th second would more than do the job. You'd need a faster shutter speed only if you moved the ISO setting to a higher sensitivity (but why would you do that?). Under less than full sunlight, 1/8,000th second is more than fast enough for any conditions you're likely to encounter.

Most sports action can be frozen at 1/2,000th second or slower, and for many sports a slower shutter speed is actually preferable—for example, to allow the wheels of a racing automobile or motorcycle, or the propeller on a classic aircraft to blur realistically.

But if you want to do some exotic action-freezing photography without resorting to electronic flash, the 7D's top shutter speed is at your disposal. Here are some things to think about when exploring this type of high-speed photography:

- **You'll need a lot of light.** High shutter speeds cut very fine slices of time and sharply reduce the amount of illumination that reaches your sensor. To use 1/8,000th second at an aperture of f/6.3, you'd need an ISO setting of 1600—even in full daylight. To use an f/stop smaller than f/6.3 or an ISO setting lower than 1600, you'd need *more* light than full daylight provides. (That's why electronic flash units work so well for high-speed photography when used as the sole illumination; they provide both the effect of a brief shutter speed and the high levels of illumination needed.)

- **Forget about reciprocity failure.** If you're an old-time film shooter, you might recall that very brief shutter speeds (as well as very high light levels and very *long* exposures) produced an effect called *reciprocity failure,* in which given exposures ended up providing less than the calculated value because of the way film responded to very short, very intense, or very long exposures of light. Solid-state sensors don't suffer from this defect, so you don't need to make an adjustment when using high shutter speeds (or brief flash bursts).

- **No elongation effect.** This is another old bugaboo that has largely been solved through modern technology, but I wanted to bring it to your attention anyway. In olden times, cameras used shutters that traveled horizontally. To achieve faster shutter speeds, focal plane shutters (located just in front of the plane of the sensor) open only a smaller-than-frame-sized slit so that, even though the shutter is already traveling at its highest rate of speed, the film/sensor is exposed for a briefer period of time as the slit moves across the surface. At very short shutter speeds, and with subjects moving horizontally at very fast velocities, it was possible for the subject to partially "keep up" with the shutter if it were traveling in the same direction as the slit, producing an elongated effect. Conversely, subjects moving in the opposite direction of shutter motion could be compressed. Today, shutters like those in the 7D move vertically and at a higher maximum rate of speed. So, unless you're photographing a rocket blasting into space, and holding the camera horizontally to boot (or shooting a racing car in vertical orientation), it's almost impossible to produce unwanted elongation/compression.

■ **Don't combine high shutter speeds with electronic flash.** You might be tempted to use an electronic flash with a high shutter speed. Perhaps you want to stop some action in daylight with a brief shutter speed and use electronic flash only as supplemental illumination to fill in the shadows. Unfortunately, under most conditions you can't use flash in subdued illumination with your 7D at any shutter speed faster than 1/250th second. That's the fastest speed at which the camera's focal plane shutter is fully open: at shorter speeds, the "slit" described previously comes into play, so that the flash will expose only the small portion of the sensor exposed by the slit during its duration. (Check out "High-Speed Sync" in Chapter 10 if you want to see how you *can* use shutter speeds shorter than 1/250th second with certain Canon Speedlites, albeit at much-reduced effective power levels.)

Working with Short Exposures

You can have a lot of fun exploring the kinds of pictures you can take using very brief exposure times, whether you decide to take advantage of the action-stopping capabilities of your built-in or external electronic flash or work with the Canon EOS 7D's faster shutter speeds. Here are a few ideas to get you started:

■ **Take revealing images.** Fast shutter speeds can help you reveal the real subject behind the façade by freezing constant motion to capture an enlightening moment in time. Legendary fashion/portrait photographer Philippe Halsman used leaping photos of famous people, such as the Duke and Duchess of Windsor, Richard Nixon, and Salvador Dali to illuminate their real selves. Halsman said, "*When you ask a person to jump, his attention is mostly directed toward the act of jumping and the mask falls so that the real person appears.*" Try some high-speed portraits of people you know in motion to see how they appear when concentrating on something other than the portrait.

■ **Create unreal images.** High-speed photography can also produce photographs that show your subjects in ways that are quite unreal. A helicopter in mid-air with its rotors frozen or a motocross cyclist leaping over a ramp, but with all motion stopped so that the rider and machine look as if they were frozen in mid-air, make for an unusual picture.

■ **Capture unseen perspectives.** Some things are *never* seen in real life, except when viewed in a stop-action photograph. Edgerton's balloon bursts were only a starting point. Freeze a hummingbird in flight for a view of wings that never seem to stop. Or, capture the splashes as liquid falls into a bowl, as shown in Figure 6.8. No electronic flash was required for this image (and wouldn't have illuminated the water in the bowl as evenly). Instead, a clutch of high-intensity lamps and an ISO setting of 1600 allowed the EOS 7D to capture this image at 1/2,000th second.

■ **Vanquish camera shake and gain new angles.** Here's an idea that's so obvious it isn't always explored to its fullest extent. A high enough shutter speed can free you from the tyranny of a tripod, making it easier to capture new angles, or to shoot quickly while moving around, especially with longer lenses. I tend to use a monopod or tripod for almost everything when I'm not using an image-stabilized lens, and I end up missing some shots because of a reluctance to adjust my camera support to get a higher, lower, or different angle. If you have enough light and can use an f/stop wide enough to permit a high shutter speed, you'll find a new freedom to choose your shots. I have a favored 170mm-500mm lens that I use for sports and wildlife photography, almost invariably with a tripod, as I don't find the "reciprocal of the focal length" rule particularly helpful in most cases. (I would *not* handhold this hefty lens at its 500mm setting with a 1/500th second shutter speed under most circumstances.) However, at 1/2,000th second or faster, it's entirely possible for a steady hand to use this lens without a tripod or monopod's extra support, and I've found that my whole approach to shooting animals and other elusive subjects changes in high-speed mode. Selective focus allows dramatically isolating my prey wide open at f/6.3, too.

Figure 6.8

A large amount of artificial illumination and an ISO 1600 sensitivity setting allowed capturing this shot at 1/2,000th second without use of an electronic flash.

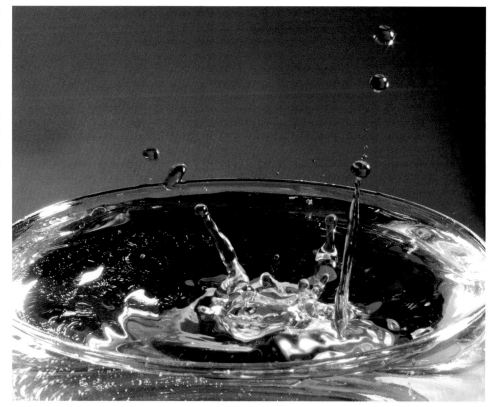

Long Exposures

Longer exposures are a doorway into another world, showing us how even familiar scenes can look much different when photographed over periods measured in seconds. At night, long exposures produce streaks of light from moving, illuminated subjects like automobiles or amusement park rides. Extra-long exposures of seemingly pitch-dark subjects can reveal interesting views using light levels barely bright enough to see by. At any time of day, including daytime (in which case you'll often need the help of neutral-density filters to make the long exposure practical), long exposures can cause moving objects to vanish entirely, because they don't remain stationary long enough to register in a photograph.

Three Ways to Take Long Exposures

There are actually three common types of lengthy exposures: *timed exposures*, *bulb exposures*, and *time exposures*. The EOS 7D offers only the first two, but once you understand all three, you'll see why Canon made the choices it did. Because of the length of the exposure, all of the following techniques should be used with a tripod to hold the camera steady.

- **Timed exposures.** These are long exposures from 1 second to 30 seconds, measured by the camera itself. To take a picture in this range, simply use Manual or Tv modes and use the Main Dial to set the shutter speed to the length of time you want, choosing from preset speeds of 1.0, 1.5, 2.0, 3.0, 4.0, 6.0, 8.0, 10.0, 15.0, 20.0, or 30.0 seconds (if you've specified 1/2 stop increments for exposure adjustments), or 1.0, 1.3, 1.6, 2.0, 2.5, 3.2, 4.0, 5.0, 6.0, 8.0, 10.0, 13.0, 15.0, 20.0, 25.0, and 30.0 seconds (if you're using 1/3 stop increments). The advantage of timed exposures is that the camera does all the calculating for you. There's no need for a stop-watch. If you review your image on the LCD and decide to try again with the exposure doubled or halved, you can dial in the correct exposure with precision. The disadvantage of timed exposures is that you can't take a photo for longer than 30 seconds.

- **Bulb exposures.** This type of exposure is so-called because in the olden days the photographer squeezed and held an air bulb attached to a tube that provided the force necessary to keep the shutter open. Traditionally, a bulb exposure is one that lasts as long as the shutter release button is pressed; when you release the button, the exposure ends. To make a bulb exposure with the 7D, set the camera to Bulb using the Mode Dial. Then, press the shutter to start the exposure, and press it again to close the shutter. If you'd like to simulate a time exposure (described next), you can use the Canon RS-80N3 or TC-80N3 remote releases that attach to the terminal on the left side of the camera under the rubber cover. Both have a shutter release lock that can be used to keep the shutter open, and the TC-80N3 includes a timer that can expose a picture for any length from 1 second to 99 hours, 59 minutes, and 59 seconds. Or, if you have a lot of money to spend and can find one, you can use the LC-4 infrared wireless transmitter and receiver. If you are able to link your camera to a computer, the EOS Utility allows taking long exposures up to 99 minutes and 59 seconds.

■ **Time exposures.** This is a setting found on some cameras to produce longer exposures. With cameras that implement this option, the shutter opens when you press the shutter release button, and remains open until you press the button again. Usually, you'll be able to close the shutter using a mechanical cable release or, more commonly, an electronic release cable. The advantage of this approach is that you can take an exposure of virtually any duration without the need for special equipment (the tethered release is optional). You can press the shutter release button, go off for a few minutes, and come back to close the shutter (assuming your camera is still there). The disadvantages of this mode are exposures must be timed manually, and with shorter exposures, it's possible for the vibration of manually opening and closing the shutter to register in the photo. For longer exposures, the period of vibration is relatively brief and not usually a problem—and there is always the release cable option to eliminate photographer-caused camera shake entirely. While the 7D does not have a built-in time exposure capability, you can simulate it with the bulb exposure technique, described previously.

WATCH OUT FOR AMP NOISE

When exposures extend past 30 seconds into the realm of several minutes—or more—all digital cameras are theoretically susceptible to a phenomenon called *amp noise*, which manifests itself as a purplish glow, often around the edges of an image, creating an aurora borealis-style ghost effect. Amp noise happens when the sensor heats up during a long exposure, and some cameras fall victim more readily than others. The EOS 7D resists this phenomenon better than most dSLRs, but you should be aware it exists, even if you'd need to use an outlandish exposure (on the order of 30 minutes or so) to create the effect with your camera.

Working with Long Exposures

Because the EOS 7D produces such good images at longer exposures, and there are so many creative things you can do with long-exposure techniques, you'll want to do some experimenting. Get yourself a tripod or another firm support and take some test shots with long exposure noise reduction both enabled and disabled (to see whether you prefer low noise or high detail) and get started.

Here are some things to try:

■ **Make people invisible.** One very cool thing about long exposures is that objects that move rapidly enough won't register at all in a photograph, while the subjects that remain stationary are portrayed in the normal way. That makes it easy to produce people-free landscape photos and architectural photos at night or, even, in full daylight if you use a neutral-density filter (or two or three) to allow an exposure of at least a few seconds. At ISO 100, f/22, and a pair of 8X (three-stop) neutral-density filters, you can use exposures of nearly two seconds; overcast days and/or even more neutral-density filtration would work even better if daylight people-vanishing is your goal. They'll have to be walking *very* briskly and across the field of view (rather than directly toward the camera) for this to work. At night, it's much easier to achieve this effect with the 20- to 30-second exposures that are possible, as you can see in Figures 6.9 and 6.10.

■ **Create streaks.** If you aren't shooting for total invisibility, long exposures with the camera on a tripod can produce some interesting streaky effects, as you can see in Figure 6.11. You don't need to limit yourself to indoor photography, however. Even a single 8X ND filter will let you shoot at f/22 and 1/6th second in full daylight at ISO 100.

■ **Produce light trails.** At night, car headlights and taillights and other moving sources of illumination can generate interesting light trails. Your camera doesn't even need to be mounted on a tripod; hand-holding the 7D for longer exposures adds movement and patterns to your trails. If you're shooting fireworks, a longer exposure may allow you to combine several bursts into one picture, as shown in Figure 6.12.

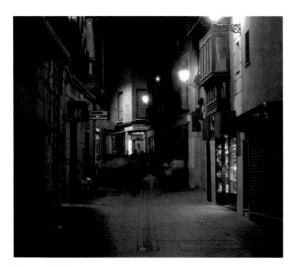

Figure 6.9 This alleyway is thronged with people, as you can see in this two-second exposure using only the available illumination.

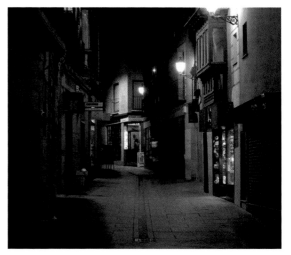

Figure 6.10 With the camera still on a tripod, a 30-second exposure rendered the passersby almost invisible.

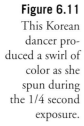

Figure 6.11
This Korean dancer produced a swirl of color as she spun during the 1/4 second exposure.

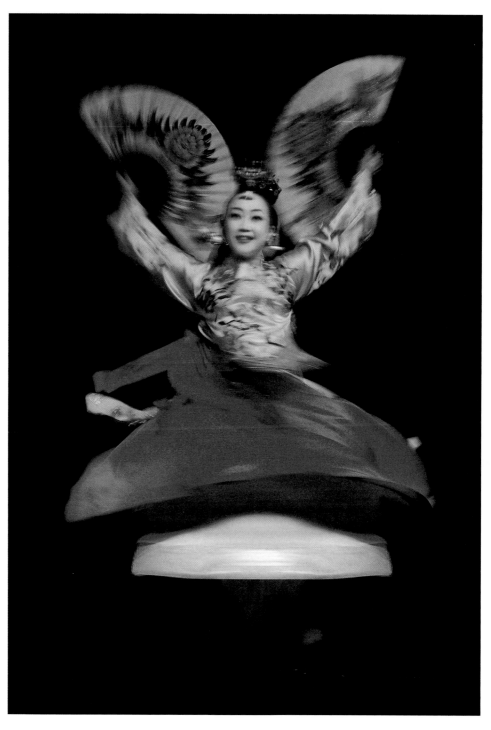

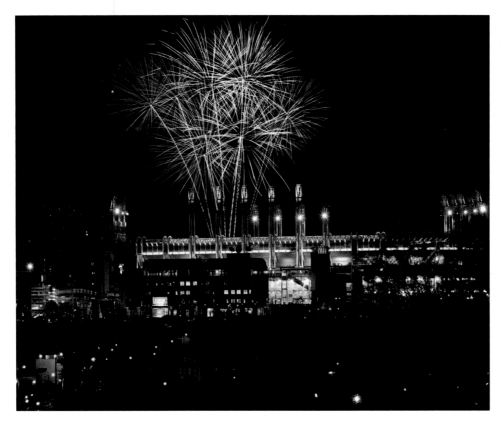

Figure 6.12
A long exposure allows capturing several bursts of fireworks in one image.

- **Blur waterfalls, etc.** You'll find that waterfalls and other sources of moving liquid produce a special type of long-exposure blur, because the water merges into a fantasy-like veil that looks different at different exposure times, and with different waterfalls. Cascades with turbulent flow produce a rougher look at a given longer exposure than falls that flow smoothly. Although blurred waterfalls have become almost a cliché, there are still plenty of variations for a creative photographer to explore, as you can see in Figure 6.13.

- **Show total darkness in new ways.** Even on the darkest, moonless nights, there is enough starlight or glow from distant illumination sources to see by, and, if you use a long exposure, there is enough light to take a picture, too. I was visiting a lakeside park after dark and saw that the dim light from the lamps in the parking lot provided sufficient light to see a distant stand of trees. A 30-second exposure with the lens almost wide open revealed the scene shown in Figure 6.14, even though in real life there was barely enough light to make out the closest tree. Although the photo appears as if it were taken at twilight or sunset, in fact the shot was made at 11 p.m. It was a new moon that night, so the main illumination was starlight, spill light from the parking lot, and a distant city (which added a sunset-like effect to the sky at the horizon that shows at the far side of the lake).

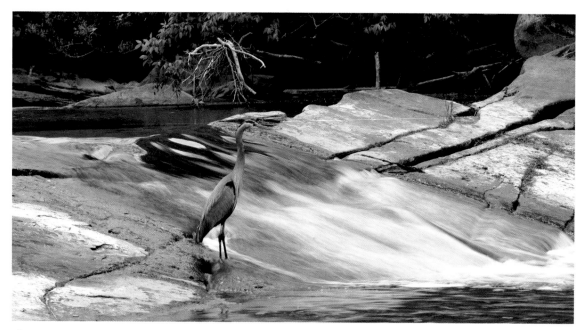

Figure 6.13 A 1/4-second exposure blurred the falling water, as the cooperative bird remained still.

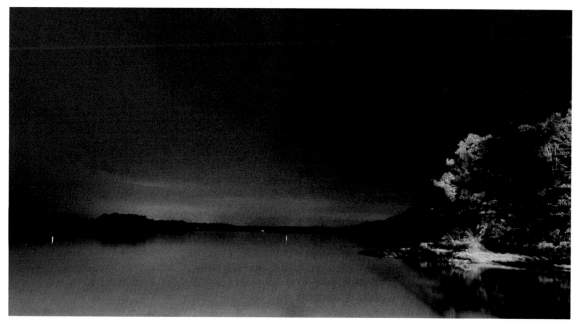

Figure 6.14 A 30-second exposure on a dark night revealed this lakeside setting, illuminated only by starlight, spill light from a parking lot adjacent to the shore, and distant city lights.

Delayed Exposures

Sometimes it's desirable to have a delay of some sort before a picture is actually taken. Perhaps you'd like to get in the picture yourself, and would appreciate it if the camera waited 10 seconds after you press the shutter release to actually take the picture. Maybe you want to give a tripod-mounted camera time to settle down and damp any residual vibration after the release is pressed to improve sharpness for an exposure with a relatively slow shutter speed. It's possible you want to explore the world of time-lapse photography. The next sections present your delayed exposure options.

Self-Timer

The EOS 7D has a built-in self-timer with 10-second and 2-second delays. Activate the timer by pressing the AF-DRIVE button and spinning the Quick Command Dial until either of the two self-timer clock icons appear on the LCD status panel. Press the shutter release button halfway to lock in focus on your subjects (if you're taking a self-portrait, focus on an object at a similar distance and use focus lock). When you're ready to take the photo, continue pressing the shutter release the rest of the way. The lamp on the front of the camera will blink slowly for eight seconds (when using the 10-second timer) and the beeper will chirp (if you haven't disabled it in the Shooting menu, as described in Chapter 7). During the final two seconds, the beeper sounds more rapidly and the lamp remains on until the picture is taken. The top-panel LCD displays a countdown while all this is going on.

Another way to use the self-timer is with the mirror lockup feature. This is something you might want to do if you're shooting close-ups, landscapes, or other types of pictures using the self-timer only to trip the shutter in the most vibration-free way possible. Forget to bring along your tripod, but still want to take a close-up picture with a precise focus setting? Set your digital camera to the self-timer function, then put the camera on any reasonably steady support, such as a fence post or a rock. When you're ready to take the picture, press the shutter release. The camera might teeter back and forth for a second or two, but it will settle back to its original position before the self-timer activates the shutter. The self-timer remains active until you turn it off—even if you power down the 7D.

Remote Control

As outlined in the "Bulb Exposure" description earlier, your Canon EOS 7D can be triggered using a plug-in remote control with an electronic or infrared connection. For example, the Remote Switch RS-80N3 allows triggering a camera attached to the end of its cable. More versatile is the Canon TC-80N3, a remote switch with a 2.6-foot cord (you can add a 33-foot extension cable) and includes a more flexible self-timer that can be set to trip the camera after a delay of anywhere from 1 second to 99 hours, 59 minutes, and 59 seconds (in other words, one second less than 100 hours). It has an LCD display that makes it easy to make and view settings.

Time-Lapse/Interval Photography

Who hasn't marveled at a time-lapse photograph of a flower opening, a series of shots of the moon marching across the sky, or one of those extreme time-lapse picture sets showing something that takes a very, very long time, such as a building under construction.

You probably won't be shooting such construction shots, unless you have a spare 7D you don't need for a few months (or are willing to go through the rigmarole of figuring out how to set up your camera in precisely the same position using the same lens settings to shoot a series of pictures at intervals). However, other kinds of time-lapse photography are entirely within reach.

Although the EOS 7D can't take time-lapse/interval photographs all by itself, if you're willing to tether the camera to a computer (a laptop will do) using the USB cable, you can take time-lapse photos using EOS Utility software furnished with your camera (see Figure 6.15).

If you want freedom to shoot anywhere, the TC-80N3 is an affordable add-on (around $135) with much more than the self-timer and remote control features mentioned previously. In fact, it has 15 different modes with an interesting array of delay/interval combinations. For example, you can set the self-timer for a specific period of time, then take a specified number of exposures at one-second intervals. Or, you can set a delay period that must elapse before the 7D begins a long exposure. Finally, you can choose to shoot a set number of pictures at intervals from 1 second to 99 hours, 59 minutes, and 59 seconds.

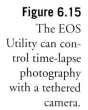
Figure 6.15
The EOS Utility can control time-lapse photography with a tethered camera.

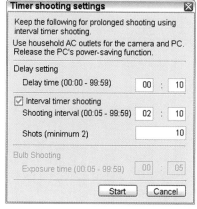

Timer shooting settings

Keep the following for prolonged shooting using interval timer shooting.
Use household AC outlets for the camera and PC. Release the PC's power-saving function.

Delay setting
Delay time (00:00 - 99:59)   00 : 10

☑ Interval timer shooting
Shooting interval (00:05 - 99:59)   02 : 10

Shots (minimum 2)   10

Bulb Shooting
Exposure time (00:05 - 99:59)   00 : 05

Start   Cancel

Here are some tips for effective time-lapse photography:

- **Use AC power.** If you're shooting a long sequence, consider connecting your camera to an AC adapter, as leaving the 7D on for long periods of time will rapidly deplete the battery.

- **Make sure you have enough storage space.** Unless your memory card has enough capacity to hold all the images you'll be taking, you might want to change to a higher compression rate or reduced resolution to maximize the image count.

- **Make a movie.** While time-lapse stills are interesting, you can increase your fun factor by compiling all your shots into a motion picture using your favorite desktop movie-making software.

- **Protect your camera.** If your camera will be set up for an extended period of time (longer than an hour or two), make sure it's protected from weather, earthquakes, animals, young children, innocent bystanders, and theft.

- **Vary intervals.** Experiment with different time intervals. You don't want to take pictures too often or less often than necessary to capture the changes you hope to image.

Part III

Advanced Tools

The next five chapters are devoted to helping you dig deeper into the capabilities of your Canon EOS 7D, so you can exploit all those cool features that your previous camera lacked. Chapters 7 and 8 list every setting and option found in the Shooting, Playback, Set-up, and Custom Functions menus. I'll not only tell you what each menu item does, I'll explain exactly when and why you should use every option. Then, in Chapter 9, I'll show you how to select the best lenses for the kinds of photography you want to do, with my recommendations for starter lenses as well as more advanced optics for specialized applications.

Chapters 10 and 11 are devoted to the magic of light—your fundamental tool in creating any photograph. There are entire books devoted to working with electronic flash, but I hope to get you started with plenty of coverage of the EOS 7D's capabilities. I'll show you how to master your camera's built-in flash—and avoid that "built-in flash" look—and offer an introduction to the use of external flash units, including the Canon Speedlite 580EX II. Because the 7D's state-of-the-art wireless flash capabilities are so new, I'm devoting an entire chapter to that technology. By the time you finish these essential chapters, you'll be well on the way to mastering your Canon EOS 7D.

7

Customizing with the Shooting and Playback Menus

The Canon EOS 7D is undoubtedly the most customizable, tweakable, fine-tunable camera Canon has offered non-professional users. In fact, this versatility has made the 7D surprisingly popular among professional photographers as well. If your camera doesn't behave in exactly the way you'd like, chances are you can make a small change in the Shooting, Playback, Set-up, and Custom menus that will tailor the 7D to your needs. In fact, if you don't like the *menus*, you can create your own using the clever My Menu system.

This chapter and the next will help you sort out the settings you can make to customize how your Canon EOS 7D uses its features, shoots photos, displays images, and processes the pictures after they've been taken. As I've mentioned before, this book isn't intended to replace the manual you received with your 7D, nor have I any interest in rehashing its contents. You'll still find the original manual useful as a standby reference that lists every possible option in exhaustive (if mind-numbing) detail—without really telling you how to use those options to take better pictures. There is, however, some unavoidable duplication between the Canon manual and this chapter, because I'm going to explain the key menu choices and the options you may have in using them. You should find, though, that this chapter gives you the information you need in a much more helpful format, with plenty of detail on why you should make some settings that are particularly cryptic.

I'm not going to waste a lot of space on some of the more obvious menu choices. For example, you can probably figure out that the Beep option in Shooting 1 menu deals with the solid-state beeper in your camera that sounds off during various activities (such as the self-timer countdown). You can certainly decipher the import of the two options available for the Beep entry (On and Off). In this chapter, I'll devote no more than a sentence or two to the blatantly obvious settings and concentrate on the more confusing aspects of 7D set-up, such as Automatic Exposure Bracketing. I'll cover the three Shooting menus and two Playback menus in this chapter, and turn to the Set-up, Custom Functions, and My Menu options in Chapter 8. Let's start off with an overview of the 7D's menus themselves.

Anatomy of the EOS 7D's Menus

If you have jumped directly to the Canon EOS 7D from an ancient model like the EOS 30D, you're in for a pleasant surprise from a menu perspective. Like all recent EOS cameras, this model abandons the time-consuming scrolling through one endless menu in favor of 11 individually tabbed menus, each with a single screen of options (so you won't need to scroll within a menu to see all the entries). The menus are much cleaner, too.

If you've used another recent EOS model, you'll find the 7D's menu system familiar, but with a more attractive look that includes "shaded" menu tabs (see Figure 7.1). Some menu items have been moved around and/or renamed. With the current system, just press the MENU button, spin the Main Dial to highlight the menu tab you want to access, and then scroll up and down within a menu with the Quick Control Dial or multi-controller. What could be easier?

Tapping the MENU button brings up a typical menu like the one shown in the figure. (If the camera goes to "sleep" while you're reviewing a menu, you may need to wake it up again by tapping the shutter release button.) When you're using any Mode Dial option other than Full Auto and Creative Auto, there are 11 menu tabs: Shooting 1, Shooting 2, Shooting 3, Playback 1, Playback 2, Set-up 1, Set-up 2, Set-up 3, Set-up 4, Custom, and My Menu.

In Full Auto and Creative Auto there are only seven tabs: the Shooting 3, Set-up 3, Set-up 4, Custom, and My Menu choices are not available, and the options within the menus are slightly different. In this chapter, I'm going to explain all the tabs and all the menu entries, and not take the time to single out those that are not available when using Full Auto and Creative Auto modes. The automatic modes are intended for situations when you don't want full control over your 7D's operation, anyway, and menu limitations go with the territory.

The 7D's tabs are color-coded: red for Shooting menus, blue for Playback menus, amber for Set-up menus, orange for the Custom menu, and green for the My Menu tab.

Figure 7.1
The EOS 7D's menus are arranged in a series of eleven tabs.

Selected menu

Inactive menus

Selected menu item

Other menu choices

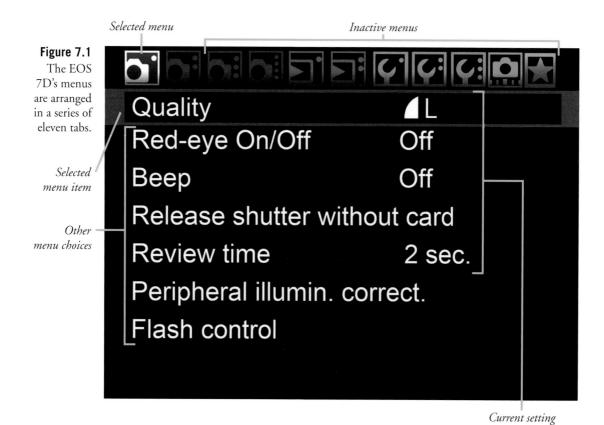

Quality
Red-eye On/Off   Off
Beep   Off
Release shutter without card
Review time   2 sec.
Peripheral illumin. correct.
Flash control

Current setting

The currently selected menu's icon is white within a white border, on a background corresponding to its color code. All the inactive menus are dimmed and the icon and their borders are color-coded.

Here are the things to watch for as you navigate the menus:

■ **Menu tabs.** In the top row of the menu screen, the menu that is currently active will be highlighted as described earlier. One, two, three, or four dots in the tab lets you know if you are in, say Shooting 1, Shooting 2, Shooting 3, or Shooting 4. Just remember that the four red camera icons stand for shooting options; the two blue right-pointing triangles represent playback options; the three yellow wrench/hammer icons stand for set-up options; the orange camera denotes Custom Functions; and the green star stands for personalized menus defined for the star of the show—you.

■ **Selected menu item.** The currently selected menu item will have a black background and will be surrounded by a box the same hue as its color code.

■ **Other menu choices.** The other menu items visible on the screen will have a dark gray background.

■ **Current setting.** The current settings for visible menu items are shown in the right-hand column, until one menu item is selected (by pressing the SET key or multi-controller). At that point all the settings vanish from the screen except for those dealing with the active menu choice.

When you've moved the menu highlighting to the menu item you want to work with, press the SET button or press the multi-controller to select it. The current settings for the other menu items in the list will be hidden, and a list of options for the selected menu item (or a submenu screen) will appear. Within the menu choices, you can scroll up or down with the Quick Control Dial or multi-controller; press SET or the multi-controller to select the choice you've made, and press the MENU button again to exit.

HYPER MENU NAVIGATION

As I mentioned, you can use the Main Dial to move from menu to menu, and the Quick Control Dial to highlight a particular menu entry. Thankfully, this is true even if the QCD Lock switch is set to LOCK. Press the SET button to select a menu item. That procedure is probably the best way to start out, because those controls are used to make so many settings with the EOS 7D that they quickly become almost intuitive. The 7D manual uses the Main Dial/Quick Control Dial method in its Menu Setting description. But, there's a better way.

If you have an agile thumb, you can do all your menu navigation with the multi-controller:

■ Shift the multi-controller left/right to jump from tab to tab.

■ Press the multi-controller up/down to move within the menu choices of a given tab.

■ Press the multi-controller in to select a menu item, and press it again to return to the menu choices.

It gets even better. You can jump from tab to tab even if you've highlighted a particular menu setting on another tab—and the 7D will remember which menu entry you've highlighted when you return to that menu. The memorization works even if you leave the menu system or turn off your camera. The 7D always remembers the last menu entry you used with a particular tab. So, if you generally use the Format command each time you access the Set-up 1 menu, that's the entry that will be highlighted when you choose that tab. The camera remembers which tab was last used, too, so, potentially, formatting your memory card might take just a couple presses (the MENU button, the SET button to select the highlighted Format command, then a click of the Quick Control Dial to choose OK, and another press of SET to start the format process).

Shooting 1, 2, 3, & 4 Menu Options

The various direct setting buttons on the top panel of the camera for AF mode, white balance, drive mode, ISO sensitivity, metering mode, and flash, along with exposure compensation (EV) adjustments are likely to be the most common settings changes you make, with changes during a particular session fairly common. You'll find that the Shooting menu options are those that you access second most frequently when you're using your EOS 7D. You might make such adjustments as you begin a shooting session, or when you move from one type of subject to another. Canon makes accessing these changes very easy.

This section explains the options of the four Shooting menus and how to use them. The options you'll find in these red-coded menus include:

- Quality
- Red-Eye On/Off
- Beep
- Release shutter without card
- Review time
- Peripheral illumination correction
- Flash control
- Exposure compensation/AEB (Automatic Exposure Bracketing)
- Auto Lighting Optimizer
- White balance
- Custom WB

- WB Shift/BKT
- Color Space
- Picture Style
- Dust Delete Data
- One-touch RAW+JPEG
- Live View shooting
- AF mode
- Grid display
- Exposure simulation
- Silent shooting
- Metering timer

Quality Settings

You can choose the image quality settings used by the 7D to store its files. You have four choices to make:

- **Resolution.** The number of pixels captured determines the absolute resolution of the photos you shoot with your 7D. Your choices range from 18 megapixels (Large or L), measuring 5184 × 3456; 8 megapixels (Medium or M), measuring 3,456 × 2,304 pixels; to 4.5 megapixels (Small or S), 2,592 × 1,728 pixels.

- **JPEG compression.** To reduce the size of your image files and allow more photos to be stored on a given memory card, the 7D uses JPEG compression to squeeze the images down to a smaller size. This compacting reduces the image quality a little, so you're offered your choice of Fine compression and Normal compression.

The symbols help you remember that Fine compression (represented by a quarter-circle) provides the smoothest results, while Normal compression (signified by a stair-step icon) provides "jaggier" images.

- **JPEG, RAW, or both.** You can elect to store only JPEG versions of the images you shoot (6.4MB each at the Large Fine resolution setting) or you can save your photos as uncompressed, loss-free RAW files, which consume about four times as much space on your memory card (up to 20MB per file). Or, you can store both at once as you shoot. Many photographers elect to save *both* a JPEG and a RAW file, so they'll have a JPEG version that might be usable as-is, as well as the original "digital negative" RAW file in case they want to do some processing of the image later. You'll end up with two different versions of the same file: one with a .jpg extension, and one with the .cr2 extension that signifies a Canon RAW file.

Table 7.1 JPEG/RAW Resolution Options

Format	RAW	M RAW	S RAW
Resolution	18 megapixels 5,184 × 3,456 pixels	10.1 megapixels 3,888 × 2,592 pixels	4.5 megapixels 2,592 × 1,728
Format	**JPEG Large**	**JPEG Medium**	**JPEG Small**
Resolution	18 megapixels 4,752 × 3,168 pixels	8.0 megapixels 3,456 × 2,304	4.5 megapixels 2,592 × 1,728

To choose the combination you want, access the menus, scroll to Quality, and press the SET button. A screen similar to the one shown in Figure 7.2 will appear with two rows of choices, one for RAW formats on top, and one for JPEG formats on the bottom. A red box appears around the currently selected choice for both RAW and JPEG formats. The " -- " (None) indicator at the left end of each row shows that you have not selected either RAW or JPEG resolution, and no file will be saved in that format.

Use the Main Dial to select any of the three RAW sizes (or leave the highlighting on None if you don't want to save a RAW version of your image). Rotate the Quick Control Dial to choose any of the six JPEG options (Large/Fine; Large/Standard; Medium/Fine; Medium/Standard; Small/Fine; Small/Standard), or None. (If you select None for *both* file formats, your 7D isn't fooled and sticks to the last format selected.) There are 27 different combinations in all. If you choose both a RAW format and a JPEG option, the screen displays the resolution of both in the second line. In practice, you'll probably use only the Large/Fine, RAW+Large/Fine, or RAW selections.

Figure 7.2
Choose your resolution, JPEG compression, and file format from this screen.

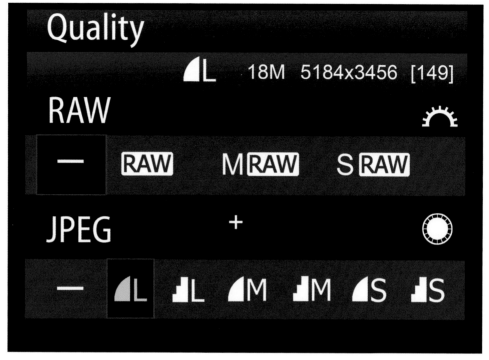

Why so many choices, then? There are some limited advantages to using the Medium and Small resolution settings, Normal JPEG compression setting, and the two lower resolution RAW formats. They all allow stretching the capacity of your Compact Flash card so you can shoehorn quite a few more pictures onto a single memory card. That can be useful when on vacation and you're running out of storage, or when you're shooting non-critical work that doesn't require full resolution (such as photos taken for real estate listings, web page display, photo ID cards, or similar applications). Some photographers like to record RAW+JPEG Standard so they'll have a moderate quality JPEG file for review only, while retaining access to the original RAW file for serious editing.

For most work, using lower resolution and extra compression is false economy. You never know when you might actually need that extra bit of picture detail. Your best bet is to have enough memory cards to handle all the shooting you want to do until you have the chance to transfer your photos to your computer or a personal storage device.

However, reduced image quality can sometimes be beneficial if you're shooting sequences of photos rapidly, as the 7D is able to hold more of them in its internal memory buffer before transferring to the Compact Flash card. Still, for most sports and other applications, you'd probably rather have better, sharper pictures than longer periods of continuous shooting.

JPEG vs. RAW

You'll sometimes be told that RAW files are the "unprocessed" image information your camera produces, before it's been modified. That's nonsense. RAW files are no more unprocessed than your camera film is after it's been through the chemicals to produce a negative or transparency. A lot can happen in the developer that can affect the quality of a film image—positively and negatively—and, similarly, your digital image undergoes a significant amount of processing before it is saved as a RAW file. Canon even applies a name (Digic 4) to the digital image processing (DIP) chips used to perform this magic (your 7D has *two* of them that work in tandem to provide high performance capabilities, including the 8 frames-per-second continuous shooting bursts).

A RAW file is more similar to a film camera's processed negative. It contains all the information, captured in 14-bit channels per color (and stored in a 16-bit space), with no compression, no sharpening, no application of any special filters or other settings you might have specified when you took the picture. Those settings are *stored* with the RAW file so they can be applied when the image is converted to a form compatible with your favorite image editor. However, using RAW conversion software such as Adobe Camera Raw or Canon's Digital Photo Professional, you can override those settings and apply settings of your own. You can select essentially the same changes there that you might have specified in your camera's picture-taking options.

RAW exists because sometimes we want to have access to all the information captured by the camera, before the camera's internal logic has processed it and converted the image to a standard file format. RAW doesn't save as much space as JPEG. What it does do is preserve all the information captured by your camera after it's been converted from analog to digital form. Of course, the 7D's M RAW and S RAW formats preserve the *settings* information, but discards some of the resolution to give you that 10.1 or 4.5-megapixel smaller RAW file.

So, why don't we always use RAW? Although some photographers do save only in RAW format, it's more common to use either RAW plus one of the JPEG options, or just shoot JPEG and eschew RAW altogether. That's because having only RAW files to work with can significantly slow down your workflow. While RAW is overwhelmingly helpful when an image needs to be fine-tuned, in other situations working with a RAW file, when all you really need is a good-quality, un-tweaked JPEG image, consumes time that you may not want to waste. For example, RAW images take longer to store on the Compact Flash card, and require more post-processing effort, whether you elect to go with the default settings in force when the picture was taken, or just make minor adjustments.

As a result, those who depend on speedy access to images or who shoot large numbers of photos at once may prefer JPEG over RAW. Wedding photographers, for example, might expose several thousand photos during a bridal affair and offer hundreds to clients as electronic proofs for possible inclusion in an album or transfer to a CD or DVD.

These wedding shooters, who want JPEG images as their final product, take the time to make sure that their in-camera settings are correct, minimizing the need to post-process photos after the event. Given that their JPEGs are so good (in most cases thanks, in large part, to the pro photographer's extensive experience), there is little need to get bogged down shooting RAW.

Sports photographers also eschew RAW files. I visited a local Division III college one sunny September afternoon while I was writing this book and managed to cover a football game, trot down a hill to shoot a women's soccer match later that afternoon, and ended up in the adjacent field house shooting a volleyball invitational tournament an hour later. I managed to shoot 1,920 photos, most of them at an 8 fps clip, in about four hours. I certainly didn't have any plans to do post-processing on very many of those shots, and firing the 7D at its maximum frame rate didn't allow RAW shooting, so carefully exposed and precisely focused JPEG images were my file format of choice that day.

JPEG was invented as a more compact file format that can store most of the information in a digital image, but in a much smaller size. JPEG predates most digital SLRs, and was initially used to squeeze down files for transmission over slow dialup connections. Even if you were using an early dSLR with 1.3 megapixel files for news photography, you didn't want to send them back to the office over a modem at 1,200 bps.

But, as I noted, JPEG provides smaller files by compressing the information in a way that loses some image data. JPEG remains a viable alternative because it offers several different quality levels. At the highest quality Fine level, you might not be able to tell the difference between the original RAW file and the JPEG version, even though the 18-megapixel RAW file occupies, by Canon's estimate, 25.1MB on your memory card, while the Fine JPEG at the same resolution takes up only 6.6MB of space. You've squeezed the image significantly without losing much visual information at all. If you don't mind losing some quality, you can use more aggressive Standard compression with JPEG to cut the size in half again, to 3.3MB.

In my case, I shoot virtually everything at RAW+JPEG Fine. Most of the time, I'm not concerned about filling up my memory cards, as I usually have a minimum of five fast 8GB Compact Flash cards with me. I also have some 32GB CF cards that are a little slower (so I don't use them for sports), but with even more capacity. If I think I may fill up all those cards, I have a tiny battery-operated personal storage device that can copy an 8GB card in about 15 minutes. As I mentioned earlier, when shooting sports I'll shift to JPEG Fine (with no RAW file) to squeeze a little extra speed out of my 7D's continuous shooting mode, and to reduce the need to wade through eight-photo bursts taken in RAW format. On the other hand, on my last trip to Europe, I took only RAW (instead of my customary RAW+JPEG) photos to fit more images onto my 160GB personal storage device, shown in Figure 7.3, as I planned on doing at least some post-processing on many of the images for a travel book I was working on.

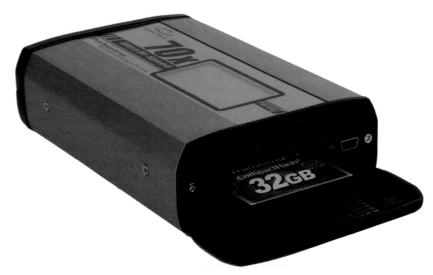

Figure 7.3
If RAW storage space is a concern, consider a portable storage device like this one.

MANAGING LOTS OF FILES

The only long-term drawback to shooting everything in RAW+JPEG is that it's easy to fill up your computer's hard drive if you are a prolific photographer. Here's what I do. My most recent photos are stored on my working hard drive in a numbered folder, say 7D-01, with subfolders named after the shooting session, such as 100501Trees, for pictures of trees taken on May 1, 2010. An automatic utility copies new and modified photos to a different hard drive for temporary backup four times daily.

When the top-level folder accumulates about 30GB of images, I back it up to DVDs and then move the folder to a 2000GB (1 terabyte) drive dedicated solely for storage of folders that have already been backed up onto DVD. Then I start a new folder, such as 7D-02, on the working hard drive and repeat the process. I always have at least one backup of every image taken, either on another hard drive or on a DVD.

Red-Eye Reduction

Your EOS 7D has a fairly effective Red-Eye Reduction flash mode. Unfortunately, your camera is unable, on its own, to *eliminate* the red-eye effects that occur when an electronic flash (or, rarely, illumination from other sources) bounces off the retinas of the eye and into the camera lens. Animals seem to suffer from yellow or green glowing pupils, instead; the effect is equally undesirable. The effect is worst under low-light conditions (exactly when you might be using a flash) as the pupils expand to allow more light to reach the retinas. The most you can hope for is to *reduce* or minimize the red-eye effect.

The best way to truly eliminate red-eye is to raise the flash up off the camera so its illumination approaches the eye from an angle that won't reflect directly back to the retina and into the lens. The extra height of the built-in flash may not be sufficient, however. That alone is a good reason for using an external flash. If you're working with your 7D's built-in flash, your only recourse may be to switch on the Red-eye reduction feature with the menu choice shown in Figure 7.4. It causes a lamp on the front of the camera to illuminate with a half-press of the shutter release button, which may cause your subjects' pupils to contract, decreasing the amount of the red-eye effect. (You may have to ask your subject to look at the lamp to gain maximum effect.) Figure 7.5 shows the effects of wider pupils (left) and those that have been contracted using the 7D's Red-eye reduction feature.

Figure 7.4
Turn on your camera's Red-eye reduction feature to help eliminate demon-red pupils.

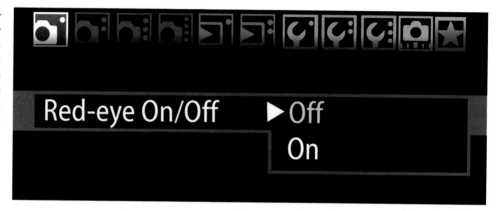

Figure 7.5
Red-eye (left) is tamed (right), thanks to the EOS 7D's Red-eye reduction lamp.

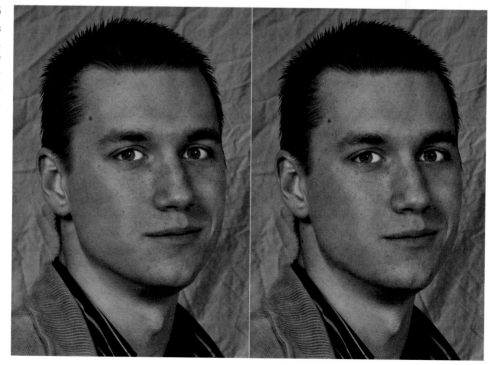

Beep

The EOS 7D's internal beeper provides a helpful chirp to signify various functions, such as the countdown of your camera's self-timer. You can switch it off if you want to avoid the beep because it's annoying, impolite, or distracting (at a concert or museum), or undesired for any other reason. It's one of the few ways to make the 7D a bit quieter, other than Live View's "silent shoot" mode. (I've actually had new dSLR owners ask me how to turn off the "shutter sound" the camera makes; such an option was available in the point-and-shoot camera they'd used previously.) Select Beep from the menu, press SET, and use the Quick Control Dial to choose On or Off, as you prefer, as shown in Figure 7.6. Press SET again to activate your choice.

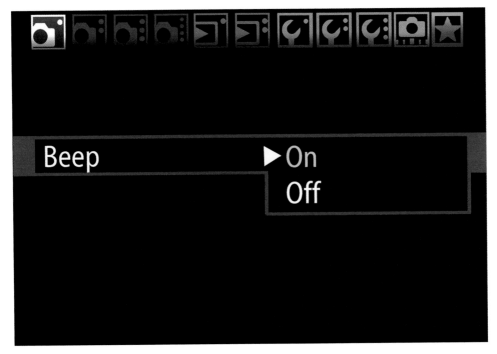

Figure 7.6
Silence your camera's beep when it might prove distracting.

Shoot without a Compact Flash Card Installed

This entry in the Set-up 1 menu (see Figure 7.7) gives you the ability to snap off "pictures" without a Compact Flash card installed—or to lock the camera shutter release if that is the case. It is sometimes called Play mode, because you can experiment with your camera's features or even hand your 7D to a friend to let him fool around, without any danger of pictures actually being taken. Back in our film days, we'd sometimes finish a roll, rewind the film back into its cassette surreptitiously, and then hand the camera to a child to take a few pictures—without actually wasting any film. It's hard to waste digital film, but Release shutter without card mode is still appreciated by some, especially

Figure 7.7
You can enable
triggering the
shutter even
when no
Compact Flash
card is present.

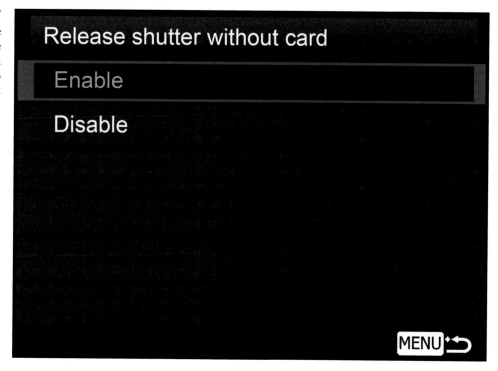

camera vendors who want to be able to demo a camera at a store or trade show, but don't want to have to equip each and every demonstrator model with a Compact Flash card. Choose this menu item, press SET, select Enable or Disable, and press SET again to turn this capability on or off.

Review Time

You can adjust the amount of time an image is displayed for review on the LCD after each shot is taken. You can elect to disable this review entirely (Off), or choose display times of 2, 4, or 8 seconds. You can also select Hold, an indefinite display, which will keep your image on the screen until you use one of the other controls, such as the shutter button, Main Dial, or Quick Control Dial. Turning the review display off or choosing a brief duration can help preserve battery power. However, the 7D will always override the review display when the shutter button is partially or fully depressed, so you'll never miss a shot because a previous image was on the screen. Choose Review time from the Shooting 1 menu, and select Off, 2 sec., 4 sec., 8 sec., or Hold, as shown in Figure 7.8. If you want to retain an image on the screen for a longer period, but don't want to use Hold as your default, press the Erase button under the LCD monitor. The image will display until you choose Cancel or Erase from the menu that pops up at the bottom of the screen.

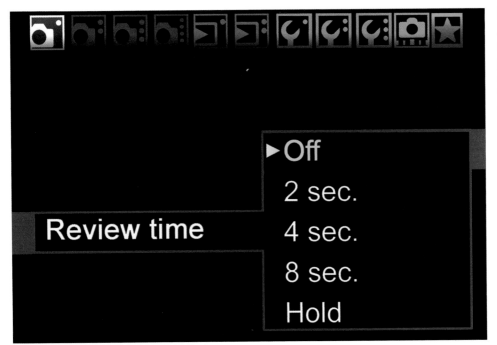

Figure 7.8
Figure 7.8
Adjust the time
an image is dis-
played on the
LCD for review
after a picture
is taken.

Peripheral Illumination Correction

With certain lenses, under certain conditions, your images might suffer from a phenomenon called *vignetting*, which is a darkening of the four corners of the frame because
of a slight amount of fall-off in illumination at those nether regions. This menu option
allows you to activate a clever feature built in to the EOS 7D that partially (or fully)
compensates for this effect. Depending on the f/stop you use, the lens mounted on the
camera, and the focal length setting, vignetting can be non-existent, slight, or may be
so strong that it appears you've used a too-small hood on your camera. (Indeed, the
wrong lens hood can produce a vignette effect of its own.) Vignetting can be affected
by the use of a telephoto converter (more on those in Chapter 9, too).

Peripheral illumination drop-off, even if pronounced, may not be much of a problem.
I actually *add* vignetting, sometimes, when shooting portraits and some other subjects.
Slightly dark corners tend to focus attention on a subject in the middle of the frame.
On the other hand, vignetting with subjects that are supposed to be evenly illuminated,
such as landscapes, is seldom a benefit.

To minimize the effects of corner light fall-off, you can process RAW files using Digital
Photo Professional (described in Chapter 12), or, if you want your JPEG files fixed as
you shoot them, by using this menu option.

Figure 7.9 shows an image without peripheral illumination correction at top, and a
corrected image at the bottom. I've exaggerated the vignetting a little to make it more

evident on the printed page. Keep in mind that the amount of correction available with Digital Photo Pro can be a little more intense than that applied in the camera. In addition, the higher the ISO speed, the less correction is applied. If you see severe vignetting with a particular lens, focal length, or ISO setting, you might want to turn off this feature, shoot RAW, and apply correction using DPP instead.

Figure 7.9
Vignetting (top) is undesirable in a landscape photo. You can correct this defect in the camera or by using Digital Photo Pro software.

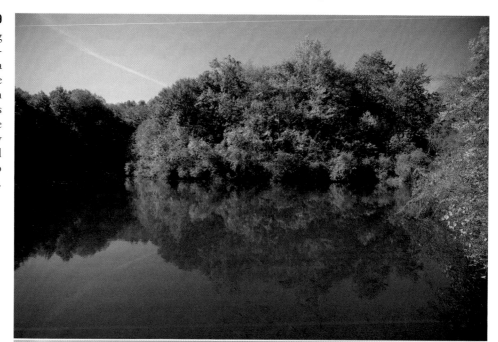

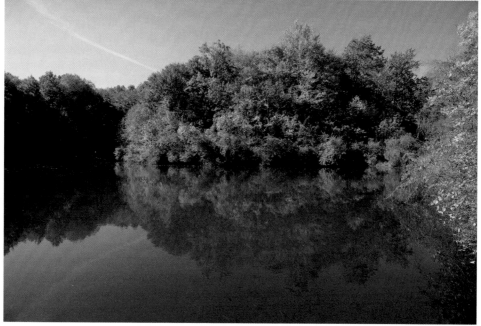

When you select this menu option from the Shooting 1 menu, the screen shown in Figure 7.10 appears. The lens currently attached to the camera is shown, along with a notation whether correction data needed to brighten the corners is already registered in the camera. (Information about 20 of the most popular lenses is included in the 7D's firmware.) If so, you can rotate the Quick Control Dial to choose Enable to activate the feature, or Disable to turn it off. Press the SET button to confirm your choice. Note that in-camera correction must be specified *before* you take the photo, so that the magical DIGIC 4 processing engine can lighten the corners of your photo before it is saved to the Compact Flash card.

If your lens is not registered in the camera, you can remedy that deficit using the EOS Utility (also described in Chapter 12). Just follow these steps:

1. Connect your 7D to your computer using the USB cable supplied with the camera.

2. Load the EOS Utility and click on Camera Settings/Remote Shooting from the splash screen that appears.

3. Choose the Shooting menu from the menu bar located about midway in the control panel that appears on your computer display. The panel is shown at left in Figure 7.11. The Shooting menu icon is the white camera on a red background.

4. Click on the Peripheral illumin. correct. choice to produce the screen shown at right in Figure 7.11.

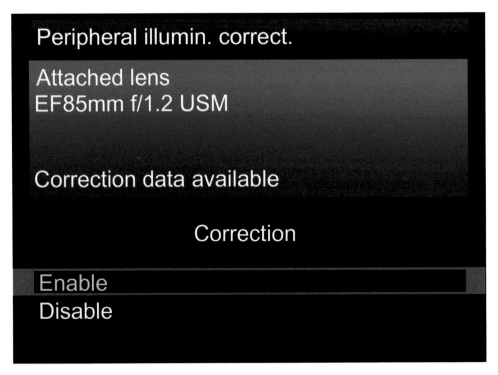

Figure 7.10

Peripheral illumination correction can fix dark corners.

Figure 7.11
Select the lenses to be corrected.

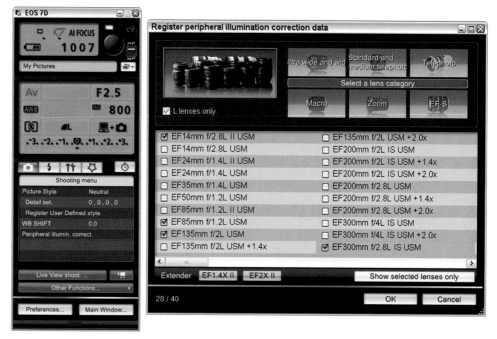

5. Select the category containing the lens you want to register from the panels at the top of the new screen; then place a check mark next to all the lenses you'd like to register in the camera.

6. Click OK to send the data from your computer to the 7D and register your lenses.

7. When a newly registered lens is mounted on the camera, you will be able to activate the anti-vignetting feature for that lens from the Set-up 1 menu.

Flash Control

This multi-level menu entry includes five settings for controlling the Canon EOS 7D's built-in, pop-up electronic flash unit, as well as accessory flash units you can attach to the camera (see Figure 7.12). I'll provide in-depth coverage of how you can use these options in Chapter 10, but will list the main options here for reference.

Flash Firing

Use this option to enable or disable the built-in electronic flash. You might want to totally disable the 7D's flash (both built-in and accessory flash) when shooting in sensitive environments, such as concerts, in museums, or during religious ceremonies. When disabled, the flash cannot fire even if you accidentally elevate it, or have an accessory flash attached and turned on. If you turn off the flash here, it is disabled in any exposure mode.

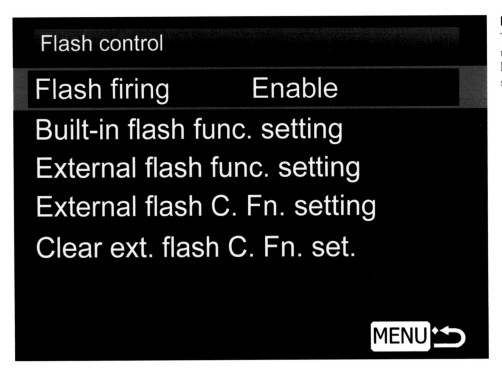

Figure 7.12
The Flash control menu entry has five setting submenus.

Built-in Flash Function Setting

There are five main choices for this menu screen, plus two additional options:

- **Flash mode.** Your choices here are E-TTL II, Manual flash, and MULTI flash, explained in detail in Chapter 10.

- **Shutter sync.** You can choose 1st curtain sync, which fires the preflash used to calculate the exposure before the shutter opens, followed by the main flash as soon as the shutter is completely open. This is the default mode, and you'll generally perceive the preflash and main flash as a single burst. Alternatively, you can select 2nd curtain sync, which fires the preflash as soon as the shutter opens, and then triggers the main flash in a second burst at the end of the exposure, just before the shutter starts to close. (If the shutter speed is slow enough, you may clearly see both the preflash and main flash as separate bursts of light.) This action allows photographing a blurred trail of light of moving objects with sharp flash exposures at the beginning and the end of the exposure. This type of flash exposure is slightly different from what some other cameras produce using 2nd curtain sync. I'll explain how it works in Chapter 10.

  If you have an external compatible Speedlite attached, you can also choose Hi-speed sync, which allows you to use shutter speeds faster than 1/250th second, using the External Flash Function Setting menu, described next and explained in Chapter 10.

- **Flash exposure compensation.** If you'd rather adjust flash exposure using a menu than with the ISO/Flash exposure compensation button, you can do that here. Select this option with the SET button, then dial in the amount of flash EV compensation you want using the multi-controller or Quick Control Dial. The EV that was in place before you started to make your adjustment is shown as a blue indicator, so you can return to that value quickly. Press SET again to confirm your change, then press the MENU button twice to exit.

- **E-TTL II.** You can choose evaluative (matrix) or average metering modes for the electronic flash exposure meter. Evaluative looks at selected areas in the scene to calculate exposure, while average calculates flash exposure by reading the entire scene.

- **Wireless functions.** These choices, which include mode, channel, firing group, and other options, are used only when you're working in wireless mode to control an external flash. If you've disabled wireless functions, the other options don't appear on the menu. I'm going to leave the explanation of these options for Chapter 11, which is an entire chapter dedicated to using the EOS 7D's new wireless shooting capabilities.

- **Clear flash settings.** When the Built-in flash func. setting (or External flash func. setting) screen is shown, you can press the INFO. button to produce a screen that allows you to clear all the flash settings.

- **Test flash firing.** If this option appears at the bottom of the screen, you can press the Picture Styles button to trigger a test flash, which is useful when you want to make sure that a wireless slave flash is active (as discussed in Chapter 11). The test flash can also be used to "wake up" a slave flash that has shut down using auto power off.

External Flash Function Setting

You can access this menu only when you have a compatible electronic flash attached and switched on. The settings available are shown in Figure 7.13. If you press the INFO. button while adjusting flash settings, both the changes made to the settings of an attached external flash and to the built-in flash will be cleared.

- **Flash mode.** This entry allows you to set the flash mode for the external flash, from E-TTL II, Manual flash, MULTI flash, TTL, AutoExtFlash, Man.Ext flash. The first three are identical to the internal flash modes described earlier. The second three are optional metering modes available with certain flash units, such as the 580 EX II, and are available for those who might need one of those less sophisticated flash metering systems. While I don't recommend any of the latter three, you can find more information about them in your flash's manual.

- **Shutter sync.** As with the 7D's internal flash, you can choose 1st curtain sync, which fires the flash as soon as the shutter is completely open (this is the default mode). Alternatively, you can select 2nd curtain sync, which fires the flash as soon as the shutter opens, and then triggers a second flash at the end of the exposure, just before the shutter starts to close.

- **FEB.** Flash Exposure Bracketing (FEB) operates similarly to ordinary exposure bracketing, providing a series of different exposures to improve your chances of getting the exact right exposure, or to provide alternative renditions for creative purposes.

- **Flash exposure compensation.** You can adjust flash exposure using a menu here. Select this option with the SET button, then dial in the amount of flash EV compensation you want using the multi-controller or Quick Control Dial. The EV that was in place before you started to make your adjustment is shown as a blue indicator, so you can return to that value quickly. Press SET again to confirm your change, then press the MENU button twice to exit.

- **E-TTL II.** You can choose evaluative (matrix) or average metering modes for the electronic flash exposure meter. Evaluative looks at selected areas in the scene to calculate exposure, while average calculates flash exposure by reading the entire scene.

- **Zoom.** Some flash units can vary their coverage to better match the field of view of your lens at a particular focal length. You can allow the external flash to zoom automatically, based on information provided, or manually, using a zoom button on the flash itself. This setting is disabled when using a flash like the Canon 420EX, which does not have zooming capability.

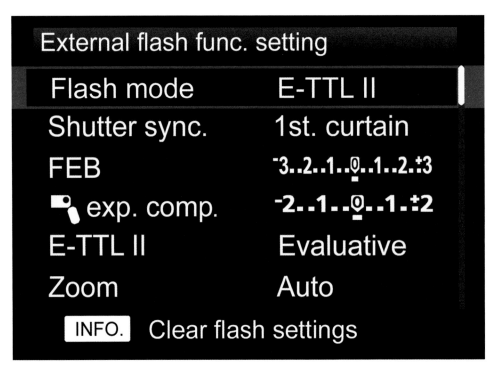

Figure 7.13
External flash units can be controlled from the Canon EOS 7D using this menu.

External Flash Custom Function Setting

Many external Speedlites from Canon include their own list of Custom Functions, which can be used to specify things like flash metering mode and flash bracketing sequences, as well as more sophisticated features, such as modeling light/flash (if available), use of external power sources (if attached), and functions of any slave unit attached to the external flash. This menu entry allows you to set an external flash unit's Custom Functions from your 7D's menu.

Clear External Flash Custom Function Setting

This entry allows you to zero-out any changes you've made to your external flash's Custom Functions, and return them to their factory default settings.

Exposure Compensation/Automatic Exposure Bracketing

The first entry on the Shooting 2 menu is Expo. comp./AEB, or exposure compensation and automatic exposure bracketing. (See Figure 7.14.) As you learned in Chapter 4, exposure compensation (added/subtracted by rotating the Quick Control Dial while this menu screen is visible) increases or decreases exposure from the metered value.

Figure 7.14
Exposure compensation/ exposure bracketing is the first entry in the Shooting 2 menu.

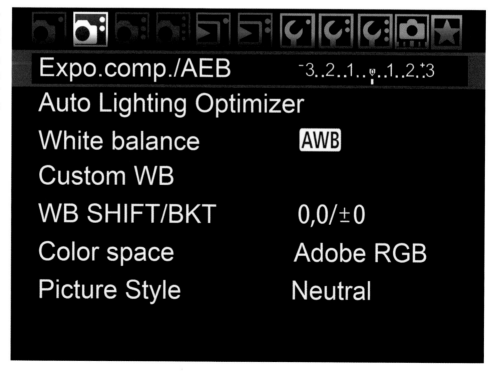

Exposure bracketing using the 7D's AEB feature is a way to shoot several consecutive exposures using different settings, to improve the odds that one will be exactly right. Automatic Exposure Bracketing is also an excellent way of creating the base exposures you'll need when you want to combine several shots to create a high dynamic range (HDR) image. (You'll find a discussion of HDR photography—one of the latest rages—in Chapter 4, too.)

To activate automatic exposure bracketing, select this menu choice, then rotate the Main Dial to spread or contract the three dots beneath the scale until you've defined the range you want the bracket to cover, shown as full-stop jumps in Figure 7.15. Then, rotate the Quick Control Dial to move the brackets right or left, biasing the bracketing towards underexposure (rotate left) or overexposure (rotate right).

When AEB is activated, the three bracketed shots will be exposed in this sequence: metered exposure, decreased exposure, increased exposure (unless you've redefined the bracketing sequence to decreased exposure, metered exposure, increased exposure using C.Fn I-05). You'll find more information about exposure bracketing in Chapter 4.

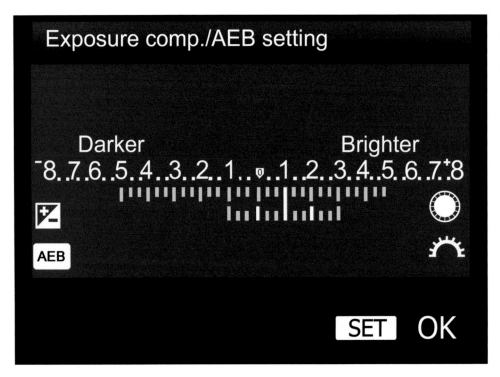

Figure 7.15
Set the range of the three bracketed exposures.

Auto Lighting Optimizer

The Auto Lighting Optimizer provides a partial fix for images that are too dark or flat. Such photos typically have low contrast, and the Auto Lighting Optimizer improves them—as you shoot—by increasing both the brightness and contrast as required. The feature can be activated in program, aperture-priority, and shutter-priority modes (but not manual mode). You can select from four settings: Standard (the default value, which is always selected when using Full Auto and Creative Auto modes, and used for Figure 7.16), plus Low, Strong, and Disable.

Figure 7.16
Auto Lighting Optimizer can brighten dark, low-contrast images (top), giving them a little extra snap and brightness (bottom).

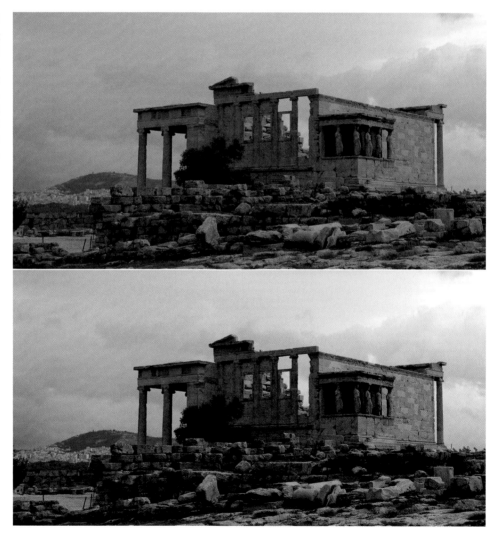

White Balance

This menu entry allows you to choose one of the white balance preset values from among Auto, Daylight, Shade, Cloudy/Twilight/Sunset, Tungsten, White Fluorescent Light, Flash, or Custom. Once you've selected White balance from the Shooting 2 menu, use the Quick Control Dial to choose a setting from the two columns of entries, then press the SET button to lock it in (see Figure 7.17). If you choose the "K" entry, you can select an exact color temperature from 2,500K to 10,000K using the Main Dial. Choosing the right white balance can have a dramatic effect on the colors of your image, as you can see in Figure 7.18.

Custom White Balance

If automatic white balance or one of the six preset settings available (Auto, Daylight, Shade, Cloudy/Twilight/Sunset, Tungsten, White Fluorescent, or Flash) aren't suitable, you can set a custom white balance using this menu option. The custom setting you establish will then be applied whenever you select Custom using the White Balance menu entry described earlier.

To set the white balance to an appropriate color temperature under the current ambient lighting conditions, focus manually (with the lens set on MF) on a plain white or gray object, such as a card or wall, making sure the object fills the spot metering circle in the center of the viewfinder. Then, take a photo. Next press the MENU button and

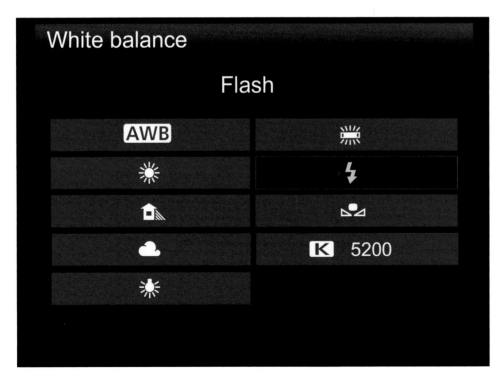

Figure 7.17
White balance presets can be chosen here.

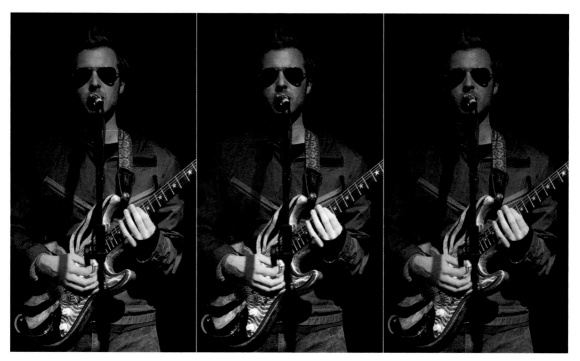

Figure 7.18 Adjusting color temperature can provide different results of the same subject at 3,400K (left), 5,000K (center), and 2,800K (right).

select Custom WB from the Shooting 2 menu. Use the Quick Control Dial until the reference image you just took appears and press the SET button to store the white balance of the image as your Custom setting.

A WHITE BALANCE LIBRARY

Shoot a selection of blank-card images under a variety of lighting conditions on a spare Compact Flash card. If you want to "recycle" one of the color temperatures you've stored, insert the card and set the Custom white balance to that of one of the images in your white balance library, as described previously.

White Balance Shift and Bracketing

White balance shift allows you to dial in a white balance color bias along the blue-yellow/amber dimensions, and/or magenta/green scale. In other words, you can set your color balance so that it is a little bluer or yellower (only), a little more magenta or green (only), or a combination of the two bias dimensions. You can also bracket exposures, taking several consecutive pictures each with a slightly different color balance biased in the directions you specify.

The process is a little easier to visualize if you look at Figure 7.19. The center intersection of lines BA and GM (remember high school geometry!) is the point of zero bias. Move the point at that intersection using the multi-controller joystick to locate it at any point on the graph using the blue-yellow/amber and green-magenta coordinates. The amount of shift will be displayed in the SHIFT box to the right of the graph.

White balance bracketing is like white balance shifting, only the bracketed changes occur along the bias axis you specify. The three squares in Figure 7.19 show that the white balance bracketing will occur in two-stop steps along the blue-yellow/amber axis. The amount of the bracketing is shown in the lower box to the right of the graph.

This form of bracketing is similar to exposure bracketing, but with the added dimension of hue. Bias bracketing can be performed in any JPEG-only mode. You can't use any RAW format or RAW+JPEG format because the RAW files already contain the information needed to fine-tune the white balance and white balance bias.

When you select WB SHIFT/BKT, the adjustment screen appears. First, you turn the Quick Control Dial to set the range of the shift in either the green/magenta dimension (turn the dial to the left to change the vertical separation of the three dots representing the separate exposures) or in the blue-yellow/amber dimension by turning the Quick Control Dial to the right. Use the multi-controller joystick to move the bracket set around within the color space, and outside the green-magenta or blue-yellow/amber axes.

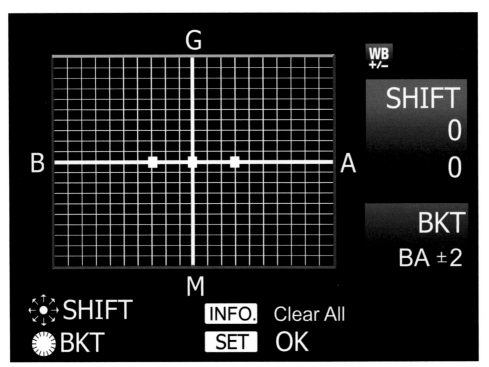

Figure 7.19
Use the Quick Control Dial to specify color balance bracketing using green-magenta bias or to specify blue-yellow/amber bias.

Use the multi-controller only after you've accumulated some experience in shifting around the white balance manually. In most cases, it's fairly easy to determine if you want your image to be more green, more magenta, more blue, or more yellow, although judging your current shots on the LCD screen can be tricky unless you view the screen in a darkened location so it will be bright and easy to see. Bracketing is covered in Chapter 4.

Color Space

When you are using one of the Creative Zone modes, you can select one of two different color spaces (also called *color gamuts*) using this menu entry, shown previously among the other menu choices in Figure 7.13. One color space is named *Adobe RGB* (because it was developed by Adobe Systems in 1998), while the other is called *sRGB* (supposedly because it is the *standard* RGB color space). These two color gamuts define a specific set of colors that can be applied to the images your 7D captures.

The color space menu choice applies directly to JPEG images shot using P, Tv, Av, and M exposure modes. When you're using Full Auto or Creative Auto modes, the 7D uses the sRGB color space for all the JPEG images you take. RAW, M RAW, or S RAW images are a special case. They have the information for *both* sRGB and Adobe RGB, but when you load such photos into your image editor, it will default to sRGB (with Full Auto or Creative Auto shots) or the color space specified here unless you change that setting while importing the photos. (See the "Best of Both Worlds" sidebar that follows for more information.)

You may be surprised to learn that the EOS 7D doesn't automatically capture *all* the colors we see. Unfortunately, that's impossible because of the limitations of the sensor and the filters used to capture the fundamental red, green, and blue colors, as well as that of the phosphors used to display those colors on your camera and computer monitors. Nor is it possible to *print* every color our eyes detect, because the inks or pigments used don't absorb and reflect colors perfectly. In short, your sensor doesn't capture all the colors that we can see, your monitor can't display all the colors that the sensor captures, and your printer outputs yet another version.

On the other hand, the 7D does capture quite a few more colors than we need. The original 14-bit RAW image contains a possible 4.4 *trillion* different hues, which are condensed down to a mere 16.8 million possible colors when converted to a 24-bit (eight bits per channel) image. While 16.8 million colors may seem like a lot, it's a small subset of 4.4 trillion captured, and an even smaller subset of all the possible colors we can see. The set of colors, or gamut, that can be reproduced or captured by a given device (scanner, digital camera, monitor, printer, or some other piece of equipment) is represented as a color space that exists within the larger full range of colors.

That full range is represented by the odd-shaped splotch of color shown in Figure 7.20, as defined by scientists at an international organization called the International Commission on Illumination (usually known as the CIE for its French name *Commission internationale de l'éclairage*) back in 1931. The colors possible with Adobe RGB are represented by the larger, black triangle in the figure, while the sRGB gamut is represented by the smaller white triangle.

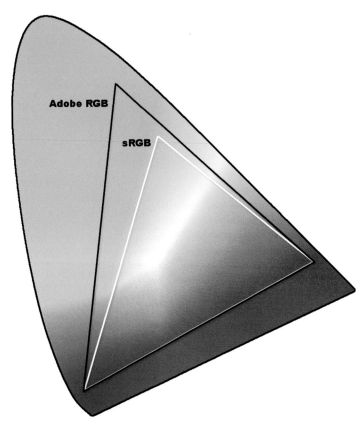

Figure 7.20
The outer figure shows all the colors we can see; the two inner outlines show the boundaries of Adobe RGB (black triangle) and sRGB (white triangle).

Regardless of which triangle—or color space—is used by the 7D, you end up with some combination of 16.8 million different colors that can be used in your photograph. (No one image will contain all 16.8 million! If each and every pixel in a 15-megapixel photo were a different color—which is extremely unlikely—you'd need only 15 million different colors.) But, as you can see from the figure, the colors available will be *different*.

Adobe RGB is what is often called an *expanded* color space, because it can reproduce a range of colors that is spread over a wider range of the visual spectrum. Adobe RGB is useful for commercial and professional printing. You don't need this range of colors if your images will be displayed primarily on your computer screen or output by your personal printer.

The other color space, sRGB, is recommended for images that will be output locally on the user's own printer, as this color space matches that of the typical inkjet printer fairly closely. While both Adobe RGB and sRGB can reproduce the exact same 16.8 million absolute colors, Adobe RGB spreads those colors over a larger portion of the visible spectrum, as you can see in the figure. Think of a box of crayons (the jumbo 16.8 million crayon variety). Some of the basic crayons from the original sRGB set have been removed and replaced with new hues not contained in the original box. Your "new" box contains colors that can't be reproduced by your computer monitor, but which work just fine with a commercial printing press.

BEST OF BOTH WORLDS

As I mentioned, if you're using Full Auto or Creative Auto, the 7D selects the sRGB color space automatically. In addition, you may choose to set the sRGB color space with this menu entry to apply that gamut to all your other photos as well. But, in either case, you can still easily obtain Adobe RGB versions of your photos if you need them. Just shoot using RAW+JPEG. You'll end up with sRGB JPEGs suitable for output on your own printer, but you can still extract an Adobe RGB version from the RAW file at any time. It's like capturing two different color spaces at once—sRGB and Adobe RGB—and getting the best of both worlds.

Of course, choosing the right color space doesn't solve the problems that result from having each device in the image chain manipulating or producing a slightly different set of colors. To that end, you'll need to investigate the wonderful world of *color management*, which uses hardware and software tools to match or *calibrate* all your devices, as closely as possible, so that what you see more closely resembles what you capture, what you see on your computer display, and what ends up on a printed hardcopy. Entire books have been devoted to color management, and most of what you need to know doesn't directly involve your Canon EOS 7D, so I won't detail the nuts and bolts here.

To manage your color, you'll need, at the bare minimum, some sort of calibration system for your computer display, so that your monitor can be adjusted to show a standardized set of colors that is repeatable over time. (What you see on the screen can vary as the monitor ages, or even when the room light changes.) I use Pantone's Huey monitor color correction system for my computer's dual 26-inch widescreen LCD displays. The Huey checks room light levels every five minutes, and reminds me to recalibrate every week or two using the small sensor device shown in Figure 7.21, which attaches temporarily to the front of the screen with tiny suction cups and interprets test patches that the Huey software displays during calibration. The rest of the time, the Huey sensor sits in the stand shown, measuring the room illumination, and adjusting my monitors for higher or lower ambient light levels.

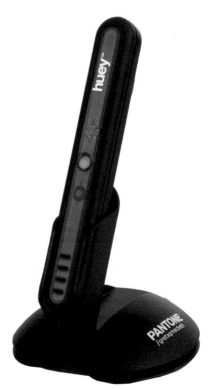

Figure 7.21
Pantone's Huey monitor color correction system is an inexpensive device for calibrating your display.

The Huey (www.pantone.com) is an inexpensive (under $100) system that does a good job of calibrating a single monitor. You can upgrade it, as I did, for use with multiple monitors using a $40 software upgrade available at the Pantone site. If you're willing to make a serious investment in equipment to help you produce the most accurate color and make prints, you'll want a more advanced system (up to $500) like the various Spyder products from Datacolor (www.datacolor.com), or Colormunki from X-Rite (www.colormunki.com).

Picture Style

The Picture Styles feature is one of the most important tools for customizing the way your Canon EOS 7D renders its photos. Picture Styles are a type of fine-tuning you can apply to your photos to change certain characteristics of each image taken using a particular Picture Style setting. The parameters you can specify for full-color images include the amount of sharpness, degree of contrast, the richness of the color, and the hue of skin tones. For black-and-white images, you can tweak the sharpness and contrast, but the two color adjustments (meaningless in a monochrome image) are replaced by controls for filter effects (which I'll explain shortly), and sepia, blue, purple, or green tone overlays.

The Canon EOS 7D has five preset color Picture Styles, for Standard, Portrait, Landscape, Neutral, and Faithful pictures, plus three user-definable settings called User Def. 1, User Def. 2, and User Def. 3, which you can define to apply to any sort of shooting situation you want, such as sports, architecture, or baby pictures. There is also a sixth Monochrome Picture Style that allows you to adjust filter effects or add color toning to your black-and-white images. See Figure 7.22 for the main Picture Style menu.

Tip

As with the Color space menu entry, the full range of Picture Styles can be applied directly *only* to JPEG images shot using P, Tv, Av, and M exposure modes. When using Full Auto, the Canon EOS 7D selects the Standard Picture Style. In Creative Auto, you can't access the full Picture Styles menu by pressing the Picture Styles button. You can choose from Standard, Portrait, Landscape, or Monochrome modes (only) using the Quick Control screen (press the Q button to access it). Any RAW format file can be adjusted to any Picture Style you want when the photo is imported into your image editor.

Figure 7.22
Nine different Picture Styles are available from this scrolling menu; these six plus three User Def. styles not shown.

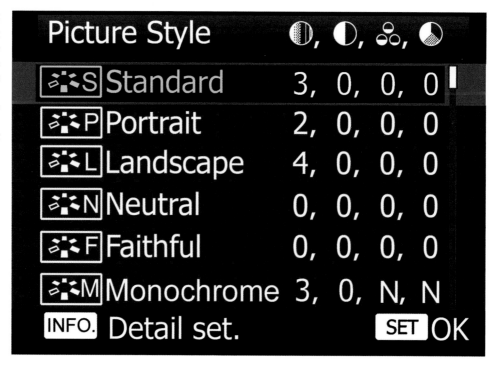

Picture Styles are extremely flexible. Canon has set the parameters for the five predefined color Picture Styles and the single monochrome Picture Style to suit the needs of most photographers. But you can adjust any of those "canned" Picture Styles to settings you prefer. Better yet, you can use those three User Definition files to create brand-new styles that are all your own. If you want rich, bright colors to emulate Velvia film or the work of legendary photographer Pete Turner, you can build your own color-soaked style. If you want soft, muted colors and less sharpness to create a romantic look, you can do that, too. Perhaps you'd like a setting with extra contrast for shooting outdoors on hazy or cloudy days.

The parameters applied when using Picture Styles follow. Figure 7.23 shows exaggerated examples of the first four (color photo) attributes, as applied by Picture Styles (your real-world tweaks may not be quite this drastic, but are more difficult to represent on the printed page):

- **Sharpness.** This parameter determines the apparent contrast between the outlines or edges in an image, which we perceive as image sharpness. You can adjust the sharpness of the image between values of 0 (no sharpening added) to 7 (dramatic additional sharpness). When adjusting sharpness, remember that more is not always a good thing. A little softness is necessary (and is introduced by a blurring "anti-alias" filter in front of the sensor) to reduce or eliminate the moiré effects that can result when details in your image form a pattern that is too close to the pattern, or frequency, of the sensor itself. The default levels of sharpening (which are, for most Picture Styles, not 0) were chosen by Canon to allow most moiré interference to be safely blurred to invisibility, at the cost of a little sharpness. As you boost sharpness (either using a Picture Style or in your image editor), moiré can become a problem, plus, you may end up with those noxious "halos" that appear around the edges of images that have been oversharpened. Use this adjustment with care.

- **Contrast.** Use this control, with values from –4 (low contrast) to +4 (higher contrast), to change the number of middle tones between the deepest blacks and brightest whites. Low contrast settings produce a flatter-looking photo, while high contrast adjustments may improve the tonal rendition while possibly losing detail in the shadows or highlights.

- **Saturation.** This parameter, adjustable from –4 (low saturation) to +4 (high saturation) controls the richness of the color, making, say, a red tone appear to be deeper and fuller when you increase saturation, and tend more towards lighter, pinkish hues when you decrease saturation of the reds. Boosting the saturation too much can mean that detail may be lost in one or more of the color channels, producing what is called "clipping." You can detect this phenomenon when using the RGB histograms, as described in Chapter 4.

- **Color tone.** This adjustment has the most effect on skin tones, making them either redder (0 to –4) or yellower (0 to +4).

- **Filter effect (Monochrome only).** Filter effects do not add any color to a black-and-white image. Instead, they change the rendition of gray tones as if the picture were taken through a color filter. I'll explain this distinction more completely in the sidebar "Filters vs. Toning" later in this section.

- **Toning effect (Monochrome only).** Using toning effects preserves the monochrome tonal values in your image, but adds a color overlay that gives the photo a sepia, blue, purple, or green cast.

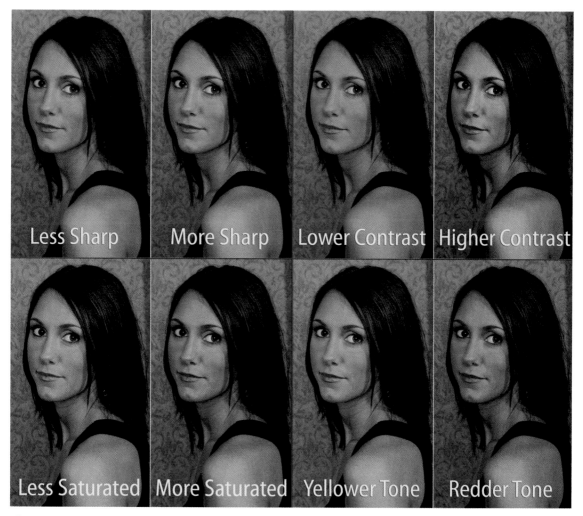

Figure 7.23 These sets of photos represent the main color image Picture Styles parameters: sharpness (upper-left pair); contrast (upper-right pair); saturation (lower-left pair); and color tone (lower-right pair).

The predefined Picture Styles are as follows:

- **Standard.** This Picture Style, the default, applies a set of parameters, including boosted sharpness, that are useful for most picture taking, and which are applied automatically when using Basic Zone modes other than Portrait or Landscape.

- **Portrait.** This style boosts saturation for richer colors when shooting portraits, which is particularly beneficial for women and children, while reducing sharpness slightly to provide more flattering skin texture. The Basic Mode Portrait setting uses this Picture Style. You might prefer the Faithful style for portraits of men when you want a more rugged or masculine look, or when you want to emphasize character lines in the faces of older subjects of either gender.

- **Landscape.** This style increases the saturation of blues and greens, and increases both color saturation and sharpness for more vivid landscape images. The Basic Zone Landscape mode uses this setting.

- **Neutral.** This Picture Style is a less-saturated and lower-contrast version of the Standard style. Use it when you want a more muted look to your images, or when the photos you are taking seem too bright and contrasty (say, at the beach on a sunny day).

- **Faithful.** The goal of this style is to render the colors of your image as accurately as possible, roughly in the same relationships as seen by the eye.

- **Monochrome.** Use this Picture Style to create black-and-white photos in the camera. If you're shooting JPEG only, the colors are gone forever. But if you're shooting JPEG+RAW, sRAW1, or sRAW2, you can convert the RAW files to color as you import them into your image editor, even if you've shot using the Monochrome Picture Style. Your 7D displays the images in black-and-white on the screen during playback, but the colors are there in the RAW file for later retrieval.

Tip

You can use the Monochrome Picture Style even if you are using one of the RAW formats alone, without a JPEG version. The EOS 7D displays your images on the screen in black-and-white, and marks the RAW image as monochrome so it will default to that style when you import it into your image editor. However, the color information is still present in the RAW file and can be retrieved, at your option, when importing the image.

Selecting Picture Styles

Canon makes selecting a Picture Style for use very easy, and, to prevent you from accidentally changing an existing style when you don't mean to, divides *selection* and *modification* functions into two separate tasks. There are actually two different ways to choose from among your existing Picture Styles.

One way is to choose Picture Styles from the Shooting 2 menu and press SET to produce the main Picture Style menu screen. Use the Quick Control Dial to rotate among the nine choices. (Neutral, Faithful, Monochrome, and User Def. 1, User Def. 2, and User Def. 3 are shown in Figure 7.24; the rest appear when you scroll using the QCD.) The current settings for each Picture Style are shown on the right half of the screen. Press SET to activate your choice. Then press the MENU button to exit the menu system. You can see that even with this method, switching among Picture Styles is fast and easy enough to allow you to shift gears as often as you like during a shooting session.

Figure 7.24

You can select a style from the Picture Style menu in Set-up 2 menu.

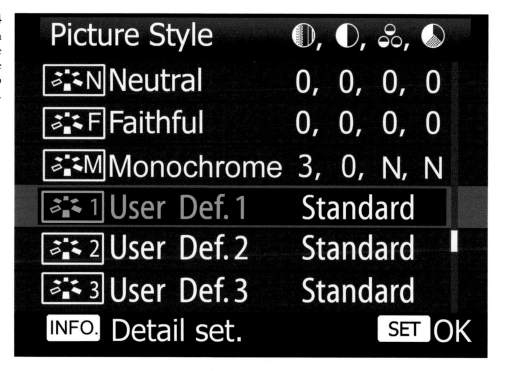

But your 7D offers an even simpler way to activate a Picture Style. Press the Picture Style button under the MENU button, and use the Quick Control Dial to scroll through the list of available styles on the screen that appears, shown in Figure 7.25. When you use this method, the current settings for a particular style are shown *only* when you've highlighted that style. Press SET or the multi-controller button to activate the style of your choice.

Defining Picture Styles

Canon makes interpreting current Picture Style settings and applying changes very easy. As you saw in Figures 7.22 and 7.24, the current settings of the visible Picture Style options are shown as numeric values on the menu screen. Some camera vendors use word descriptions, like Sharp, Extra Sharp, or Vivid, More Vivid that are difficult to

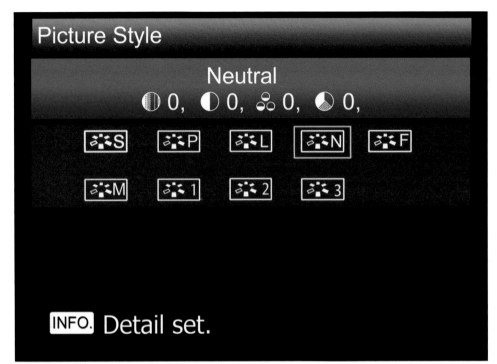

Figure 7.25
Press the
Picture Style
button to the
left of the LCD
to choose a
style from this
fast-access
screen.

relate to. The 7D's settings, on the other hand, are values on uniform scales, with seven steps (from 1 to 7) for sharpness, and plus/minus four steps clustered around a zero (no change) value for contrast and saturation (so you can change from low contrast/low saturation, –4, to high contrast/high saturation, +4), as well as color tone (–4/reddish to +4/yellowish). The individual icons at the top of Figures 7.22 and 7.24 represent (left to right) Sharpness, Contrast, Saturation, and Color Tone.

You can change one of the existing Picture Styles or define your own whenever the Shooting 2 menu version of the Picture Styles menu, or the pop-up selection screen shown in Figure 7.25, is visible. Just press the INFO. button when either screen is on the LCD. Follow these steps:

1. Use the Quick Control Dial to scroll to the style you'd like to adjust.

2. Press the INFO. button to choose Detail set. If you're coming from the Shooting 2 menu, the screen that appears next will look like the one shown in Figure 7.26 for the five color styles or three User Def. styles. If you've accessed the adjustment screen by pressing the Picture Style button first, the screen looks much the same, but has blue highlighting instead of red.

3. Use the Quick Control Dial to scroll among the four parameters, plus Default set, at the bottom of the screen, which restores the values to the preset numbers.

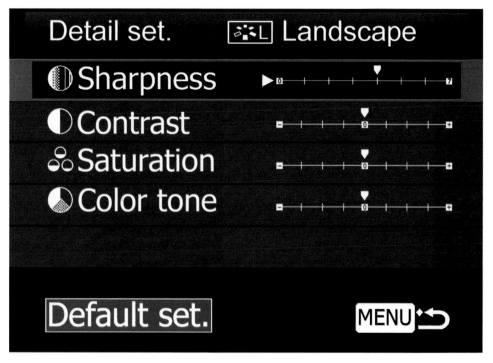

4. Press SET to change the values of one of the four parameters. If you're redefining one of the default presets, the menu screen will look like the figure (Figure 7.26), which represents the Landscape Picture Style.

5. Use the Quick Control Dial to move the triangle to the value you want to use. Note that the previous value remains on the scale, represented by a gray triangle. This makes it easy to return to the original setting if you want.

6. Press the SET button to lock in that value, then press the MENU button three times to back out of the menu system.

Any Picture Style that has been changed from its defaults will be shown in the Picture Style menu with blue highlighting the altered parameter. You don't have to worry about changing a Picture Style and then forgetting that you've modified it. A quick glance at the Picture Style menu will show you which styles and parameters have been changed.

Making changes in the Monochrome Picture Style is slightly different, as the Saturation and Color tone parameters are replaced with Filter effect and Toning effect options. (Keep in mind that once you've taken a photo using a Monochrome Picture Style, you can't convert the image back to full color.) You can choose from Yellow, Orange, Red, Green filters, or None, and specify Sepia, Blue, Purple, or Green toning, or None. You can still set the Sharpness and Contrast parameters that are available with the other Picture Styles. Figure 7.27 shows filter effects being applied to the Monochrome Picture Style.

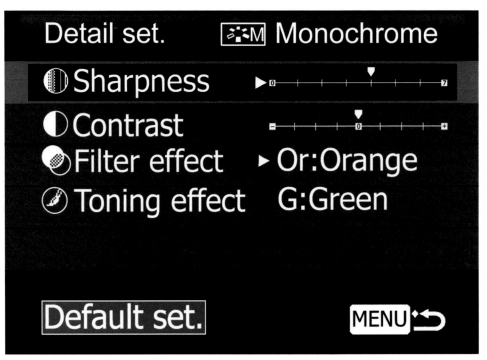

Figure 7.27
Apply changes to the Monochrome Picture Style.

FILTERS VS. TONING

Although some of the color choices overlap, you'll get very different looks when choosing between Filter Effects and Toning Effects. Filter Effects add no color to the monochrome image. Instead, they reproduce the look of black-and-white film that has been shot through a color filter. That is, Yellow will make the sky darker and the clouds will stand out more, whereas Orange makes the sky even darker and sunsets more full of detail. The Red filter produces the darkest sky of all and darkens green objects, such as leaves. Human skin may appear lighter than normal. The Green filter has the opposite effect on leaves, making them appear lighter in tone. Figure 7.28 shows the same scene shot with no filter, then Yellow, Green, and Red filters.

The Sepia, Blue, Purple, and Green toning effects, on the other hand, all add a color cast to your monochrome image. Use these when you want an old-time look or a special effect, without bothering to recolor your shots in an image editor. Figure 7.29 shows the various toning effects available.

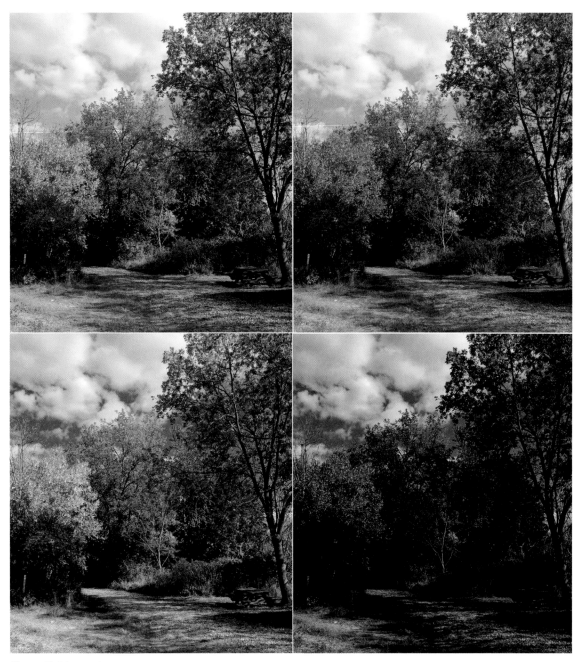

Figure 7.28 No filter (upper left); Yellow filter (upper right); Green filter (lower left), and Red filter (lower right).

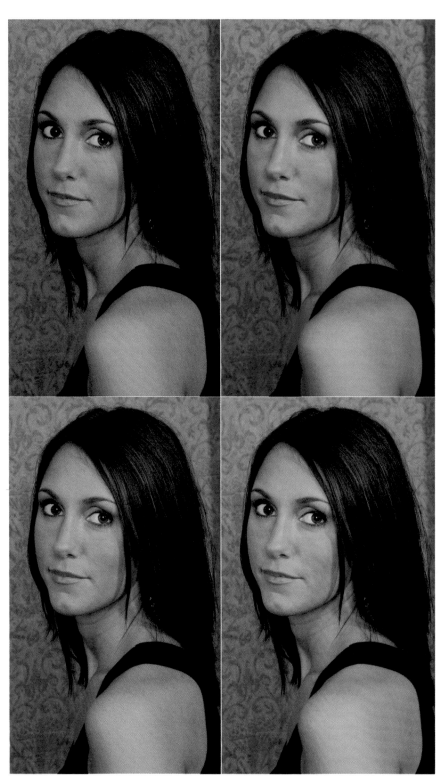

Figure 7.29
Select from among four color filters in the Mono-chrome Picture Style, including Sepia (top left); Blue (top right); Purple (lower left); and Green (lower right).

Adjusting Styles with the Picture Style Editor

The Picture Style Editor, shown in Figure 7.30, allows you to create your own custom Picture Styles, or edit existing styles, including the Standard, Landscape, Faithful, and other predefined settings already present in your EOS 7D. You can change sharpness, contrast, color saturation, and color tone—and a lot more—and then save the modifications as a PF2 file that can be uploaded to the camera, or used by Digital Photo Professional (described in Chapter 12) to modify a RAW image as it is imported.

To create and load your own Picture Style, just follow these steps:

1. **Load the editor.** Launch the Picture Style Editor (PSE, not to be confused with the *other* PSE, Photoshop Elements).

2. **Access a RAW file.** Load a RAW .cr2 image you'd like to use as a reference into PSE. You can drag a file from a folder into the editor's main window, or use the Open command in the File menu.

3. **Choose an existing style to base your new style on.** Select any of the base styles except for Standard. Your new style will begin with all the attributes of the base style you choose, so start with one that already is fairly close to the look you want to achieve ("tweaking" is easier than building a style from the ground up).

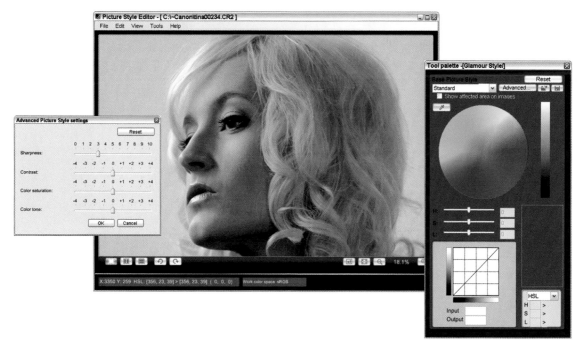

Figure 7.30 The Picture Style Editor lets you create your own Picture Styles for use by the 7D or Digital Photo Professional when importing image files.

4. **Split the screen.** You can compare the appearance of your new style with the base style you are working from. Near the lower-left edge of the display pane are three buttons you can click to split the old/new styles vertically, horizontally, or return to a single image.

5. **Dial in basic changes.** Click the Advanced button in the Tool palette, shown at right in Figure 7.30 to pop up the Advanced Picture Style Settings dialog box that appears at left in the figure. These are the same parameters you can change in the camera. Click OK when you're finished.

6. **Make advanced changes.** The Tool palette has additional functions for adjusting hue, tonal range, and curves. Use of these tools is beyond the scope of a single chapter, let alone a notation in a list, but if you're familiar with the advanced tools in Photoshop, Photoshop Elements, Digital Photo Pro, or another image editor, you can experiment to your heart's content. Note that these modifications go way beyond what you can do with Picture Styles in the camera itself, so learning how to work with them is worth the effort.

7. **Save your Picture Style.** When you're finished, choose Save Picture Style File from the File menu to store your new style as a PF2 file on your hard disk. Add a caption and copyright information to your style in the boxes provided. If you click Disable Subsequent Editing, your style will be "locked" and protected from further changes, and the modifications you did make will be hidden from view (just in case you dream up your own personal, "secret" style). But you'll be unable to edit that style later on. If you think you might want to change your custom Picture Style, save a second copy without marking the Disable Subsequent Editing box.

Now it's time to upload your new style to your Canon EOS 7D using one of your three User Def. slots in the Picture Style array. Just follow these steps:

1. **Link your camera for upload.** Connect your camera to your computer using the USB cable, turn the 7D on, launch the EOS Utility, and click the Camera Settings/Remote Shooting choice in the splash screen.

2. **Choose the Shooting menu.** It's marked with an icon of a white camera on a red background, from the menu bar located about midway in the control panel that appears on your computer display.

3. **Access the Picture Style.** Click on the Picture Style choice to produce the screen shown at left in Figure 7.31. Highlight one of the three User Def. choices and click Detail set. (Note that you could also click one of the predefined Picture Styles, such as Standard or Landscape, and change their parameters, too.) The Picture Style settings dialog box, at right in Figure 7.31, appears.

4. **Specify your new style.** In the Picture Style settings dialog box, click the Open button, and navigate to the new Picture Style that you named and saved in Step 7 above.

Figure 7.31
Upload your new style to your EOS 7D using the EOS Utility.

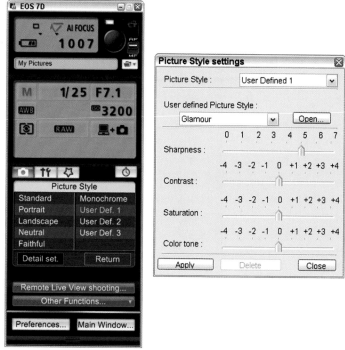

5. **Upload to your camera.** Click the Apply button and your Picture Style will be uploaded to the 7D into the User Defined slot indicated at the top of the dialog box.

6. **Exit EOS Utility.** Click Close to quit the Picture Style settings dialog, and exit the EOS Utility. Disconnect your camera from your computer, and your new style is ready to use.

Get More Picture Styles

I've found that careful Googling can unearth other Picture Styles that helpful fellow EOS owners have made available, and even a few from the helpful Canon company itself. My own search turned up this link: http://web.canon.jp/imaging/picturestyle/file/index.html, where Canon offers a half dozen or more useful PF2 files you can download and install on your own. Remember that Picture Style files are compatible between various Canon EOS camera models (that is, you can use a style created for the Canon 40D with your 7D), but you should be working with the latest software versions to work with the latest cameras and Picture Styles. If you installed your software from the CDs that came with your EOS 7D, you're safe. If you owned an earlier EOS and haven't re-installed the software since your camera upgrade, you might need to re-install the software. It's available for download from the Canon website.

Try the additional styles Canon offers. They include:

- **Studio Portrait.** Compared to the Portrait style built into the camera, this one, Canon says, expresses translucent skin in smooth tones, but with less contrast. (Similar to films in the pre-digital age that were intended for studio portraiture.)

- **Snapshot Portrait.** This is another "translucent skin" style, but with enhanced contrast indoors or out.

- **Nostalgia.** This style adds an amber tone to your images, while reducing the saturation of blue and green tones.

- **Clear.** This style adds contrast for what Canon says is additional "depth and clarity."

- **Twilight.** Adds a purple tone to the sky just before and after sunset or sunrise.

- **Emerald.** Emphasizes blues and greens.

- **Autumn Hues.** Increases the richness of browns and red tones seen in Fall colors.

Dust Delete Data

This menu choice is the first of two that appear in the Shooting 3 menu. (See Figure 7.32.) It lets you "take a picture" of any dust or other particles that may be adhering to

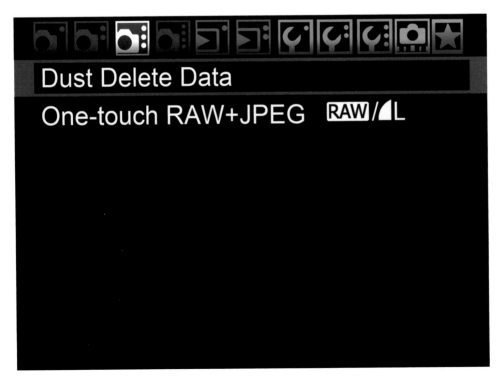

Figure 7.32
Dust Delete Data is the first choice in the Shooting 3 menu.

your sensor. The 7D will then append information about the location of this dust to your photos, so that the Digital Photo Professional software can use this reference information to identify dust in your images and remove it automatically. You should capture a Dust Delete Data photo from time to time as your final line of defense against sensor dust.

To use this feature, select Dust Delete Data to produce the screen shown in Figure 7.33. Select OK and press the SET button. The camera will first perform a self-cleaning operation by applying ultrasonic vibration to the low-pass filter that resides on top of the sensor. Then, a screen will appear asking you to press the shutter button. Point the 7D at a solid-white card with the lens set on manual focus and rotate the focus ring to infinity. When you press the shutter release, the camera takes a photo of the card using aperture-priority and f/22 (which provides enough depth-of-field [actually, in this case, *depth-of-focus*] to image the dust sharply). The "picture" is not saved to your Compact Flash card but, rather, is stored in a special memory area in the camera. Finally, a "Data obtained" screen appears.

The Dust Delete Data information is retained in the camera until you update it by taking a new "picture." The 7D adds the information to each image file automatically.

Figure 7.33
Capture updated dust data for your sensor to allow Digital Photo Professional to remove it automatically.

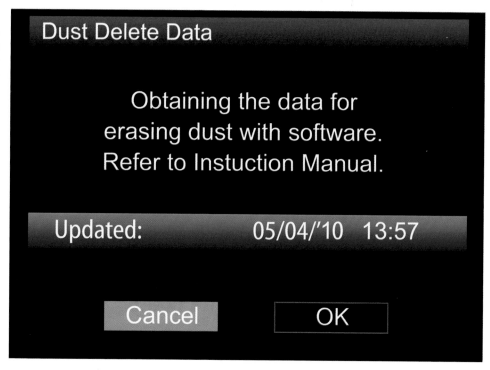

One-Touch RAW+JPEG

I described how to use the One-touch RAW+JPEG button in Chapter 3, but will recap the discussion here, to cover this menu entry, which is where you define exactly what RAW and JPEG formats you want to use for your next shot when the button is pressed.

As I noted earlier, the One-touch RAW+JPEG button provides a useful capability. When you're shooting either RAW or JPEG format (only), it allows you to capture the alternate file format for the next picture you take. Earlier in this chapter you learned that you can choose to shoot three types of RAW files: standard RAW (RAW), Medium RAW (MRAW), or Small RAW (SRAW), either alone or simultaneously with any of six different types of JPEG files (Large, Medium, and Small, each in Fine or Standard image quality). Alternatively, you can elect to shoot using one of those six JPEG settings, with no RAW files at all.

If you've chosen to shoot only RAW or only JPEG, you can press this button and capture the other format, using a quality setting you define with this menu entry. For example, you can tell the EOS 7D to capture a Small RAW (SRAW) image when pressed while you're shooting JPEG only, or to capture, say, a Medium JPEG Standard file when you're shooting RAW and decide you need a reduced-resolution JPEG version of a shot. To select the quality level for your alternate shot, just access this menu item and highlight either Simultaneous RAW or Simultaneous JPEG, as shown in Figure 7.34, using

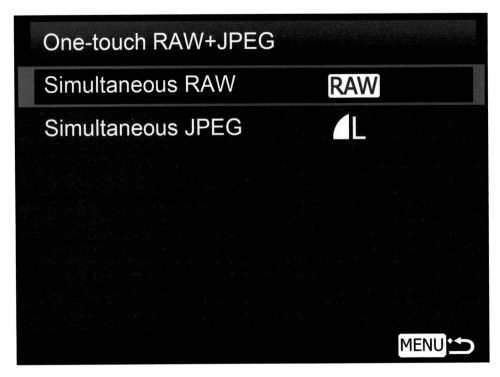

Figure 7.34
Set quality level for your simultaneous RAW or JPEG shots.

the Quick Control Dial or multi-controller. Press SET, and in the screen that appears, choose the default simultaneous quality setting you want to use by rotating the QCD, then press SET to confirm. Use the same procedure to specify both RAW and JPEG settings.

Then, each time you press the One-touch RAW+JPEG button when shooting RAW or JPEG (only), the next shot (only) will be taken using the alternate setting at the quality level you've just defined. The simultaneous shooting is cancelled after that one shot is taken. A reminder: the button has no effect if you're already using a RAW+JPEG quality setting.

Live View Shooting Settings

This menu entry is the first in the Shooting 4 menu (see Figure 7.35). All of the settings on this tab pertain to the 7D's Live View functions, which I explained in detail in the last chapter. This first one is easy; it has just two options, Enable and Disable. When set to Enable, you can activate Live View by pressing the Start/Stop button on the back of the camera (it's located immediately to the right of the viewfinder window) when the Live View switch (concentric with the button) is rotated all the way to the clockwise position. Choose Disable, and use of Live View is blocked.

Figure 7.35
Most of the settings on the Shooting 4 menu involve Live View functions.

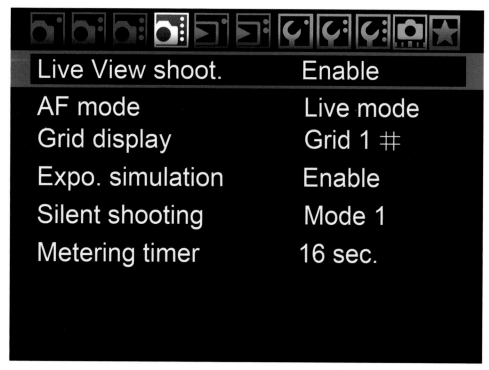

AF Mode

Indicates the autofocus mode used for Live View shooting: Quick mode, Live mode, and Live mode (face detection), as described in Chapter 6.

Grid Display

In Chapter 6, I showed you how to activate either of two "rule of thirds" grids on the LCD to help with alignment and composition. You can enable a separate grid for the optical viewfinder, using the VF Grid Display option in the Set-up 2 menu, described in Chapter 8.

Exposure Simulation

Causes the Live View LCD to mimic the amount of exposure, underexposure, or over-exposure your image will have when taken using the current f/stop, shutter speed, and ISO setting. Your choices are Enable and Disable. I showed you how to use this feature in Chapter 6.

Silent Shooting

Provides a quieter shutter sound when taking pictures using Live View. You can select from two modes: Mode 1 reduces the noise level of the shutter, but allows taking several shots in succession, including continuous shooting at about 6 fps. Mode 2 reduces the noise even further by delaying the action when you press the shutter release down (only a slight click is heard). When you let up slightly on the shutter release, the shot is taken, producing another soft click. Continuous shooting is not possible in Mode 2. Silent shooting can also be disabled entirely.

Metering Timer

This option turns off the exposure meter after a specified period of time (4, 16, or 30 seconds, plus 1, 10, and 30 minutes) to save power, as Live View can be quite a juice hog when you're displaying an image on the LCD for more than a few seconds at a time.

Playback 1 & 2 Menu Options

The two blue-coded Playback menus are where you select options related to the display, review, and printing of the photos you've taken. The choices you'll find include:

- Protect images
- Rotate
- Erase images
- Print order
- Highlight alert
- AF point disp.
- Histogram
- Slide show
- Image Jump

Protect

This is the first of four entries in Playback 1 menu (see Figure 7.36). If you want to keep an image from being accidentally erased (either with the Erase button or by using the Erase menu), you can mark that image for protection. To protect one or more images, press the MENU button and choose Protect. Then use the Quick Control Dial to view the image to be protected. Press the SET button to apply the protection. A key icon will appear at the upper edge of the information display while still in the protection screen, and when reviewing that image later (see Figure 7.37). To remove protection, repeat the process. You can scroll among the other images on your memory card and protect/unprotect them in the same way. Image protection will not save your images from removal when the card is reformatted.

Rotate

While you can set the EOS 7D to automatically rotate images taken in a vertical orientation using the Auto rotate option in the Set-up 1 menu (as described in Chapter 8), you can manually rotate an image during playback using this menu selection. Select Rotate from the Playback 1 menu, use the Quick Control Dial to page through the available images on your memory card until the one you want to rotate appears, then press SET. The image will appear on the screen rotated 90 degrees, as shown in Figure 7.38. Press SET again, and the image will be rotated 270 degrees.

Figure 7.36
The Playback
1 menu.

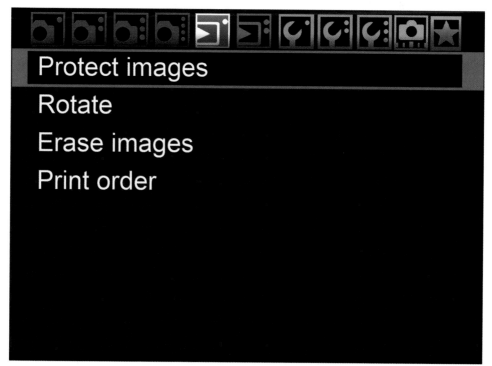

Protect images

Rotate

Erase images

Print order

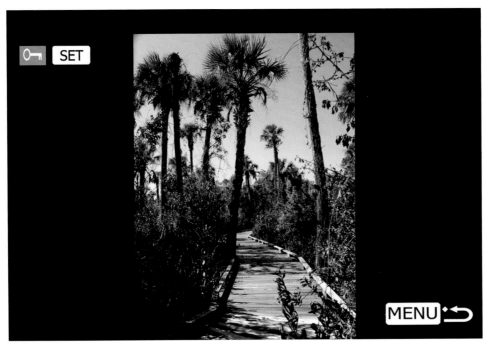

Figure 7.37
Protected
images can be
locked against
accidental era-
sure (but not
preserved from
formatting).

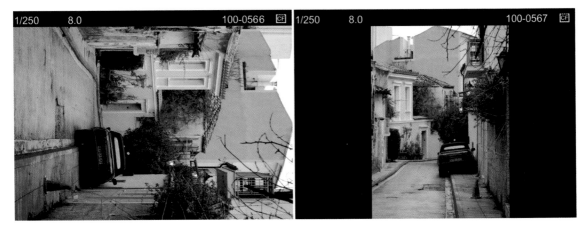

Figure 7.38 A vertically oriented image that isn't rotated appears larger on the LCD, but rotation allows viewing the photo without turning the camera.

Erase Images

Choose this menu entry and you'll be given two choices: Select and erase images and All images on card. The former option displays the most recent image. Press SET to mark that image for deletion, and then rotate the Quick Control Dial to view other images, using the SET button to mark those you want to delete. When finished marking pictures, press the Trash button, and you'll see a screen that says Erase selected images with two options, Cancel and OK. Use the Quick Control Dial to choose OK, then press the SET button to erase the images, or select Cancel and press the SET button to return to the selection screen. Press the MENU button to unmark your selections and return to the menu.

The All images on card choice removes all the pictures on the card, except for those you've marked with the Protect command, and does not reformat the memory card.

Print Order

The EOS 7D supports the DPOF (Digital Print Order Format) that is now almost universally used by digital cameras to specify which images on your memory card should be printed, and the number of prints desired of each image. This information is recorded on the memory card, and can be interpreted by a compatible printer when the camera is linked to the printer using the USB cable, or when the memory card is inserted into a card reader slot on the printer itself. Photo labs are also equipped to read this data and make prints when you supply your memory card to them.

You can read more about assembling print orders in Chapter 12.

Highlight Alert

This menu entry, the first item on the Playback 2 menu tab (shown in Figure 7.39), has just two options: Enable and Disable. When set to Enable, overexposed highlight areas in your image will blink during picture review. That's your cue to consider using exposure compensation to reduce exposure, unless a minus-EV setting will cause loss of shadow detail that you want to preserve. You can read more about correcting exposure in Chapter 4.

Autofocus Points Display

The 7D can display the autofocus point (or points) that was active when the picture was taken as a tiny red square when the full information display is chosen for playback. (Some users mistake the red square in the playback thumbnail as a "hot" pixel.) Choose AF point disp. in the Playback 2 menu and select Enable or Disable. There is little reason not to view this information, so most leave this setting switched on at all times. There's more about choosing autofocus points in Chapter 5.

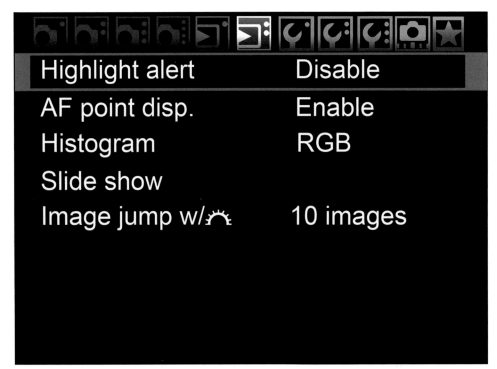

Figure 7.39
Choose Highlight alert to enable on-screen "blinkies" that represent overexposed areas of your image.

Histogram

The 7D can show either a Brightness histogram or set of three separate Red, Green, and Blue histograms in the full information display during picture review, or, it can show you both types of histogram in the partial information display.

Brightness histograms give you information about the overall tonal values present in the image. The RGB histograms can show more advanced users valuable data about specific channels that might be "clipped" (details are lost in the shadows or highlights). This menu choice determines only how they are displayed during picture review. The amount of information displayed cycles through the following list as you repeatedly press the INFO. button:

- **Single image display.** Only the image itself is shown, with basic shooting information displayed in a band across the top of the image, as you can see at upper left in Figure 7.40.

- **Single image display+Image-recording quality.** Identical to Single image display, except that the image size, RAW format (if selected), and JPEG compression (if selected) are overlaid on the image in the lower-left corner of the frame.

■ **Histogram display.** Both RGB and brightness histograms are shown, along with partial shooting information. This menu choice has no effect on the histograms shown in this display, which you can see at upper right in Figure 7.40.

■ **Shooting information display.** Full shooting data is shown, along with either a brightness histogram (bottom left in Figure 7.40) or RGB histogram (bottom right in Figure 7.40). The type of histogram on view in this screen is determined by the setting you make in this menu choice. Select Histogram from the Playback 2 menu and choose Brightness or RGB. You can read more about *using* histograms in Chapter 4.

Figure 7.40
Press the INFO. button to cycle between Single image display (upper left); Single image display+ Image-recording quality (not shown); Histogram display (upper right); Shooting information display with brightness histogram (bottom left); or RGB histogram (bottom right).

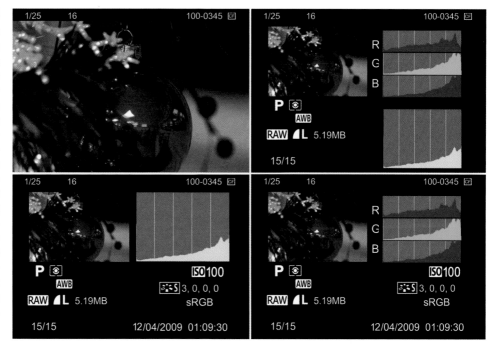

Slide Show

Slide show (also called Auto Playback) is a convenient way to review images one after another, without the need to manually switch between them. To activate, just choose Slide show from the Playback 2 menu. During playback, you can press the SET button to pause the "slide show" (in case you want to examine an image more closely), or the INFO. button to change the amount of information displayed on the screen with each image. For example, you might want to review a set of images and their histograms to judge the exposure of the group of pictures. To set up your slide show, follow these steps:

1. **Begin set up.** Choose Slide show from the Playback 2 menu, pressing SET to display the screen shown in Figure 7.41.

2. **Choose image selection method.** Rotate the Quick Command Dial to All images, and press SET. Then rotate the QCD to choose from All images, Folder, or Date. Press SET to activate that selection mode. If you selected All images, skip to Step 4.

3. **Choose images.** If you've selected Folder or Date, press the INFO. button to produce a screen that allows you to select from the available folders, or the available image creation dates on your memory card. When you've chosen a folder or date, press SET to confirm your choice.

4. **Choose Play time and Repeat options.** Rotate the Quick Command Dial to highlight Set-up and press SET to produce a screen with playing time (1, 2, 3, or 5 seconds per image), and repeating options (On or Off). When you've specified either value, press the MENU button to confirm your choice, and then MENU once more to go back to the main Slide show screen.

5. **Start the show.** Rotate the QCD to highlight Start and press SET to begin your show. (If you'd rather cancel the show you've just set up, press MENU instead.)

6. **Use show options during display.** Press SET to pause/restart; Info to cycle among the four information displays described in the section before this one; MENU to stop the show.

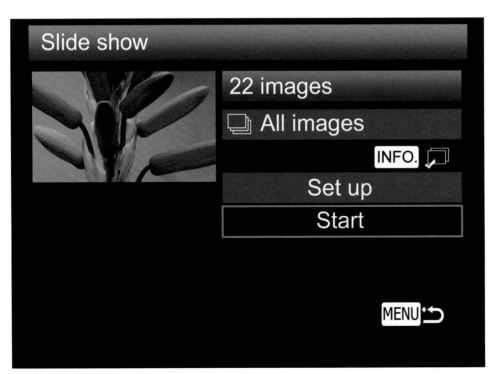

Figure 7.41
Set up your slide show using this screen.

Image Jump with Main Dial

As first described in Chapter 2, you can leap ahead or back during picture review by rotating the Main Dial, using a variety of increments that you can select using this menu entry. The Jump method is shown briefly on the screen as you leap ahead to the next image displayed, as shown in Figure 7.42. Your options are as follows:

- **1 image.** Rotating the Main Dial one click jumps forward or back 1 image.

- **10 images.** Rotating the Main Dial one click jumps forward or back 10 images.

- **100 images.** Rotating the Main Dial one click jumps forward or back 100 images.

- **Screen.** Rotating the Main Dial one click jumps forward or back one screen full of images when viewing in Index mode.

- **Date.** Rotating the Main Dial one click jumps forward or back to the first image taken on the next or previous calendar date.

- **Folder.** Rotating the Main Dial one click jumps forward or back to the first image in the next folder available on your memory card (if one exists).

Figure 7.42
The Jump method is shown on the LCD briefly when you leap forward or back using the Main Dial.

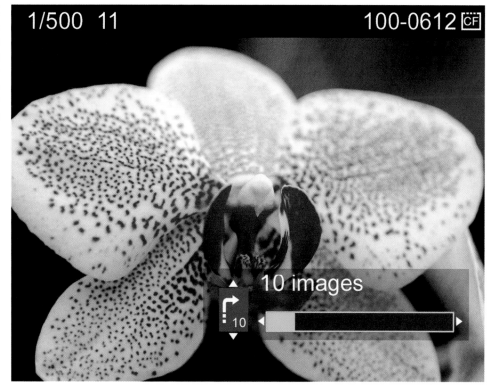

8

Customizing with Set-up, Custom Functions, and My Menus

In the last chapter, I introduced you to the layout and general functions of the Canon EOS 7D's menu system, with specifics on how to customize your camera with the Shooting 1, Shooting 2, Shooting 3, Shooting 4, Playback 1, and Playback 2 menus. In this chapter, you'll learn how to work with the three (count 'em) Set-up menus, the Custom Functions menu, and how to assemble your own roster of favorite menu listings with the My Menu feature.

If you're jumping directly to this chapter and need some guidance on how to navigate the 7D's menu system, review the first few pages of Chapter 7. Otherwise, you're welcome to dive right in.

Set-up 1, 2, and 3 Menu Options

There are three amber-coded set-up menus where you make adjustments on how your camera *behaves* during your shooting session, as differentiated from the Shooting menu, which adjusts how the pictures are actually taken.

Your choices include:

- Auto power off
- Auto rotate
- Format
- File numbering
- Select folder
- LCD brightness

- Date/Time
- Language
- Video system
- Sensor cleaning
- VF grid display
- Battery info.

- INFO. button
- Camera user setting
- Copyright information
- Clear all camera settings
- Firmware Ver.

Auto Power Off

This setting, the first in Set-up 1 menu (see Figure 8.1), allows you to determine how long the EOS 7D remains active before shutting itself off. As you can see in Figure 8.2, you can select 1, 2, 4, 8, 15, or 30 minutes or Off, which leaves the camera turned on indefinitely. However, even if the camera has shut itself off, if the power switch remains in the On position, you can bring the camera back to life by pressing the shutter button.

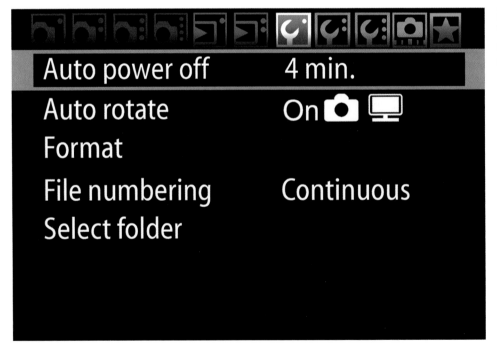

Figure 8.1
The Set-up 1 menu has five options.

Figure 8.2

Select an automatic shut-off period to save battery power.

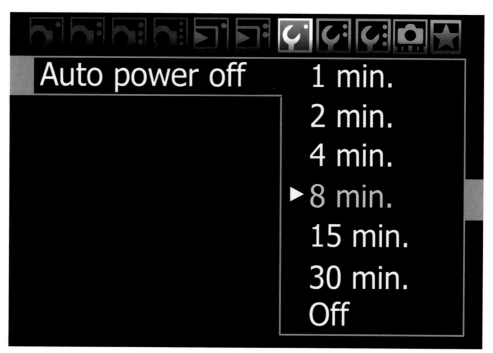

SAVING POWER WITH THE EOS 7D

There are three settings and several techniques you can use to help stretch the longevity of your 7D's battery. The first setting is the Review time option described in Chapter 7 under the Shooting 1 menu. That big 3-inch LCD uses a lot of juice, so reducing the amount of time it is used (either for automatic review or for manually playing back your images) can boost the effectiveness of your battery. Auto Power Off turns off most functions (metering and autofocus shut off by themselves about six seconds after you release the shutter button or take a picture) based on the delay you specify. The third setting is the LCD Brightness adjustment described later in this section. If you're willing to shade the LCD with your hand, you can often get away with lower brightness settings outdoors, which will further increase the useful life of your battery. The techniques? Use the internal flash as little as possible; no flash at all or fill flash use less power than a full blast. Turn off image stabilization if your lens has that feature and you feel you don't need it. When transferring pictures from your 7D to your computer, use a card reader instead of the USB cable. Linking your camera to your computer and transferring images using the cable takes longer and uses a lot more power.

Auto Rotate

You can turn this feature On or Off. When activated, the EOS 7D rotates pictures taken in vertical orientation on the LCD screen so you don't have to turn the camera to view them comfortably. However, this orientation also means that the longest dimension of the image is shown using the shortest dimension of the LCD, so the picture is reduced in size. (You can see examples of horizontal and rotated vertical shots in Figure 7.38 in the previous chapter.) You have three options, shown in Figure 8.3. The image can be autorotated when viewing in the camera *and* on your computer screen using your image editing/viewing software. The image can be marked to autorotate *only* when reviewing your image in your image editor or viewing software. This option allows you to have rotation applied when using your computer, while retaining the ability to maximize the image on your LCD in the camera. The third choice is Off. The image will not be rotated when displayed in the camera or with your computer. Note that if you switch Auto Rotate off, any pictures shot while the feature is disabled will not be automatically rotated when you turn Auto Rotate back on; information embedded in the image file when the photo *is taken* is used to determine whether autorotation is applied.

Format

Use this item to erase everything on your memory card and set up a fresh file system ready for use. When you select Format, you'll see a display like Figure 8.4, showing the capacity of the card, how much of that space is currently in use, and two choices at the bottom of the screen to Cancel or OK (proceed with the format). A blue-green bar appears on the screen to show the progress of the formatting step.

File Numbering

The EOS 7D will automatically apply a file number to each picture you take, using consecutive numbering for all your photos over a long period of time, spanning many different memory cards, starting over from scratch when you insert a new card, or when you manually reset the numbers. Numbers are applied from 0001 to 9999, at which time the camera creates a new folder on the card (100, 101, 102, and so forth), so you can have 0001 to 9999 in folder 100, then numbering will start over in folder 101.

The camera keeps track of the last number used in its internal memory. That can lead to a few quirks you should be aware of. For example, if you insert a memory card that had been used with a different camera, the 7D may start numbering with the next number after the highest number used by the previous camera. (I once had a brand new 7D start numbering files in the 8,000 range.) I'll explain how this can happen next.

Figure 8.3
Choose auto rotation both in the camera and on your computer display (top); only on your computer display (middle); or no automatic rotation (bottom).

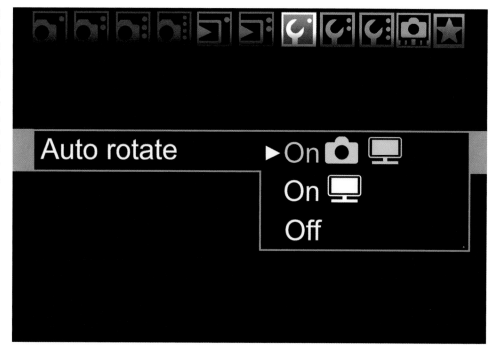

Figure 8.4
You must confirm the format step before the camera will erase a memory card.

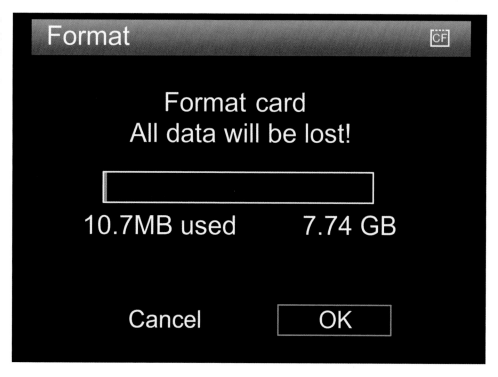

On the surface, the numbering system seems simple enough: In the menu, you can choose Continuous, Automatic reset, or Manual reset. Here is how each works:

- **Continuous.** If you're using a blank/reformatted memory card, the 7D will apply a number that is one greater than the number stored in the camera's internal memory. If the card is not blank and contains images, then the next number will be one greater than the highest number on the card *or* in internal memory. (In other words, if you want to use continuous file numbering consistently, you must always use a card that is blank or freshly formatted.) Here are some examples.

  - You've taken 4,235 shots with the camera, and you insert a blank/reformatted memory card. The next number assigned will be 4,236, based on the value stored in internal memory.

  - You've taken 4,235 shots with the camera, and you insert a memory card with a picture numbered 2,728. The next picture will be numbered 4,236.

  - You've taken 4,235 shots with the camera, and you insert a memory card with a picture numbered 8,281. The next picture will be numbered 8,282, and that value will be stored in the camera's menu as the "high" shot number (and will be applied when you next insert a blank card).

- **Automatic reset.** If you're using a blank/reformatted memory card, the next photo taken will be numbered 0001. If you use a card that is not blank, the next number will be one greater than the highest number found on the memory card. Each time you insert a memory card, the next number will either be 0001 or one higher than the highest already on the card.

- **Manual reset.** The 7D creates a new folder numbered one higher than the last folder created, and restarts the file numbers at 0001. Then, the camera uses the numbering scheme that was previously set, either Continuous or Automatic reset, each time you subsequently insert a blank or non-blank memory card.

Select Folder

Choose this menu option to create a folder where the images you capture will be stored on your memory card, or to switch between existing folders. Just follow these steps:

1. **Choose Select folder.** Access the option from the Set-up 1 menu.

2. **View list of available folders.** The Select folder screen pops up with a list of the available folders on your memory card, with names like 100EOS7D, 101EOS7D, etc.

3. **Choose a different folder.** To store subsequent images in a different existing folder, rotate the Quick Control Dial to highlight the label for the folder you want to use. When a folder that already has photos is selected, two thumbnails representing images in that folder are displayed at the right side of the screen.

4. **Confirm the folder.** Press SET to confirm your choice of an existing folder.

5. **Create new folder.** If you'd rather create a new folder, highlight Create folder in the Select folder screen and press SET. The name of the folder that will be created is displayed, along with a choice to Cancel or OK creating the folder. Press SET to confirm your choice.

6. **Exit.** Press MENU to return to the Set-up 1 menu.

LCD Brightness

Choose this menu option, the first on the second Set-up menu tab (see Figure 8.5), and a thumbnail image with a grayscale strip appears on the LCD, as shown in Figure 8.6. You can select both automatic brightness and manually set brightness.

■ **Automatic brightness.** Use the Main Dial to toggle between Auto and Manual brightness settings. You may see the LCD dim when switching to Auto, as the camera adjusts for the light level.

■ **Manual brightness.** If you select Manual, you can use the Quick Control Dial or the multi-controller to adjust the brightness to a comfortable viewing level. Use the gray bars as a guide; you want to be able to see both the lightest and darkest steps at top and bottom, and not lose any of the steps in the middle. Brighter settings use more battery power, but can allow you to view an image on the LCD outdoors in bright sunlight. When you have the brightness you want, press the SET button to lock it in and return to the menu.

Figure 8.5
The Set-up 2 menu includes six options.

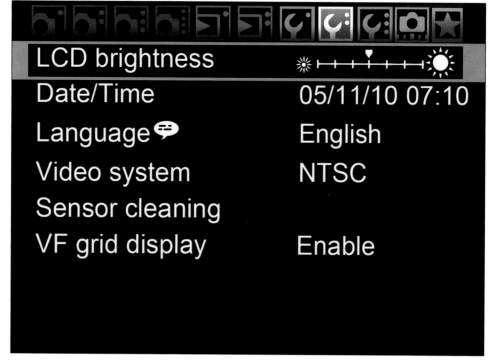

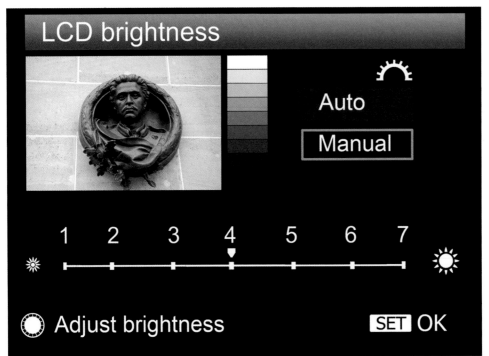

Figure 8.6
Adjust LCD brightness for easier viewing under varying ambient lighting conditions.

Date/Time

Use this option to set the date and time, which will be embedded in the image file along with exposure information and other data. As first outlined in Chapter 1, you can set the date and time by following these steps:

1. Access this menu entry from the Set-up 2 menu.

2. Rotate the (QCD) to move the highlighting down to the Date/Time entry.

3. Press the SET button in the center of the QCD to access the Date/Time setting screen, shown in Figure 8.7.

4. Rotate the QCD to select the value you want to change. When the gold box highlights the month, day, year, hour, minute, second, or year format you want to adjust, press the SET button to activate that value. A pair of up/down pointing triangles appears above the value.

5. Rotate the QCD to adjust the value up or down. Press the SET button to confirm the value you've entered.

6. Repeat steps 4 and 5 for each of the other values you want to change. The date format can be switched from the default mm/dd/yy to yy/mm/dd or dd/mm/yy.

Figure 8.7
Adjust the time
and date.

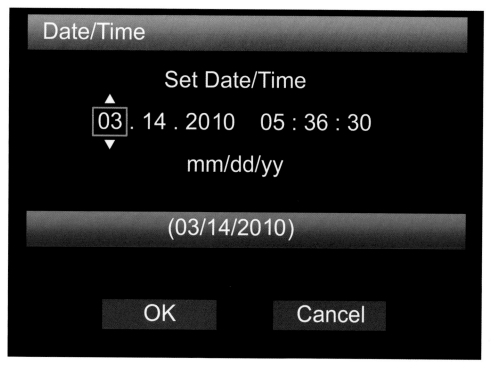

7. When finished, rotate the QCD to select either OK (if you're satisfied with your changes) or Cancel (if you'd like to return to the Set-up 2 menu without making any changes). Press SET to confirm your choice.

8. When finished setting the date and time, press the MENU button to exit, or just tap the shutter release.

Language

Choose from 25 languages for menu display, rotating the Quick Control Dial or using the multi-controller joystick until the language you want to select is highlighted. Press the SET button to activate. Your choices include English, German, French, Dutch, Danish, Portuguese, Finnish, Italian, Ukrainian, Norwegian, Swedish, Spanish, Greek, Russian, Polish, Czech, Magyar, Romanian, Turkish, Arabic, Thai, Simplified Chinese, Traditional Chinese, Korean, and Japanese.

If you accidentally set a language you don't read and find yourself with incomprehensible menus, don't panic. Just choose the third option from the top of the Set-up 2 menu, and select the idioma, sprache, langue, or kieli of your choice. English is the first selection in the list.

Video System

This setting controls the output of the 7D through the AV cable when you're displaying images on an external monitor. You can select either NTSC, used in the United States, Canada, Mexico, many Central, South American, and Caribbean countries, much of Asia, and other countries or PAL, which is used in the UK, much of Europe, Africa, India, China, and parts of the Middle East.

VIEWING ON A TELEVISION

Canon makes it quite easy to view your images on a standard television screen, and not much more difficult on a high-definition television (HDTV). (You have to buy a separate cable for HDTV.) For regular TV, just open the right port cover on the left side of the camera, plug in the cable supplied with the camera into the socket labeled Video, and connect the other end to the yellow VIDEO RCA composite jack on your television or monitor.

For HDTV display, purchase the optional HDMI Cable HTC-100 and connect it to the HDMI OUT terminal just below the standard video terminal on the left side of the camera. Connect the other end to an HDMI input port on your television or monitor (my 42-inch HDTV has three of them; my 26-inch monitor has just two). Then turn on the camera and press the Playback button. The image will appear on the external TV/HDTV/monitor and will not be displayed on the camera's LCD. HDTV systems automatically show your images at the appropriate resolution for that set.

Sensor Cleaning

One of the Canon EOS 7D's most useful features is the automatic sensor cleaning system that reduces or eliminates the need to clean your camera's sensor manually using brushes, swabs, or bulb blowers (you'll find instructions on how to do that in Chapter 13). Canon has applied anti-static coatings to the sensor and other portions of the camera body interior to counter charge build-ups that attract dust. A separate filter over the sensor vibrates ultrasonically each time the 7D is powered on or off, shaking loose any dust, which is captured by a sticky strip beneath the sensor.

Use this menu entry (see Figure 8.8) to enable or disable automatic sensor cleaning on power up (select Auto cleaning to choose) to activate automatic cleaning during a shooting session (select Clean now). You can also choose the Clean manually option to flip up the mirror and clean the sensor yourself with a blower, brush, or swab, as described in Chapter 13. If the battery level is too low to safely carry out the cleaning operation, the 7D will let you know and refuse to proceed, unless you use the optional AC Adapter Kit ACK-E6.

Figure 8.8

Use this menu choice to activate automatic sensor cleaning or enable/disable it on power up.

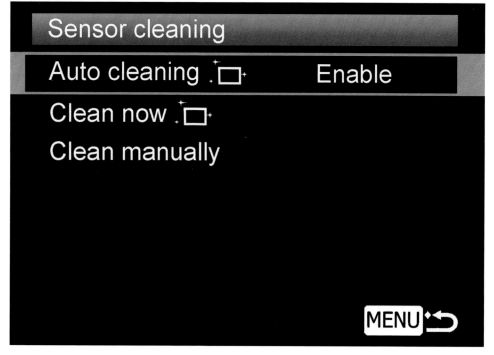

VF Grid Display

This entry allows you to enable or disable the optical viewfinder grid display. To activate/deactivate the grid display visible on the LCD when using Live View, use the Grid display choice in the Shooting 4 menu, as described in Chapter 7. You can use the viewfinder grid to align horizontal or vertical lines in your frame, or as an aid to composition.

Battery Info.

This entry, the first in the Set-up 3 menu (see Figure 8.9) is an exceptionally useful feature that allows you to view battery condition information and performance, and track the data among several different batteries. Your EOS 7D can keep track of multiple LP-E6 batteries because each of them is given a unique serial number (which is printed on an included sticker you can affix to the battery). The camera reads this serial number and stores information about each of the batteries that you use and have "registered" separately. I always recommend owning at least two and, preferably three or more batteries. That's especially true if you use the Battery Grip BG-E7, which holds two battery packs itself. This feature makes it possible to see exactly how each battery you own is performing, allows you to rotate them to even out the usage, and helps you know when it's time to replace a battery.

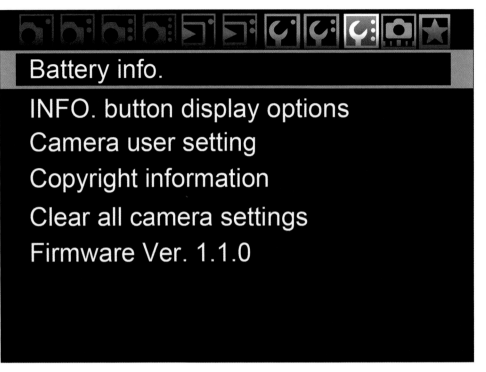

When you select this menu choice, a Battery info screen like the one shown in Figure 8.10 appears, with a wealth of information (if you use two LP-E6 packs in a BG-E7 grip, information about both packs will appear):

- **Battery position.** The second line of the screen includes an icon that shows where the battery currently being evaluated is installed (usually the handgrip if you're not using the BG-E7).

- **Power type.** Next to the position icon is an indicator that shows the model number of the battery installed, or shows that the DC power adapter is being used instead.

- **Remaining capacity.** The Battery check icon appears showing the remaining capacity visually, along with a percentage number that reads out in 1% increments. You can use this as a rough gauge of how much power you have remaining. If you're in the middle of an important shooting session, you might want to switch to a fully charged battery at the 25-33% level to avoid interruptions at the worst probable time. (If you're using six AA batteries in the BG-E7 grip instead of LP-E6 packs, only this battery capacity notice will appear; the other indicators are not shown.)

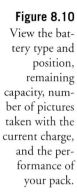

Figure 8.10
View the battery type and position, remaining capacity, number of pictures taken with the current charge, and the performance of your pack.

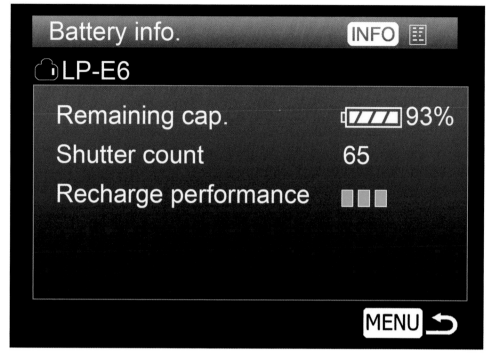

- **Shutter count.** Displays how many times the shutter has been actuated with the current charged battery. This info can help you learn just how much certain features cost you in terms of power. For example if a battery has only 50 percent of its power remaining, but you've taken only a few dozen photos, you know that your power is being sapped by picture review, lots of autofocus, frequent image stabilization because of lower shutter speeds, or (a major culprit) that flip-up flash you've been using. While in most cases knowledge is power, in this instance knowledge can help you *save* power, with a tip-off to use fewer juice-sapping features if the current battery pack must be stretched as far as possible.

- **Recharge performance.** This indicator shows how well your battery pack is accepting and holding a charge. Three green bars mean that the pack's performance is fine; two bars show that recharge performance is degraded a little. A red bar indicates that your pack is on its last legs and should be replaced soon. To lengthen the service time of your batteries, you might want to rotate usage among several different packs, so they all "age" at roughly the same rate.

Registering Your Battery Packs

The EOS 7D can "remember" information about up to six LP-E6 battery packs, and provide readouts of their status individually.

To register the battery currently in your camera, follow these steps:

1. Access the Battery info. screen (shown in Figure 8.10) from the Shooting 3 menu.

2. Press the INFO. button, located to the left of the LCD screen.

3. Information about the current battery, including its serial number and the current date will be shown on a new screen.

4. Choose Register to log the battery; if the pack has already been registered, you can choose Delete info. to remove the battery from the list. (You'd want to do this if you already had registered the limit of six batteries and want to add another one.)

5. Press SET to add the battery to the registry.

6. If you're deleting a battery, the 7D shows you a Battery info. delete screen instead. (You can delete a battery pack without having that battery installed in the camera—which could come in handy if you lose one.) Just select the battery (by serial number) and delete.

7. Press MENU to back out of any of the Battery info. screens.

8. Once a battery has been registered, you can check on its remaining capacity at any time (even if it isn't currently installed in the 7D) from the Battery info page. The camera remembers and updates the status of each registered battery whenever it is inserted in the 7D. The date the battery was last used is also shown.

Tip

Use this info with caution, however, as a given battery may have self-discharged slightly during storage and, of course, you may have fully recharged it since the last time it was inserted in the camera. However, this data can be useful in tracking the remaining capacity of several different battery packs during a single shooting session, or over the course of several days when you're not recharging the packs at the conclusion of each session.

INFO. Button

The INFO. button on the back panel of the Canon EOS 7D by default rotates among the display of several different screens, which can vary, depending on how you've set up this menu option. Just follow these steps:

1. When you select the menu entry, the INFO. button display options screen appears with three choices (described next). Use the Quick Control Dial or multi-controller to highlight any of the three and press SET to mark or unmark that option.

2. Always mark at least one of the three. The 7D won't allow you to disable all of the display options.

3. When finished, use the QCD to move highlighting down to OK (to confirm your changes) or Cancel (to exit without making any changes).

4. Press SET to OK or Cancel and exit the screen. (If you exit in any other way, your changes will not be entered.) Once you've left this options screen, you can press MENU or tap the shutter release to return to shooting mode.

5. Thereafter, the 7D will cycle among the choices you've activated, plus a blank screen, each time you press the INFO. button.

Select at least one and up to three of the following displays:

- **Displays camera settings.** Shows basic camera settings (see Figure 8.11, top).

- **Electronic level.** Indicates how the camera is tilted (see Figure 8.12).

- **Displays shooting functions.** Shows you the current shooting settings of the camera (see Figure 8.11, bottom).

Figure 8.11
Camera settings (top) and Shooting functions (bottom) can be displayed when you press the INFO. button.

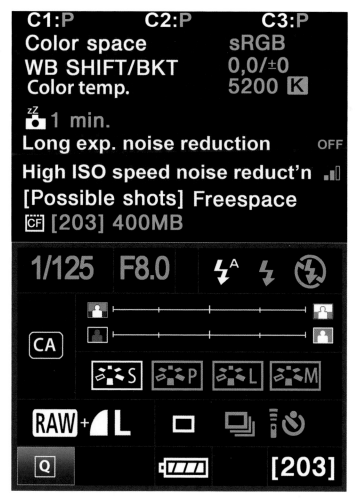

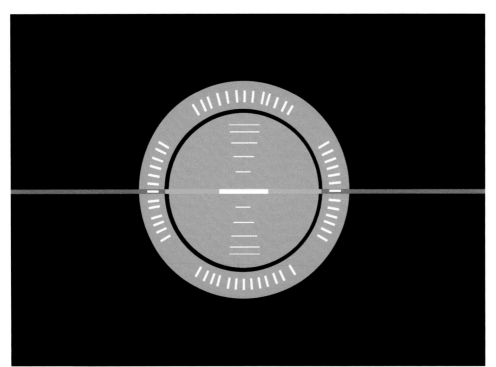

Figure 8.12
The electronic level shows the orientation of the camera.

Camera User Setting

This entry allows you to register your EOS 7D's current camera shooting settings and file them away in the C1, C2, or C3 positions on the Mode Dial. Doing this overwrites any settings previously stored at that Camera user position. You can also clear the settings for any of the two Mode Dial positions individually, returning them to their factory default values. Table 8.1 shows the settings you can store.

Register your favorite settings for use in particular situations. I have one for sports, one for portraits, and another for landscapes. If you switch to C1, C2, or C3 and forget what settings you've made for that slot, just press the INFO. button to view the current settings. Keep in mind that My Menu settings (described later in this chapter) are not stored individually. You can have only one roster of My Menu entries available for all of the Mode Dial's positions.

This menu choice has only two options: Register (which stores your current settings in your choice of C1, C2, or C3) and Clear settings (which erases the settings in C1, C2, or C3). Note that you must use this menu entry to clear your settings; when using C1, C2, or C3, the Clear settings option in the Set-up 3 menu is disabled. The Clear all Custom Func. (C.Fn.) option in the Custom Functions menu is disabled as well.

Table 8.1 Stored Camera User Settings

Shooting Settings	Menu Settings
Shooting mode	Shooting 1: Image quality; Red-eye; Beep; Release shutter without card; Review time; Peripheral illumination correction; Flash control settings.
ISO sensitivity	Shooting 2: Exposure compensation/AEB; Auto Lighting Optimizer; White balance settings; Color space; Picture Style.
Autofocus mode	Shooting 3: One-touch RAW+JPEG.
Autofocus point	Shooting 4: Live View settings; AF mode; Grid display; Exposure simulation; Silent shooting; Metering timer.
Metering mode	Playback 2: Highlight alert; AF point display; Histogram; Slide show; Image jump.
Drive mode	Set-up 1: Auto power off; Auto rotate; File numbering.
Exposure compensation value	Set-up 2: LCD brightness; Sensor cleaning; VF grid display.
Flash exposure compensation value	Set-up 3: INFO. button display options. Custom Functions: All C.Fn. settings.

To perform either of these tasks, just follow these steps:

1. **Make your settings.** Set the EOS 7D to an exposure mode other than Full Auto or Creative Auto.

2. **Access Camera user settings.** Navigate to the Camera user setting option in Set-up 3 menu, and press SET.

3. **Choose function.** Rotate the Quick Control Dial to choose Register if you want to store your 7D's current settings in C1, C2, or C3; or select Clear settings if you want to erase the settings stored in either location. Press SET to access the settings screen for your choice.

4. **Store/Clear settings.** The individual screens for storing/clearing are virtually identical (see Figure 8.13). Use the QCD to highlight Mode dial: C1, Mode dial: C2, or Mode dial: C3, and press SET to store or clear the settings for that position. (You'll be given a choice to proceed or cancel first.)

5. **Exit.** When you confirm, you'll be returned to the Setting 3 menu. Press the MENU button or tap the shutter release button to exit the menu system entirely.

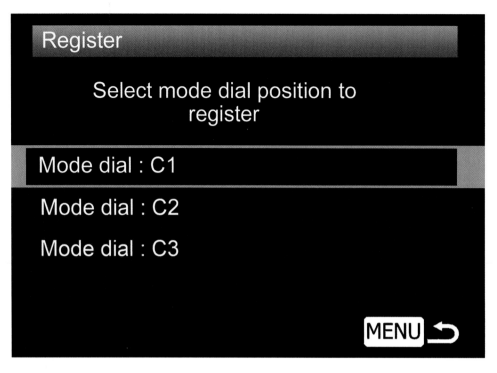

Figure 8.13
Register your current settings in Camera user 1 or Camera user 2 on the Mode Dial.

Copyright Settings

You can embed your name (as "author" or *auteur* of the image) and copyright information in the Exif (Exchangeable Image File format) data appended to each photo that you take. When you choose this menu entry (see Figure 8.14), you have four options:

- **Display copyright info.** Shows the current author and copyright data.

- **Enter author's name.** Produces a text entry screen like the one shown in Figure 8.15. See "Entering Text" for instructions on how to type in text for this screen and the Copyright details screen.

- **Enter copyright details.** Produces the same text entry screen, allowing you to enter copyright details. Oddly enough, no copyright symbol is available (although the @ sign is provided so you can type in your e-mail address!). Just use the parentheses and a lowercase c: (c).

- **Delete copyright information.** Removes the current copyright information (both author and copyright data). Once you delete the data, or if you haven't entered it yet, this option and the Display copyright info. option are grayed out and unavailable.

Figure 8.14
Access text entry screens for entering the name of the photographer and copyright details here.

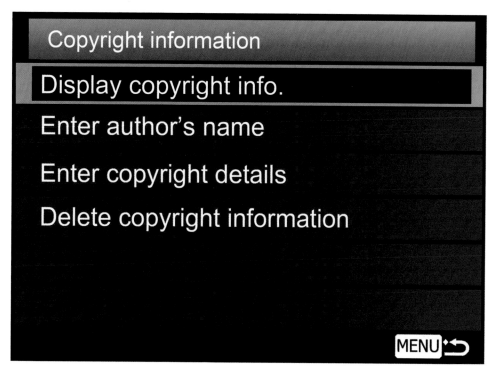

Figure 8.15
Select the alphanumeric characters for your text entry.

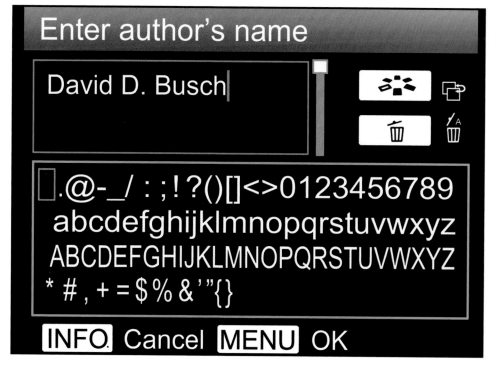

Entering Text

Entering text into the Author's name or Copyright details screens is done in the same way, using a screen like the one shown in Figure 8.15. Just use these instructions:

- **Choose areas.** Either the text area (at top left) or available characters area (bottom half of the screen) will be highlighted with a blue outline. Switch between them by pressing the Picture Styles button located at the left of the back-panel LCD.

- **Scroll among text.** When the text area is highlighted, you can scroll among the text using the Quick Control Dial or multi-controller. Up to 63 alphanumeric characters can be entered/displayed. A scroll bar to the right of the text area shows the position of the gold-colored cursor within the text that's already been entered.

- **Enter characters.** When the available characters list is highlighted, use the QCD or multi-controller to move among the alphanumeric characters shown. Press the SET button or the multi-controller to enter that character at the cursor position in the text area above. You can delete the current character by pressing the Delete/Trash button.

- **Finish/Cancel.** When finished entering text, press the MENU button to confirm your choice, or press the INFO. button to cancel and return to the Copyright information screen.

Clear All Camera Settings

This menu choice resets all the settings to their default values. Regardless of how you've set up your EOS 7D, it will be adjusted for One-Shot AF mode, automatic AF point selection, evaluative metering, JPEG Fine Large image quality, automatic ISO, sRGB color mode, automatic white balance, and Standard Picture Style. Any changes you've made to exposure compensation, flash exposure compensation, and white balance will be canceled, and any bracketing for exposure or white balance nullified. Custom white balances and Dust Delete Data will be erased.

However, Custom Functions and Camera user settings will *not* be cleared. If you want to cancel those, as well, you'll need to use the Camera user setting option (described previously) and the Custom Functions clearing option, which I'll describe shortly. Table 8.2 shows the settings defaults after using this menu option.

Firmware Version

You can see the current firmware release in use in the menu listing. If you want to update to a new firmware version, insert a memory card containing the binary file, and press the SET button to begin the process. You can read more about firmware updates in Chapter 13.

Table 8.2 Camera Setting Defaults

Shooting Settings	Default Value
AF mode	One-Shot AF
AF area selection mode	Auto selection 19-point AF
Metering mode	Evaluative
ISO speed	Auto
Drive mode	Single shooting
Exposure compensation/AEB	Canceled
Flash exposure compensation	0
Custom Functions	Unchanged

Camera Settings	Default Value
VF grid display	Disable
Auto power off	1 minute
Beep	On
Release shutter without card	Enable
Review time	2 seconds
Highlight alert	Disable
AF point display	Disable
Histogram	Brightness
Image jump with Main Dial	10 images
Auto rotate	On/Camera/Display
LCD brightness	Auto:Standard
Date/Time	Unchanged
Language	Unchanged
Video system	Unchanged
Camera user settings	Unchanged
Copyright information	Unchanged
My Menu settings	Unchanged

Image-Recording Settings	Default Value
Quality	JPEG Large/Fine
One-touch RAW+JPEG	RAW, JPEG Large/Fine
Picture Style	Standard
Auto Lighting Optimizer	Standard
Peripheral illumination correction	Enable/correction data preserved
Color space	sRGB
White balance	Auto
White balance correction	Cancelled
WB-BKT	Cancelled
File numbering	Continuous
Auto cleaning	Enable
Dust Delete Data	Erased

Live View Settings	Default
Live view shooting	Enable
AF mode	Live mode
Grid display	Off
Exposure simulation	Enable
Silent shooting	Mode 1
Metering timer	16 seconds

Movie Settings	Default
AF mode	Live mode
Grid display	Off
Movie-recording size	1920 × 1080, 30fps
Sound recording	On
Silent shooting	Mode 1
Metering timer	16 sec.

Custom Functions I/II/III/IV

Custom Functions let you customize the behavior of your camera in a variety of different ways, ranging from whether or not the flash fires automatically to the function carried out when the SET button is pressed. If you don't like the default way the camera carries out a particular task, you just may be able to do something about it. You can find the Custom Functions in their own menu, color-coded orange.

Unlike Canon's entry-level cameras, which crowd all the Custom Functions onto a single screen, recent advanced Canon models like the EOS 7D have allocated them onto four separate screens with multiple options each, plus the main screen with its Clear all Custom Func. entry. There are 27 C.Fn entries in all, which can be set when using P, Tv, Av, and M modes.

Unfortunately, the entries are still somewhat cryptic. Within a given Custom Function menu, you can tell at a glance that the numeral 1 underneath Setting 02 meant…uh, that Setting 02, whatever it was, was adjusted to something other than its default value (because 0s always represent the defaults). It's hard enough to figure out what a setting means by examining a row of numbers, and even more difficult to find the setting you want to change quickly. The good news is that when a particular Custom Function is highlighted within its menu, the purpose of that function is shown at the top of the screen. You can scroll quickly through the options in any particular menu to find the one you want.

As I noted, Canon has made adjusting these options slightly less unwieldy by dividing them into submenus that, at least, give you a fighting chance of finding the Custom Function you want by organizing them by type of feature. The four categories, shown in Figure 8.16, are Exposure, Image, Autofocus/Drive, Operation/Others. The menu also has an option for clearing all the Custom Functions and returning them to their default values. I'm going to explain each of the categories of Custom Functions separately, but first you need your introduction into the mysteries of Canon's method of setting them.

Each of the Custom Functions is set in exactly the same way, except for C.Fn III-06 and IV-01, so I'm not going to bog you down with a bunch of illustrations showing how to make this setting or that. One quick run-through using Figure 8.17 should be enough. Here are the key parts of the Custom Function screen:

- **Custom Function category.** At the top of the Settings screen is a label that tells you which category that screen represents.
- **Current Function name.** Use the Quick Control Dial to select the function you want to adjust. The name of the function currently selected appears at the top of the screen, and its number is marked with an overscore in the row of numbers at the bottom of the screen. You don't need to memorize the function numbers.

Figure 8.16
The 27 Custom Functions are divided into submenus in four categories.

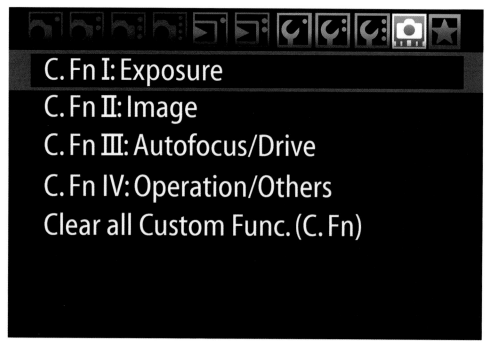

Figure 8.17
Each C.Fn screen has multiple settings, represented by the numbers at the bottom of the screen.

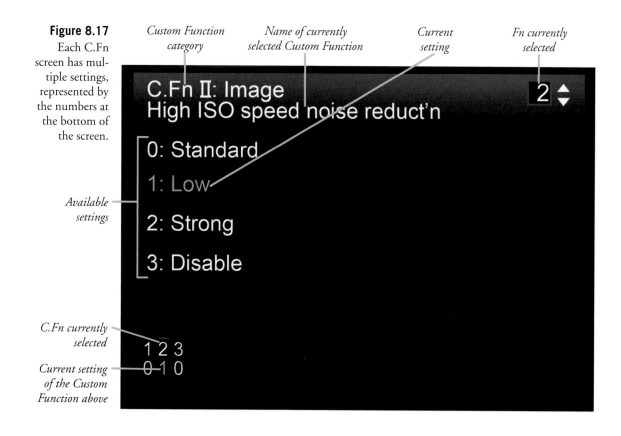

Custom Function category

Name of currently selected Custom Function

Current setting

Fn currently selected

Available settings

C.Fn currently selected

Current setting of the Custom Function above

- **Function number.** The function number appears in two places. In the upper-right corner, you'll find a box with the current function clearly designated. In the lower half of the screen are two lines of numbers, from 1 to 13 (or fewer). The currently selected function will have an orange superscore above it.

- **Available settings.** Within the dark gray blocks appear numbered setting options. The current setting is highlighted in blue. Press the SET button, rotate the Quick Control Dial to highlight the setting option you want, then press the SET button to select it, and finally press the MENU button twice to back out of the Custom Functions menus. (Only C.Fn IV-04 has more than five options available, and a scroll bar appears at the right, and you can use the Quick Control Dial to scroll down to the hidden option.)

- **Current setting.** Underneath each Custom Function is a number from 0 to 6 that represents the current setting for that function.

- **Option selection.** When a function is selected, the currently selected option appears in a highlighted box. As you scroll up and down the option list, the setting in the box changes to indicate an alternate value.

In the listings that follow, I'm going to depart from the sometimes-cryptic labels Canon assigns to each Custom Function in the menu, and instead categorize them by what they really do. The actual label will be listed immediately underneath. I'm also going to provide you with a great deal more information on each option and what it means to your photography. If the function is a simple one, I'll explain the options in detail in this section. For more complex functions, such as autofocus options (covered in Chapter 5), I'll refer you back to the chapter devoted to that feature, and list only a brief description of the options themselves.

Custom Function I (C.Fn I): Exposure

This is the Custom Function category you can use to set the increments for exposure and ISO, define bracketing parameters, and other settings.

C.Fn I-01: Size of Exposure Adjustments

Exposure level increments. This setting tells the EOS 7D the size of the "jumps" it should use when making exposure adjustments—either one-third or one-half stop. The increment you specify here applies to f/stops, shutter speeds, EV changes, and autoexposure bracketing.

- **0: 1/3 stop.** Choose this setting when you want the finest increments between shutter speeds and/or f/stops. For example, the 7D will use shutter speeds such as 1/60th, 1/80th, 1/100th, and 1/125th second, and f/stops such as f/5.6, f/6.3, f/7.1, and f/8, giving you (and the autoexposure system) maximum control.

- **1: 1/2 stop.** Use this setting when you want larger and more noticeable changes between increments. The 7D will apply shutter speeds such as 1/60th, 1/125th, 1/250th, and 1/500th second, and f/stops including f/5.6, f/6.7, f/8, f/9.5, and f/11. These coarser adjustments are useful when you want more dramatic changes between different exposures (as when shooting for HDR), or if you make frequent changes and find that half-stop increments can be made more quickly.

C.Fn I-02: Size of ISO Sensitivity Adjustments

ISO speed setting increments. This setting determines the size of the "jumps" it should use when making ISO adjustments—either one-third or one full stop.

- **0: 1/3 stop.** Choose this setting when you want the finest increments between ISO settings. That's useful if you frequently use ISO settings to fine-tune exposure, or need just a small "boost" in sensitivity. For example, perhaps you want to shoot an action shot at 1/500th of a second (to stop action) and f/4 (because that's the maximum aperture of your lens). You find that your image is just a bit too dark. Rather than change the shutter speed or aperture, you can dial in an extra 1/3 or 2/3 stop of sensitivity. (The amount of visual noise doesn't change much with such small modifications.) At the one-third stop setting, typical ISO values would be 100, 125, 160, 200, and so forth.

- **1: 1 stop.** This setting is useful when you just want to bump the ISO sensitivity up or down, and want to do it quickly. Switch to the one-stop setting, and typical ISO values would be 100, 200, 400, 800, and so forth. The larger increment can help you leap from one ISO setting to one that's twice (or half) as sensitive with one click.

C.Fn I-03: Whether ISO 12,800 Is Available or Disabled

ISO expansion. Ordinarily, only ISO settings from 100 to 6400 are available (ISO 200-6400 if Highlight tone priority [C.Fn II-3] is enabled). The ISO Expansion function is disabled by default to prevent you from unintentionally using ISO settings higher than ISO 6400. If you want to use the H (ISO 12,800) setting, it must be activated using this Custom Function. I've found the noise produced at the ISO 12,800 setting on my EOS 7D to be quite acceptable under certain situations. That's particularly so with images of subjects that have a texture of their own that tends to hide or mask the noise. Figure 8.18 is an example of this type of shot. It was taken indoors at a jellyfish exhibit, with the back illumination so dim and ethereal that I needed a high ISO 12,800 setting with this Custom Function enabled to provide shutter speed fast enough to freeze the pulsating motion of the creatures. Although there is a fair amount of noise in the image, the multicolored speckles are not objectionable. (That's not a black-and-white shot; those are ghostly-white monochrome jellyfish!)

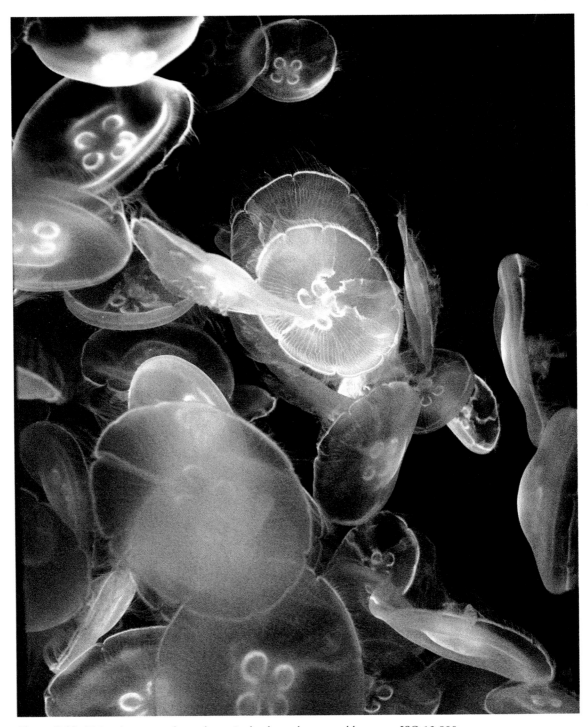

Figure 8.18 This enlargement shows that noise levels can be acceptable even at ISO 12,800.

> **CAUTION**
>
> Be aware that if you've activated Highlight tone priority (described later), the H setting (and ISO values less than ISO 200) will not be available even if you have enabled ISO expansion.

- **0: Off.** The H (ISO 12,800) setting is locked out and not available when using the ISO button or menu options.
- **1: On.** The H setting (equivalent to ISO 12,800) can be selected.

C.Fn I-04: Whether Bracketing Is Cancelled Automatically

Bracketing auto cancel. You can set the EOS 7D so that AEB (Auto Exposure Bracketing) and WB-BKT (White Balance Bracketing) are turned off automatically, or whether they remain in effect until you manually disable them. I know a photographer who brackets *everything*, and prefers that her camera keep her bracketing settings active all the time. It's more efficient not to have to remember to activate bracketing each time she uses the camera.

On the other hand there are photographers who bracket frequently, forget to turn the feature off, and then are annoyed when the camera acts "funny," producing varying exposures the next day—because bracketing is still in effect. For hurried or forgetful photographers of that ilk (such as me!) having the 7D turn off bracketing at the end of a session is the best option. The two available settings are as follows:

- **0: On.** When Auto cancel is activated (the default), AEB (Auto Exposure Bracketing) and WB-BKT (White Balance Bracketing) are cancelled when you turn the 7D off, change lenses, or use the flash.
- **1: Off.** When Auto cancel is deactivated, bracketing remains in effect until you manually turn it off or use the flash. When Auto cancel is switched off, the AEB and WB-BKT settings will be kept even when the power switch is turned to the Off position. The flash still cancels autoexposure bracketing, but your settings are retained.

C.Fn I-05: Order in Which Bracketing Changes Are Applied

Bracketing sequence. You can define the sequence in which AEB and WB-BKT series are exposed. Some photographers, particularly those from the film era, are accustomed to using manual bracketing. They may start with the metered exposure, then shift the shutter speed to one speed increment slower, then click twice in the opposite direction and shoot a third image at one increment faster than the "ideal" exposure. The same procedure might be used to fire off a manual bracket sequence by varying the aperture: one at the metered exposure, one a stop less, a third at a stop more. (At least, that's how I used to do it.)

Of course, in the electronic age, it's more efficient to let the camera change the settings, and shoot the trio of images starting with "under" exposure, metered exposure, and "over" exposure. This Custom Function lets you choose either exposure pattern, as you prefer.

It also controls the order in which white balance bracketing is done. For example, if your bias preference is set to Blue/Amber, the white balance sequence when option 0 is selected will be: current WB, more blue, more amber. If your bias preference is set to magenta/green, then the sequence for option 0 will be: current WB, more magenta, more green. The options are

- **0:** Exposure sequence is metered exposure, decreased exposure, increased exposure (0, –, +). White balance sequence is current standard WB, more blue/more magenta (depending on how your bias is set), more amber/more green (ditto).

- **1:** The sequence is decreased exposure, metered exposure, increased exposure (–, 0, +). White balance sequence is more blue/more magenta, current standard WB, more amber/more green.

C.Fn I-06: Overriding Your Preference in Aperture-Priority or Shutter-Priority Modes

Safety shift. Ordinarily, both aperture-priority and shutter-priority modes work fine, because you'll select an f/stop or shutter speed that allows the 7D to produce a correct exposure using the other type of setting (shutter speed for Av; aperture for Tv). However, when lighting conditions change, it may not be possible to select an appropriate setting with the available exposure options, and the camera will be unable to take a picture at all.

For example, you might be at a concert shooting the performers and, to increase your chances of getting a sharp image, you've selected Tv mode and a shutter speed of 1/250th second. Under bright lights and with an appropriate ISO setting, the 7D might select f/5.6, f/4, or even f/2.8. Then, in a dramatic moment, the stage lights are dimmed significantly. An exposure of 1/250th second at f/2 is called for, but your lens has an f/2.8 maximum aperture. If you've used this Custom Function to allow the 7D to override your selection, the camera will automatically switch to 1/125th second to allow the picture to be taken at f/2.8.

Safety shift will make similar adjustments if your scene suddenly becomes too bright; although, in practice, you'll find that the override will be needed most often when using Tv mode. It's easier to "run out of" f/stops, which generally range no smaller than f/22 or f/32, than to deplete the available supply of shutter speeds, which can be as brief as 1/8,000th second. For example, if you're shooting at ISO 400 in Tv mode at 1/1,000th second, an extra-bright beach scene could easily call for an f/stop smaller than f/22, causing overexposure. However, Safety shift would bump your shutter speed up to 1/2,000th second with no problem.

On the other hand, if you were shooting under the same illumination in Av mode with the preferred aperture set to f/16, the EOS 7D could use 1/1,000th, 1/2,000th, 1/4,000th, or 1/8,000th second shutter speeds to retain that f/16 aperture under conditions that are 2X, 4X, 8X, or 16X as bright as normal daylight. No Safety shift would be needed, even if the ISO were (for some unknown reason) set much higher than the ISO 400 used in this example.

- **0: Disable.** Turn off Safety shift. Your specified shutter speed or f/stop remains locked in, even if conditions are too bright or too dim for an appropriate exposure.

- **1: Enable.** Safety shift is activated. The 7D will adjust the preferred shutter speed or f/stop to allow a correct exposure.

C.Fn I-07: Flash Synchronization Speed when Using Aperture-Priority

Flash sync. speed in Av mode. You'll find this setting useful when using flash. When you're set to aperture-priority mode, you select a fixed f/stop and the EOS 7D chooses an appropriate shutter speed. That works fine when you're shooting by available light. However, when you're using flash, the flash itself provides virtually all of the illumination that makes the main exposure, and the shutter speed determines how much, if any, of the ambient light contributes to a second, non-flash exposure. Indeed, if the camera or subject is moving, you can end up with two distinct exposures in the same frame: the sharply defined flash exposure, and a second, blurry "ghost" picture created by the ambient light.

If you *don't* want that second exposure, you should use the highest shutter speed that will synchronize with your flash (that's 1/250th second with the EOS 7D). If you do want the ambient light to contribute to the exposure (say, to allow the background to register in night shots, or to use the ghost image as a special effect), use a slower shutter speed. For brighter backgrounds, you'll need to put the camera on a tripod or other support to avoid the blurry ghosts.

- **0: Auto.** The 7D will vary the shutter speed in Av mode, allowing ambient light to partially illuminate the scene in combination with the flash exposure, as at right in Figure 8.19.

- **1: 1/250-1/60 sec. auto.** In this mode, the 7D varies the shutter speed (as in Auto mode), but won't use a speed slower than 1/60th second, helping to minimize blur caused by camera shake. The background may be dark if the ambient light isn't strong enough to supplement the flash exposure.

- **2: 1/250 sec. (fixed).** The camera always uses 1/250th second as its shutter speed in Av mode, reducing the effect of ambient light and, probably, rendering the background dark.

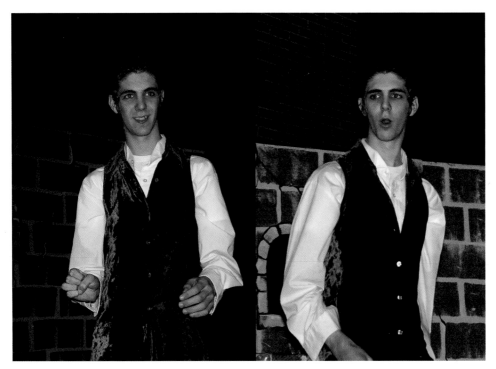

Figure 8.19
At left, a 1/250th second shutter speed eliminated ambient light so only the flash illuminated the scene; at right, a 1/60th second shutter speed let the ambient light supplement the electronic flash.

Custom Function II (C.Fn II): Image

There are only three settings in the C.Fn II: Image section; two for controlling noise reduction features, and one for enabling or disabling Highlight tone priority.

C.Fn II-01: Reducing Noise Effects at Shutter Speeds of One Second or Longer

Long exposure noise reduction. Visual noise is that awful graininess that shows up as multicolored specks in images, and this setting helps you manage it. In some ways, noise is like the excessive grain found in some high-speed photographic films. However, while photographic grain is sometimes used as a special effect, it's rarely desirable in a digital photograph.

The visual noise-producing process is something like listening to a CD in your car, and then rolling down all the windows. You're adding sonic noise to the audio signal, and while increasing the CD player's volume may help a bit, you're still contending with an unfavorable signal to noise ratio that probably mutes tones (especially higher treble notes) that you really want to hear.

The same thing happens when the analog signal is amplified: You're increasing the image information in the signal, but boosting the background fuzziness at the same time. Tune in a very faint or distant AM radio station on your car stereo. Then turn up the volume. After a certain point, turning up the volume further no longer helps you hear better. There's a similar point of diminishing returns for digital sensor ISO increases and signal amplification as well.

These processes create several different kinds of noise. Noise can be produced from high ISO settings. As the captured information is amplified to produce higher ISO sensitivities, some random noise in the signal is amplified along with the photon information. Increasing the ISO setting of your camera raises the threshold of sensitivity so that fewer and fewer photons are needed to register as an exposed pixel. Yet, that also increases the chances of one of those phantom photons being counted among the real-life light particles, too.

Fortunately, the EOS 7D's sensor and its digital processing chip are optimized to produce the low noise levels, so ratings as high as ISO 1600 can be used routinely (although there will be some noise, of course), and even ISO 3200 can generate good results.

A second way noise is created is through longer exposures. Extended exposure times allow more photons to reach the sensor, but increase the likelihood that some photosites will react randomly even though not struck by a particle of light. Moreover, as the sensor remains switched on for the longer exposure, it heats, and this heat can be mistakenly recorded as if it were a barrage of photons. This Custom Function can be used to tailor the amount of noise cancelling performed by the digital signal processor.

- **0: Off.** Disables long exposure noise reduction. Use this setting when you want the maximum amount of detail present in your photograph, even though higher noise levels will result. This setting also eliminates the extra time needed to take a picture caused by the noise reduction process. If you plan to use only lower ISO settings (thereby reducing the noise caused by ISO amplification), the noise levels produced by longer exposures may be acceptable. For example, you might be shooting waves crashing on the shore at ISO 100 with the camera mounted on a tripod, using a neutral-density filter and long exposure to cause the water to blur, as shown in Figure 8.20. To maximize detail in the non-moving portions of your photos, you can switch off long exposure noise reduction.

- **1: Auto.** The EOS 7D examines your photo taken with an exposure of one second or longer, and if long exposure noise is detected, a second, blank exposure is made and compared to the first image. Noise found in the "dark frame" image is subtracted from your original picture, and only the noise-corrected image is saved to your memory card. Because the noise-reduction process effectively doubles the time required to take a picture, this is a good setting to use when you want to avoid this delay when possible, but still have noise reduction applied when appropriate.

- **2: On.** When this setting is activated, the 7D applies dark frame subtraction to all exposures longer than 1 second. You might want to use this option when you're working with high ISO settings (which will already have noise boosted a bit) and want to make sure that any additional noise from long exposures is eliminated, too. Noise reduction will be applied to some exposures that would not have caused it to kick in using the Auto setting.

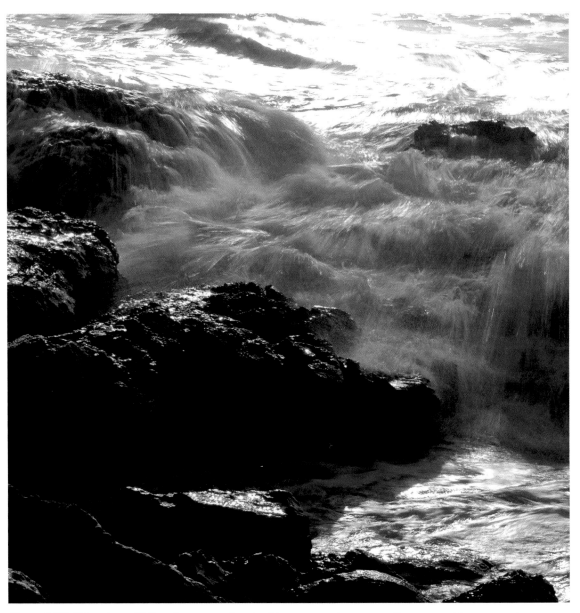

Figure 8.20 When lower ISO settings are used, as in this two-second exposure of a wave crashing on a rocky Mediterranean shore, long exposure noise reduction might not be needed.

C.Fn II-02: Eliminating Noise Caused by Higher ISO Sensitivities

High ISO speed noise reduction. This setting applies noise reduction that is especially useful for pictures taken at high ISO sensitivity settings. For the EOS 7D, Canon has supplied four different options (compared with simply On and Off with some earlier models).

The default is 0 (Standard), but you can specify additional values of 1 to 2 for increasingly potent noise reduction measures. At lower ISO values, noise reduction improves the appearance of shadow areas without affecting highlights; at higher ISO settings, noise reduction is applied to the entire photo. Note that when the Strong option is selected, the maximum number of continuous shots that can be taken will decrease significantly, because of the additional processing time for the images.

- **0: Standard.** Activates minimal ISO noise reduction. At lower ISO values, noise reduction is applied primarily to shadow areas; at higher ISO settings, noise reduction affects the entire image.

- **1: Low.** Uses more noticeable ISO noise reduction, which may mask some detail in the image.

- **2: Strong.** Applies more aggressive ISO noise reduction, which minimizes graininess at the cost of noticeable image detail.

- **3: Disable.** No additional noise reduction will be applied.

C.Fn II-03: Improving Detail in Highlights

Highlight tone priority. This setting concentrates the available tones in an image from the middle grays up to the brightest highlights, in effect expanding the dynamic range of the image at the expense of shadow detail. You'd want to activate this option when shooting subjects in which there is lots of important detail in the highlights, and less detail in shadow areas. Highlight tones will be preserved, while shadows will be allowed to go dark more readily. Bright beach or snow scenes, especially those with few shadows (think high noon, when the shadows are smaller) can benefit from using Highlight tone priority.

- **0: Disable.** The EOS 7D's normal dynamic range is applied.

- **1: Enable.** Highlight areas are given expanded tonal values, while the tones available for shadow areas are reduced. The ISO 3200 (H) setting is disabled, even if ISO Expansion has been activated.

Custom Function III (C.Fn III): Autofocus/Drive

Here you'll find the important options for controlling how the Canon EOS 7D's autofocus system operates, along with settings for Live View and mirror lockup.

C.Fn III-01: AI Servo Tracking Sensitivity

AI Servo tracking sensitivity. This setting controls how the 7D's autofocus system in AI Servo AF (also known as continuous autofocus) handles the sudden intrusion of new subjects that interject themselves in the frame temporarily. Perhaps you're shooting an architectural photo from across the street and a car passes in front of the camera. Or, at a football game, a referee dashes past just as a receiver is about to make a catch. This setting lets you specify how quickly the EOS 7D reacts to these transient interruptions that would cause relatively large changes in focus before refocusing on the "new" subject matter. You can specify a long delay, so that the interloper is ignored, a shorter delay, or turn lock-on off completely so that the 7D immediately refocuses when a new subject moves into the frame.

This is one of the few Custom Functions that doesn't use a strictly numeric option list. Instead, you're shown a scale with Slow at one end and Fast at the other, with intermediate settings between them. (See Figure 8.21.) You can choose any of the five points on the scale. The options are

- **Slow.** The longest delay causes the 7D to ignore the intervening subject matter for a significant period of time. Use this setting when shooting subjects, such as sports, in which focus interruptions are likely to be frequent and significant. You can set either Slow or the setting between Slow and the "normal" (zero) position.

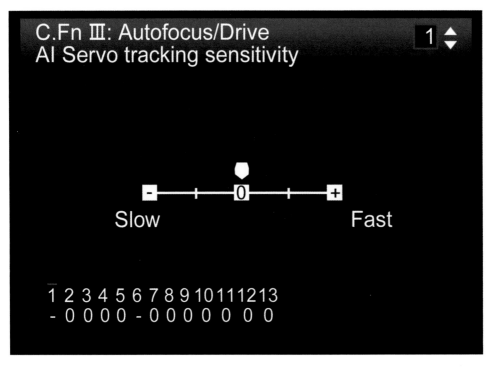

Figure 8.21
Choose the tracking sensitivity of the 7D when using AI Servo mode.

- **Normal.** This default (center of the scale) setting provides an intermediate delay before the camera refocuses on the new subject. It's usually the best choice when shooting sports in continuous shooting mode, as the long delay can throw off autofocus accuracy at higher fps settings.

- **Fast.** Choose this setting to tell the 7D to wait only a moment before refocusing. Very high frame rates may work better when you allow refocusing to take place rapidly, without a lock-on delay. You can set either the Fast or the mark between normal and Fast.

C.Fn III-02: How the Autofocus System Prioritizes Focus/Shutter Release in Continuous Shooting

AI Servo 1st/2nd image priority. This menu entry allows you to specify what takes precedence when you press the shutter release all the way down to take a picture during continuous shooting in AI Servo (continuous autofocus) mode: either focus (called *focus priority*) or the release button (called *release priority*). It makes it possible to give different priorities to the first picture exposed in a continuous series and the second and additional photos in a series.

In an ideal world, autofocus would operate quickly enough that when you press the shutter the camera would automatically lock in focus on the correct subject. The 7D can usually do that when you're using One-Shot autofocus, because focus is fixed at the moment you press the shutter halfway, and freezes at that point until you let go of the shutter button, or press the rest of the way down to take the picture. But when you've selected AI Servo AF, the camera attempts to focus once when the shutter release is pressed halfway, then *continue refocusing* while the button is held down, even if your subject moves. In that mode, when (or if) you finally press the shutter all the way to take a picture, one of two things can happen: a.) The subject is in focus at that instant, and the picture can be taken without incident, or b.) the camera has not quite finished focusing. In the latter case, should the 7D go ahead and take the picture, or should it delay a few fractions of a second until focus is actually achieved?

The answer isn't as easy as you think. For photojournalism, action shots, and other situations, getting *any* picture at the right instant is more important than getting a technically perfect picture. In such cases, you'd want to use *release priority*. When the button is pressed, the picture is taken. If you'd rather get the sharpest picture possible (under the circumstances) you might want to opt for *focus priority*, accepting a slight delay to give the 7D time to focus precisely.

This Custom Function lets you specify how the camera handles a variety of different situations when using AI Servo focus mode and continuous shooting. Your four choices follow:

- **0: AF priority/Tracking priority.** With this setting, the first shot is taken with focus priority; there may be a slight delay before the shutter triggers, to allow the camera to precisely focus the subject. The second and subsequent shots of the continuous sequence are also given focus priority, which may slow down the continuous shooting frame per second rate, to allow the camera to track moving subjects for the entire series. Use this setting to make sure that as many images in your series as possible are in focus.

- **1: AF priority/Drive speed priority.** The first shot is taken using focus priority, ensuring that the first image in the series is precisely focused. The second and subsequent shots will be taken at the selected fps rate, using release priority. Fast-moving subjects in the images after the first one may (or may not) be slightly out of focus if the camera is not able to track the focus changes quickly during the continuous shooting. (Remember, the 7D can fire off 8 frames per second.) Use this setting to ensure that your first image will be sharply focused, but you're willing to take your chances with the other shots in the series. They may all be within acceptable focus—but, again, they may not.

- **2: Release/Drive speed priority.** With this setting, the shutter release is given priority over optimum focus for all images in the series. Your pictures will be taken at the camera's selected frame rate with no delay waiting for sharpest focus. Use this setting when you can't predict when in a sequence your "money" shot will be captured and you're willing to accept less than perfect focus to get the shot.

- **3: Release/Tracking priority.** In this mode, the first shot is given shutter release priority (it's taken immediately), while the second and subsequent images in the series are given focus priority, allowing the camera to track a moving subject more accurately. Use this setting to ensure that you'll get *some* kind of shot at the instant you press the shutter all the way, while allowing a slightly slower continuous frame rate and optimum focusing for the other images in the series.

C.Fn III-03: Whether the Camera Switches to a Closer Subject That Appears in AI Servo AF Mode

AI Servo tracking sensitivity. This setting works hand-in-hand with C.Fn III-01 when using AF Servo (continuous autofocus) mode. The latter Custom Function controls how quickly the camera switches to an intervening subject that enters the frame (Slow, Fast, or in-between). This one determines whether the camera makes the switch at all. If a subject—such as that referee mentioned earlier—crosses in front of your main subject, you can tell the 7D to ignore it entirely. Or, if you think the new subject might be something of interest, you can tell the camera to switch to that new point. Your options are

- **0: Main focus point priority.** With this setting, if a closer subject appears in the frame, the 7D will switch the active AF point to that subject and continue tracking it. Use this setting if you think the closest subject in your frame will be the one you want to follow. In many sports, if you position yourself appropriately, the closest subject will often be the person with the ball and, absent any referees, the person you want to lock focus on. C.Fn. III-01 can be set to assign a time interval before the focus point switch takes place.

- **1: Continuous AF track priority.** In this mode, the 7D will ignore close subjects and continue to track the original subject. Use this setting when you feel you'll be satisfied with the focus point selection you or the camera makes and are not interested in switching to a closer subject that may intervene. For example, if you're shooting scenery from a moving vehicle, you'd want to ignore trees, telephone poles, and other objects that pass in front of the lens as you're taking pictures.

C.Fn III-04: How the Autofocus System Behaves when Autofocus Fails

Lens drive when AF impossible. This setting controls how the 7D's autofocus system handles hard-to-autofocus (or impossible-to-autofocus) situations. Canon's AF system operates on differences in contrast using a phase detection system described in more detail in Chapter 5. When a subject displays the greatest amount of contrast, the camera's rangefinder-like system can "line up" details in the image, and the subject is deemed to be in sharp focus. When a scene has little inherent contrast (say, a blank wall or the sky) or if there isn't enough illumination to allow determining contrast accurately (in low light levels, or with lenses having maximum apertures of less than f/5.6), a lens may be unable to achieve autofocus. Very long telephoto lenses suffer from this syndrome because their depth-of-field is so shallow that the correct point of focus may zip past during the AF process before the AF system has a chance to register it.

Use this setting to tell the 7D either to keep trying to focus if AF seems to be impossible or to stop seeking focus.

- **0: Focus search on.** The 7D will keep trying to focus, even if the effort causes the lens to become grossly out of focus. Use this default setting if you'd prefer that the lens keep trying. Sometimes you can point the lens at an object with sufficient contrast at approximately the same distance to let the AF system lock on, then reframe your original subject with the hope that accurate focus will now be achieved.

- **1: Focus search off.** When this option is selected, the camera will stop trying to focus uselessly, allowing you to attempt to manually bring the subject into focus. Very long telephoto lenses often get "lost" when trying to focus, and this setting can keep them from "wandering off" into non-focusland, so to speak.

C.Fn III-05: Fine-tuning Your Autofocus Lenses

AF microadjustment. Caution! Use this control, which allows you to tweak the point of focus of individual lenses, with care. Well-intentioned, but inaccurate, adjustments can turn slight focus problems into major ones. I covered this drastic correctional step in detail in Chapter 5. For now, I'll just provide a list of the options. You can read how to use them in the chapter, which also covers other autofocus topics in depth.

- **0: Disable.** No adjustments are made to the focus points of your lenses.

- **1: Adjust all by the same amount.** You can select an amount of adjustment over 20 steps in front of/behind the default point of focus for all your lenses.

- **2: Adjust by lens.** You can specify the adjustment individually for each lens that you feel needs some focus point compensation.

C.Fn III-06: Choose Which AF Area Settings Are Available

Select AF area selection mode. This Custom Function allows you to turn various autofocus zone settings on or off. Three AF area selection modes are available by default, as described in Chapter 5. Those three can still be selected if you choose Disable in this Custom Function.

- **19-point AF.** Of the five choices shown with check boxes next to them in Figure 8.22, this one is at left in the top row. The 7D chooses one or more AF points from the 19 available to use for focusing automatically. It is active during Full Auto and Creative Auto shooting, and can be selected when using other exposure modes. In One-Shot AF mode, the camera focuses on the closest subject and displays the AF point(s) in the viewfinder; in AI Servo AF mode, you manually select the initial point used to start autofocus; the camera selects additional points if the subject moves and focus tracking begins. You'll find a full description of this mode in Chapter 5.

- **Zone AF (Manual select).** You select any of the five zones, and the 7D chooses the AF point(s) in that zone. I showed you how to choose the zone in Chapter 5.

- **Single point AF selectable.** In this mode, you choose which of the 19 AF points are used for automatic focus.

These three AF selection modes are always available when you're using P, Av, Tv, or M exposure modes. You can add one or two additional selection modes using this Custom Function, or disable any of the three that are available by default. Those additional modes are as follows:

- **Spot AF (Manual point selection).** If you have enabled this mode, the active AF point becomes smaller (roughly representing the area shown as autofocus points in the viewfinder), rather than a larger area that is larger than the viewfinder AF point.

Figure 8.22

Single point AF (Manual point selection)   *Spot AF (Manual point selection)*

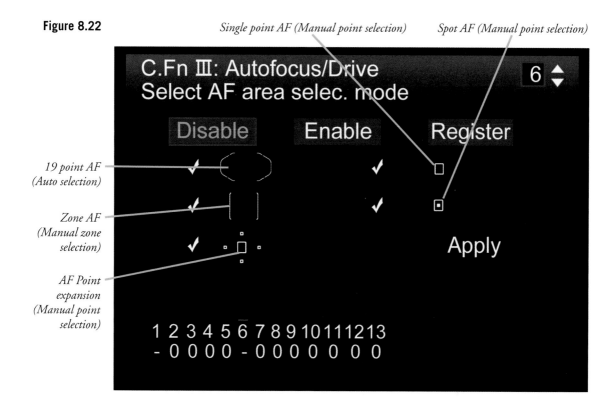

19 point AF (Auto selection)

Zone AF (Manual zone selection)

AF Point expansion (Manual point selection)

Use this mode to focus precisely on a particular point in your image; for that reason, it's not your best choice for fast-moving subjects (which call for AF points that are larger and can track the subject more easily).

■ **AF-point expansion (Manual point selection).** Enable this mode to tell the 7D to use points adjacent to the AF point you manually select, effectively increasing the size of the autofocus area. It's a handy mode for fast-moving subjects, to increase focus-tracking capabilities. I showed you how to use this mode in Chapter 5.

To enable or disable AF specific selection modes, just follow these steps:

1. **Access Custom Function.** Navigate to Custom Function III-06 and press the SET button to activate the screen shown in Figure 8.22.

2. **Choose Register to activate/deactivate modes.** Rotate the Quick Control Dial to Register and press SET. That will give you access to the five check boxes shown in the center of the figure.

3. **Select/Deselect modes to be used.** Use the Quick Control Dial to scroll among the five different AF point selection modes. When a mode you want to activate/deactivate is highlighted, press SET to mark the check box, or to unmark a box that is already checked.

4. **Confirm your selections.** When finished marking/unmarking the AF modes you want to activate/deactivate, rotate the QCD to Apply and press SET. Note: You must always have at least one mode check marked. You can't deactivate all AF point selection modes.

5. **Enable your choices, or use the defaults.** Rotate the QCD and select Disable if you want only the three default AF point selection modes described earlier to be available. (I know this is confusing; disable doesn't deactivate modes, it just limits your choices to the three default modes.) If you choose Enable instead, then *only* the AF point selection modes with check marks will be available. If you use Spot AF and 19-point AF most of the time, you can deactivate the other choices.

6. **Choose a mode while shooting.** When you're ready to take photos, you can cycle among the one to five AF selection modes you've chosen to activate by holding down the AF point selection/Magnify button (on the upper-right-back corner of the camera), while pressing the M-Fn button repeatedly until the choice you want is indicated in the viewfinder.

C.Fn III-07: Whether Manual Focus Point Selection Wraps around Edges of the Frame

Manual AF point selection pattern. This setting is purely a personal preference parameter. When you manually select a focus point, the EOS 7D can be told to stop when the selection reaches the edge of the AF 19-point array—or, it can continue, wrapping around to the opposite edge, like Pac-Man leaving the playing area on one side or top/bottom to re-emerge on the other. (I hope I'm not revealing my age, here.) Your choices are simple; decide which behavior you prefer:

- **0: Stops at AF area edges.** Continuing to attempt to move the focus point stops at the outer edge of the array. This setting has no effect when using 19-point AF auto selection or Zone AF (the 7D selects the actual focus point automatically in both cases, either from the full 19-point array or from the selected zone).

- **1: Continuous.** When you've reached the edge of the focus point array, the display wraps the selection to the opposite side, still moving in the same direction.

C.Fn III-08: Whether the Autofocus Points, Grid, etc. Are Illuminated in the Viewfinder

VF display illumination. The C.Fn-08 superimposed display function can control whether the AF points, grid, and other elements are illuminated in the viewfinder in red under low-light levels. Some people find the glowing red elements distracting and like to disable the function.

- **0: Auto.** One or more focus points and the grid glow in red when ambient light levels are low.

- **1: Enable.** The red highlighting is used regardless of light levels.

- **2: Disable.** The red highlighting is never used.

C.Fn III-09: Display All AF Points During Point Selection/Shooting

Display all AF points. This controls whether all AF points are displayed in the viewfinder when selecting a focus point, or only the active AF points are shown.

- **0: Disable.** All AF points are shown during AF point selection, but when shooting, only the active AF point(s) can be seen. This allows you to monitor which points are being used to determine autofocus.

- **1: Enable.** All AF points are shown during AF point selection and when shooting. Some would rather see what parts of the frame are covered by the AF points (especially when using AF 19-point auto selection) rather than the exact point or points active at the current time.

C.Fn III-10: Focus Display in AI SERVO/MF

Focus Display in AI Servo/MF. This controls whether all AF points are displayed in the viewfinder when shooting, or only the active AF points are shown.

- **0: Enable.** When using AI Servo AF and Zone AF and 19-point auto selection, the highlighted focus point will track the subject. In manual focus, the focus confirmation indicator will illuminate.

- **1: Disable.** No focus confirmation illuminator is shown.

C.Fn III-11: Activation of the Autofocus Assist Lamp

AF-assist beam firing. This setting determines when the AF assist lamp or bursts from an electronic flash are used to emit a pulse of light that helps provide enough contrast for the EOS 7D to focus on a subject.

- **0: Enable.** The AF assist light is emitted by the camera's built-in flash or from a Canon Speedlite whenever light levels are too low for accurate focusing using the ambient light.

- **1: Disable.** The AF assist illumination is disabled. You might want to use this setting when shooting at concerts, weddings, or darkened locations where the light might prove distracting or discourteous.

- **2: Only external flash emits.** The built-in AF assist light is disabled, but if a Canon EX dedicated flash unit is attached to the camera, its AF assist feature will be used when needed. Because the flash unit's AF assist is more powerful, you'll find this option useful when you're using flash and are photographing objects in dim light that are more than a few feet away from the camera (and thus not likely to be illuminated usefully by the EOS 7D's built-in light source). If you've disabled the AF-assist beam *on your external flash*, it will still be disabled even if option 0: Enable or 2: Only external flash emits are active.

- **3: IR AF assist beam only.** Deactivates the use of an external flash's series of small flash bursts as an AF assist light. Only Canon Speedlites that have an infrared AF-assist light (such as the 580EX II) will be used as an autofocus aid when this option is selected. Use this option when you want to avoid the distraction of a visible electronic flash burst used as an AF assist light.

C.Fn III-12: Choose AF Area Selection Mode and Manually-Selected AF Point/Zone for Horizontal and Vertical Shots

Orientation linked AF point. This Custom Function allows you to use the same AF area selection mode and manually selected AF point/zone for vertically and horizontally composed shots—or to select a different mode and point/zone for vertical and horizontal shots. It's a really cool feature I explained in detail in Chapter 5. To recap, your options are

- **0: Same for both vertical/horizontal.** The AF area selection mode and manually selected AF point or Zone (when using Zone AF) that you specify are used for any camera orientation.
- **1: Select different AF points.** You can choose a specific AF area selection mode and AF point/zone for each orientation.

C.Fn III-13: Whether It Is Possible to Lock Up the Viewing Mirror Prior to an Exposure

Mirror lockup. The Mirror lockup function determines whether the reflex viewing mirror will be flipped up out of the way in advance of taking a picture, thereby eliminating any residual blurring effects caused by the minuscule amount of camera shake that can be produced if (as is the case normally) the mirror is automatically flipped up an instant before the actual exposure. When shooting telephoto pictures with a very long lens, or close-up photography at extreme magnifications, even this tiny amount of vibration can have an impact.

You'll want to make this adjustment immediately prior to needing the mirror lockup function, because once it's been enabled, the mirror *always* flips up, and picture taking becomes a two-press operation. That is, you press the shutter release once to lock exposure and focus, and to swing the mirror out of the way. Your viewfinder goes blank (of course, the mirror's blocking it). Press the shutter release a second time to actually take the picture. Because the goal of mirror lockup is to produce the sharpest picture possible, and because of the viewfinder blackout, you can see that the camera should be mounted on a tripod prior to taking the picture, and, to avoid accidentally shaking the camera yourself, using an off-camera shutter release mechanism, such as the Canon Remote Switch RS-80N3 or Timer Remote Controller TC-80N3, is a good idea.

- **0: Disable.** Mirror lockup is not possible.

- **1: Enable.** Mirror lockup is activated and will be used for every shot until disabled.

Canon lists some important warnings and techniques related to using mirror lockup in the EOS 7D manual, and I want to emphasize them here and add a few of my own, even if it means a bit of duplication. Better safe than sorry!

- **Don't use ML for sensor cleaning.** Though locked up, the mirror will flip down again automatically after 30 seconds, which you don't want to happen while you're poking around the sensor with a brush, swab, or air jet. There's a separate menu item—sensor cleaning—for sensor housekeeping. You can find more about this topic in Chapter 13.

- **Avoid long exposure to extra-bright scenes.** The shutter curtain, normally shielded from incoming light by the mirror, is fully exposed to the light being focused on the focal plane by the lens mounted on the 7D. When the mirror is locked up, you certainly don't want to point the camera at the sun, and even beach or snow scenes may be unsafe if the shutter curtain is exposed to their illumination for long periods. (This advice also applies to Live View, of course, because the sensor is similarly exposed while you're previewing the image on the LCD.)

- **ML can't be used in continuous shooting modes.** The EOS 7D will use single shooting mode for mirror lockup exposures, regardless of the sequence mode you've selected.

- **Use self-timer to eliminate second button press.** If you've activated the self-timer, the mirror will flip up when you press down the shutter button all the way, and then the picture will be taken two seconds later. This technique can help reduce camera shake further if you don't have a remote release available and have to use a finger to press the shutter button.

- **Watch for bulb/self-timer interaction.** When using mirror lockup while using bulb exposures and the self-timer, be aware that the click you hear if you release the shutter before the self-timer's countdown is complete is *not* a picture being taken. The actual exposure doesn't begin until the timer has finished its delay, so hold down the release button for the length of time of the self-timer's delay, plus your intended bulb exposure.

Custom Function IV (C.Fn IV): Operation/Others

Within this category of Custom Functions, you'll find four options for adjusting the behavior of controllers and buttons, specifying the focusing screen in use and other features.

C.Fn IV-01: Custom Controls

Custom controls. This setting allows you to assign common functions to various camera buttons and dials, up to and including changing the functions of the Quick Control Dial, Main Dial, and multi-controller. Your choices are shown in Table 8.3.

Which functions are assigned to which controls is strictly a matter of personal preference, and should be thought out carefully. If you own several cameras, or if someone else uses your camera, changing the controls around can cause a great deal of confusion!

Table 8.3 Camera Controls Functions

Button/Control	Default Function/Shooting Mode	Alternate Functions Assignable
Shutter button/half press	Metering and AF start	Metering start/AE lock
AF-ON button	Metering and AF start	AE lock/AF stop/Flash exposure lock/No function
AE lock button	Auto exposure lock	Metering and AF start/AF stop/ Flash exposure lock/No function
DOF preview button	Depth-of-field preview	AF stop/AE lock/One Shot-AI servo toggle/IS start/Switch to registered AF func.
Lens AF stop button	AF stop (only on lenses equipped with this control)	Metering and AF start/AE lock/ One-Shot AI servo toggle/IS start/Switch to registered AF func.
Multi-function button	Flash exposure lock	AE lock/One-touch RAW+JPEG/ Viewfinder electronic level
SET button	No function	Image quality/Picture Style/ Menu display/Image display/ Quick control screen
Main Dial	Shutter speed in Tv/Manual mode Flexible Program in P mode	Aperture set in Av/Manual mode
Quick Control Dial	Aperture set in Av/Manual mode	Shutter speed in Tv/ Manual Mode AF point direct selection
Multi-controller	No function	AF point direct selection

If you want to go ahead and change the functions of your controls, just follow these steps:

1. Navigate to this menu entry and press SET to access the two columns containing the ten icons representing the individual controls described in the table. A miniature camera diagram appears at the left side of the screen with the location of the control you've selected highlighted.

2. Use the Main Dial or Quick Control Dial to highlight the control you want to change.

3. Press the SET button. A screen will appear with the default and alternate settings listed.

4. For some controls and settings, an INFO. icon will appear at the bottom of the screen, indicating you can press the INFO. button to specify related options for that control and setting. For example, if you want to assign Metering and AF start to the AF-ON button (which is its default function), you can press the INFO. button and tell the 7D to use either a manually selected AF point *or* a registered AF point when the AF-ON button is pressed.

5. When you've specified the function for a control, press the SET button to confirm it.

C.Fn IV-02: Reverse Dial Direction when Using Shutter-Priority or Aperture-Priority

Dial direction during Tv/Av. This setting reverses the result when rotating the Quick Control Dial and Main Dial when using Shutter-priority or Aperture-priority (Tv and Av). That is, rotating the Main Dial to the right will decrease the shutter speed rather than increase it; f/stops will become larger rather than smaller. Use this if you find the default rotation scheme in Tv and Av modes are not to your liking. Activating this option also reverses the dial direction in Manual exposure mode. In other shooting modes, only the Main Dial's direction will be reversed.

■ **0: Normal.** The Main Dial and Quick Control Dial change shutter speed and aperture normally.

■ **1: Reverse direction.** The dials adjust shutter speed and aperture in the reverse direction when rotated.

C.Fn IV-03: Activating Data Verification Feature

Add original decision data. The EOS 7D has a special feature that allows determining whether a specific image has been modified using a special Canon Data Verification Kit OSK-E3, which consists of a dedicated SM (secure mobile) card reader-writer and verification software that must be used with a computer to verify an image. The

C.Fn-19 setting, Add original decision data function determines whether the information needed to verify an image is included in the image file. Data verification is especially useful for law enforcement, legal, and scientific purposes, but not required for everyday shooting (which is why the feature is turned off by default).

- **0: Off.** Data verification information is not added to the image file.
- **1: On.** Data verification information is included in the image file.

C.Fn IV-04: Specify an Aspect Ratio in the Image File

Add aspect ratio information. While the EOS 7D can't shoot images "cropped" to specific proportions, or aspect ratios, it can do the next best thing. When shooting in Live View mode, you can display a grid that includes vertical lines that show the limits of various aspect ratios that correspond to the proportions of photographic film sizes, such as medium format 6×6 cm or 6×4.5 cm, and sheet film sizes such as 4×5 inches. These ratios may also correspond to that of some common print sizes, such as 4×5, 5×7, and 8×10 inches. That makes it easier to compose your images to conform to those proportions.

This Custom Function allows you to tell the 7D to add one of the available aspect ratios to the image file, so when the photo is displayed using Digital Photo Pro software (described in Chapter 12), the picture will be displayed in the aspect ratio you specified. You can then manually crop it to those proportions.

Your options include:

- **0: Off.** No aspect ratio will be appended to the image file.
- **1: Aspect ratio 6:6.**
- **2: Aspect ratio 3:4.**
- **3: Aspect ratio 4:5.**
- **4: Aspect ratio 6:7.**
- **5: Aspect ratio 10:12.**
- **6: Aspect ratio 5:7.**

Clear All Custom Func (C.Fn) Settings

This choice, located at the same level as the Custom Function categories, can be used to clear all camera Custom Functions. Press the SET button, then rotate the Quick Control Dial to choose either Cancel or OK. Press the SET button to confirm. All Custom Functions will be reset to their default 0 values.

My Menu

The Canon EOS 7D has a great feature that allows you to define your own menu, with just the items listed that you want. Remember that the 7D always returns to the last menu and menu entry accessed when you press the MENU button. So you can set up My Menu to include just the items you want, and jump to those items instantly by pressing the MENU button. Or, you can set your camera so that My Menu appears when the MENU button has been pressed, regardless of what other menu entry you accessed last.

To create your own My Menu, you have to *register* the menu items you want to include. Just follow these steps:

1. Press the MENU button and use the Main Dial or multi-controller to select the My Menu tab. When you first begin, the personalized menu will be empty except for the My Menu Settings entry. Press the SET button to select it. You'll then see a screen like the one shown in Figure 8.23.

2. Rotate the Quick Control Dial to select Register; then press the SET button.

3. Use the Quick Control Dial to scroll down through the continuous list of menu entries to find one you would like to add. Press Set.

4. Confirm your choice by selecting OK in the next screen and pressing SET again.

Figure 8.23
In the My Menu Settings screen you can add menu items, delete them, and specify whether My Menu always pops up when the MENU button is pressed.

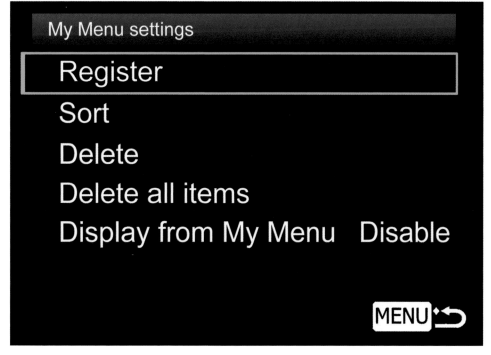

5. Continue to select up to six menu entries for My Menu.

6. When you're finished, press the MENU button twice to return to the My Menu screen to see your customized menu, which might look like Figure 8.24.

In addition to registering menu items, you can perform other functions at the My Menu Settings screen:

■ **Changing the order.** Choose Sort to reorder the items in My Menu. Select the menu item and press the SET button. Rotate the Quick Control Dial to move the item up and down within the menu list. When you've placed it where you'd like it, press the MENU button to lock in your selection and return to the previous screen.

■ **Delete/Delete all items.** Use these to remove an individual menu item or all menu items you've registered in My Menu.

■ **Display from My Menu.** As I mentioned earlier, the 7D (almost) always shows the last menu item accessed. That's convenient if you used My Menu last, but if you happen to use another menu, then pressing the MENU button will return to that item instead. If you enable the Display from My Menu option, pressing the MENU button will *always* display My Menu first. You are free to switch to another menu tab if you like, but the next time you press the MENU button, My Menu will come up again. Use this option if you work with My Menu a great deal and make settings with other menu items less frequently.

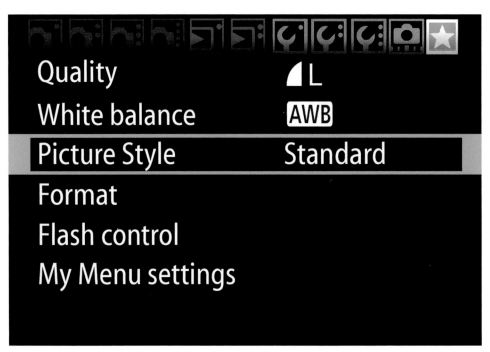

Figure 8.24
You can add one to six menu entries to My Menu.

9

Working with Lenses

Several years ago, Canon announced that it had produced its 40 millionth EF-series lens, a mere 21 years after the company's current autofocus mount was introduced (back in the film era). Considering that it took 11 years for Canon to sell its first 10 million copies of its EF lens line, but only two years and three months to peddle its most recent 10 million lenses, it's easy to see that the digital photography revolution can take credit for the most recent explosion.

With more than five dozen lenses in its current lineup, Canon is catering to the wide-ranging needs of a broad user base, from novice photo enthusiasts to advanced amateur and professional photographers. It's this mind-bending assortment of high-quality lenses available to enhance the capabilities of cameras like the Canon EOS 7D that make the product line so appealing. Thousands of current and older lenses introduced by Canon and third-party vendors since 1987 can be used to give you a wider view, bring distant subjects closer, let you focus closer, shoot under lower-light conditions, or provide a more detailed, sharper image for critical work. Other than the sensor itself, the lens you choose for your dSLR is the most important component in determining image quality and perspective of your images.

This chapter explains how to select the best lenses for the kinds of photography you want to do.

But Don't Forget the Crop Factor

From time to time you've heard the term *crop factor*, and you've probably also heard the term *lens multiplier factor*. Both are misleading and inaccurate terms used to describe the same phenomenon: the fact that cameras like the 7D (and most other affordable digital SLRs) provide a field of view that's smaller and narrower than that produced by certain other (usually much more expensive) cameras, when fitted with exactly the same lens.

Figure 9.1 quite clearly shows the phenomenon at work. The outer rectangle, marked 1X, shows the field of view you might expect with a 28mm lens mounted on a Canon EOS 1Ds Mark III or EOS 5D Mark II camera, so-called "full-frame" models. The rectangle marked 1.3X shows the effective field of view from the same vantage point with the exact same lens mounted on a Canon EOS 1D Mark III camera, while the area marked 1.6X shows the field of view you'd get with that 28mm lens installed on a 7D. It's easy to see from the illustration that the 1X rendition provides a wider, more expansive view, while the other two are, in comparison, *cropped*.

The cropping effect is produced because the sensors of the latter two cameras are smaller than the sensors of the 1Ds Mark III. The "full-frame" camera has a sensor that's the size of the standard 35mm film frame, 24mm × 36mm. Your 7D's sensor does *not* measure 24mm × 36mm; instead, it specs out at 22.3mm × 14.9mm, or about 62.5 percent of the area of a full-frame sensor, as shown by the yellow boxes in the figure. You can calculate the relative field of view by dividing the focal length of the lens by .625. Thus, a 100mm lens mounted on a 7D has the same field of view as a 160mm lens on the 1Ds Mark III. We humans tend to perform multiplication operations in our heads more easily than division, so such field of view comparisons are usually calculated using the reciprocal of .625—1.6—so we can multiply instead. (100 / .625=160; 100 × 1.6=160)

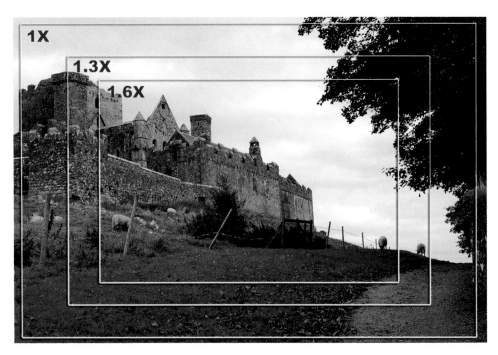

Figure 9.1
Canon offers digital SLRs with full-frame (1X) crops, as well as 1.3X and 1.6X crops.

This translation is generally useful only if you're accustomed to using full-frame cameras (usually of the film variety) and want to know how a familiar lens will perform on a digital camera. I strongly prefer *crop factor* over *lens multiplier*, because nothing is being multiplied; a 100mm lens doesn't "become" a 160mm lens—the depth-of-field and lens aperture remain the same. (I'll explain more about these later in this chapter.) Only the field of view is cropped. But *crop factor* isn't much better, as it implies that the 24 × 36mm frame is "full" and anything else is "less." I get e-mails all the time from photographers who point out that they own full-frame cameras with 36mm × 48mm sensors (like the Mamiya 645ZD or Hasselblad H3D-39 medium format digitals). By their reckoning, the "half-size" sensors found in cameras like the 1Ds Mark III and 5D Mark II are "cropped."

If you're accustomed to using full-frame film cameras, you might find it helpful to use the crop factor "multiplier" to translate a lens's real focal length into the full-frame equivalent, even though, as I said, nothing is actually being multiplied. Throughout most of this book, I've been using actual focal lengths and not equivalents, except when referring to specific wide-angle or telephoto focal length ranges and their fields of view.

Your First Lens

Back in ancient times (the pre-zoom, pre-autofocus era before the mid-1980s), choosing the first lens for your camera was a no-brainer: you had few or no options. Canon cameras (which used a different lens mount in those days) were sold with a 50mm f/1.4, a 50mm f/1.8, or, if you had deeper pockets, a super-fast 50mm f/1.2 lens. It was also possible to buy a camera as a body alone, which didn't save much money back when a film SLR like the Canon A-1 sold for $435—*with lens*. (Thanks to the era of relatively cheap optics, I still own a total of *eight* 50mm f/1.4 lenses.)

Today, your choices are more complicated, and Canon lenses, which now include zoom, autofocus, and, more often than not, built-in image stabilization (IS) features, tend to cost a lot more compared to the price of a camera. (Adjusted for inflation, that $435 A-1 cost $879 in today's dollars.)

The Canon EOS 7D is frequently purchased with a lens, even now, often the Canon EF-S 18-200mm f/3.5-5.6 IS lens (about $575) that provides a very useful 11X zoom range. Some buyers don't need quite that zoom range, and save a few dollars by purchasing the EF-S 18-135 f3.5-5.6 IS Lens (about $450) or Canon EF 28-135mm f/3.5-5.6 IS USM Lens ($409). (The latter lens has one advantage. *EF* lenses like the 28-135mm zoom can also be used with any *full-frame* camera you add/migrate to at a later date. You'll learn the difference later in this chapter.)

True budget-hunters might go for the highly limited (but cheap) Canon EF-S 18-55mm f/3.5-5.6 IS autofocus lens. It adds only about $100 to the price tag of the body alone, and is thus an irresistible bargain. You can also buy the 7D body with no optics if you already have some lenses. Other more upscale Canon models, including the EOS 1D Mark III, EOS 1Ds Mark III, and EOS 5D Mark II, are most often purchased without a lens by veteran Canon photographers who already have a complement of optics to use with their cameras.

I bought my EOS 7D as a body only, because I already had a collection of lenses. However, you'll also find many purchasers who fall into one of the following categories: Those who are upgrading from the Digital Rebel/Rebel models or an EOS 10D/20D/30D/40D/50D; from a Canon film camera; or who are buying the 7D as a second camera body to complement their other Canon camera. These owners, too, generally already have lenses they can use with their new 7D.

So, depending on which category you fall into, you'll need to make a decision about what kit lens to buy, or decide what other kind of lenses you need to fill out your complement of Canon optics. This section will cover "first lens" concerns, while later in the chapter we'll look at "add-on lens" considerations.

When deciding on a first lens, there are several factors you'll want to consider:

- **Cost.** You might have stretched your budget a bit to purchase your 7D, so you might want to keep the cost of your first lens fairly low. Fortunately, there are excellent lenses available that will add from $100 to $500 to the price of your camera if purchased at the same time.

- **Zoom range.** If you have only one lens, you'll want a fairly long zoom range to provide as much flexibility as possible. Fortunately, the two most popular basic lenses for the 7D have 3X to 5X zoom ranges, extending from moderate wide-angle/normal out to medium telephoto. These are fine for everyday shooting, portraits, and some types of sports.

- **Adequate maximum aperture.** You'll want an f/stop of at least f/3.5 to f/4 for shooting under fairly low-light conditions. The thing to watch for is the maximum aperture when the lens is zoomed to its telephoto end. You may end up with no better than an f/5.6 maximum aperture. That's not great, but you can often live with it.

- **Image quality.** Your starter lens should have good image quality, befitting a camera with 18MP of resolution, because that's one of the primary factors that will be used to judge your photos. Even at a low price, the several different lenses sold with the 7D as a kit include extra-low dispersion glass and aspherical elements that minimize distortion and chromatic aberration; they are sharp enough for most applications. If you read the user evaluations in the online photography forums, you know that owners of the kit lenses have been very pleased with their image quality.

- **Size matters.** A good walking-around lens is compact in size and light in weight.

- **Fast/close focusing.** Your first lens should have a speedy autofocus system (which is where the ultrasonic motor/USM found in nearly all moderately priced lenses is an advantage). Close focusing (to 12 inches or closer) will let you use your basic lens for some types of macro photography.

You can find comparisons of the lenses discussed in the next section, as well as third-party lenses from Sigma, Tokina, Tamron, and other vendors, in online groups and websites. I'll provide my recommendations, but more information is always helpful.

Buy Now, Expand Later

The 7D is commonly available with several good, basic lenses that can serve you well as a "walk-around" lens (one you keep on the camera most of the time, especially when you're out and about without your camera bag). The number of options available to you is actually quite amazing, even if your budget is limited to about $100-$500 for your first lens. One other vendor, for example, offers only 18mm-70mm and 18mm-55mm kit lenses in that price range, plus a 24mm-85mm zoom. Two popular starter lenses Canon offers are shown in Figures 9.2 and 9.3. Canon's best-bet first lenses are as follows:

- **Canon EF-S 18-55mm f/3.5-5.6 IS Autofocus lens.** This lens has image stabilization that can counter camera shake by providing the vibration-stopping capabilities of a shutter speed four stops faster than the one you've dialed in. That is, with image stabilization activated, you can shoot at 1/30th second and eliminate camera shake as if you were using a shutter speed of 1/250th second. (At least, that's what Canon claims; I usually have slightly less impressive results.) Of course, IS doesn't freeze subject motion—that basketball player driving for a layup will still be blurry at 1/30th second, even though the effects of camera shake will be effectively nullified. But this lens is an all-around good choice if your budget is tight.

- **Canon EF-S 17-85mm f/4-5.6 IS USM Autofocus lens.** This lens is a very popular "basic" lens sold for the 7D. The allure here is the longer telephoto range, coupled with the built-in image stabilization, which allows you to shoot rock-solid photos at shutter speeds that are at least two or three notches slower than you'd need normally (say, 1/8th second instead of 1/30th or 1/60th second), as long as your subject isn't moving. It also has a quiet, fast, reliable ultrasonic motor (more on that later, too). This is another lens designed for the 1.6X crop factor; all but one of the remaining lenses in this list can also be used on full-frame cameras. (I'll tell you why later in this chapter.) This lens is shown in Figure 9.3.

- **Canon EF-S 18-200mm f/3.5-5.6 IS Autofocus lens.** This one, priced at about $600, has been wildly popular as a basic lens for the 7D, because it's light, compact, and covers a full range from true wide-angle to long telephoto. Image stabilization keeps your pictures sharp at the long end of the zoom range, allowing the longer shutter speeds that the f/5.6 maximum aperture demands at 200mm. Automatic panning detection turns the IS feature off when panning in both horizontal and vertical directions. An improved "Super Spectra Coating" minimizes flare and ghosting, while optimizing color rendition. Can you tell that I like this lens?

■ **Canon EF-S 18-135mm f/3.5-5.6 IS Autofocus lens.** This one, priced at about $450, is also popular as a basic lens. It's also light, compact, and covers a useful range from true wide-angle to intermediate telephoto. As with the 18-200mm lens, image stabilization partially compensates for the slow f/5.6 maximum aperture at the telephoto end, by allowing you to use longer shutter speeds to capture an image under poor lighting conditions.

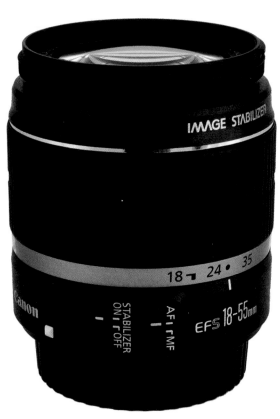

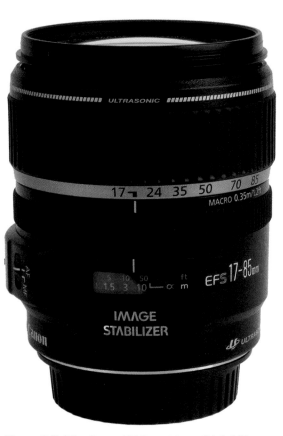

Figure 9.2 The Canon EF-S 18-55mm f/3.5-5.6 IS Autofocus lens ships as a basic kit lens for entry-level Canon cameras; you can also purchase it for the 7D if your budget is strapped.

Figure 9.3 The Canon EF-S 17-85mm f/4-5.6 IS USM Autofocus lens is another popular starter lens for the 7D.

- **Canon EF 55-200mm f/4.5-5.6 II USM Autofocus Lightweight Compact Telephoto Zoom lens.** If you bought the 18-55mm kit lens, this one picks up where that one leaves off, going from short telephoto to medium long (88mm-320mm full-frame equivalent). It features a desirable ultrasonic motor. Best of all, it's very affordable at around $225. If you can afford only two lenses, the 18-55mm and this one make a good basic set.

- **EF-S 55-250mm f/4-5.6 IS Telephoto Zoom lens.** This is an image-stabilized EF-S lens (which means it can't be used with Canon's 1.3X and 1.0X crop-factor pro cameras), providing the longest focal range in the EF-S range to date, and that 4-stop Image Stabilizer. Again, at about $250, it's more money than the older, non-stabilized EF version, but it's worth the extra cost.

- **Canon EF 24-85mm f/3.5-4.5 USM Autofocus Wide-Angle Telephoto Zoom lens.** If you can get by with normal focal length to medium telephoto range, Canon offers four affordable lenses, plus one more expensive killer lens that's worth the extra expenditure. All of them can be used on full-frame or cropped-frame digital Canons, which is why they include "wide angle" in their product names. They're really wide-angle lenses only when mounted on a full-frame camera. This one, priced in the $300 range, offers a useful range of focal lengths, extending from the equivalent of 38mm to 136mm.

- **Canon EF 28-105mm f/3.5-4.5 II USM Autofocus Wide-Angle Telephoto Zoom lens.** If you want to save about $100 and gain a little reach, this 45mm-168mm (equivalent lens) might be what you are looking for.

- **Canon EF 28-135mm f/3.5-5.6 IS USM Image-Stabilized Autofocus Wide-Angle Telephoto Zoom lens.** Image stabilization is especially useful at longer focal lengths, which makes this 45mm-216mm (equivalent) lens worth its $400-plus price tag. Several retailers are packing this lens with the 7D as a kit.

- **Canon EF 28-200mm f/3.5-5.6 USM Autofocus Wide-Angle Telephoto Zoom lens.** If you want one lens to do everything except wide-angle photography, this 7X zoom lens costs less than $400 and takes you from the equivalent of 45mm out to a long 320mm.

- **Canon Zoom Wide-Angle-Telephoto EF 24-70mm f/2.8L USM Autofocus lens.** I couldn't leave this premium lens out of the mix, even though it costs well over $1,000. As part of Canon's L-series (Luxury) lens line, it offers the best sharpness over its focal range than any of the other lenses in this list. Best of all, it's fast (for a zoom), with an f/.2.8 maximum aperture that *doesn't change* as you zoom out. Unlike the other lenses, which may offer only an f/5.6 maximum f/stop at their longest zoom setting, this is a *constant aperture* lens, which retains its maximum f/stop. The added sharpness, constant aperture, and ultra-smooth USM motor are what you're paying for with this lens.

What Lenses Can You Use?

The previous section helped you sort out what lens you need to buy with your 7D (assuming you already didn't own any Canon lenses). Now, you're probably wondering what lenses can be added to your growing collection (trust me, it will grow). You need to know which lenses are suitable and, most importantly, which lenses are fully compatible with your 7D.

With the Canon 7D, the compatibility issue is a simple one: It accepts any lens with the EF or EF-S designation, with full availability of all autofocus, autoaperture, autoexposure, and image-stabilization features (if present). It's comforting to know that any EF (for full-frame or cropped sensors) or EF-S (for cropped sensor cameras only) will work as designed with your camera. As I noted at the beginning of the chapter, that's more than 40 million lenses!

But wait, there's more. You can also attach Nikon F mount, Leica R, Olympus OM, and M42 ("Pentax screw mount") lenses with a simple adapter, if you don't mind losing automatic focus and aperture control. If you use one of these lenses, you'll need to focus manually (even if the lens operates in Autofocus mode on the camera it was designed for), and adjust the f/stop to the aperture you want to use to take the picture. That means that lenses that don't have an aperture ring (such as Nikon G-series lenses) must be used only at their maximum aperture if you use them with a simple adapter. However, Novoflex makes expensive adapter rings (the Nikon-Lens-on-Canon-Camera version is called EOS/NIK NT) with an integral aperture control that allows adjusting the aperture of lenses that do not have an old-style aperture ring. Expect to pay as much as $300 for an adapter of this type.

Because of these limitations, you probably won't want to make extensive use of "foreign" lenses on your 7D, but an adapter can help you when you really, really need to use a particular focal length but don't have a suitable Canon-compatible lens. For example, I occasionally use an older 400mm lens that was originally designed for the Nikon line on my 7D. The lens needs to be mounted on a tripod for steadiness anyway, so its slower operation isn't a major pain. Another good match is the 105mm Micro-Nikkor I sometimes use with my Canon 7D. Macro photos, too, are most often taken with the camera mounted on a tripod, and manual focus makes a lot of sense for fine-tuning focus and depth-of-field. Because of the contemplative nature of close-up photography, it's not much of an inconvenience to stop down to the taking aperture just before exposure.

The limitations on use of lenses within Canon's own product line (as well as lenses produced for earlier Canon SLRs by third-party vendors) are fairly clear-cut. The 7D cannot be used with any of Canon's earlier lens mounting schemes for its film cameras, including the immediate predecessor to the EF mount, the FD mount (introduced with the Canon F1 in 1964 and used until the Canon T60 in 1990), FL (1964-1971), or

WHY SO MANY LENS MOUNTS?

Four different lens mounts in 40-plus years might seem like a lot of different mounting systems, especially when compared to the Nikon F mount of 1959, which retained quite a bit of compatibility with that company's film and digital camera bodies during that same span. However, in digital photography terms, the EF mount itself is positively ancient, having remained reasonably stable for almost two decades. Lenses designed for the EF system work reliably with every EOS film and digital camera ever produced.

However, at the time, yet another lens mount switch, especially a change from the traditional breech system to a more conventional bayonet-type mount, was indeed a daring move by Canon. One of the reasons for staying with a particular lens type is to "lock" current users into a specific camera system. By introducing the EF mount, Canon in effect cut loose every photographer in its existing user base. If they chose to upgrade, they were free to choose another vendor's products and lenses. Only satisfaction with the previous Canon product line and the promise of the new system would keep them in the fold.

the original Canon R mount (1959-1964). That's really all you need to know. While you'll find FD-to-EF adapters for about $40, you'll lose so many functions that it's rarely worth the bother.

In retrospect, the switch to the EF mount seems like a very good idea, as the initial EOS film cameras can now be seen as the beginning of Canon's rise to eventually become the leader in film and (later) digital SLR cameras. By completely revamping its lens mounting system, the company was able to take advantage of the latest advances in technology without compromise.

For example, when the original EF bayonet mount was introduced in 1987, the system incorporated new autofocus technology (EF actually stands for "electro focus") in a more rugged and less complicated form. A tiny motor was built into the lens itself, eliminating the need for mechanical linkages with the camera. Instead, electrical contacts are used to send power and the required focusing information to the motor. That's a much more robust and resilient system that made it easier for Canon to design faster and more accurate autofocus mechanisms just by redesigning the lenses.

EF vs. EF-S

Today, in addition to its EF lenses, Canon offers lenses that use the EF-S (the S stands for "short back focus") mount, with the chief difference being (as you might expect) lens components that extend farther back into the camera body of some of Canon's latest digital cameras (specifically those with smaller than full-frame sensors), such as the 7D. As I'll explain next, this refinement allows designing more compact, less-expensive lenses especially for those cameras, but not for models like the EOS 5D Mark II, 1Ds

Mark III, or 1D Mark III (even though the latter camera does have a sensor that is slightly smaller than full frame).

Canon's EF-S lens mount variation was born in 2003, when the company virtually invented the consumer-oriented digital SLR category by introducing the original EOS 300D/Digital Rebel, a dSLR that cost less than $1,000 *with lens* at a time when all other interchangeable lens digital cameras (including the 7D's "grandparent," the original EOS 10D) were priced closer to $2,000 with a basic lens. Like the EOS 10D the EOS 7D features a smaller than full-frame sensor with a 1.6X crop factor (Canon calls this format APS-C). But the EOS Digital Rebel accepted lenses that took advantage of the shorter mirror found in APS-C cameras, with elements of shorter focal length lenses (wide angles) that extended *into* the camera, space that was off limits in other models because the mirror passed through that territory as it flipped up to expose the shutter and sensor. (Canon even calls its flip-up reflector a "half mirror.")

In short (so to speak), the EF-S mount made it easier to design less-expensive wide-angle lenses that could be used *only* with 1.6X-crop cameras, and featured a simpler design and reduced coverage area suitable for those non-full-frame models. The new mount made it possible to produce lenses like the ultra-wide EF-S 10-22mm f/3.5-4.5 USM lens, which has the equivalent field of view as a 16mm-35mm zoom on a full-frame camera. (See Figure 9.4.)

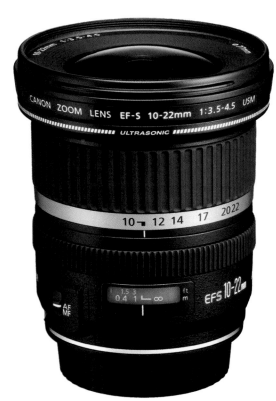

Figure 9.4
The EF-S 10-22mm ultra-wide lens was made possible by the shorter back focus difference offered by the original Digital EOS 7D and subsequent Canon 1.6X "cropped sensor" models.

Suitable cameras for EF-S lenses include all the entry-level models from the original Digital Rebel to the latest Rebel XSi/XS and the Canon EOS 20D/30D/40D/7D. The EF-S lenses cannot be used on the APS-C-sensor EOS 10D, the 1D Mark II N/Mark III (which have a 28.7mm × 19.1mm APS-H sensor with a 1.3X crop factor), or any of the full-frame digital or film EOS models, such as the EOS 1Ds Mark III or EOS 5D Mark II. It's easy to tell an EF lens from an EF-S lens: The latter incorporate EF-S into their name! Plus, EF lenses have a raised red dot on the barrel that is used to align the lens with a matching dot on the camera when attaching the lens. EF-S lenses and compatible bodies use a white square instead. Some EF-S lenses also have a rubber ring at the attachment end that provides a bit of weather/dust sealing and protects the back components of the lens if a user attempts to mount it on a camera that is not EF-S compatible.

Ingredients of Canon's Alphanumeric Soup

The actual product names of individual Canon lenses are fairly easy to decipher; they'll include either the EF or EF-S designation, the focal length or focal length range of the lens, its maximum aperture, and some other information. Additional data may be engraved or painted on the barrel or ring surrounding the front element of the lens, as shown in Figure 9.5.

Figure 9.5
Most of the key specifications of the lens are marked on the ring around the front element.

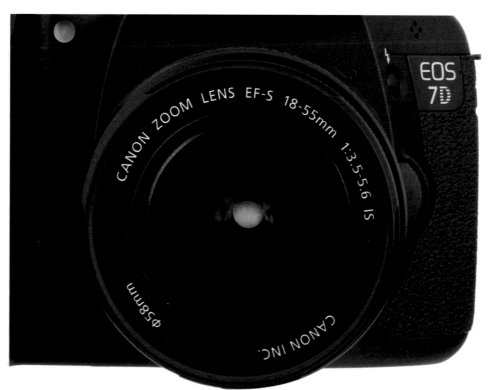

Here's a decoding of what the individual designations mean:

- **EF/EF-S.** If the lens is marked EF, it can safely be used on any Canon EOS camera, film or digital. If it is an EF-S lens, it should be used only on an EF-S compatible camera, such as the EOS 7Ds, EOS 20D/30D/40D, and any newer APS-C cameras introduced after the publication of this book.

- **Focal length.** Given in millimeters or a millimeter range, such as 60mm in the case of a popular Canon macro lens, or 17-55mm, used to describe a medium-wide to short-telephoto zoom.

- **Maximum aperture.** The largest f/stop available with a particular lens is given in a string of numbers that might seem confusing at first glance. For example, you might see 1:1.8 for a fixed-focal length (prime) lens, and 1:4.5-5.6 for a zoom. The initial 1: signifies that the f/stop given is actually a ratio or fraction (in regular notation, f/ replaces the 1:), which is why a 1:2 (or f/2) aperture is larger than an 1:4 (or f/4) aperture—just as 1/2 is larger than 1/4. With most zoom lenses, the maximum aperture changes as the lens is zoomed to the telephoto position, so a range is given instead: 1:4.5-5.6. (Some zooms, called constant aperture lenses, keep the same maximum aperture throughout their range.)

- **Autofocus type.** Most newer Canon lenses that aren't of the bargain-basement type use Canon's *ultrasonic motor* autofocus system (more on that later) and are given the USM designation. If USM does not appear on the lens or its model name, the lens uses the less sophisticated AFD (arc-form drive) autofocus system or the micro-motor (MM) drive mechanism.

- **Series.** Canon adds a Roman numeral to many of its products to represent an updated model with the same focal length or focal length range, so some lenses will have a II or III added to their name.

- **Pro quality.** Canon's more expensive lenses with more rugged construction and higher optical quality, intended for professional use, include the letter L (for "luxury") in their product name. You can further differentiate these lenses visually by a red ring around the lens barrel and the off-white color of the metal barrel itself in virtually all telephoto L-series lenses. (Some L-series lenses have shiny or textured black plastic exterior barrels.) Internally, every L lens includes at least one lens element that is built of ultra-low dispersion glass, is constructed of expensive fluorite crystal, or uses an expensive ground (not molded) aspheric (non-spherical) lens component.

- **Filter size.** You'll find the front lens filter thread diameter in millimeters included on the lens, preceded by a Ø symbol, as in Ø67 or Ø72.

■ **Special-purpose lenses.** Some Canon lenses are designed for specific types of work, and they include appropriate designations in their names. For example, close-focusing lenses such as the Canon EF-S 60mm f/2.8 Macro USM lens incorporate the word *Macro* into their name. Lenses with perspective control features preface the lens name with T-S (for tilt-shift). Lenses with built-in image-stabilization features, such as the nifty EF 28-300mm f/3.5-5.6L IS USM Telephoto Zoom include *IS* in their product names.

SORTING THE MOTOR DRIVES

Incorporating the autofocus motor inside the lens was an innovative move by Canon, and this allowed the company to produce better and more sophisticated lenses as technology became available to upgrade the focusing system. As a result, you'll find four different types of motors in Canon-designed lenses, each with cost and practical considerations.

■ **AFD (Arc-form drive)** and **Micromotor (MM)** drives are built around tiny versions of electromagnetic motors, which generally use gear trains to produce the motion needed to adjust the focus of the lens. Both are slow, noisy, and not particularly effective with larger lenses. Manual focus adjustments are possible only when the motor drive is disengaged.

■ **Micromotor ultrasonic motor (USM)** drives use high-frequency vibration to produce the motion used to drive the gear train, resulting in a quieter operating system at a cost that's not much more than that of electromagnetic motor drives. With the exception of a couple lenses that have a slipping clutch mechanism, manual focus with this kind of system is possible only when the motor drive is switched off and the lens is set in Manual mode. This is the kind of USM system you'll find in lower-cost lenses.

■ **Ring ultrasonic motor (USM)** drives, available in two different types (*electronic focus ring USM* and *ring USM*), also use high-frequency movement, but generate motion using a pair of vibrating metal rings to adjust focus. Both variations allow a feature called Full Time Manual (FTM) focus, which lets you make manual adjustments to the lens's focus even when the autofocus mechanism is engaged. With electronic focus ring USM, manual focus is possible only when the lens is mounted on the camera and the camera is turned on; the focus ring of lenses with ring USM can be turned at any time.

Your Second (and Third...) Lens

There are really only two advantages to owning just a single lens. One of them is creative. Keeping one set of optics mounted on your 7D all the time forces you to be especially imaginative in your approach to your subjects. I once visited Europe with only a single camera body and a 35mm f/2 lens. The experience was actually quite exciting, because I had to use a variety of techniques to allow that one lens to serve for landscapes, available light photos, action, close-ups, portraits, and other kinds of images. Canon makes an excellent 35mm f/2 lens (which focuses down to 9.6 inches) that's perfect for that kind of experiment; although, today, my personal choice would be the sublime (and expensive) Canon Wide-Angle EF 35mm f/1.4L USM Autofocus lens. I also own the Canon EF 50mm f/1.8 II lens, which I favor as a very compact and light walkaround/short telephoto/portrait lens, especially indoors. It makes a great close-up/macro lens, too, and, at $100, is my choice as a very good second lens.

Of course, it's more likely that your "single" lens is actually a zoom, which is, in truth, many lenses in one, taking you from, say, 17mm to 85mm (or some other range) with a rapid twist of the zoom lever. You'll still find some creative challenges when you stick to a single zoom lens's focal lengths.

The second advantage of the unilens camera is only a marginal technical benefit since the introduction of the 7D. If you don't exchange lenses, the chances of dust and dirt getting inside your 7D and settling on the sensor is reduced (but *not* eliminated entirely). Although I've known some photographers who minimized the number of lens changes they made for this very reason, reducing the number of lenses you work with is not a productive or rewarding approach for most of us. The 7D's automatic sensor cleaning feature has made this "advantage" much less significant than it was in the past.

It's more likely that you'll succumb to the malady known as *Lens Lust*, which is defined as an incurable disease marked by a significant yen for newer, better, longer, faster, sharper, anything-er optics for your camera. (And, it must be noted, this disease can *cost* you significant yen—or dollars, or whatever currency you use.) In its worst manifestations, sufferers find themselves with lenses that have overlapping zoom ranges or capabilities, because one or the other offers a slight margin in performance or suitability for specific tasks. When you find yourself already lusting after a new lens before you've really had a chance to put your latest purchase to the test, you'll know the disease has reached the terminal phase.

What Lenses Can Do for You

A saner approach to expanding your lens collection is to consider what each of your options can do for you and then choosing the type of lens that will really boost your creative opportunities. Here's a general guide to the sort of capabilities you can gain by adding a lens to your repertoire.

■ **Wider perspective.** Your 18-55mm f/3.5-5.6 or 17-85mm f/4-5.6 or 18-200mm lens has served you well for moderate wide-angle shots. Now you find your back is up against a wall and you *can't* take a step backwards to take in more subject matter. Perhaps you're standing on the rim of the Grand Canyon, and you want to take in as much of the breathtaking view as you can. You might find yourself just behind the baseline at a high school basketball game and want an interesting shot with a little perspective distortion tossed in the mix. There's a lens out there that will provide you with what you need, such as the EF-S 10-22mm f/3.5-4.5 USM Zoom. If you want to stay in the sub-$600 price category, you'll need something like the Sigma Super Wide-Angle 10-20mm f/4-5.6 EX DC HSM Autofocus lens. The two lenses provide the equivalent of a 16mm to 32/35mm wide-angle view. For a distorted view, there is the Canon Fisheye EF 15mm f/2.8 Autofocus, with a similar lens available from Sigma, which offers an extra-wide circular fisheye, and the Sigma Fisheye 8mm f/3.5 EX DG Circular Fisheye. Your extra-wide choices may not be abundant, but they are there. Figure 9.6 shows the perspective you get from an ultra-wide-angle, non-fisheye lens.

■ **Bring objects closer.** A long lens brings distant subjects closer to you, offers better control over depth-of-field, and avoids the perspective distortion that wide-angle lenses provide. They compress the apparent distance between objects in your frame. In the telephoto realm, Canon is second to none, with a dozen or more offerings in the sub-$600 range, including the Canon EF 100-300mm f/4.5-5.6 USM Autofocus and Canon EF 70-300mm f/4-5.6 IS USM Autofocus Telephoto Zoom lenses, and a broad array of zooms and fixed-focal length optics if you're willing to spend up to $1,000 or a bit more. Don't forget that the 7D's crop factor narrows the field of view of all these lenses, so your 70-300mm lens looks more like a 112mm-480mm zoom through the viewfinder. Figures 9.7 and 9.8 were taken from the same position as Figure 9.6, but with an 85mm and 500mm lens, respectively.

■ **Bring your camera closer.** Macro lenses allow you to focus to within an inch or two of your subject. Canon's best close-up lenses are all fixed focal length optics in the 50mm to 180mm range (including the well-regarded Canon EF-S 60mm f/2.8 Compact and Canon EF 100mm f/2.8 USM Macro Autofocus lenses). But you'll find macro zooms available from Sigma and others. They don't tend to focus quite as close, but they provide a bit of flexibility when you want to vary your subject distance (say, to avoid spooking a skittish creature).

■ **Look sharp.** Many lenses, particularly Canon's luxury "L" line, are prized for their sharpness and overall image quality. While your run-of-the-mill lens is likely to be plenty sharp for most applications, the very best optics are even better over their entire field of view (which means no fuzzy corners), are sharper at a wider range of focal lengths (in the case of zooms), and have better correction for various types of distortion. That's why the Canon EF 28-105mm f/3.5-4.5 II USM Zoom lens costs

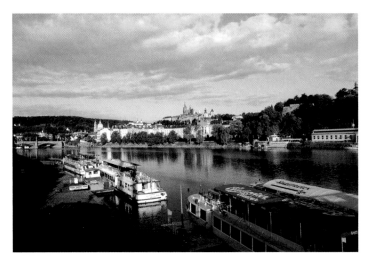

Figure 9.6
An ultrawide-angle lens provided this view of a castle in Prague, Czech Republic.

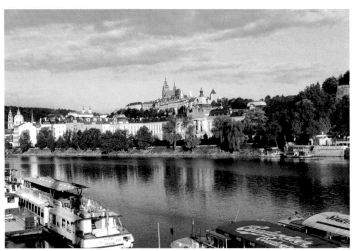

Figure 9.7
This photo, taken from roughly the same distance, shows the view using a short telephoto lens.

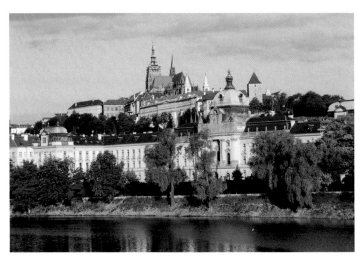

Figure 9.8
A longer telephoto lens captured this closer view of the castle from approximately the same shooting position.

a couple hundred dollars, while the "similar" (in zoom range only) Canon EF 24-105mm f/4L IS USM Zoom is priced $1,000 higher.

- **More speed.** Your Canon EF 100-300mm f/4.5-5.6 Telephoto Zoom lens might have the perfect focal length and sharpness for sports photography, but the maximum aperture won't cut it for night baseball or football games, or, even, any sports shooting in daylight if the weather is cloudy or you need to use some ungodly fast shutter speed, such as 1/4,000th second. You might be happier with the Canon EF 100mm f/2 Medium Telephoto for close-range stuff, or even the pricier Canon EF 135mm f/2L. If money is no object, you can spring for Canon's 400mm f/2.8 and 600mm f/4 L-series lenses (both with image stabilization and priced in the $6,500-and-up stratosphere). Or, maybe you just need the speed and can benefit from an f/1.8 or f/1.4 lens in the 20mm-85mm range. They're all available in Canon mounts (there's even an 85mm f/1.2 and 50mm f/1.2 for the real speed demons). With any of these lenses you can continue photographing under the dimmest of lighting conditions without the need for a tripod or flash.

- **Special features.** Accessory lenses give you special features, such as tilt/shift capabilities to correct for perspective distortion in architectural shots. Canon offers four of these TS-E lenses in 17mm, 24mm, 45mm, and 90mm focal lengths, at more than $1,000 each. You'll also find macro lenses, including the MP-E 65mm f/2.8 1-5x Macro Photo lens, a manual focus lens that shoots *only* in the 1X to 5X life-size range. If you want diffused images, check out the EF 135mm f/2.8 with two soft-focus settings. The fisheye lenses mentioned earlier and all IS (image-stabilized) lenses also count as special-feature optics.

Zoom or Prime?

Zoom lenses have changed the way serious photographers take pictures. One of the reasons that I own 12 SLR film bodies is that in ancient times it was common to mount a different fixed focal length prime lens on various cameras and take pictures with two or three cameras around your neck (or tucked in a camera case) so you'd be ready to take a long shot or an intimate close-up or wide-angle view on a moment's notice, without the need to switch lenses. It made sense (at the time) to have a half dozen or so bodies (two to use, one in the shop, one in transit, and a couple backups). Zoom lenses of the time had a limited zoom range, were heavy, and not very sharp (especially when you tried to wield one of those monsters hand-held).

That's all changed today. Lenses like the razor-sharp Canon EF 28-300mm f/3.5-5.6L IS USM can boast 10X or longer zoom ranges, in a package that's about 7 inches long, and while not petite at 3.7 pounds, quite usable hand-held (especially with IS switched on). Although such a lens might seem expensive at $2,200-plus, it's actually much less costly than the six or so lenses it replaces.

When selecting between zoom and prime lenses, there are several considerations to ponder. Here's a checklist of the most important factors. I already mentioned image quality and maximum aperture earlier, but those aspects take on additional meaning when comparing zooms and primes.

- **Logistics.** As prime lenses offer just a single focal length, you'll need more of them to encompass the full range offered by a single zoom. More lenses mean additional slots in your camera bag, and extra weight to carry. Just within Canon's line alone you can select from about a dozen general-purpose prime lenses in 28mm, 35mm, 50mm, 85mm, 100mm, 135mm, 200mm, and 300mm focal lengths, all of which are overlapped by the 28-300mm zoom I mentioned earlier. Even so, you might be willing to carry an extra prime lens or two in order to gain the speed or image quality that lens offers.

- **Image quality.** Prime lenses usually produce better image quality at their focal length than even the most sophisticated zoom lenses at the same magnification. Zoom lenses, with their shifting elements and f/stops that can vary from zoom position to zoom position, are in general more complex to design than fixed focal length lenses. That's not to say that the very best prime lenses can't be complicated as well. However, the exotic designs, aspheric elements, low-dispersion glass, and Canon's new diffraction optics (DO) technology (a three-layer diffraction grating to better control how light is captured by a lens) can be applied to improving the quality of the lens, rather than wasting a lot of it on compensating for problems caused by the zoom process itself.

- **Maximum aperture.** Because of the same design constraints, zoom lenses usually have smaller maximum apertures than prime lenses, and the most affordable zooms have a lens opening that grows effectively smaller as you zoom in. The difference in lens speed verges on the ridiculous at some focal lengths. For example, the 18mm-55mm basic zoom gives you a 55mm f/5.6 lens when zoomed all the way out, while prime lenses in that focal length commonly have f/1.8 or faster maximum apertures. Indeed, the fastest f/2, f/1.8, f1/4, and f/1.2 lenses are all primes, and if you require speed, a fixed focal length lens is what you should rely on. Figure 9.9 shows an image taken with a Canon 85mm f 1.8 Series EF USM Telephoto lens.

- **Speed.** Using prime lenses takes time and slows you down. It takes a few seconds to remove your current lens and mount a new one, and the more often you need to do that, the more time is wasted. If you choose not to swap lenses, when using a fixed focal length lens you'll still have to move closer or farther away from your subject to get the field of view you want. A zoom lens allows you to change magnifications and focal lengths with the twist of a ring and generally saves a great deal of time.

Figure 9.9
An 85mm f/1.8 lens was perfect for this hand-held photo of a musician.

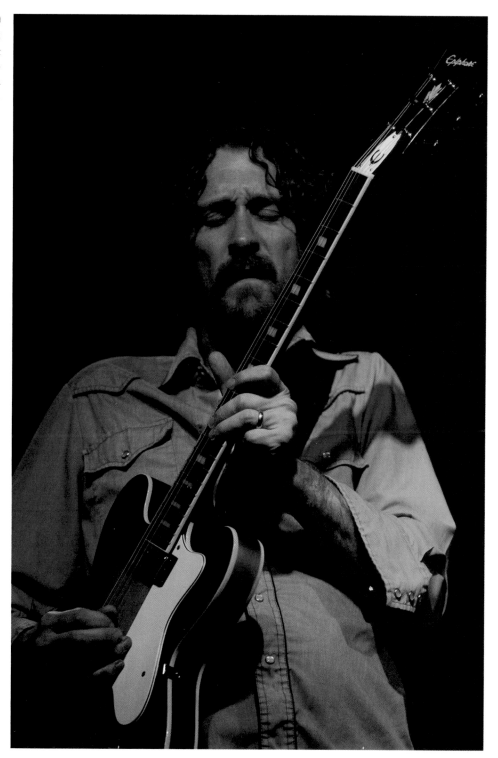

Categories of Lenses

Lenses can be categorized by their intended purpose—general photography, macro photography, and so forth—or by their focal length. The range of available focal lengths is usually divided into three main groups: wide-angle, normal, and telephoto. Prime lenses fall neatly into one of these classifications. Zooms can overlap designations, with a significant number falling into the catch-all wide-to-telephoto zoom range. This section provides more information about focal length ranges, and how they are used.

Any lens with an equivalent focal length of 10mm to 20mm is said to be an *ultrawide-angle lens*; from about 20mm to 40mm (equivalent) is said to be a *wide-angle lens*. *Normal lenses* have a focal length roughly equivalent to the diagonal of the film or sensor, in millimeters, and so fall into the range of about 45mm to 60mm (on a full-frame camera). *Telephoto lenses* usually fall into the 75mm and longer focal lengths, while those from about 300mm-400mm and longer often are referred to as *super-telephotos*.

Using Wide-Angle and Wide-Zoom Lenses

To use wide-angle prime lenses and wide zooms, you need to understand how they affect your photography. Here's a quick summary of the things you need to know.

- **More depth-of-field.** Practically speaking, wide-angle lenses offer more depth-of-field at a particular subject distance and aperture. (But see the sidebar later in this section for an important note.) You'll find that helpful when you want to maximize sharpness of a large zone, but not very useful when you'd rather isolate your subject using selective focus (telephoto lenses are better for that).

- **Stepping back.** Wide-angle lenses have the effect of making it seem that you are standing farther from your subject than you really are. They're helpful when you don't want to back up, or can't because there are impediments in your way.

- **Wider field of view.** While making your subject seem farther away, as implied above, a wide-angle lens also provides a larger field of view, including more of the subject in your photos. Table 9.1 shows the diagonal field of view offered by an assortment of lenses, taking into account the crop factor introduced by the 7D's smaller-than-full-frame sensor.

- **More foreground.** As background objects retreat, more of the foreground is brought into view by a wide-angle lens. That gives you extra emphasis on the area that's closest to the camera. Photograph your home with a normal lens/normal zoom setting, and the front yard probably looks fairly conventional in your photo (that's why they're called "normal" lenses). Switch to a wider lens and you'll discover that your lawn now makes up much more of the photo. So, wide-angle lenses are great when you want to emphasize that lake in the foreground, but problematic when your intended subject is located farther in the distance.

Table 9.1 Field of View at Various Focal Lengths

Diagonal Field of View	Focal Length at 1X Crop	Focal Length Needed to Produce Same Field of View at 1.6X Crop
107 degrees	16mm	10mm
94 degrees	20mm	12mm
84 degrees	24mm	15mm
75 degrees	28mm	18mm
63 degrees	35mm	22mm
47 degrees	50mm	31mm
28 degrees	85mm	53mm
18 degrees	135mm	85mm
12 degrees	200mm	125mm
8.2 degrees	300mm	188mm

- **Super-sized subjects.** The tendency of a wide-angle lens to emphasize objects in the foreground, while de-emphasizing objects in the background can lead to a kind of size distortion that may be more objectionable for some types of subjects than others. Shoot a bed of flowers up close with a wide angle, and you might like the distorted effect of the larger blossoms nearer the lens. Take a photo of a family member with the same lens from the same distance, and you're likely to get some complaints about that gigantic nose in the foreground.

- **Perspective distortion.** When you tilt the camera so the plane of the sensor is no longer perpendicular to the vertical plane of your subject, some parts of the subject are now closer to the sensor than they were before, while other parts are farther away. So, buildings, flagpoles, or NBA players appear to be falling backwards, as you can see in Figure 9.10. While this kind of apparent distortion (it's not caused by a defect in the lens) can happen with any lens, it's most apparent when a wide angle is used.

- **Steady cam.** You'll find that you can hand-hold a wide-angle lens at slower shutter speeds, without need for image stabilization, than you can with a telephoto lens. The reduced magnification of the wide-lens or wide-zoom setting doesn't emphasize camera shake like a telephoto lens does.

- **Interesting angles.** Many of the factors already listed combine to produce more interesting angles when shooting with wide-angle lenses. Raising or lowering a telephoto lens a few feet probably will have little effect on the appearance of the distant subjects you're shooting. The same change in elevation can produce a dramatic effect for the much-closer subjects typically captured with a wide-angle lens or wide-zoom setting.

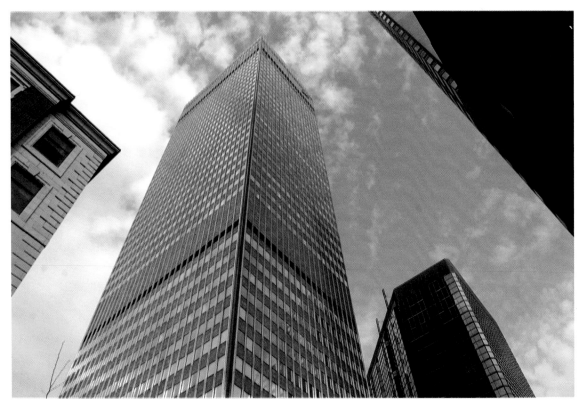

Figure 9.10 Tilting the camera back produces this "falling back" look in architectural photos.

The crop factor strikes again! You can see from Table 9.1 that wide-angle lenses provide a broader field of view, and that, because of the 7D's 1.6 crop factor, lenses must have a shorter focal length to provide the same field of view. If you like working with a 28mm lens with your full-frame camera, you'll need an 18mm lens for your 7D to get the same field of view. (Some focal lengths have been rounded slightly for simplification.)

DOF IN DEPTH

The depth-of-field (DOF) advantage of wide-angle lenses is diminished when you enlarge your picture; believe it or not, a wide-angle image enlarged and cropped to provide the same subject size as a telephoto shot would have the *same* depth-of-field. Try it: take a wide-angle photo of a friend from a fair distance, and then zoom in to duplicate the picture in a telephoto image. Then, enlarge the wide shot so your friend is the same size in both. The wide photo will have the same DOF (and will have much less detail, too).

Avoiding Potential Wide-Angle Problems

Wide-angle lenses have a few quirks that you'll want to keep in mind when shooting so you can avoid falling into some common traps. Here's a checklist of tips for avoiding common problems:

- **Symptom: converging lines.** Unless you want to use wildly diverging lines as a creative effect, it's a good idea to keep horizontal and vertical lines in landscapes, architecture, and other subjects carefully aligned with the sides, top, and bottom of the frame. That will help you avoid undesired perspective distortion. Sometimes it helps to shoot from a slightly elevated position so you don't have to tilt the camera up or down.

- **Symptom: color fringes around objects.** Lenses are often plagued with fringes of color around backlit objects, produced by *chromatic aberration*, which comes in two forms: *longitudinal/axial*, in which all the colors of light don't focus in the same plane; and *lateral/transverse*, in which the colors are shifted to one side. Axial chromatic aberration can be reduced by stopping down the lens, but transverse chromatic aberration cannot. Both can be reduced by using lenses with low diffraction index glass (or UD elements, in Canon nomenclature) and by incorporating elements that cancel the chromatic aberration of other glass in the lens. For example, a strong positive lens made of low-dispersion crown glass (made of a soda-lime-silica composite) may be mated with a weaker negative lens made of high-dispersion flint glass, which contains lead.

- **Symptom: lines that bow outward.** Some wide-angle lenses cause straight lines to bow outwards, with the strongest effect at the edges. In fisheye (or *curvilinear*) lenses, this defect is a feature, as you can see in Figure 9.11, which was an experimental shot where I set the white balance on tungsten and used flash for the foreground, producing a mixed-color look. When distortion is not desired, you'll need to use a lens that has corrected barrel distortion. Manufacturers like Canon do their best to minimize or eliminate it (producing a *rectilinear* lens), often using *aspherical* lens elements (which are not cross-sections of a sphere). You can also minimize less severe barrel distortion simply by framing your photo with some extra space all around, so the edges where the defect is most obvious can be cropped out of the picture.

- **Symptom: dark corners and shadows in flash photos.** The Canon EOS 7D's built-in electronic flash is designed to provide even coverage for lenses as wide as 17mm. If you use a wider lens, you can expect darkening, or *vignetting*, in the corners of the frame. At wider focal lengths, the lens hood of some lenses (my 17mm-85mm lens is a prime offender) can cast a semi-circular shadow in the lower portion of the frame when using the built-in flash. Sometimes removing the lens hood or zooming in a bit can eliminate the shadow. Mounting an external flash unit, such as the mighty Canon 580EX II can solve both problems, as it has zoomable coverage up to 114 degrees with the included adapter, sufficient for a 15mm rectilinear lens. Its higher vantage point eliminates the problem of lens hood shadow, too.

■ **Symptom: light and dark areas when using polarizing filter.** If you know that polarizers work best when the camera is pointed 90 degrees away from the sun and have the least effect when the camera is oriented 180 degrees from the sun, you know only half the story. With lenses having a focal length of 10mm to 18mm (the equivalent of 16mm-28mm), the angle of view (107 to 75 degrees diagonally, or 97 to 44 degrees horizontally) is extensive enough to cause problems. Think about it: when a 10mm lens is pointed at the proper 90-degree angle from the sun, objects at the edges of the frame will be oriented at 135 to 41 degrees, with only the center at exactly 90 degrees. Either edge will have much less of a polarized effect. The solution is to avoid using a polarizing filter with lenses having an actual focal length of less than 18mm (or 28mm equivalent).

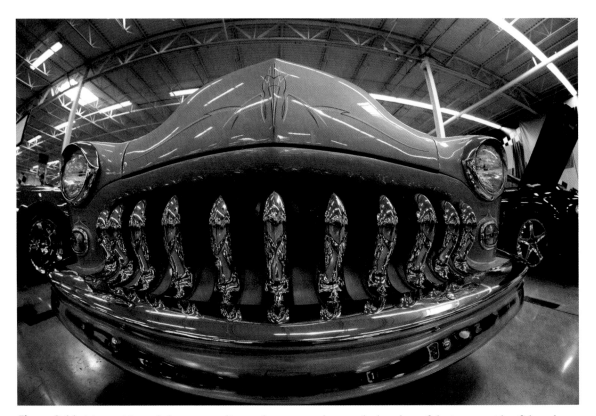

Figure 9.11 Many wide-angle lenses cause lines to bow outwards towards the edges of the image; with a fisheye lens, this tendency is especially useful for creating special effects, as in this shot.

Using Telephoto and Tele-Zoom Lenses

Telephoto lenses also can have a dramatic effect on your photography, and Canon is especially strong in the long-lens arena, with lots of choices in many focal lengths and zoom ranges. You should be able to find an affordable telephoto or tele-zoom to enhance your photography in several different ways. Here are the most important things you need to know. In the next section, I'll concentrate on telephoto considerations that can be problematic—and how to avoid those problems.

■ **Selective focus.** Long lenses have reduced depth-of-field within the frame, allowing you to use selective focus to isolate your subject. You can open the lens up wide to create shallow depth-of-field (see Figure 9.12), or close it down a bit to allow more to be in focus. The flip side of the coin is that when you *want* to make a range of objects sharp, you'll need to use a smaller f/stop to get the depth-of-field you need. Like fire, the depth-of-field of a telephoto lens can be friend or foe.

Figure 9.12
A wide f/stop helped isolate the lemur from its background.

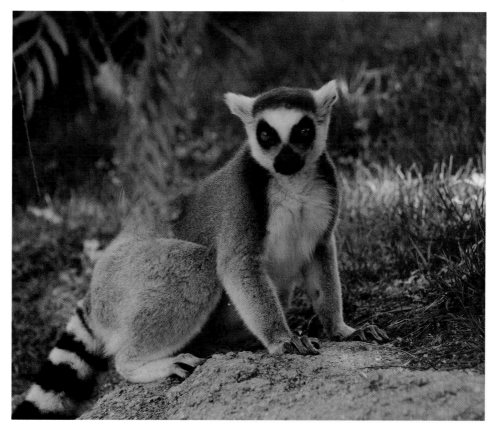

- **Getting closer.** Telephoto lenses bring you closer to wildlife, sports action, and candid subjects. No one wants to get a reputation as a surreptitious or "sneaky" photographer (except for paparazzi), but when applied to candids in an open and honest way, a long lens can help you capture memorable moments while retaining enough distance to stay out of the way of events as they transpire.

- **Reduced foreground/increased compression.** Telephoto lenses have the opposite effect of wide angles: they reduce the importance of things in the foreground by squeezing everything together. This compression even makes distant objects appear to be closer to subjects in the foreground and middle ranges. You can use this effect as a creative tool.

- **Accentuates camera shakiness.** Telephoto focal lengths hit you with a double-whammy in terms of camera/photographer shake. The lenses themselves are bulkier, more difficult to hold steady, and may even produce a barely perceptible see-saw rocking effect when you support them with one hand halfway down the lens barrel. Telephotos also magnify any camera shake. It's no wonder that image stabilization is popular in longer lenses.

- **Interesting angles require creativity.** Telephoto lenses require more imagination in selecting interesting angles, because the "angle" you do get on your subjects is so narrow. Moving from side to side or a bit higher or lower can make a dramatic difference in a wide-angle shot, but raising or lowering a telephoto lens a few feet probably will have little effect on the appearance of the distant subjects you're shooting.

Avoiding Telephoto Lens Problems

Many of the "problems" that telephoto lenses pose are really just challenges and not that difficult to overcome. Here is a list of the seven most common picture maladies and suggested solutions.

- **Symptom: flat faces in portraits.** Head-and-shoulders portraits of humans tend to be more flattering when a focal length of 50mm to 85mm is used. Longer focal lengths compress the distance between features like noses and ears, making the face look wider and flat. A wide-angle might make noses look huge and ears tiny when you fill the frame with a face. So stick with 50mm to 85mm focal lengths, going longer only when you're forced to shoot from a greater distance, and wider only when shooting three-quarters/full-length portraits, or group shots.

- **Symptom: blur due to camera shake.** Use a higher shutter speed (boosting ISO if necessary), consider an image-stabilized lens, or mount your camera on a tripod, monopod, or brace it with some other support. Of those three solutions, only the first will reduce blur caused by *subject* motion; an IS lens or tripod won't help you freeze a racecar in mid-lap.

- **Symptom: color fringes.** Chromatic aberration is the most pernicious optical problem found in telephoto lenses. There are others, including spherical aberration, astigmatism, coma, curvature of field, and similarly scary-sounding phenomena. The best solution for any of these is to use a better lens that offers the proper degree of correction, or stop down the lens to minimize the problem. But that's not always possible. Your second-best choice may be to correct the fringing in your favorite RAW conversion tool or image editor. Photoshop's Lens Correction filter offers sliders that minimize both red/cyan and blue/yellow fringing.

- **Symptom: lines that curve inwards.** Pincushion distortion is found in many telephoto lenses. You might find after a bit of testing that it is worse at certain focal lengths with your particular zoom lens. Like chromatic aberration, it can be partially corrected using tools like Photoshop's Lens Correction filter and Photoshop Elements' Correct Camera Distortion filter.

- **Symptom: low contrast from haze or fog.** When you're photographing distant objects, a long lens shoots through a lot more atmosphere, which generally is muddied up with extra haze and fog. That dirt or moisture in the atmosphere can reduce contrast and mute colors. Some feel that a skylight or UV filter can help, but this practice is mostly a holdover from the film days. Digital sensors are not sensitive enough to UV light for a UV filter to have much effect. So you should be prepared to boost contrast and color saturation in your Picture Styles menu or image editor if necessary.

- **Symptom: low contrast from flare.** Lenses are furnished with lens hoods for a good reason: to reduce flare from bright light sources at the periphery of the picture area, or completely outside it. Because telephoto lenses often create images that are lower in contrast in the first place, you'll want to be especially careful to use a lens hood to prevent further effects on your image (or shade the front of the lens with your hand).

- **Symptom: dark flash photos.** Edge-to-edge flash coverage isn't a problem with telephoto lenses as it is with wide angles. The shooting distance is. A long lens might make a subject that's 50 feet away look as if it's right next to you, but your camera's flash isn't fooled. You'll need extra power for distant flash shots, and probably more power than your 7D's built-in flash provides. The shoe-mount Canon 580EX II Speedlite, for example, can automatically zoom its coverage down to that of a medium telephoto lens, providing a theoretical full-power shooting aperture of about f/8 at 50 feet and ISO 400. (Try *that* with the built-in flash!)

Telephotos and Bokeh

Bokeh describes the aesthetic qualities of the out-of-focus parts of an image and whether out-of-focus points of light—circles of confusion—are rendered as distracting fuzzy discs or smoothly fade into the background. *Boke* is a Japanese word for "blur," and the h was added to keep English speakers from rendering it monosyllabically to rhyme with *broke.* Although bokeh is visible in blurry portions of any image, it's of particular concern with telephoto lenses, which, thanks to the magic of reduced depth-of-field, produce more obviously out-of-focus areas.

Bokeh can vary from lens to lens, or even within a given lens depending on the f/stop in use. Bokeh becomes objectionable when the circles of confusion are evenly illuminated, making them stand out as distinct discs, or, worse, when these circles are darker in the center, producing an ugly "doughnut" effect. A lens defect called spherical aberration may produce out-of-focus discs that are brighter on the edges and darker in the center, because the lens doesn't focus light passing through the edges of the lens exactly as it does light going through the center. (Mirror or *catadioptric* lenses also produce this effect.)

Other kinds of spherical aberration generate circles of confusion that are brightest in the center and fade out at the edges, producing a smooth blending effect, as you can see at right in Figure 9.13. Ironically, when no spherical aberration is present at all, the discs are a uniform shade, which, while better than the doughnut effect, is not as pleasing as the bright center/dark edge rendition. The shape of the disc also comes into play, with round smooth circles considered the best, and nonagonal or some other polygon (determined by the shape of the lens diaphragm) considered less desirable.

If you plan to use selective focus a lot, you should investigate the bokeh characteristics of a particular lens before you buy. Canon user groups and forums will usually be full of comments and questions about bokeh, so the research is fairly easy.

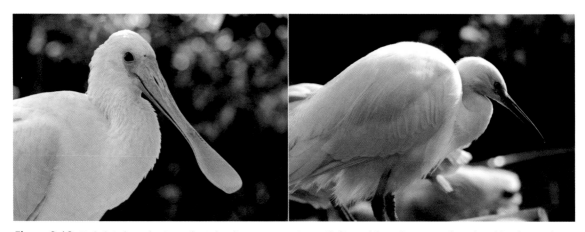

Figure 9.13 Bokeh is less pleasing when the discs are prominent (left), and less obtrusive when they blend into the background (right).

Add-ons and Special Features

Once you've purchased your telephoto lens, you'll want to think about some appropriate accessories for it. There are some handy add-ons available that can be valuable. Here are a couple of them to think about.

Lens Hoods

Lens hoods are an important accessory for all lenses, but they're especially valuable with telephotos. As I mentioned earlier, lens hoods do a good job of preserving image contrast by keeping bright light sources outside the field of view from striking the lens and, potentially, bouncing around inside that long tube to generate flare that, when coupled with atmospheric haze, can rob your image of detail and snap. In addition, lens hoods serve as valuable protection for that large, vulnerable, front lens element. It's easy to forget that you've got that long tube sticking out in front of your camera and accidentally whack the front of your lens into something. It's cheaper to replace a lens hood than it is to have a lens repaired, so you might find that a good hood is valuable protection for your prized optics.

When choosing a lens hood, it's important to have the right hood for the lens, usually the one offered for that lens by Canon or the third-party manufacturer. You want a hood that blocks precisely the right amount of light: neither too much light nor too little. A hood with a front diameter that is too small can show up in your pictures as vignetting. A hood that has a front diameter that's too large isn't stopping all the light it should. Generic lens hoods may not do the job.

When your telephoto is a zoom lens, it's even more important to get the right hood, because you need one that does what it is supposed to at both the wide-angle and telephoto ends of the zoom range. Lens hoods may be cylindrical, rectangular (shaped like the image frame), or petal shaped (that is, cylindrical, but with cut-out areas at the corners which correspond to the actual image area). Lens hoods should be mounted in the correct orientation (a bayonet mount for the hood usually takes care of this).

Telephoto Extenders

Telephoto extenders (often called teleconverters outside the Canon world), multiply the actual focal length of your lens, giving you a longer telephoto for much less than the price of a lens with that actual focal length. These extenders fit between the lens and your camera and contain optical elements that magnify the image produced by the lens. Available in 1.4X and 2.0X configurations from Canon, an extender transforms, say, a 200mm lens into a 280mm or 400mm optic, respectively. Given the 7D's crop factor, your 200mm lens now has the same field of view as a 448mm or 640mm lens on a full-frame camera. At around $300 each, they're quite a bargain, aren't they?

Actually, there are some downsides. While extenders retain the closest focusing distance of your original lens, autofocus is maintained only if the lens's original maximum aperture is f/4 or larger (for the 1.4X extender) or f/2.8 or larger (for the 2X extender). The components reduce the effective aperture of any lens they are used with, by one f/stop with the 1.4X extender, and 2 f/stops with the 2X extender. So, your EF 200mm f/2.8L II USM becomes a 280mm f/4 or 400mm f/5.6 lens. Although Canon extenders are precision optical devices, they do cost you a little sharpness, but that improves when you reduce the aperture by a stop or two. Each of the extenders is compatible only with a particular set of lenses of 135mm focal length or greater, so you'll want to check Canon's compatibility chart to see if the component can be used with the lens you want to attach to it.

If your lenses are compatible and you're shooting under bright lighting conditions, the Canon Extender EF 1.4x II, and Canon Extender EF 2x II make handy accessories.

Macro Focusing

Some telephotos and telephoto zooms available for the 7D have particularly close focusing capabilities, making them *macro* lenses. Of course, the object is not necessarily to get close (get too close and you'll find it difficult to light your subject). What you're really looking for in a macro lens is to magnify the apparent size of the subject in the final image. Camera-to-subject distance is most important when you want to back up farther from your subject (say, to avoid spooking skittish insects or small animals). In that case, you'll want a macro lens with a longer focal length to allow that distance while retaining the desired magnification.

Canon makes 50mm, 60mm, 65mm, 100mm, and 180mm lenses with official macro designations. You'll also find macro lenses, macro zooms, and other close-focusing lenses available from Sigma, Tamron, and Tokina. If you want to focus closer with a macro lens, or any other lens, you can add an accessory called an *extension tube*, like the one shown in Figure 9.14. These add-ons move the lens farther from the focal plane, allowing it to focus more closely. Canon also sells add-on close-up lenses, which look like filters, and allow lenses to focus more closely.

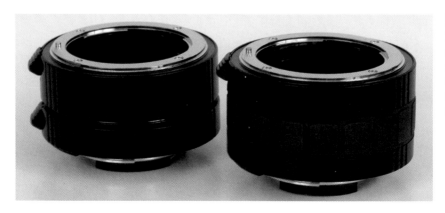

Figure 9.14
Extension tubes enable any lens to focus more closely to the subject.

Image Stabilization

Canon has a burgeoning line of more than a dozen lenses with built-in image stabilization (IS) capabilities. This feature uses lens elements that are shifted internally in response to the motion of the lens during hand-held photography, countering the shakiness the camera and photographer produce and which telephoto lenses magnify. However, IS is not limited to long lenses; the feature works like a champ at the 17mm zoom position of Canon's EF-S 17-85mm f4-5.6 IS USM and EF-S 17-55 f/2.8 IS USM lenses. Other Canon IS lenses provide stabilization with zooms that are as wide as 24-28mm.

Image stabilization provides you with camera steadiness that's the equivalent of at least two or three shutter speed increments. (Canon claims four, which I feel may be optimistic.) This extra margin can be invaluable when you're shooting under dim lighting conditions or hand-holding a long lens for, say, wildlife photography. Perhaps that shot of a foraging deer calls for a shutter speed of 1/1,000th second at f/5.6 with your EF 100-400mm f/4.5-5.6L IS USM lens. Relax. You can shoot at 1/250th second at f/11 and get virtually the same results, as long as the deer doesn't decide to bound off.

Or, maybe you're shooting a high school play without a tripod or monopod, and you'd really, really like to use 1/15th second at f/4. Assuming the actors aren't flitting around the stage at high speed, your 17mm-85mm IS lens can grab the shot for you at its wide-angle position. However, keep these facts in mind:

- **IS doesn't stop action.** Unfortunately, no IS lens is a panacea to replace the action-stopping capabilities of a higher shutter speed. Image stabilization applies only to camera shake. You still need a fast shutter speed to freeze action. IS works great in low light, when you're using long lenses, and for macro photography. It's not always the best choice for action photography (unless you're willing to let subject motion become part of your image, as in Figure 9.15). In other situations, you may need enough light to allow a sufficiently high shutter speed. But in that case, IS can make your shot even sharper.

- **IS slows you down.** The process of adjusting the lens elements takes time, just as autofocus does, so you might find that IS adds to the lag between when you press the shutter and when the picture is actually taken. That's another reason why image stabilization might not be a good choice for sports.

- **Use when appropriate.** Some IS lenses produce worse results if you use them while you're panning, although newer Canon IS lenses have a mode that works fine when the camera is deliberately moved from side to side (or up and down) during exposure. Older lenses can confuse the motion with camera shake and overcompensate. You might want to switch off IS when panning or when your camera is mounted on a tripod.

- **Do you need IS at all?** Remember that an inexpensive monopod might be able to provide the same additional steadiness as a IS lens, at a much lower cost.

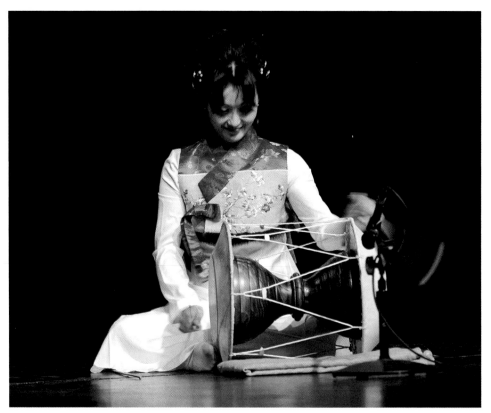

Figure 9.15
Image stabilization made it possible to shoot this concert photo with a 200mm lens at 1/60th second. Note that the drummer's hands are still a blur, but her beautiful costume is vividly sharp.

IMAGE STABILIZATION: IN THE CAMERA OR IN THE LENS?

Sony's acquisition of Konica Minolta's dSLR assets and the introduction of an improved in-camera image-stabilization system has revised an old debate about whether IS belongs in the camera or in the lens. Perhaps it's my Canon bias showing, but I am quite happy not to have image stabilization available in the body itself. Here are some reasons:

- Should in-camera IS fail, you have to send the whole camera in for repair, and camera repairs are generally more expensive than lens repairs. I like being able to simply switch to another lens if I have an IS problem.

- IS in the camera doesn't steady your view in the viewfinder, whereas an IS lens shows you a steadied image as you shoot.

- You're stuck with the IS system built into your camera. If an improved system is incorporated into a lens and the improvements are important to you, just trade in your old lens for the new one.

- Optimized stabilization. Canon claims that it is able to produce the best possible image stabilization for each lens it introduces, something that would not be possible if a "one size fits all lenses" stabilization scheme had to be built into the camera.

10

Working with Light

Successful photographers and artists have an intimate understanding of the importance of light in shaping an image. Rembrandt was a master of using light to create moods and reveal the character of his subjects. Artist Thomas Kinkade's official tagline is "Painter of Light." The late Dean Collins, co-founder of Finelight Studios, revolutionized how a whole generation of photographers learned and used lighting. Photo guru Ed Pierce has a popular seminar called "Captivated by the Light." It's impossible to underestimate how the use of light adds to—and how misuse can detract from—your photographs.

All forms of visual art use light to shape the finished product. Sculptors don't have control over the light used to illuminate their finished work, so they must create shapes using planes and curved surfaces so that the form envisioned by the artist comes to life from a variety of viewing and lighting angles. Painters, in contrast, have absolute control over both shape and light in their work, as well as the viewing angle, so they can use both the contours of their two-dimensional subjects and the qualities of the "light" they use to illuminate those subjects to evoke the image they want to produce.

Photography is a third form of art. The photographer may have little or no control over the subject (other than posing human subjects) but can often adjust both viewing angle *and* the nature of the light source to create a particular compelling image. The direction and intensity of the light sources create the shapes and textures that we see. The distribution and proportions determine the contrast and tonal values: whether the image is stark or high key, or muted and low in contrast. The colors of the light (because even "white" light has a color balance that the sensor can detect), and how much of those colors the subject reflects or absorbs, paint the hues visible in the image.

As an EOS 7D photographer, you must learn to be a painter and sculptor of light if you want to move from *taking* a picture to *making* a photograph. This chapter introduces using the two main types of illumination: *continuous* lighting (such as daylight, incandescent, or fluorescent sources) and the brief, but brilliant snippets of light we call *electronic flash.*

Continuous Illumination versus Electronic Flash

Continuous lighting is exactly what you might think: uninterrupted illumination that is available all the time during a shooting session. Daylight, moonlight, and the artificial lighting encountered both indoors and outdoors count as continuous light sources (although all of them can be "interrupted" by passing clouds, solar eclipses, a blown fuse, or simply by switching off a lamp). Indoor continuous illumination includes both the lights that are there already (such as incandescent lamps or overhead fluorescent lights indoors) and fixtures you supply yourself, including photoflood lamps or reflectors used to bounce existing light onto your subject.

Electronic flash is notable because it can be much more intense than continuous lighting, lasts only a brief moment, and can be much more portable than supplementary incandescent sources. It's a light source you can carry with you and use anywhere. Indeed, your EOS 7D has a flip-up electronic flash unit built in, as shown in Figure 10.1.

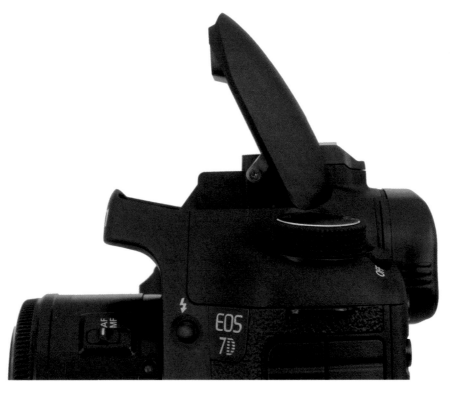

Figure 10.1
One form of light that's always available is the flip-up flash on your EOS 7D.

But you can also use an external flash, either mounted on the 7D's accessory shoe or used off-camera and linked with a cable or triggered by a slave light (which sets off a flash when it senses the firing of another unit). Studio flash units are electronic flash, too, and aren't limited to "professional" shooters, as there are economical "monolight" (one-piece flash/power supply) units available in the $200 price range. You can buy a couple to store in a closet and use to set up a home studio, or use as supplementary lighting when traveling away from home.

There are advantages and disadvantages to each type of illumination. Here's a quick checklist of pros and cons:

- **Lighting preview—Pro: continuous lighting.** With continuous lighting, you always know exactly what kind of lighting effect you're going to get and, if multiple light sources are used, how they will interact with each other, as shown in Figure 10.2, where the main light was the sun, but a bit of fill was provided by a gold reflector held up a few feet off-camera to her left. With electronic flash, the general effect you're going to see may be a mystery until you've built some experience, and you may need to review a shot on the LCD, make some adjustments, and then reshoot to get the look you want. (In this sense, a digital camera's review capabilities replace the Polaroid test shots pro photographers relied on in decades past.)

- **Exposure calculation—Pro: continuous lighting.** Your 7D has no problem calculating exposure for continuous lighting, because the illumination remains constant and can be measured through a sensor that interprets the light reaching the viewfinder. The amount of light available just before the exposure will, in almost all cases, be the same amount of light present when the shutter is released. The 7D's spot metering mode can be used to measure and compare the proportions of light in the highlights and shadows, so you can make an adjustment (such as using more or less fill light) if necessary. You can even use a hand-held light meter to measure the light yourself.

- **Exposure calculation—Con: electronic flash.** Electronic flash illumination doesn't exist until the flash fires and so can't be measured by the 7D's exposure sensor when the mirror is flipped up during the exposure. Instead, the light must be measured metering the intensity of a preflash triggered an instant before the main flash, as it is reflected back to the camera and through the lens. An alternative is to use a sensor built into the flash itself and measure reflected light that has not traveled through the lens. If you have a do-it-yourself bent, there are hand-held flash meters, too, including models that measure both flash and continuous light.

- **Evenness of illumination—Pro/con: continuous lighting.** Of continuous light sources, daylight, in particular, provides illumination that tends to fill an image completely, lighting up the foreground, background, and your subject almost equally. Shadows do come into play, of course, so you might need to use reflectors or fill-in light sources to even out the illumination further, but barring objects that block large sections of your image from daylight, the light is spread fairly evenly. Indoors, however, continuous lighting is commonly less evenly distributed. The average living room, for example, has hot spots and dark corners. But on the plus side, you can *see* this uneven illumination and compensate with additional lamps.

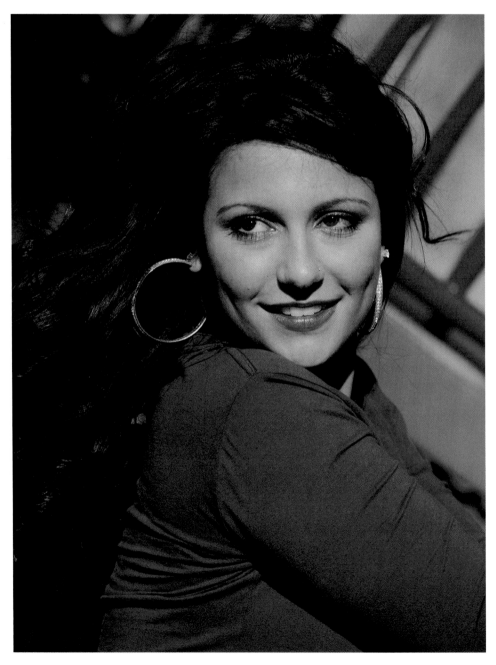

Figure 10.2
You always know how the lighting will look when using continuous illumination.

■ **Evenness of illumination—Con: electronic flash.** Electronic flash units (like continuous light sources such as lamps that don't have the advantage of being located 93 million miles from the subject) suffer from the effects of their proximity. The *inverse square law,* first applied to both gravity and light by Sir Isaac Newton, dictates that as a light source's distance increases from the subject, the amount of light reaching the subject falls off proportionately to the square of the distance. In plain English, that means that a flash or lamp that's eight feet away from a subject provides only one-quarter as much illumination as a source that's four feet away (rather than half as much). (See Figure 10.3.) This translates into relatively shallow "depth-of-light."

Figure 10.3
A light source that is twice as far away provides only one-quarter as much illumination.

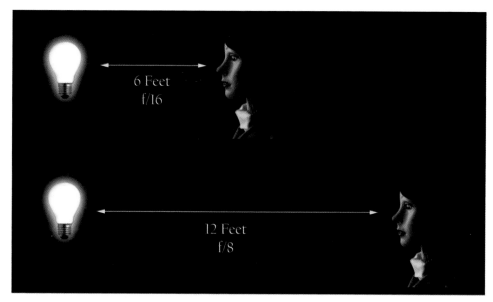

■ **Action stopping—Con: continuous lighting.** Action stopping with continuous light sources is completely dependent on the shutter speed you've dialed in on the camera. And the speeds available are dependent on the amount of light available and your ISO sensitivity setting. Outdoors in daylight, there will probably be enough sunlight to let you shoot at 1/2,500th second and f/6.3 with a non-grainy sensitivity setting of ISO 400. That's a fairly useful combination of settings if you're not using a super-telephoto with a small maximum aperture. But inside, the reduced illumination quickly has you pushing your EOS 7D to its limits. For example, if you're shooting indoor sports, there probably won't be enough available light to allow you to use a 1/2,000th second shutter speed (although I routinely shoot indoor basketball with my 7D at ISO 1600 and 1/500th second at f/4). In many indoor sports situations, you may find yourself limited to 1/500th second or slower.

■ **Action stopping—Pro: electronic flash.** When it comes to the ability to freeze moving objects in their tracks, the advantage goes to electronic flash. The brief duration of electronic flash serves as a very high "shutter speed" when the flash is the main or only source of illumination for the photo. Your EOS 7D's shutter speed may be set for 1/250th second during a flash exposure, but if the flash illumination predominates, the *effective* exposure time will be the 1/1,000th to 1/50,000th second or less duration of the flash, as you can see in Figure 10.4, because the flash unit reduces the amount of light released by cutting short the duration of the flash. The only fly in the ointment is that, if the ambient light is strong enough, it may produce a secondary, "ghost" exposure, as I'll explain later in this chapter.

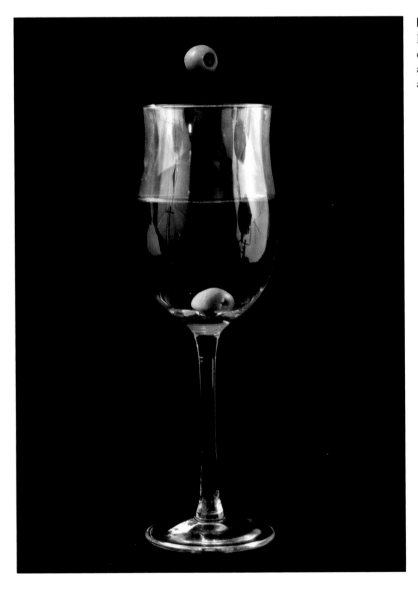

Figure 10.4
Electronic flash can freeze almost any action.

- **Cost—Pro: continuous lighting.** Incandescent or fluorescent lamps are generally much less expensive than electronic flash units, which can easily cost several hundred dollars. I've used everything from desktop hi-intensity lamps to reflector floodlights for continuous illumination at very little cost. There are lamps made especially for photographic purposes, too, priced up to $50 or so. Maintenance is economical, too: many incandescent or fluorescents use bulbs that cost only a few dollars.

- **Cost—Con: electronic flash.** Electronic flash units aren't particularly cheap. The lowest-cost dedicated flash designed specifically for the Canon dSLRs is about $110. Such units are limited in features, however, and intended for those with entry-level cameras. Plan on spending some money to get the features that a sophisticated electronic flash offers.

- **Flexibility—Con: continuous lighting.** Because incandescent and fluorescent lamps are not as bright as electronic flash, the slower shutter speeds required (see Action stopping) mean that you may have to use a tripod more often, especially when shooting portraits. The incandescent variety of continuous lighting gets hot, especially in the studio, and the side effects range from discomfort (for your human models) to disintegration (if you happen to be shooting perishable foods like ice cream). The heat also makes it more difficult to add filtration to incandescent sources.

- **Flexibility—Pro: electronic flash.** Electronic flash's action-freezing power allows you to work without a tripod in the studio (and elsewhere), adding flexibility and speed when choosing angles and positions. Flash units can be easily filtered, and, because the filtration is placed over the light source rather than the lens, you don't need to use high quality filter material. For example, a couple sheets of unexposed, processed Ektachrome film can make a dandy infrared-pass filter for your flash unit. Roscoe or Lee lighting gels, which may be too flimsy to use in front of the lens, can be mounted or taped in front of your flash with ease.

Continuous Lighting Basics

While continuous lighting and its effects are generally much easier to visualize and use than electronic flash, there are some factors you need to take into account, particularly the color temperature of the light. (Color temperature concerns aren't exclusive to continuous light sources, of course, but the variations tend to be more extreme and less predictable than those of electronic flash.)

Color temperature, in practical terms, is how "bluish" or how "reddish" the light appears to be to the digital camera's sensor. Indoor illumination is quite warm, comparatively, and appears reddish to the sensor. Daylight, in contrast, seems much bluer to the sensor. Our eyes (our brains, actually) are quite adaptable to these variations, so white objects don't appear to have an orange tinge when viewed indoors, nor do they seem excessively blue outdoors in full daylight. Yet, these color temperature variations are real and the sensor is not fooled. To capture the most accurate colors, we need to take the color temperature into account in setting the color balance (or *white balance*) of the 7D—either automatically using the camera's smarts or manually, using our own knowledge and experience.

Color temperature can be confusing, because of a seeming contradiction in how color temperatures are named: warmer (more reddish) color temperatures (measured in degrees Kelvin) are the *lower* numbers, while cooler (bluer) color temperatures are *higher* numbers. It might not make sense to say that 3,400K is warmer than 6,000K, but that's the way it is. If it helps, think of a glowing red ember contrasted with a white-hot welder's torch, rather than fire and ice.

The confusion comes from physics. Scientists calculate color temperature from the light emitted by a mythical object called a black body radiator, which absorbs all the radiant energy that strikes it, and reflects none at all. Such a black body not only *absorbs* light perfectly, but it *emits* it perfectly when heated (and since nothing in the universe is perfect, that makes it mythical).

At a particular physical temperature, this imaginary object always emits light of the same wavelength or color. That makes it possible to define color temperature in terms of actual temperature in degrees on the Kelvin scale that scientists use. Incandescent light, for example, typically has a color temperature of 3,200K to 3,400K. Daylight might range from 5,500K to 6,000K. Each type of illumination we use for photography has its own color temperature range—with some cautions. The next sections will summarize everything you need to know about the qualities of these light sources.

Daylight

Daylight is produced by the sun, and so is moonlight (which is just reflected sunlight). Daylight is present, of course, even when you can't see the sun. When sunlight is direct, it can be bright and harsh. If daylight is diffused by clouds, softened by bouncing off objects such as walls or your photo reflectors, or filtered by shade, it can be much dimmer and less contrasty.

Daylight's color temperature can vary quite widely. It is highest (most blue) at noon when the sun is directly overhead, because the light is traveling through a minimum amount of the filtering layer we call the atmosphere. The color temperature at high noon may be 6,000K. At other times of day, the sun is lower in the sky and the particles in the air provide a filtering effect that warms the illumination to about 5,500K for most of the day. Starting an hour before dusk and for an hour after sunrise, the warm appearance of the sunlight is even visible to our eyes when the color temperature may dip below 4,500K, as shown in Figure 10.5

Figure 10.5 At dawn and dusk, the color temperature of daylight may dip below 4,500K, providing this reddish rendition.

Because you'll be taking so many photos in daylight, you'll want to learn how to use or compensate for the brightness and contrast of sunlight, as well as how to deal with its color temperature. I'll provide some hints later in this chapter.

Incandescent/Tungsten Light

The term incandescent or tungsten illumination is usually applied to the direct descendents of Thomas Edison's original electric lamp. Such lights consist of a glass bulb that contains a vacuum, or is filled with a halogen gas, and contains a tungsten filament that is heated by an electrical current, producing photons and heat. Tungsten-halogen lamps are a variation on the basic light bulb, using a more rugged (and longer-lasting) filament that can be heated to a higher temperature, housed in a thicker glass or quartz envelope, and filled with iodine or bromine ("halogen") gases. The higher temperature allows tungsten-halogen (or quartz-halogen/quartz-iodine, depending on their construction) lamps to burn "hotter" and whiter. Although popular for automobile headlamps today, they are also popular for photographic illumination.

Although incandescent illumination isn't a perfect black body radiator, it's close enough that the color temperature of such lamps can be precisely calculated and used for photography without concerns about color variation (at least, until the very end of the lamp's life).

The other qualities of this type of lighting, such as contrast, are dependent on the distance of the lamp from the subject, type of reflectors used, and other factors that I'll explain later in this chapter.

Fluorescent Light/Other Light Sources

Fluorescent light has some advantages in terms of illumination, but some disadvantages from a photographic standpoint. This type of lamp generates light through an electro-chemical reaction that emits most of its energy as visible light, rather than heat, which is why the bulbs don't get as hot. The type of light produced varies depending on the phosphor coatings and type of gas in the tube. So, the illumination fluorescent bulbs produce can vary widely in its characteristics.

That's not great news for photographers. Different types of lamps have different "color temperatures" that can't be precisely measured in degrees Kelvin, because the light isn't produced by heating. Worse, fluorescent lamps have a discontinuous spectrum of light that can have some colors missing entirely. A particular type of tube can lack certain shades of red or other colors (see Figure 10.6), which is why fluorescent lamps and other

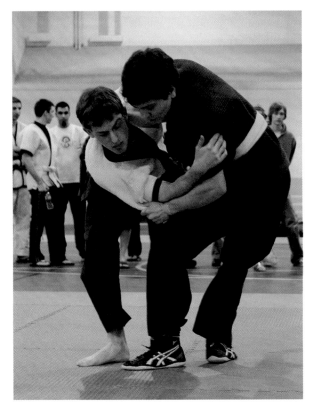

Figure 10.6
The fluorescent lighting in this gym added a distinct greenish cast to the image.

alternative technologies such as sodium-vapor illumination can produce ghastly look-ing human skin tones. Their spectra can lack the reddish tones we associate with healthy skin and emphasize the blues and greens popular in horror movies.

Adjusting White Balance

I showed you how to adjust white balance in Chapter 4, using the 7D's built-in presets, white balance shift capabilities, and white balance bracketing (there's more on bracket-ing in Chapter 4, too).

In most cases, however, the EOS 7D will do a good job of calculating white balance for you, so Auto can be used as your choice most of the time. Use the preset values or set a custom white balance that matches the current shooting conditions when you need to. The only really problematic light sources are likely to be fluorescents. Vendors, such as GE and Sylvania, may actually provide a figure known as the *color rendering index* (or CRI), which is a measure of how accurately a particular light source represents standard colors, using a scale of 0 (some sodium-vapor lamps) to 100 (daylight and most incan-descent lamps). Daylight fluorescents and deluxe cool white fluorescents might have a CRI of about 79 to 95, which is perfectly acceptable for most photographic applica-tions. Warm white fluorescents might have a CRI of 55. White deluxe mercury vapor lights are less suitable with a CRI of 45, while low-pressure sodium lamps can vary from CRI 0-18.

Remember that if you shoot RAW, you can specify the white balance of your image when you import it into Photoshop, Photoshop Elements, or another image editor using your preferred RAW converter. While color-balancing filters that fit on the front of the lens exist, they are primarily useful for film cameras, because film's color balance can't be tweaked as extensively or as easily as that of a sensor.

Electronic Flash Basics

Until you delve into the situation deeply enough, it might appear that serious photog-raphers have a love/hate relationship with electronic flash. You'll often hear that flash photography is less natural looking, and that the built-in flash in most cameras should never be used as the primary source of illumination because it provides a harsh, garish look. Indeed, most "pro" cameras like the Canon EOS 1D Mark III and 1Ds Mark III don't have a built-in flash at all. Available ("continuous") lighting is praised, and built-in flash photography seems to be roundly denounced.

In truth, however, the bias is against *bad* flash photography. Indeed, flash has become the studio light source of choice for pro photographers, because it's more intense (and its intensity can be varied to order by the photographer), freezes action, frees you from using a tripod (unless you want to use one to lock down a composition), and has a snappy, consistent light quality that matches daylight. (While color balance changes as the flash duration shortens, some Canon flash units can communicate to the camera the exact white balance provided for that shot.) And even pros will cede that the built-in flash of the Canon EOS 7D has some important uses as an adjunct to existing light, particularly to illuminate dark shadows using a technique called *fill flash*.

But electronic flash isn't as inherently easy to use as continuous lighting. As I noted earlier, electronic flash units are more expensive, don't show you exactly what the lighting effect will be (unless you use a second source called a *modeling light* for a preview), and the exposure of electronic flash units is more difficult to calculate accurately.

How Electronic Flash Works

The bursts of light we call electronic flash are produced by a flash of photons generated by an electrical charge that is accumulated in a component called a *capacitor* and then directed through a glass tube containing xenon gas, which absorbs the energy and emits the brief flash. For the pop-up flash built into the EOS 7D, the full burst of light lasts about 1/1,000th of a second and provides enough illumination to shoot a subject 10 feet away at f/4 using the ISO 100 setting. In a more typical situation, you'd use ISO 200, f/5.6 to f/8 and photograph something 8 to 10 feet away. As you can see, the built-in flash is somewhat limited in range; you'll see why external flash units are often a good idea later in this chapter.

An electronic flash (whether built in or connected to the EOS 7D through the PC terminal or a cable plugged into a hot shoe adapter) is triggered at the instant of exposure, during a period when the sensor is fully exposed by the shutter. As I mentioned earlier in this book, the 7D has a vertically traveling shutter that consists of two curtains. The first curtain opens and moves to the opposite side of the frame, at which point the shutter is completely open. The flash can be triggered at this point (so-called *1st curtain sync*), making the flash exposure. Then, after a delay that can vary from 30 seconds to 1/250th second (with the EOS 7D; other cameras may sync at a faster or slower speed), a second curtain begins moving across the sensor plane, covering up the sensor again. If the flash is triggered just before the second curtain starts to close, then *2nd curtain sync* is used. In both cases, though, a shutter speed of 1/250th second is the maximum that can be used to take a photo.

Figure 10.7 illustrates how this works. At upper left, you can see a fanciful illustration of a generic shutter (your EOS 7D's shutter does *not* look like this), with both curtains tightly closed. At upper right, the first curtain begins to move downwards, starting to expose a narrow slit that reveals the sensor behind the shutter. At lower left, the first curtain moves downwards farther until, as you can see at lower right in the figure, the sensor is fully exposed.

When 1st curtain sync is used, the flash is triggered at the instant that the sensor is completely exposed. The shutter then remains open for an additional length of time

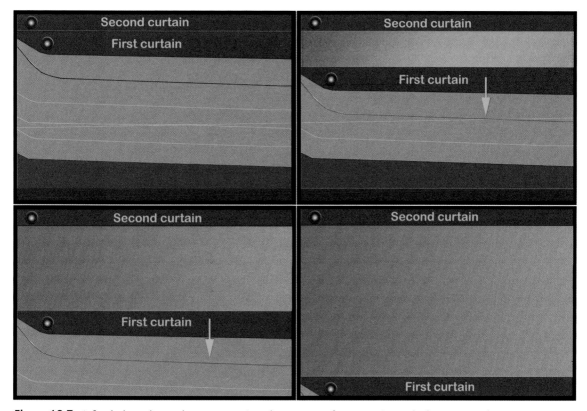

Figure 10.7 A focal plane shutter has two curtains, the upper, or front curtain, and a lower, second curtain.

(from 30 seconds to 1/250th second), and the second curtain begins to move downward, covering the sensor once more. When 2nd curtain sync is activated, the flash is triggered *after* the main exposure is over, just before the second curtain begins to move downward.

Ghost Images

The difference between triggering the flash when the shutter just opens, or just when it begins to close might not seem like much. But whether you use 1st curtain sync (the default setting) or 2nd curtain sync (an optional setting) can make a significant difference to your photograph *if the ambient light in your scene also contributes to the image.* You can set either of these sync modes in the Shooting 1 menu, under Flash Control and the Built-in flash func. setting and External flash func. setting options.

At faster shutter speeds, particularly 1/250th second, there isn't much time for the ambient light to register, unless it is very bright. It's likely that the electronic flash will provide almost all the illumination, so 1st curtain sync or 2nd curtain sync isn't very important. However, at slower shutter speeds, or with very bright ambient light levels, there is a significant difference, particularly if your subject is moving, or the camera isn't steady.

In any of those situations, the ambient light will register as a second image accompanying the flash exposure, and if there is movement (camera or subject), that additional image will not be in the same place as the flash exposure. It will show as a ghost image and, if the movement is significant enough, as a blurred ghost image trailing in front of or behind your subject in the direction of the movement.

As I noted, when you're using 1st curtain sync, the flash's main burst goes off the instant the shutter opens fully (a preflash used to measure exposure in auto flash modes fires *before* the shutter opens). This produces an image of the subject on the sensor. Then, the shutter remains open for an additional period (30 seconds to 1/250th second, as I said). If your subject is moving, say, towards the right side of the frame, the ghost image produced by the ambient light will produce a blur on the right side of the original subject image, making it look as if your sharp (flash-produced) image is chasing the ghost. For those of us who grew up with lightning-fast superheroes who always left a ghost trail *behind them*, that looks unnatural (see Figure 10.8).

So, Canon uses 2nd curtain sync to remedy the situation. In that mode, the shutter opens, as before. The shutter remains open for its designated duration, and the ghost image forms. If your subject moves from the left side of the frame to the right side, the ghost will move from left to right, too. *Then*, about 1.5 milliseconds before the second shutter curtain closes, the flash is triggered, producing a nice, sharp flash image *ahead* of the ghost image. Voilà! We have monsieur *Speed Racer* outdriving his own trailing image.

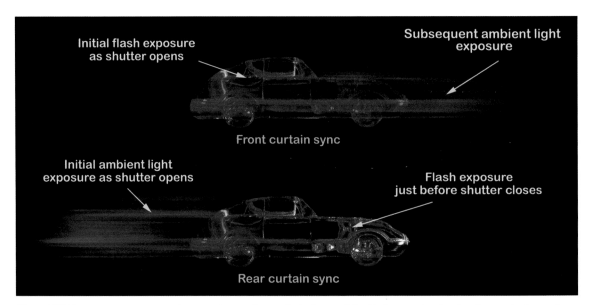

Figure 10.8 1st curtain sync produces an image that trails in front of the flash exposure (top), whereas 2nd curtain sync creates a more "natural looking" trail behind the flash image.

Avoiding Sync Speed Problems

Using a shutter speed faster than 1/250th second can cause problems. Triggering the electronic flash only when the shutter is completely open makes a lot of sense if you think about what's going on. To obtain shutter speeds faster than 1/250th second, the 7D exposes only part of the sensor at one time, by starting the second curtain on its journey before the first curtain has completely opened, as shown in Figure 10.9. That effectively provides a briefer exposure as a slit, narrower than the full height of the sensor, passes over it. If the flash were to fire during the time when the first and second curtains partially obscured the sensor, only the slit that was actually open would be exposed.

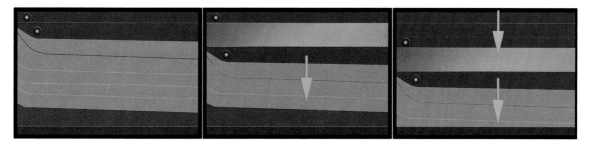

Figure 10.9 A closed shutter (left); partially open shutter as the first curtain begins to move downward (middle); only part of the sensor is exposed as the slit moves (right).

You'd end up with only a narrow band, representing the portion of the sensor that was exposed when the picture is taken. For shutter speeds *faster* than 1/250th second, the second curtain begins moving *before* the first curtain reaches the bottom of the frame. As a result, a moving slit, the distance between the first and second curtains, exposes one portion of the sensor at a time as it moves from the top to the bottom. Figure 10.9 shows three views of our typical (but imaginary) focal plane shutter. At left is pictured the closed shutter; in the middle version you can see the first curtain has moved down about 1/4 of the distance from the top; and in the right-hand version, the second curtain has started to "chase" the first curtain across the frame towards the bottom.

If the flash is triggered while this slit is moving, only the exposed portion of the sensor will receive any illumination. You end up with a photo like the one shown in Figure 10.10. Note that a band across the bottom of the image is black. That's a shadow of the second shutter curtain, which had started to move when the flash was triggered. Sharp-eyed readers will wonder why the black band is at the *bottom* of the frame rather than at the top, where the second curtain begins its journey. The answer is simple: your lens flips the image upside down and forms it on the sensor in a reversed position. You never notice that, because the camera is smart enough to show you the pixels that make up your photo in their proper orientation. But this image flip is why, if your sensor gets

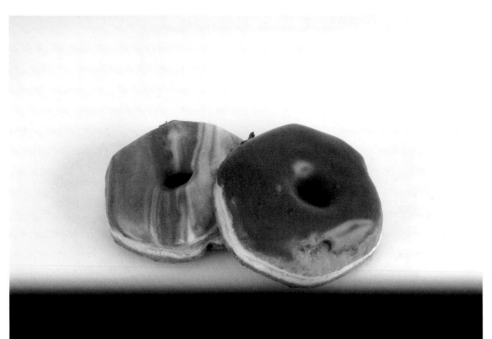

Figure 10.10
If a shutter speed faster than 1/250th second is used, you can end up photographing only a portion of the image.

dirty and you detect a spot of dust in the upper half of a test photo, if cleaning manually, you need to look for the speck in the *bottom* half of the sensor.

I generally end up with sync speed problems only when shooting in the studio, using studio flash units rather than my 7D's built-in flash or a Canon-dedicated Speedlite. That's because if you're using either type of "smart" flash, the camera knows that a strobe is attached, and remedies any unintentional goof in shutter speed settings. If you happen to set the 7D's shutter to a faster speed in Tv or M mode, the camera will automatically adjust the shutter speed down to 1/250th second. In Av, P, or any of the automatic modes, where the 7D selects the shutter speed, it will never choose a shutter speed higher than 1/250th second when using flash. In P mode, shutter speed is automatically set between 1/60th to 1/250th second when using flash.

But when using a non-dedicated flash, such as a studio unit plugged into the 7D's PC/X connector, the camera has no way of knowing that a flash is connected, so shutter speeds faster than 1/250th second can be set inadvertently. Note that the 7D can use a feature called *high-speed sync* that allows shutter speeds faster than 1/250th second with certain external dedicated Canon flash units. When using high-speed sync, the flash fires a continuous serious of bursts at reduced power for the entire duration of the exposure, so that the illumination is able to expose the sensor as the slit moves. High-speed sync is set using the controls on the attached and powered-up compatible external flash.

Determining Exposure

Calculating the proper exposure for an electronic flash photograph is a bit more complicated than determining the settings by continuous light. The right exposure isn't simply a function of how far away your subject is (which the 7D can figure out based on the autofocus distance that's locked in just prior to taking the picture). Various objects reflect more or less light at the same distance so, obviously, the camera needs to measure the amount of light reflected back and through the lens. Yet, as the flash itself isn't available for measuring until it's triggered, the 7D has nothing to measure.

The solution is to fire the flash twice. The initial shot is a preflash that can be analyzed, then followed by a main flash that's given exactly the calculated intensity needed to provide a correct exposure. As a result, the primary flash may be longer for distant objects and shorter for closer subjects, depending on the required intensity for exposure. This through-the-lens evaluative flash exposure system is called E-TTL II, and it operates whenever the pop-up internal flash is used, or you have attached a Canon dedicated flash unit to the 7D.

Guide Numbers

Guide numbers, usually abbreviated GN, are a way of specifying the power of an electronic flash in a way that can be used to determine the right f/stop to use at a particular shooting distance and ISO setting. In fact, before automatic flash units became prevalent, the GN was actually used to do just that. A GN is usually given as a pair of numbers for both feet and meters that represent the range at ISO 100. For example, the EOS 7D's built-in flash has a GN of 12/39 (meters/feet) at ISO 100. To calculate the right exposure at that ISO setting, you'd divide the guide number by the distance to arrive at the appropriate f/stop.

Using the 7D's built-in flash as an example, at ISO 100 with its GN of 39, if you wanted to shoot a subject at a distance of 10 feet, you'd use f/3.9 (39 divided by 10; round to f/4 for simplicity's sake). At 8 feet, an f/stop of f/4.8 (round up to f/5.6) would be used. Some quick mental calculations with the GN will give you any particular electronic flash's range. You can easily see that the built-in flash would begin to peter out at about 15 feet, where you'd need an aperture of roughly f/2.8 at ISO 100. Of course, in the real world you'd probably bump the sensitivity up to a setting of ISO 400 so you could use a more practical f/5.6 at that distance.

Today, guide numbers are most useful for comparing the power of various flash units. You don't need to be a math genius to see that an electronic flash with a GN of, say, 190 would be *a lot* more powerful than your built-in flash (at ISO 100, you could use f/13 instead of f/2.8 at 15 feet).

Getting Started with the Built-In Flash

The Canon EOS 7D's built-in flash is a handy accessory because it is available as required, without the need to carry an external flash around with you constantly. The next sections explain how to use the flip-up flash.

When the 7D is set to Full Auto mode, the flash will pop up and fire automatically, as required. If you're using Creative Auto mode, you can set the flash to operate in that automatic manner, or set it to function only on request:

1. With the Mode Dial set to CA, press the Q button to invoke the Quick Control screen.

2. Use the multi-controller, if necessary, to navigate to the Flash settings at the upper-right corner of the screen.

3. Rotate the Main Dial or Quick Control Dial to select Auto fire, Flash On, or Flash Off. (See Figure 10.11.)

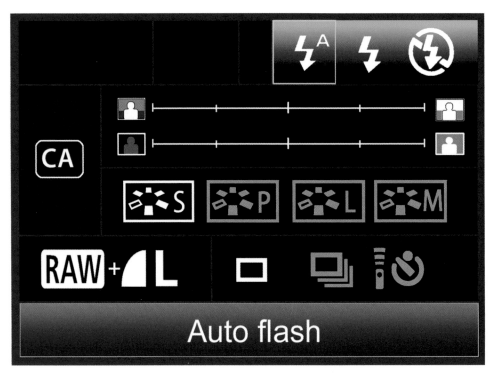

Figure 10.11
Choose Auto fire, Flash On, or Flash Off in the Quick Control menu.

When you're using P, Av, Tv, B, or Manual exposure modes, you'll have to judge for yourself when flash might be useful, and flip it up yourself by pressing the Flash button on the side of the pentaprism. The behavior of the internal flash varies, depending on which exposure mode you're using.

■ **P.** In Program mode, the 7D fully automates the exposure process, giving you subtle fill flash effects in daylight, and fully illuminating your subject under dimmer lighting conditions. The camera selects a shutter speed from 1/60th to 1/250th second and sets an appropriate aperture.

■ **Av.** In Aperture-priority mode, you set the aperture as always, and the 7D chooses a shutter speed from 30 seconds to 1/250th second. Use this mode with care, because if the camera detects a dark background, it will use the flash to expose the main subject in the foreground, and then leave the shutter open long enough to allow the background to be exposed correctly, too. If you're not using an image-stabilized lens, you can end up with blurry ghost images even of non-moving subjects at exposures longer than 1/30th second, and if your camera is not mounted on a tripod, you'll see these blurs at exposures longer than about 1/8th second even if you are using IS.

To disable use of a slow shutter speed with flash, access C.Fn I-7 Flash sync. Speed in Av mode, and change from the default setting (0: Auto) to either 1: 1/250-1/60sec. auto or 2:1/250sec. (fixed), as described in Chapter 8.

■ **Tv.** When using flash in Tv mode, you set the shutter speed from 30 seconds to 1/250th second, and the 7D will choose the correct aperture for the correct flash exposure. If you accidentally set the shutter speed higher than 1/250th second, the camera will reduce it to 1/250th second when you're using the flash.

■ **M/B.** In Manual or Bulb exposure modes, you select both shutter speed (30 seconds to 1/250th second) and aperture. The camera will adjust the shutter speed to 1/250th second if you try to use a faster speed with the internal flash. The E-TTL II system will provide the correct amount of exposure for your main subject at the aperture you've chosen (if the subject is within the flash's range, of course). In Bulb mode, the shutter will remain open for as long as the release button on top of the camera is held down, or the release of your remote control is activated.

Flash Range

The illumination of the EOS 7D's built-in flash varies with distance, focal length, and ISO sensitivity setting.

■ **Distance.** The farther away your subject is from the camera, the greater the light fall-off, thanks to the inverse square law discussed earlier. Keep in mind that a subject that's twice as far away receives only one-quarter as much light, which is two f/stops' worth.

■ **Focal length.** The built-in flash "covers" only a limited angle of view, which doesn't change. So, when you're using a lens that is wider than the default focal length, the frame may not be covered fully, and you'll experience dark areas, especially in the corners. As you zoom in using longer focal lengths, some of the illumination is outside the area of view and is "wasted." (This phenomenon is why some external flash units, such as the 580EX II, "zoom" to match the zoom setting of your lens to concentrate the available flash burst onto the actual subject area.)

■ **ISO setting.** The higher the ISO sensitivity, the more photons captured by the sensor. So, doubling the sensitivity from ISO 100 to 200 produces the same effect as, say, opening up your lens from f/8 to f/5.6.

Red-Eye Reduction and Autofocus Assist

The 7D's built-in flash (and some external flashes) can fire a preburst that can be used to reduce red-eye effects and to assist the camera in achieving automatic focus.

When Red-eye reduction is turned on in the Shooting 1 menu (as described in Chapter 7), the red-eye reduction preflash will illuminate for about 1.5 seconds when you press down the shutter release halfway, theoretically causing your subjects' irises to contract (if they are looking toward the camera), and thereby reducing the red-eye effect in your photograph.

The flash can also function to provide additional illumination in low-light situations, so that the EOS 7D can focus automatically. You can still use the Autofocus assist beam function even when you don't want the flash to contribute to the exposure by disabling flash while enabling autofocus assist, using one of the Flash control options in the Shooting 1 menu. Just follow these steps:

1. Press the MENU button and navigate to the Shooting 1 menu.

2. Rotate the Quick Control Dial and select the Flash control entry.

3. Select Flash firing, press SET, and choose Disable. That option disables both the built-in flash and any external dedicated flash you may have attached.

4. Press the MENU button twice to exit. (Or just tap the shutter release button.)

Use C.Fn III-11, as described in Chapter 8 to choose whether the AF-assist beam is emitted by the built-in flash or the external Speedlite. I'll review other Flash Control functions later in this chapter.

Using FE Lock and Flash Exposure Compensation

If you want to lock flash exposure for a subject that is not centered in the frame, you can use the FE lock (the M-Fn button) to lock in a specific flash exposure. Just depress and hold the shutter button halfway to lock in focus, then center the viewfinder on the subject you want to correctly expose and press the M-Fn button. The preflash fires and calculates exposure, displaying the FEL (flash exposure lock) message in the viewfinder. The 7D remembers the correct exposure until you take a picture, and the FEL indicator in the viewfinder is your reminder. If you want to recalculate your flash exposure, just press the M-Fn button again. When you're ready to shoot, recompose your photo and press the shutter down the rest of the way to take the picture.

You can also manually add or subtract exposure to the flash exposure calculated by the 7D. Press the ISO-Flash exposure compensation button on the top of the camera, and rotate the Quick Control Dial to the right (to add exposure) or to the left (to subtract exposure). The exposure index scale on the LCD and in the viewfinder will indicate the change you've made, and a flash exposure compensation icon will appear when the shutter button is pressed halfway to warn you that an adjustment has been made. If you're using a Canon Speedlite, you can set exposure compensation on the external flash instead, using the *flash unit's* Custom Function 13 (not to be confused with the 7D's similarly numbered C.Fn in the Custom Function menu). This overrides any setting you've made with the camera. To avoid confusion, avoid making FEC settings on both the camera and an external flash unit.

Flash exposure compensation can work in tandem with non-flash exposure compensation, so you can adjust the amount of light registered from the scene by ambient light even while you're tweaking the amount of illumination absorbed from your flash unit.

As with non-flash exposure compensation, the compensation you make remains in effect for the pictures that follow, and even when you've turned the camera off, remember to cancel the flash exposure compensation adjustment by reversing the steps used to set it when you're done using it.

Tip

If you've enabled the Auto Lighting Optimizer in the Shooting 2 menu, as described in Chapter 7, it may cancel out any EV you've subtracted using flash exposure compensation. Disable the Auto Lighting Optimizer if you find your images are still too bright when using flash exposure compensation.

More on Flash Control Settings

I introduced the Shooting 1 menu's Flash control settings in Chapter 7. This next section offers additional information for using the Flash control menu. The menu includes five options (see Figure 10.12): Flash firing, Built-in flash function settings, External flash function settings, External flash C.Fn settings, and Clear external flash C.Fn settings.

Flash Firing

This menu entry has two options: Enable and Disable. It can be used to activate or deactivate the built-in electronic flash and any attached external electronic flash unit. When disabled, the flash cannot fire even if you accidentally elevate it, or have an accessory flash attached and turned on. However, you should keep in mind that the AF-assist beam can still be used. If you want to disable that, too, you'll need to turn it off using C.Fn III-11.

Here are some applications where I always disable my flash and AF-assist beam, even though my 7D won't pop up the flash and fire without my intervention anyway. Some situations are too important to take chances. (Who knows, maybe I've accidentally set the Mode Dial to Creative Auto?)

- **Venues where flash is forbidden.** I've discovered that many No Photography signs actually mean "No Flash Photography," either because those who make the decisions feel that flash is distracting or they fear it may potentially damage works of art. Tourists may not understand the difference between flash and available light photography, or may be unable to set their camera to turn off the flash. One of the first phrases I learn in any foreign language is "Is it permitted to take photos if I do not use flash?" A polite request, while brandishing an advanced camera like the 7D (which may indicate you know what you are doing), can often result in permission to shoot away.

- **Venues where flash is ineffective anyway.** We've all seen the concertgoers who stand up in the last row to shoot flash pictures from 100 yards away. I tend to not tell friends that their pictures are not going to come out, because they usually come back to me with a dismal, grainy shot (actually exposed by the dim available light) that they find satisfactory, just to prove I was wrong.

- **Venues where flash is annoying.** If I'm taking pictures in a situation where flash is permitted, but mostly supplies little more than visual pollution, I'll disable or avoid using it. Concerts or religious ceremonies may *allow* flash photography, but who needs to add to the blinding bursts when you have a camera that will take perfectly good pictures at ISO 3200? Of course, I invariably see one or two people flashing away at events where flash is not allowed, but that doesn't mean I am eager to join in the festivities.

Figure 10.12
The Flash
Control menu
has settings for
both built-in
and external
flash.

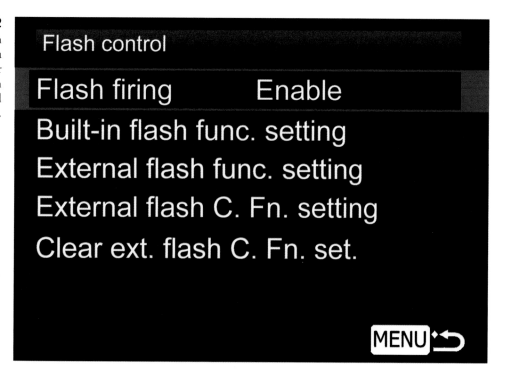

Flash control

Flash firing   Enable

Built-in flash func. setting

External flash func. setting

External flash C. Fn. setting

Clear ext. flash C. Fn. set.

MENU ↰

Built-in Flash Function Setting

There are five main choices for this menu choice, which normally appears as shown in Figure 10.13. Pressing the INFO. button to the left of the LCD while this menu screen is visible clears the current flash settings. There are also additional settings that apply when using an external flash, such as Channel and Firing group, which I'll address in the sections on external flash. Here's a quick summary of the five main built-in flash selections. I'll explain each in more detail in the sections that follow this one, and in Chapter 11.

- **Flash mode.** Your choices here are E-TTL II, Manual flash, MULTI Flash, explained in the following section.

- **Shutter sync.** You can choose 1st curtain sync (which fires the main flash as soon as the shutter is completely open) or 2nd curtain sync (which waits until just before the shutter starts to close to fire the main flash). I'll explain how they work in more detail later in this chapter. If you have a compatible Canon Speedlite attached, you can also select High-speed sync (HSS), which allows using shutter speeds faster than 1/250th second, from the External flash function setting menu. You can't select it here, and HSS cannot be used in wireless mode (wireless mode is covered in Chapter 11).

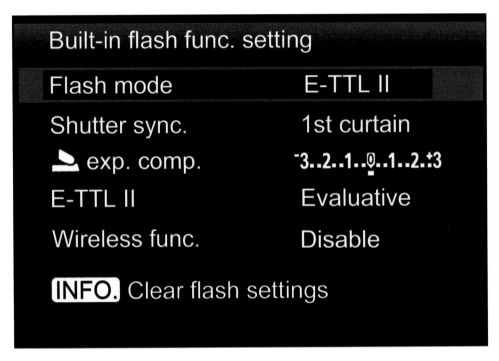

Built-in flash func. setting

Flash mode   E-TTL II

Shutter sync.   1st curtain

🔻 exp. comp.   ⁻3..2..1..0̲..1..2.⁺3

E-TTL II   Evaluative

Wireless func.   Disable

[INFO.] Clear flash settings

Figure 10.13
Five entries are available from the Built-in flash functions menu.

- **E-TTL II.** When you're using E-TTL II mode, you can specify here whether the 7D uses evaluative (matrix) or average metering modes for the electronic flash exposure meter. Evaluative metering intelligently looks at selected areas in the scene and compares its measurements to a database of typical scene "layouts" to calculate exposure, while average calculates flash exposure by reading the entire scene. Your choice becomes active when you select E-TTL II as your flash mode, using the entry listed first on this menu screen, and described in more detail in the next section.

- **Flash exposure compensation.** If you'd rather adjust flash exposure using a menu than with the ISO-Flash exposure compensation button, you can do that here. Select this option with the SET button, then dial in the amount of flash EV compensation you want using the multi-controller or Quick Control Dial. The EV that was in place before you started to make your adjustment is shown as a blue indicator, so you can return to that value quickly. Press SET again to confirm your change, then press the MENU button twice to exit.

- **Wireless functions.** These choices, which include mode, channel, firing group, and other options are used only when you're working with an external flash in wireless mode. I'm going to leave the explanation of these options for Chapter 11, which is an entire chapter dedicated to using the EOS 7D's new wireless shooting capabilities.

Using Flash Mode

In choosing Flash mode, you have three choices when working with Built-in flash function settings. (These options are identical with External flash function settings, plus you have two more, described in the next section.) The available modes are E-TTL II, the standard mode for EX-series Speedlites; Manual flash, which you can use to set a fixed flash output, from full power (1/1) to 1/128th power; and MULTI flash, used to produce stroboscopic effects.

E-TTL II

You'll leave Flash mode at this setting most of the time. In this mode, the camera fires a preflash prior to the exposure, and measures the amount of light reflected to calculate the proper settings. As noted earlier, when you've selected the E-TTL II flash mode, you can also choose either evaluative or average metering methods. If you select Manual flash or MULTI flash, that option is removed from the Built-in flash func. setting menu.

Manual Flash

Use this setting when you want to specify exactly how much light is emitted by the flash, and don't want the 7D's E-TTL II exposure system to calculate the f/stop for you. When you activate this option, a new entry appears in the Built-in flash func. setting menu, with a sliding scale from 1/1 (full power) to 1/128th power. (See Figure 10.14.)

Figure 10.14
When Manual flash mode is chosen, a flash output selection scale appears.

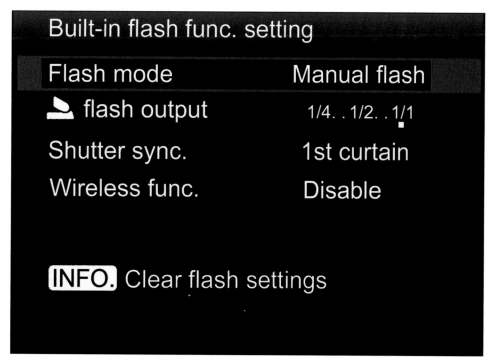

Highlight the scale and press the SET button. You can then rotate the Quick Control Dial and choose any of the settings. (Only 1/4, 1/2, 1/1, and the intermediate settings between them appear when 1/1 is chosen; view the other power settings by rotating the QCD counterclockwise.) A blue dot appears under the 1/1 setting, and a white dot under your new setting, a reminder that you've chosen something other than full power.

Here are some situations where you might want to use manual flash settings:

- **Close-ups.** You're shooting macro photos and the E-TTL II exposure is not precisely what you'd like. You can dial in exposure compensation, or set the output manually. Close-up photos are problematic, because the power of the built-in flash may be too much (choose 1/128 power to minimize the output), or the reflected light may not be interpreted accurately by the through-the-lens metering system. Manual flash gives you greater control.

- **Fill flash.** Although E-TTL II can be used in full daylight to provide fill flash to brighten shadows, using manual flash allows you to tweak the amount of light being emitted in precise steps. Perhaps you want just a little more illumination in the shadows to retain a dramatic lighting effect without the dark portions losing all detail. Again, you can try using exposure compensation to make this adjustment, but I prefer to use manual flash settings. (See Figure 10.15.)

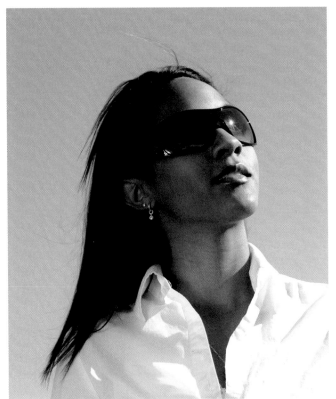

Figure 10.15
You can fine-tune fill illumination by adjusting the output of your camera's built-in flash manually.

- **Action stopping.** The lower the power of the flash, the shorter the effective exposure. Use 1/128th power in a darkened room (so that there is no ambient light to contribute to the exposure and cause a "ghost" image) and you can end up with a "shutter speed" that's the equivalent of 1/50,000th second! Figure 10.16 shows what you can do. It's an image captured by Cleveland photographer Kris Bosworth (a long-time Canon shooter), who used a sound trigger device to activate the flash during a Bulb exposure.

Figure 10.16
At 1/128th power, the duration of the flash is very brief, producing the same effect as a fast shutter speed.

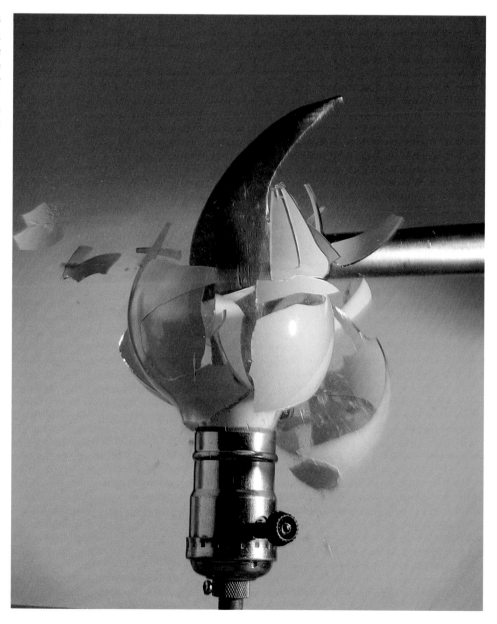

MULTI Flash

The MULTI flash setting makes it possible to shoot cool stroboscopic effects, with the flash firing several times in quick succession. You can use the capability to produce multiple images of moving objects, to trace movement (say, your golf swing). I put the feature to work for Figure 10.17, which shows multiple positions of the trigger and spout of a spray bottle, along with droplets of water as they spew forth. It was taken in a darkened room with the camera mounted on a tripod, and the shutter set for a one-second exposure. Only the three flash bursts illuminated the scene. (I used an off-camera flash positioned to the right for this particular image, but MULTI flash with the built-in flash produce similar effects.) When you've activated MULTI flash, three parameters appear on the Built-in flash function setting menu, as shown in Figure 10.18. They include:

- **Flash output.** Similar to the Flash output option in Manual mode, you can choose the intensity of each individual flash in your multiple flash sequence, from 1/4 to 1/128th power (the 1/1 and 1/2 power settings are not available). I selected 1/128th power when I shot Figure 10.17, which is a close-up.

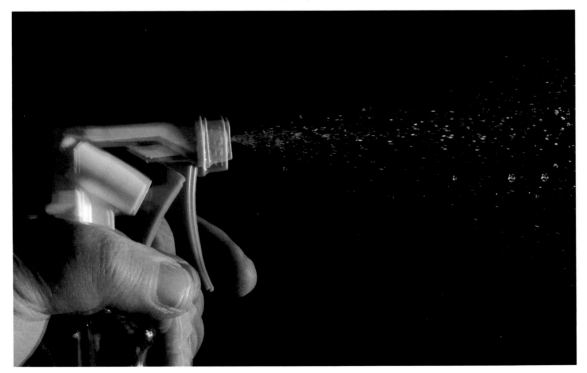

Figure 10.17 Three consecutive flashes within a short period of time produced this stroboscopic effect.

Figure 10.18
Chose Flash
mode here.

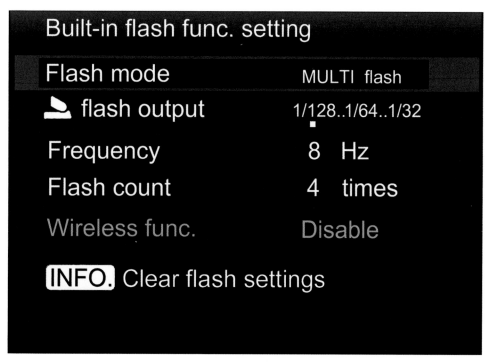

- **Frequency.** This figure specifies the number of bursts per second. With the built-in flash, you can choose (theoretically) 1 to 199 bursts per second. The actual number of flashes produced will be determined by your flash count (which turns off the flash after the specified number of flashes), and flash output (higher output levels will deplete the available energy in your flash unit), and your shutter speed.

- **Flash count.** This setting determines the number of flashes in a given burst, and can be set from 1 to 30 flashes.

These factors work together to determine the maximum number of flashes you can string together in a single shot. The exact number will vary, depending on your settings. Here are some guidelines you can use:

- **Output.** As you cut the power from 1/4 to 1/128th, the output of the flash drops dramatically, and so does the maximum distance you can shoot at any particular f/stop. The 1/4 power setting, the most powerful setting available with MULTI flash, will give you the greatest flash range in this mode. With your 7D's sensitivity set to ISO 1600, your built-in flash will allow you to photograph a subject at 10 feet using f/8 and one-quarter power. (If you remember the discussion of guide numbers from earlier in this chapter, the flash would have an effective GN of 80 at ISO 1600.)

  If you wanted to use the 1/16th power setting instead, you'd need to use f/4 to account for the reduced output of the flash. By the time you dial down to 1/128th power, your built-in flash has a feeble guide number of about 14 (at ISO 1600!), so to shoot at f/4 you'd be able to locate your subject *no farther* than 3.5 feet from the camera.

The output level also determines the maximum number of flashes that are possible before the charge stored in your flash's capacitor is depleted The capacitor partially recharges itself as you shoot, so the number of flashes also varies by the flashes-per-second rate. At the 1Hz (one flash per second) rate, and 1/4 power you can expect about 6-7 flashes before the unit's power poops out. By the time you reach 10Hz (10 flashes per second) and higher, the unit can crank out no more than two flashes per second at 1/4 power.

Logically, as output levels decrease, more flashes can be pumped out in a given time period. At 1/128th power, you can expect as many as 100 flashes at the 1Hz rate, and up to 40 consecutive flashes at the 20-199Hz frequency.

- **Flashes per second.** Cycles per second are, by convention, measured using an increment called *Hertz*. The more flashes you want during the time the shutter is open, the higher the rate you must select. You can select rates of 1 to 199Hz, or 1 to 199 flashes per second, plus "- -" (more on that later). To maximize the number of flashes in a second, you'll also need to choose the lowest power output level that you find acceptable. The flash unit can emit a lot more fractional 1/128th power bursts in a given period of time than it can more robust (relatively) 1/4 power bursts.

When you choose "- -" for your frequency, the flash will continue firing until the shutter closes, or its internal storage is depleted. (In any case, you should not use the MULTI flash feature for more than 10 consecutive pictures. At that point, you should allow the flash to "rest" for at least 15 minutes. But don't worry, the unit will shut down automatically to avoid overheating.)

- **Flash count.** Chose the number of flashes, from 1 to 30, that you want in your multiple exposure, given the output and flash frequency constraints described previously.

External Flash Function Setting

You can access this menu only when you have a compatible electronic flash attached and switched on. The settings available are shown in Figure 10.19. If you press the INFO. button while adjusting flash settings, both the changes made to the settings of an attached external flash and to the built-in flash will be cleared.

- **Flash mode.** This entry allows you to set the flash mode for the external flash, from E-TTL II, Manual flash, MULTI flash, TTL, AutoExFlash, ManEx flash. The first three are identical to the modes described earlier. The second three are optional metering modes available with certain flash units, such as the 580 EX II, and are available for those who might need one of those less sophisticated flash metering systems. TTL measures light bouncing back from your subject through the lens to calculate exposure but, unlike E-TTL II, does not use a preflash or intelligent evaluation of the measurements to adjust for different types of scenes. AutoExFlash and ManEx flash don't measure light through the lens at all, but, instead, meter the illumination falling on an external sensor (with an unvarying 20-degree angle of view) that's built into the flash. The former method performs automatic exposure calculation using this information, while the latter provides data you can use for manual flash exposure. While I don't recommend any of the three, you can find more information about them in your flash's manual.

■ **Shutter sync.** As with the 7D's internal flash, you can choose 1st curtain sync, which fires the flash as soon as the shutter is completely open (this is the default mode). Alternatively, you can select 2nd curtain sync, which fires the flash as soon as the shutter opens, and then triggers a second flash at the end of the exposure, just before the shutter starts to close. If a compatible Canon flash, such as the Speedlite 580EX II is attached and turned on, you can also select High-speed sync. and shoot using shutter speeds faster than 1/250th second. HSS does not work in wireless mode, as I'll explain in Chapter 11.

■ **FEB.** Flash Exposure Bracketing (FEB) operates similarly to ordinary exposure bracketing, providing a series of different exposures to improve your chances of getting the exact right exposure, or to provide alternative renditions for creative purposes.

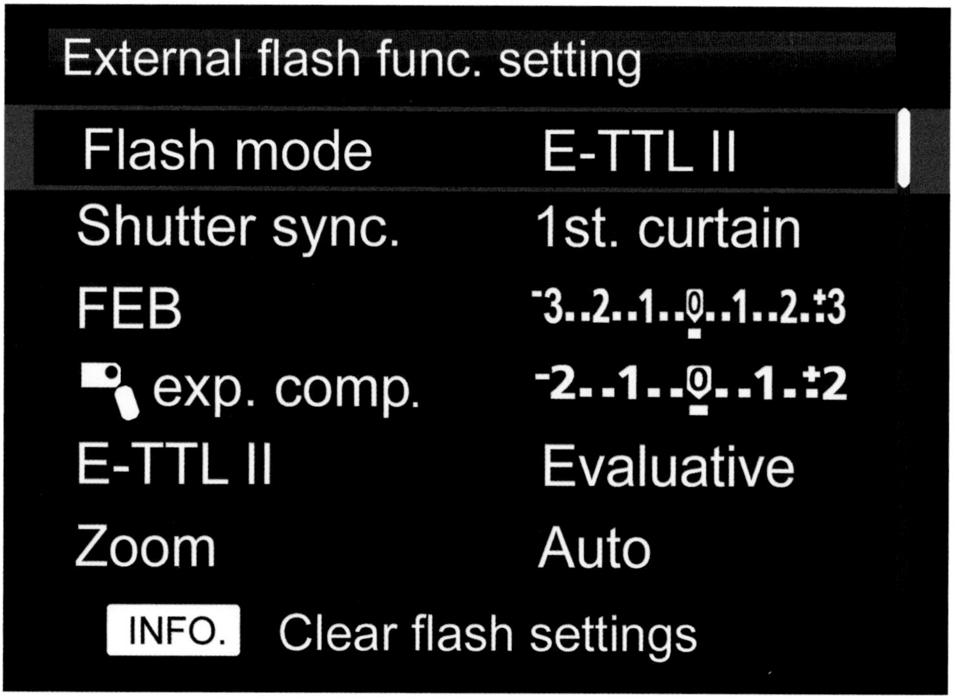

Figure 10.19
External flash units can be controlled from the Canon EOS 7D using this menu.

External flash func. setting	
Flash mode	E-TTL II
Shutter sync.	1st. curtain
FEB	⁻3..2..1..0..1..2.⁺3
📸 exp. comp.	⁻2..1..0..1.⁺2
E-TTL II	Evaluative
Zoom	Auto
INFO. Clear flash settings	

- **Flash exposure compensation.** You can adjust flash exposure for external flash using a menu here. Select this option with the SET button, then dial in the amount of flash EV compensation you want using the multi-controller or Quick Control Dial. The EV that was in place before you started to make your adjustment is shown as a blue indicator, so you can return to that value quickly. Press SET again to confirm your change, then press the MENU button twice to exit.

- **E-TTL II.** You can choose evaluative (matrix) or average metering modes for the electronic flash exposure meter. Evaluative looks at selected areas in the scene to calculate exposure, while average calculates flash exposure by reading the entire scene.

- **Zoom.** Some flash units can vary their coverage to better match the field of view of your lens at a particular focal length. You can allow the external flash to zoom automatically, based on information provided, or manually, using a zoom button on the flash itself. This setting is disabled when using a flash like the Canon 420EX, which does not have zooming capability.

- **Wireless func.** These functions are available when using wireless flash, and will be explained in Chapter 11.

High-Speed Sync

High-speed sync is a special mode that allows you to synchronize an external flash at all shutter speeds, rather than just 1/250th second and slower. The entire frame is illuminated by a series of continuous bursts as the shutter opening moves across the sensor plane, so you do *not* end up with a horizontal black band, as shown earlier in Figure 10.10.

HSS is especially useful in three situations, all related to problems associated with high ambient light levels:

- **Eliminate "ghosts" with moving images.** When shooting with flash, the primary source of illumination may be the flash itself. However, if there is enough available light, a secondary image may be recorded by that light (as described under "Ghost Images" earlier in this chapter). If your main subject is not moving, the secondary image may acceptable or even desirable. Indeed, the 7D has a provision for Slow Sync that allows using a slow shutter speed to record the ambient light and help illuminate dark backgrounds. But if your subject is moving, the secondary image creates a ghost image.

  High-speed sync gives you the ability to use a higher shutter speed. If ambient light produces a ghost image at 1/250th second, upping the shutter speed to 1/500th or 1/1000th second may eliminate it.

  Of course, HSS *reduces* the amount of light the flash produces. If your subject is not close to the camera, the waning illumination of the flash may force you to use a larger f/stop to capture the flash exposure. So, while shifting from 1/250th second at f/8 to 1/500th second at f/8 *will* reduce ghost images, if you switch to 1/500th second at f/5.6 (because the flash is effectively less intense), you'll end up with the same ambient light exposure. Still, it's worth a try.

■ **Improved fill flash in daylight.** The 7D can use the built-in flash or an attached unit to fill in inky shadows—both automatically and using manually specified power ratios, as described earlier in this chapter. However, both methods force you to use a 1/250th second (or slower) shutter speed. That limitation can cause three complications.

First, in very bright surroundings, such as beach or snow scenes, it may be difficult to get the correct exposure at 1/250th second. You might have to use f/16 or a smaller f/stop to expose a given image, even at ISO 100. If you want to use a larger f/stop for selective focus, then you encounter the second problem—1/250th second won't allow apertures wider than f/8 or f/5.6 under many daylight conditions at ISO 100. (See the discussion of fill flash with aperture-priority in the next bullet.)

Finally, if you're shooting action, you'll probably want a shutter speed faster than 1/250th second, if at all possible under the current lighting. That's because, in fill flash situations, the ambient light (often daylight) provides the primary source of illumination. For many sports and fast moving subjects, 1/500th second, or faster, is desirable. HSS allows you to increase your shutter speed and still avail yourself of fill flash. This assumes that your subject is close enough to your camera that the fill flash has some effect; forget about using fill and HSS with subjects a dozen feet away or farther. The flash won't be powerful enough to have much effect on the shadows.

■ **When using fill flash with aperture-priority.** The difficulties of using selective focus with fill flash, mentioned earlier, become particularly acute when you switch to Av exposure mode. Selecting f/5.6, f/4, or a wider aperture when using flash is guaranteed to create problems when photographing close-in subjects, particularly at ISO settings higher than ISO 100. If you own an external flash unit, HSS may be the solution you are looking for.

To use High-speed sync, just follow these steps:

1. **Attach the flash.** Mount/connect the external flash on the 7D, using the hot shoe or a cable. (HSS cannot be used in wireless mode, nor with a flash linked through the PC terminal.)

2. **Power up.** Turn the flash and camera on.

3. **Select HSS in the camera.** Set the External flash function setting *in the camera* to HSS as the 7D's sync mode.

4. **Choose HSS on the flash.** Activate HSS (FP flash) on your attached external flash. With the 580EX II, press the High-speed sync button on the back of the flash unit (it's the second from the right under the LCD). (See Figure 10.20.)

5. **Confirm HSS is active.** The HSS icon will be displayed on the flash unit's LCD (at the upper-left side with the 580EX II), and at bottom left in the 7D's viewfinder. If you choose a shutter speed of 1/250th second or slower, the indicator will not appear in the viewfinder, as HSS will not be used at slower speeds.

6. **View minimum/maximum shooting distance.** Choose a distance based on the maximum shown in the line at the bottom of the flash's LCD display (from 0.5 to 18 meters).

7. **Shoot.** Take the picture. To turn off HSS press the button on the flash again. Remember that you can't use MULTI flash or Wireless flash when working with High-speed sync.

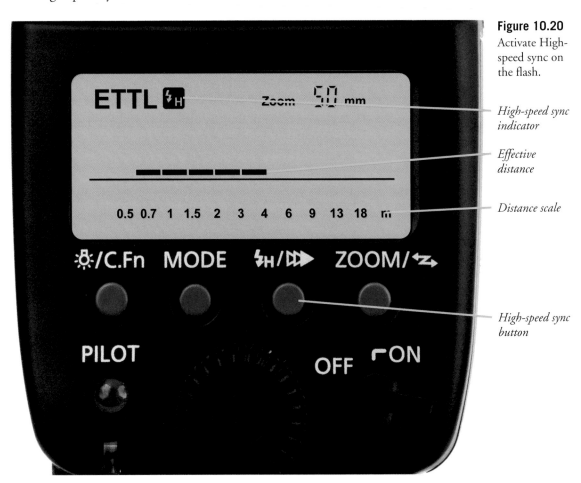

Figure 10.20
Activate High-speed sync on the flash.

High-speed sync indicator

Effective distance

Distance scale

High-speed sync button

External Flash Custom Function Setting

Many external Speedlites from Canon include their own list of Custom Functions, which can be used to specify things like flash metering mode and flash bracketing sequences, as well as more sophisticated features, such as modeling light/flash (if available), use of external power sources (if attached), and functions of any slave unit attached to the external flash. This menu entry allows you to set an external flash unit's Custom Functions from your 7D's menu. The settings available in the 7D for the Speedlite 580EX II are shown later in the section that describes that flash.

Clear External Flash Custom Function Setting

This entry allows you to zero-out any changes you've made to your external flash's Custom Functions, and return them to their factory default settings.

Using External Electronic Flash

Canon offers a broad range of accessory electronic flash units for the EOS 7D. They can be mounted to the flash accessory shoe, or used off-camera with a dedicated cord that plugs into the flash shoe to maintain full communications with the camera for all special features. (Non-dedicated flash units, such as studio flash, can be connected using the PC terminal.) They range from the Speedlite 580EX II (see Figure 10.21), which

Figure 10.21
The Canon Speedlite 580EX II is the most powerful shoe-mount flash Canon offers.

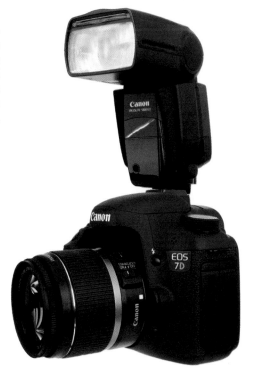

can correctly expose subjects up to 24 feet away at f/11 and ISO 200, to the 220EX, which is good out to 9 feet at f/11 and ISO 200. (You'll get greater ranges at even higher ISO settings, of course.) There are also two electronic flash units specifically for specialized close-up flash photography.

Speedlite 580EX II

This flagship of the Canon accessory flash line is the most powerful unit the company offers, with a GN of 190, and a manual/automatic zoom flash head that covers the full frame of lenses from 24mm wide angle to 105mm telephoto. (There's a flip-down wide-angle diffuser that spreads the flash to cover a 14mm lens' field of view, too.) All angle specifications given by Canon refer to full-frame sensors, but this flash unit automatically converts its field of view coverage to accommodate the crop factor of the EOS 7D and the other 1.6X crop Canon dSLRs. Compared to the 580 EX it replaces, the Mark II model recycles (inaudibly—no more hum!) 20 percent faster, and has improved dust- and water-resistance so you can use it in harsher environments.

The unit offers full-swivel, 180-degrees in either direction, and has its own built-in AF assist beam and an exposure system that's compatible with the nine focus points of the 7D. Powered by economical AA-size batteries, the unit recycles in 0.1 to 6 seconds, and can squeeze 100 to 700 flashes from a set of alkaline batteries.

The 580EX II automatically communicates white balance information to your camera, allowing it to adjust WB to match the flash output. You can even simulate a modeling light effect: When you press the Depth-of-field preview button on the 7D, the 580EX II emits a one-second burst of light that allows you to judge the flash effect. If you're using multiple flash units with Canon's wireless E-TTL system, this model can serve as a master flash that controls the slave units you've set up (more about this later) or function as a slave itself.

It's easy to access all the features of this unit, because it has a large backlit LCD panel on the back that provides information about all flash settings. There are 14 Custom Functions that can be controlled from the flash, numbered from 00 to 14. These functions are (the first setting is the default value):

C.Fn-00   Distance indicator display (Meters/Feet)

C.Fn-01   Auto power off (Enabled/Disabled)

C.Fn-02   Modeling flash (Enabled-DOF Preview button/Enabled-Test Firing button/Enabled-Both buttons/Disabled)

C.Fn-03   FEB Flash exposure bracketing auto cancel (Enabled/Disabled)

C.Fn-04   FEB Flash Exposure Bracketing Sequence (Metered > Decreased > Increased Exposure/Decreased > Metered > Increased Exposure)

C.Fn-05   Flash metering mode (E-TTL II-E-TTL/TTL/External metering: Auto/External metering: Manual)

C.Fn-06   Quickflash with continuous shot (Disabled/Enabled)

C.Fn-07   Test firing with autoflash (1/32/Full power)

C.Fn-08   AF-assist beam firing (Enabled/Disabled)

C.Fn-09   Auto zoom adjusted for image/sensor size (Enabled/Disabled)

C.Fn-10   Slave auto power off timer (60 minutes/10 minutes)

C.Fn-11   Cancellation of slave unit auto power off by master unit (Within 8 Hours/Within 1 Hour)

C.Fn-12   Flash recycling on external power (Use internal and external power/Use only external power)

C.Fn-13   Flash exposure metering setting button (Speedlite button and dial/Speedlite dial only)

Speedlite 430EX II

This less pricey electronic flash has a GN of 141, with automatic and manual zoom coverage from 24mm to 105mm, and the same wide-angle pullout panel found on the 580EX II that covers the area of a 14mm lens on a full-frame camera, and automatic conversion to the cropped frame area of the 7D and other 1.6X crop Canon dSLRs. The 430EX also communicates white balance information with the camera, and has its own AF assist beam. Compatible with Canon's wireless E-TTL system, it makes a good slave unit, but cannot serve as a master flash. It, too, uses AA batteries, and offers recycle times of 0.1 to 3.7 seconds for 200 to 1,400 flashes, depending on subject distance.

Speedlite 220EX

Unlike the other two units, this one offers automatic operation only, and none of the fancy features of its more expensive siblings. Its 72 guide number is a little beefier than the 7D's built-in flash, making it a good choice as a low-power auxiliary flash unit. It lacks a zoomable flash head and offers fixed coverage equivalent to the field of view of a 28mm full-frame lens. Expect 250 to 1,700 flashes from a set of four AA batteries and recycle times of 0.1 to 4.5 seconds. The built-in AF assist beam is linked to the center focusing point of the 7D only.

Ringlights

Canon offers two ringlights, the Macro Ringlite MR-14EX, and Macro Twin Lite Ringlite flash MR-24 EX. As you might guess from their names, ringlights are especially suitable for close-up, or macro photography, because they provide a relatively shadowless illumination. It's always tricky photographing small subjects up close, because there often isn't room enough between the camera lens and the subject to position lights effectively. Ringlights, especially those with their own modeling lamps to help you visualize the illumination you're going to get, mount around the lens at the camera position, and help solve many close-up lighting problems.

But, in recent years, the ringlight has gone far beyond the macro realm and is now probably even more popular as a light source for fashion and glamour photography. The right ringlight, properly used, can provide killer illumination for glamour shots, while eliminating the need to move and reset lights for those shots that lend themselves to ringlight illumination. As you, the photographer, move around your subject, the ringlight moves with you.

One of the key drawbacks to ringlights (whether used for macro or glamour photography) is that they are somewhat bulky and clumsy to use (they must be fastened around the camera lens itself, or the photographer must position the ringlight, and then shoot "through" the opening or ring). That means that you might not be moving round your subject as much as you thought and will, instead, mount the ringlight and camera on a tripod, studio stand, or other support.

Another drawback is the cost. The MR-14EX and MR-24-EX are priced in the $500 and $700 range, respectively. You have to be planning a *lot* of macro or fashion work to pay for one of those. Specialists take note. I tend to favor a third-party substitute, the Alien Bees ABR800 Ringflash, shown in Figure 10.22. It's priced at about $400, and, besides, it integrates very well with my other Alien Bees studio flash units.

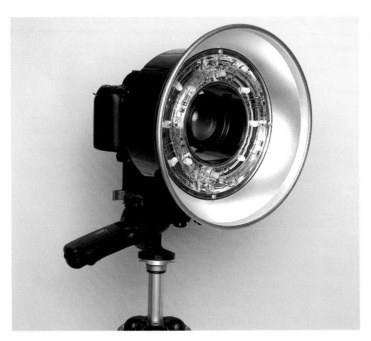

Figure 10.22
This Alien Bees ringflash is a more economical alternative to Canon's own units.

More Advanced Lighting Techniques

As you advance in your Canon EOS 7D photography, you'll want to learn more sophisticated lighting techniques, using more than just straight-on flash, or using just a single flash unit. Check out *David Busch's Quick Snap Guide to Lighting* if you want to delve further. I'm going to provide a quick introduction to some of the techniques you should be considering.

Diffusing and Softening the Light

Direct light can be harsh and glaring, especially if you're using the flash built into your camera, or an auxiliary flash mounted in the hot shoe and pointed directly at your subject. The first thing you should do is stop using direct light (unless you're looking for a stark, contrasty appearance as a creative effect). There are a number of simple things you can do with both continuous and flash illumination.

- **Use window light.** Light coming in a window can be soft and flattering, and a good choice for human subjects. Move your subject close enough to the window that its light provides the primary source of illumination. You might want to turn off other lights in the room, particularly to avoid mixing daylight and incandescent light (see Figure 10.23).

Figure 10.23
Window light makes the perfect diffuse illumination for informal soft-focus portraits like this one.

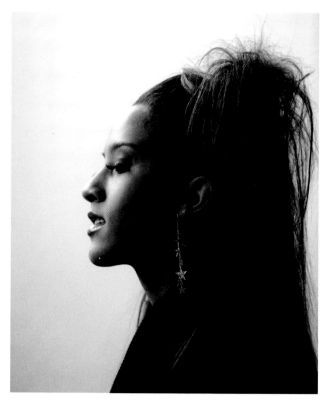

- **Use fill light.** Your 7D's built-in flash makes a perfect fill-in light for the shadows, brightening inky depths with a kicker of illumination (see Figure 10.15, earlier in the chapter).

- **Bounce the light.** External electronic flash units mounted on the 7D usually have a swivel that allows them to be pointed up at a ceiling for a bounce light effect. You can also bounce the light off a wall. You'll want the surface to be white or have a neutral gray color to avoid a color cast.

- **Use reflectors.** Another way to bounce the light is to use reflectors or photo umbrellas that you can position yourself to provide a greater degree of control over the quantity and direction of the bounced light. Good reflectors can be pieces of foamboard, Mylar, or a reflective disk held in place by a clamp and stand. Although some expensive photo umbrellas and reflectors are available, spending a lot isn't necessary. A simple piece of white foamboard does the job beautifully. Umbrellas have the advantage of being compact and foldable, while providing a soft, even kind of light. They're relatively cheap, too, with a good 40-inch umbrella designed specifically for photographic applications available for as little as $20.

- **Use diffusers.** Sto-Fen and some other vendors offer clip-on diffusers like the one shown in Figures 10.24 and 10.25, that fit over your electronic flash head and provide a soft, flattering light. These add-ons are more portable than umbrellas and other reflectors, yet provide a nice diffuse lighting effect.

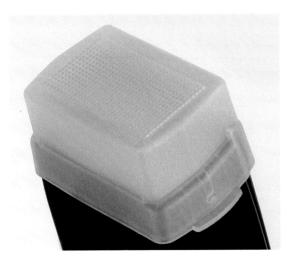

Figure 10.24 The Sto-Fen OmniBounce is a clip-on diffuser that softens the light of an external flash unit.

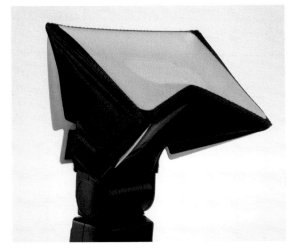

Figure 10.25 Soft boxes use Velcro strips to attach them to third-party flash units (like the one shown) or any Canon external flash.

Using Multiple Light Sources

Once you gain control over the qualities and effects you get with a single light source, you'll want to graduate to using multiple light sources. Using several lights allows you to shape and mold the illumination of your subjects to provide a variety of effects, from backlighting to side lighting to more formal portrait lighting. You can start simply with several incandescent light sources, bounced off umbrellas or reflectors that you construct. Or you can use more flexible multiple electronic flash setups.

Effective lighting is the one element that differentiates great photography from candid or snapshot shooting. Lighting can make a mundane subject look a little more glamorous. Make subjects appear to be soft when you want a soft look, or bright and sparkly when you want a vivid look, or strong and dramatic if that's what you desire. As you might guess, having control over your lighting means that you probably can't use the lights that are already in the room. You'll need separate, discrete lighting fixtures that can be moved, aimed, brightened, and dimmed on command.

Selecting your lighting gear will depend on the type of photography you do, and the budget you have to support it. It's entirely possible for a beginning 7D photographer to create a basic, inexpensive lighting system capable of delivering high-quality results for a few hundred dollars, just as you can spend megabucks ($1,000 and up) for a sophisticated lighting system.

Basic Flash Setups

If you want to use multiple electronic flash units, the Canon Speedlites described earlier will serve admirably. The two higher-end models can be used with Canon's wireless E-TTL feature, which allows you to set up to three separate groups of flash units (several flashes can be included in each group) and trigger them using a master flash (such as the 580EX II) and the camera. Just set up one master unit (there's a switch on the unit's foot that sets it for master mode) and arrange the compatible slave units around your subject. You can set the relative power of each unit separately, thereby controlling how much of the scene's illumination comes from the main flash, and how much from the auxiliary flash units, which can be used as fill flash, background lights, or, if you're careful, to illuminate the hair of portrait subjects. You'll find more about wireless flash in Chapter 11.

Studio Flash

If you're serious about using multiple flash units, a studio flash setup might be more practical. The traditional studio flash is a multi-part unit, consisting of a flash head that mounts on your light stand, and is tethered to an AC (or sometimes battery) power supply. A single power supply can feed two or more flash heads at a time, with separate control over the output of each head.

When they are operating off AC power, studio flash don't have to be frugal with the juice, and are often powerful enough to illuminate very large subjects or to supply lots and lots of light to smaller subjects. The output of such units is measured in watt seconds (ws), so you could purchase a 200ws, 400ws, or 800ws unit, and a power pack to match.

Their advantages include greater power output, much faster recycling, built-in modeling lamps, multiple power levels, and ruggedness that can stand up to transport, because many photographers pack up these kits and tote them around as location lighting rigs. Studio lighting kits can range in price from a few hundred dollars for a set of lights, stands, and reflectors, to thousands for a high-end lighting system complete with all the necessary accessories.

A more practical choice these days are *monolights* (see Figure 10.26), which are "all-in-one" studio lights that sell for about $200-$400. They have the flash tube, modeling light, and power supply built into a single unit that can be mounted on a light stand. Monolights are available in AC-only and battery-pack versions, although an external battery eliminates some of the advantages of having a flash with everything in one unit. They are very portable, because all you need is a case for the monolight itself, plus the stands and other accessories you want to carry along. Because these units are so popular with photographers who are not full-time professionals, the lower-cost monolights are often designed more for lighter duty than professional studio flash. That doesn't mean they aren't rugged; you'll just need to handle them with a little more care, and, perhaps, not expect them to be used eight hours a day for weeks on end. In most other respects, however, monolights are the equal of traditional studio flash units in terms of fast recycling, built-in modeling lamps, adjustable power, and so forth.

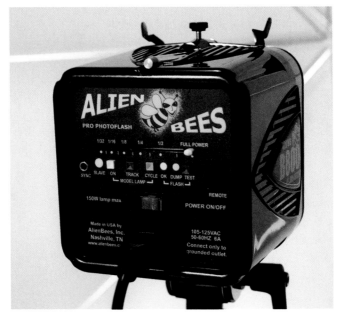

Figure 10.26
All-in-one "monolights" contain flash, power supply, and a modeling light in one compact package (umbrella not included).

Connecting Multiple Units to Your Canon EOS 7D

Non-dedicated electronic flash units can't use the automated E-TTL II features of your EOS 7D; you'll need to calculate exposure manually, through test shots evaluated on your camera's LCD or by using an electronic flash meter. Moreover, you don't have to connect them to the accessory shoe on top of the camera. Instead, you can use the 7D's PC terminal, or use an adapter in the hot shoe to provide a PC/X connector (perhaps with a voltage regulator), and use a shutter speed of 1/60th second or slower.

You should be aware that older electronic flash units sometimes use a triggering voltage that is too much for your 7D to handle. You can actually damage the camera's electronics if the voltage is too high. You won't need to worry about this if you purchase brand new units from Alien Bees, Adorama, or other vendors. But if you must connect an external flash with an unknown triggering voltage, I recommend using a Wein Safe Sync (see Figure 10.27), which isolates the flash's voltage from the camera triggering circuit, and provides a PC/X adapter for plugging in non-dedicated flash units.

Another safe way to connect external cameras is through a radio-control device, such as the popular Pocket Wizard products, or the generic transmitter/receiver set shown in Figure 10.28. It piggybacks onto the 7D's PC/X connector and transmits a signal to a matching receiver that's connected to your flash unit. The receiver has both a PC connector of its own as well as a "monoplug" connector (it looks like a headphone plug) that links to a matching port on compatible flash units.

Finally, some flash units have an optical slave trigger built in, or can be fitted with one, so that they fire automatically when another flash, including your camera's built-in unit, fires.

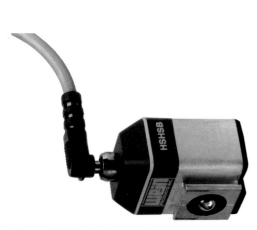

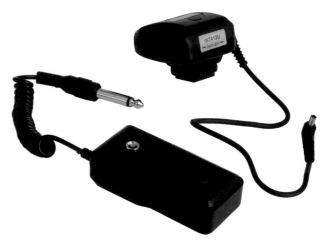

Figure 10.27 A voltage isolator can prevent frying your 7D's flash circuits if you use an older electronic flash, and provides a PC/X connector, which the EOS 7D lacks.

Figure 10.28 A radio-control device frees you from a sync cord tether between your flash and camera.

Other Lighting Accessories

Once you start working with light, you'll find there are plenty of useful accessories that can help you. Here are some of the most popular that you might want to consider.

Soft Boxes

Soft boxes are large square or rectangular devices that may resemble a square umbrella with a front cover, and produce a similar lighting effect. They can extend from a few feet square to massive boxes that stand five or six feet tall—virtually a wall of light. With a flash unit or two inside a soft box, you have a very large, semi-directional light source that's very diffuse and very flattering for portraiture and other people photography.

Soft boxes are also handy for photographing shiny objects. They not only provide a soft light, but if the box itself happens to reflect in the subject (say you're photographing a chromium toaster), the box will provide an interesting highlight that's indistinct and not distracting.

You can buy soft boxes (like the one shown in Figure 10.29) or make your own. Some lengths of friction-fit plastic pipe and a lot of muslin cut and sewed just so may be all that you need.

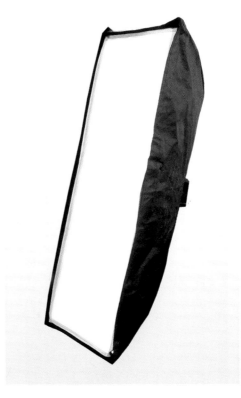

Figure 10.29
Soft boxes provide an even, diffuse light source.

Light Stands

Both electronic flash and incandescent lamps can benefit from light stands. These are lightweight, tripod-like devices (but without a swiveling or tilting head) that can be set on the floor, tabletops, or other elevated surfaces and positioned as needed. Light stands should be strong enough to support an external lighting unit, up to and including a relatively heavy flash with soft box or umbrella reflectors. You want the supports to be capable of raising the lights high enough to be effective. Look for light stands capable of extending six to seven feet high. The nine-foot units usually have larger, steadier bases, and extend high enough that you can use them as background supports. You'll be using these stands for a lifetime, so invest in good ones. I bought the light stand shown in Figure 10.30 when I was in college, and I have been using it for decades.

Figure 10.30
Light stands can hold lights, umbrellas, backdrops, and other equipment.

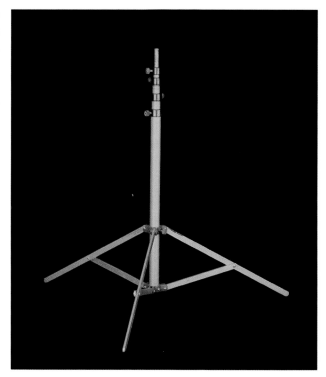

Backgrounds

Backgrounds can be backdrops of cloth, sheets of muslin you've painted yourself using a sponge dipped in paint, rolls of seamless paper, or any other suitable surface your mind can dream up. Backgrounds provide a complementary and non-distracting area behind subjects (especially portraits) and can be lit separately to provide contrast and separation that outlines the subject, or which helps set a mood.

I like to use plain-colored backgrounds for portraits, and white seamless backgrounds for product photography. You can usually construct these yourself from cheap materials and tape them up on the wall behind your subject, or mount them on a pole stretched between a pair of light stands.

Snoots and Barn Doors

These fit over the flash unit and direct the light at your subject. Snoots are excellent for converting a flash unit into a hair light, while barn doors give you enough control over the illumination by opening and closing their flaps that you can use another flash as a background light, with the capability of feathering the light exactly where you want it on the background. A barn door unit is shown in Figure 10.31.

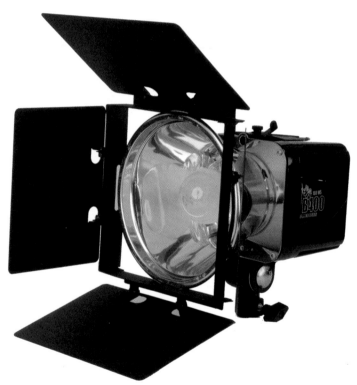

Figure 10.31
Barn doors allow you to modulate the light from a flash or lamp, and they are especially useful for hair lights and background lights.

11

Using the EOS 7D's Wireless Flash Controller

As I mentioned in the last chapter, one of the chief objections to the use of electronic flash is the stark, flat look of direct/on-camera flash, as you can see in Figure 11.1. But as flash wizard Joe McNally, author of *The Hotshoe Diaries*, has proven, small flash units can produce amazingly creative images when used properly.

The key to effective flash photography is to get the flash off the camera, so its illumination can be used to paint your subject in interesting and subtle ways from a variety of angles. But, sometimes, using a cable to liberate your flash from the accessory shoe isn't enough. Nor is the use of just a single electronic flash always the best solution. What we really have needed is a way to trigger one—or more—flash units wirelessly, giving us the freedom to place the electronic flash anywhere in the scene and, if our budgets and time allow, to work in this mode with multiple flashes.

Canon shooters who owned cameras introduced before the EOS 7D have long had wireless flash capabilities. The complication was that wireless triggering was not built into the camera itself. To control other flash units, it was necessary to use either a Canon Speedlite Transmitter ST-E2 (a $250 accessory that uses hard-to-find and expensive 2CR5 batteries) or dedicate a 580EX II (at a cost of around $400) to your camera just to trigger your wireless strobes.

So, I was very pleased when Canon introduced the EOS 7D, which is Canon's first camera to offer built-in wireless flash control through its pop-up flash. It's an improvement many photographers have welcomed. Anytime a new feature eliminates the need to carry a costly accessory and its unusual batteries, the manufacturer has made life simpler and easier for the photographer.

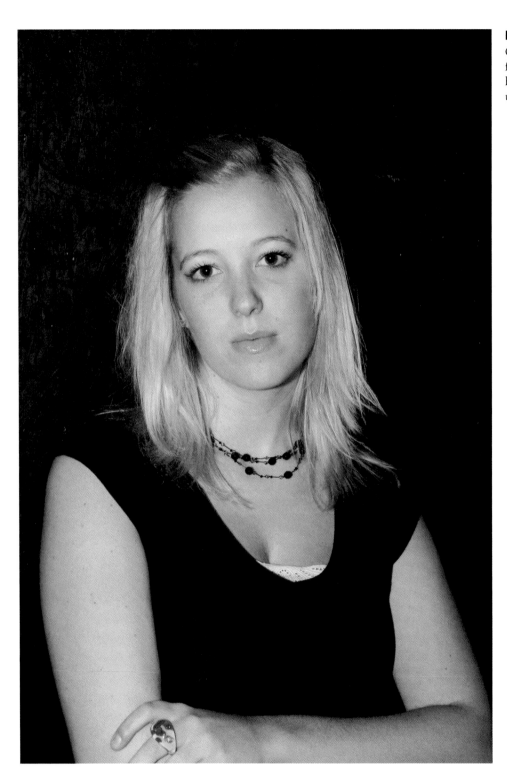

Figure 11.1
On-camera flash is often harsh and unflattering.

It's not possible to cover every aspect of wireless flash in one chapter. There are too many permutations involved. For example, you can use the 7D's built-in flash, an external flash, or the ST-E2 transmitter as the master. You may have one external "slave" flash, or use several. It's possible to control all your wireless flash units as if they were one multi-headed flash, or you can allocate them into "groups" that can be managed individually. You may select one of four "channels" to communicate with your strobes. These are all aspects that you'll want to explore as you become used to working with the 7D's amazing wireless capabilities.

What I hope to do in this chapter is provide the introduction to the basics that you won't find in the other guidebooks, so you can learn how to operate the 7D's new wireless capabilities quickly, and then embark on your own exploration of the possibilities.

Elements of Wireless Flash

Here are some of the key concepts to electronic flash and wireless flash that I'll be describing in this chapter:

- **Built-in flash used alone.** I covered the use of the pop-up flash alone in Chapter 10.

- **Built-in flash used simultaneously with off-camera flash.** You can use the off-camera flash as a *main light* and supply *fill light* from the built-in flash to produce interesting effects and pleasing portraits.

- **Built-in flash used as a trigger only for off-camera flash.** Use the 7D's built-in wireless flash controller to command single or multiple Speedlites for studio-like lighting effects, without having the pop-up flash contribute to the exposure itself.

- **Using flash ratios.** You can control the power of multiple off-camera Speedlites to adjust each unit's relative contribution to the image, for more dramatic portraits and other effects.

- **Channel controls.** Canon's wireless flash system offers users the ability to determine on which of four possible channels the flash units can communicate. (The pilots, ham radio operators, or scanner listeners among you can think of the channels as individual communications frequencies.) The channel ability is important when you're working around other photographers who are also using the same system. Each photographer sets his flash units to a different channel so as to not accidentally trigger other users' strobes. (At big events with more than four photographers using Canon flash, you may need to negotiate.)

- **Groups.** Canon's wireless flash system lets you designate multiple flash units in separate groups (as many as three groups with the 7D's built-in controller). You can then have flash units in one group fire at a different output than flash units in another group. This lets you create different styles of lighting for portraits and other shots.

Getting Started

Canon's wireless flash system gives you a number of advantages that include the ability to use directional lighting, which can help bring out detail or emphasize certain aspects of the picture area. It also lets you operate multiple strobes, as many as four flash units in each of three groups, or 12 in all (although most of us won't own 12 Canon Speedlites). You can set up complicated portrait or location lighting setups. Since the top-of-the line Canon Speedlite 580EX II pumps out a lot of light for a shoe mount flash, a set of these units can give you near studio-quality lighting. Of course, the cost of these high-end Speedlites approaches that of some studio monolights—but the Canon battery-powered units are more portable and don't require an external AC power source.

This chapter builds on the information in Chapter 10 and shows how to take advantage of the 7D's built-in wireless controller. While it may seem complicated at first, it really isn't. Learning the 7D's controls doesn't take a lot of effort, and once you get the hang of it, you'll be able to make changes quickly.

Since it's necessary to set up both the camera and the strobes for wireless operation, this guide will help you with both, starting with prepping the camera. To configure your camera for wireless flash, just follow these steps (I'm going to condense them a bit, because many of these settings have been introduced in previous chapters):

1. **Using the built-in flash as a wireless flash controller.** Start by popping up the camera's built-in flash. You can use this flash either in conjunction with your remote, off-camera strobes (adding some illumination to your photos) or just to control them (with no illumination from your pop-up flash contributing to the exposure). The built-in flash needs to be in the up position to use the 7D's wireless flash controller either way.

2. **Enable internal flash.** Press the MENU button and navigate to the Shooting 1 menu. Choose the Flash control entry, as described in Chapter 10, and press the SET button (it's the one in the center of the Quick Control Dial). This brings up the Flash control menu (which is at the bottom of the menu). Press the SET button to enter the Flash control menu. Next, select the Flash firing setting (by turning the Quick Control Dial) and set the camera to Enable. This activates the built-in flash, which makes wireless flash control with the 7D possible. (See Figure 11.2.)

3. **Confirm/Enable E-TTL II exposure.** Although you can use wireless flash techniques and manual flash exposure, you're better off learning to use wireless features with the EOS 7D set to automatic exposure. So, from the Flash control menu, use the Quick Control Dial to move to the Built-in flash func. setting option (second from the top in Figure 11.2) and press the SET button again. If Flash mode is not already set for E-TTL II, select the entry, press SET, and change from Manual flash or MULTI Flash back to E-TTL II. (See Figure 11.3.)

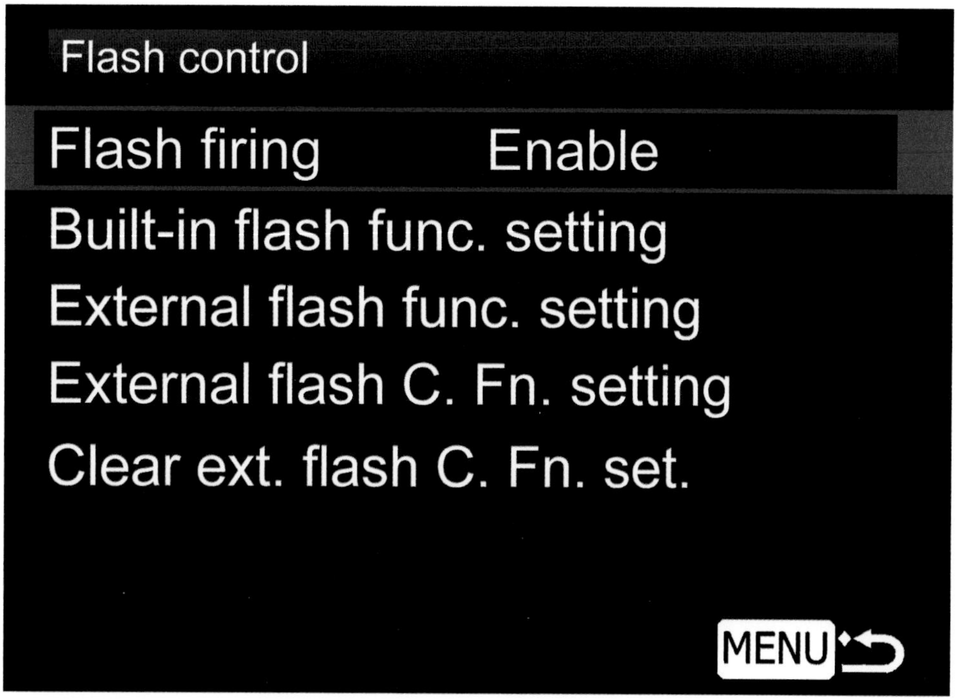

Figure 11.2
Enable the
internal flash
unit.

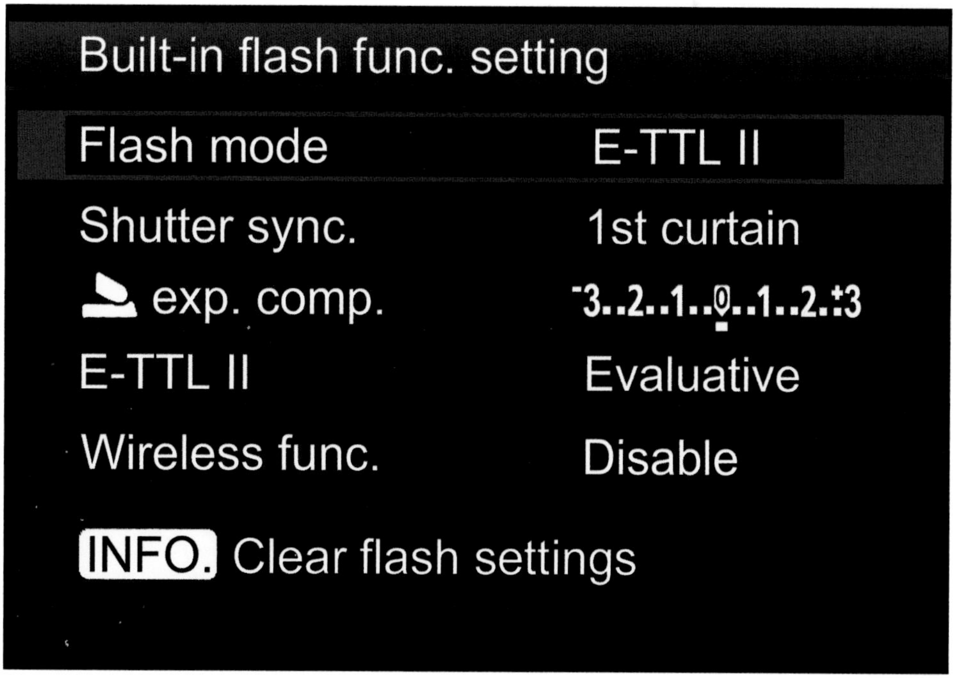

Flash control

Flash firing   Enable

Built-in flash func. setting
External flash func. setting
External flash C. Fn. setting
Clear ext. flash C. Fn. set.

MENU ⟵

Figure 11.3
Set flash expo-
sure to the
automatic
E-TTL II
mode.

Built-in flash func. setting

Flash mode   E-TTL II

Shutter sync.   1st curtain

⬑ exp. comp.   ‾3..2..1..0..1..2.‡3

E-TTL II   Evaluative

Wireless func.   Disable

INFO. Clear flash settings

4. **Enable wireless functions.** Back at the Built-in flash func. setting menu, use the QCD to scroll down to the Wireless func. entry and press SET. The four options available are Disable, Ratio set, Wireless (external) flash only, and Wireless (external) flash plus built-in flash. To use wireless, flash, you'll need to switch from Disable to one of the three other choices, which I will explain in the following sections.

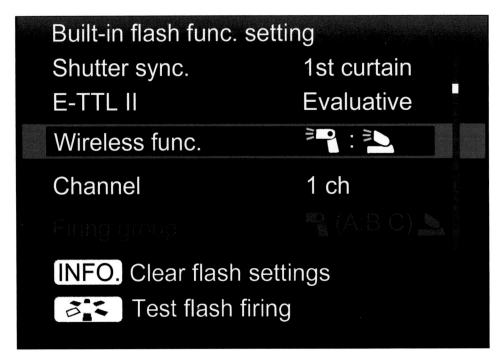

Figure 11.4
Enable wireless flash by choosing one of three wireless flash functions (described next).

Once you've completed the four steps above, your 7D is set up to begin using wireless flash. But first, you'll need to specify a few other options, including wireless functions, channels, and groups. I'll show you each of these one at a time.

Selecting Wireless Functions

As I noted, the Wireless func. entry in the Built-in flash func. setting menu has four options: Disable, plus Internal/external flash ratio setting, Wireless flash only, and Wireless flash plus built-in flash. You probably understand the function of Disable fairly well, but here's a discussion of the other three choices.

Internal/External Flash Ratio Setting

This option lets you choose a power ratio between your built-in flash and your wireless flash units—the relative strength of each. It can be especially useful if you want to use the built-in flash for just a little fill light while letting your off-camera units do the heavy work.

Having the ability to vary the power of each flash unit or group of flash units wirelessly gives you greater flexibility and control. Varying the light output of each flash unit makes it possible to create specific types of lighting (such as traditional portrait lighting which frequently calls for a 3:1 lighting ratio between main light and fill light) or to use illumination to highlight one part of the photo while reducing contrast in another.

Lighting ratios determine the contrast between the main (sometimes called a "key" light) and fill light. For portraiture, usually the main light is typically placed at a 45-degree angle to the subject (although there are some variations), with the fill-in light on the opposite side or closer to the camera position. Choosing the right lighting ratio can do a lot to create a particular look or mood. For instance, a 1:1 ratio produces what's known as "flat" lighting. While this is good for copying or documentation, it's not usually as interesting for portraiture. Instead, making the main light more powerful than the fill light creates interesting shadows for more dramatic images. (See Figure 11.5.)

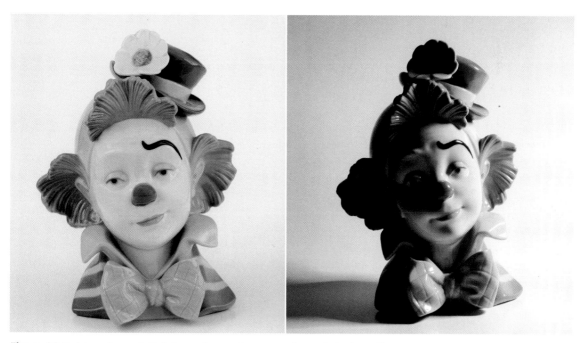

Figure 11.5 More dramatic lighting ratios produce more dramatic-looking illumination.

By selecting the power ratio between the flash units, you can change the relative illumination between them. Figure 11.6 shows a series of four images with a single main flash located at a 45-degree angle off to the right and slightly behind the model. The built-in flash at the camera provided illumination to fill in the shadows on the side of the face closest to the camera. The ratio between the external and internal flash were varied using 2:1 (upper left), 3:1 (upper right), 4:1 (lower left), and 5:1 (lower right) ratios.

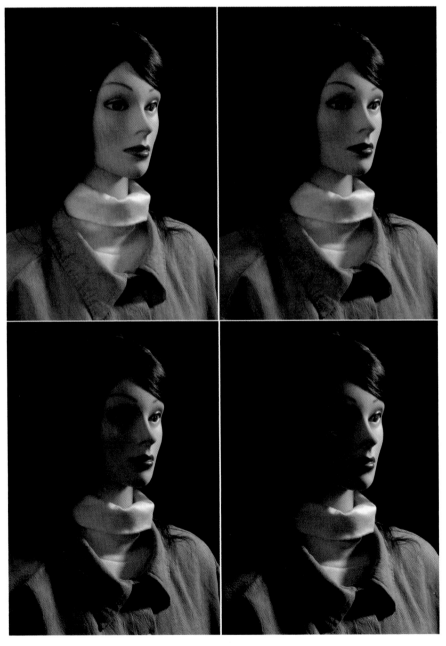

Figure 11.6
The main light (to the right and behind the model) and fill light (at the camera position) were varied using 2:1 and 3:1 (top row, left to right) as well as 4:1 and 5:1 (bottom row, left to right) ratios.

Here's how to set the lighting ratio between the internal flash and one external wireless flash unit:

1. **Choose Ratio setting in Wireless func. menu.** In the Built-in flash func. setting menu, highlight Wireless func., press SET, and choose Ratio setting (it's the first entry under Disable, as shown in Figure 11.7). Press SET again to confirm and return to the previous menu.

2. **Access the Power ratio entry.** Now you can set the power ratio by scrolling down just below the Firing group entry, represented by a pair of icons corresponding to an external and internal flash unit.

3. **Set the control.** Press the SET button.

4. **Choose the desired ratio.** Then use the Quick Control Dial to choose the setting you want. (See Figure 11.8.) Your choices range from 1:1 (the off-camera and built-in flash have equal output) to 8:1 (the off-camera flash supplies 8X output compared to the internal flash). Set the ratio to 4:1, for example, and the external flash will produce four times as much light as the on-camera flash, which is then used as fill illumination. For most subjects, ratios of 2:1 to 5:1 will produce the best results, as shown earlier in Figure 11.6.

5. **Confirm.** Press SET to confirm your ratio.

Figure 11.7
Choose Ratio setting to adjust the relative power of the external and internal flash units.

External/internal flash ratio

External flash only

External+ internal flash

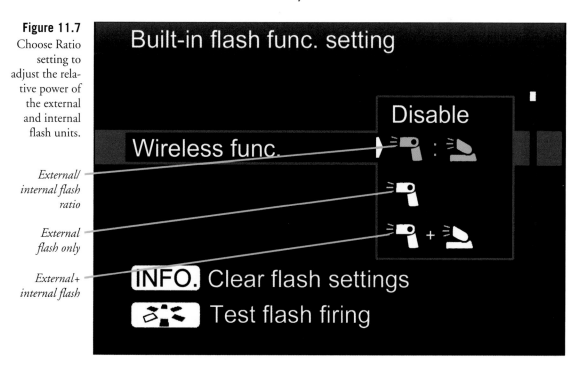

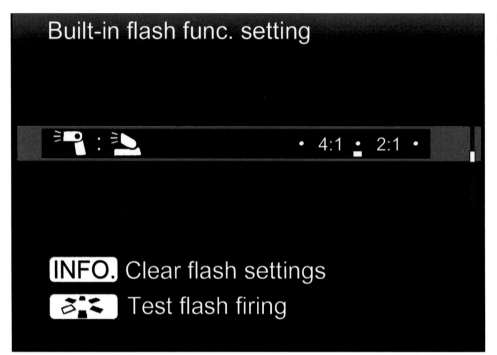

Figure 11.8
Select a ratio
from 8:1 to
1:1.

Wireless Flash Only

This setting allows you to turn off the flash output of your 7D's built-in flash, while allowing it to emit a wireless controller flash that signals the external flash units you're working with. You'll still see a burst from your camera's built-in flash, but that burst will not contribute to the exposure. It will only be used to tell the remote/slave flash units to fire.

This is the setting to choose if you only want to use the flash controller to operate your remote flashes. It's probably the most commonly used choice when you don't want to use the internal flash for fill light, since firing the built-in flash increases the risk of red eye effects.

Photographers prefer this mode in part because Canon's portable shoe mount flash units are much more powerful than a camera's built-in flash. They want to avoid using a light source that is directly above the lens and close to the lens because the chances of red-eye are much greater since it is caused by light from the flash unit reflecting off the subject's retinas and bouncing back into the lens.

Using off-camera flash lets the photographer precisely control light direction and effect. It also makes it possible for the photographer to move around within the constraints of the flash units' ability to illuminate a scene, without worrying about getting too far from the subject for the flash unit(s) to be effective. Only the camera to subject position changes and not the light to subject position and ratio. Once you've set up the flash units relative to your subject, you can move around freely.

Being able to control lighting direction is a very useful capability since it can lead to more dramatic images. In Figures 11.9 and 11.10, a single flash unit was used to light the model. A snoot (a small cylindrical light modifier) or a grid was placed on the flash head to restrict the light from the unit. In each case, the lighting effect is dramatic.

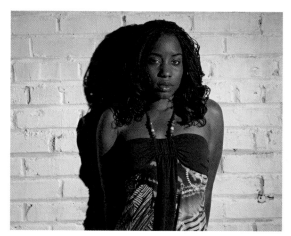

Figure 11.9 Chevon Hill lit by a Canon 580EX II flash unit with a Zoot Snoot mounted on it. The flash was mounted on a light stand placed at a 45-degree angle to the model.

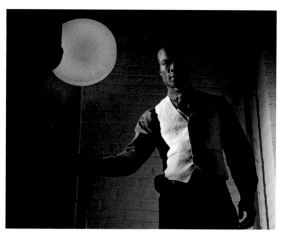

Figure 11.10 Belito was lit by a Canon 580EX II flash unit with a Honl Speed Grid. The flash unit was placed on a light stand positioned to the left of the model and angled slightly downward. The white bricks reflected some of the light from the flash unit back into the model's opposite side providing a little fill lighting.

Here are the steps to follow when using wireless flash only (whether you're working with a single external flash, or multiple units).

1. **Choose wireless flash only.** Navigate to the Wireless func. menu as you did earlier, but choose Wireless flash only (the single-flash icon two rows below the Disable setting).

2. **Confirm.** Press the SET button to confirm the Wireless flash only setting.

3. **Set the Power ratio (optional).** If you are using more than one external flash, and have assigned flash units to different groups (Groups A, B, and C are available), you can then set the power ratios between groups. (I'll explain groups later in this chapter.) If you are using only one flash, or all the flash units are assigned to the same group, you don't need to do this; setting a power ratio won't make any difference. (Remember to change the power ratio back to normal when you are finished with a session; Canon's Speedlites retain the settings you make, even after a quick battery change.)

Using Wireless and Built-in Flash

This option in the Wireless func. screen adds the built-in flash to whatever wireless groups you're using. You can then use the built-in flash in conjunction with whatever firing groups you've set up. In this case you're still using the external flash units as the main sources of light, but the built-in flash can either serve to provide some extra fill (such as to illuminate the face under the brim of a hat) or to provide a second light when you only have one off-camera flash available.

It is also possible to set up a two-light portrait using an off-camera flash as a main light (about 45 degrees to the model) and the built-in flash as the fill light, as discussed earlier. Use the External/Internal flash ratio setting to adjust their relative contribution to the image.

Some photographers do like to position their fill light directly above the camera and straight towards the model. The lighting ratio for such a setup would either have the built-in and external strobes set to 1:1 or 2:1. Keep in mind that if using such a configuration, the light from the built-in flash is striking the subject head on and needs to be added to your calculations for the main light. In other words, setting your lighting ratio to 1:1 would actually provide a 2:1 effective lighting ratio since you would have 1 part light from the main light and 1 part light from the built-in flash illuminating one side of the subject and just 1 part light from the built-in flash illuminating the other side. Setting your lighting ratio to 2:1 would effectively provide a 3:1 lighting ratio this way. If you have set the camera to E-TTL II exposure as recommended, the lighting you choose will be automatically accounted for in the exposure selected by the camera, so no calculations are necessary by the photographer.

Working with Groups

With what you've already learned, you can shoot wirelessly using your camera's built-in flash and one or more external flash units. All these strobes will work together with the 7D for automatic exposure using E-TTL II exposure mode. You can vary the power ratio between your built-in flash and the external units. As you become more comfortable with wireless flash photography, you can even switch the individual external flash units into manual mode, and adjust their lighting ratios manually.

But there's a lot more you can do if you've splurged and own two or more compatible external flash units (some photographers I know own five or six Speedlite 580EX II units). Canon wireless photography lets you collect individual strobes into *groups*, and control all the Speedlites within a given group together. You can operate as few as two strobes in two groups or three strobes in three groups, while controlling more units if desired. You can also have them fire at equal output settings (A+B+C mode) versus using them at different power ratios (A:B or A:B C modes). Setting each group's strobes to different power ratios gives you more control over lighting for portraiture and other uses.

This is one of the more powerful options of the EOS wireless flash system. I prefer to keep my Speedlites set to different groups normally. I can always set the power ratio to 1:1 if I want to operate the flash units all at the same power. If I change my mind and need to make adjustments, I can just change the wireless flash controller and then be able to manipulate the different groups' output as desired.

Canon's wireless flash system works with a number of Canon flashes and even some third-party units. I routinely mix a 580EX II, 550EX, and 420EX plus sometimes add a Sigma EF-500 Super. I control these flash units either with the EOS 7D's built-in wireless capabilities or using a Canon ST-E2 Speedlite Transmitter.

The ST-E2 is a hot shoe mount device that offers wireless flash control for a wide variety of Canon wireless flash capable strobes and can even control flash units wirelessly for high speed sync (HSS) photography (a capability the 7D doesn't offer). (HSS is described in Chapter 10.) The ST-E2 can only control two flash groups though, not three like the 7D and also can support flash exposure bracketing. Its range isn't as great as the 7D's though.

Canon flash units that can be operated wirelessly include: 580EX II, 580EX, 550EX, 430EX, 420EX, MR-14EX, MT-24EX. The 270EX, 220EX, 380EX and earlier Canon flash units cannot be operated wirelessly via Canon's wireless flash system. There are third-party flash units that can (such as the Sigma I use), but you must use one designed to work with Canon's wireless flash system only.

Here's how you set up groups:

1. **Determine lighting setup.** Decide whether you're using the built-in flash as part of your lighting scheme or just using the external flash units. If you do want the internal flash to contribute to the exposure, then you can scroll down to the external flash/built-in flash lighting ratio control (if you're using lighting ratios) and set that control (from 8:1 to 2:1, as noted earlier).

2. **Access lighting groups.** If you're not using the built-in flash, scroll down to the Firing group entry and press SET. The screen shown in Figure 11.11 appears.

3. **Select the group configuration you want.** From top to bottom, the choices shown in Figure 11.11 are:

   A+B+C. Multiple external flash units functioning as one big flash.

   A:B. Multiple external units in two groups.

   A:B C. Multiple external strobes in three groups.

   I'll explain exactly what these three configurations do next.

4. **Allocate flash units into groups.** You must do this at the flash unit itself. You'll need to tell each flash which group it "belongs" to, so it will respond, along with any other strobes (if any) in its group, to wireless commands directed at that particular group. The procedure for setting each flash unit's slave ID/group varies depending on what flash you are using, so consult your Speedlite's manual.

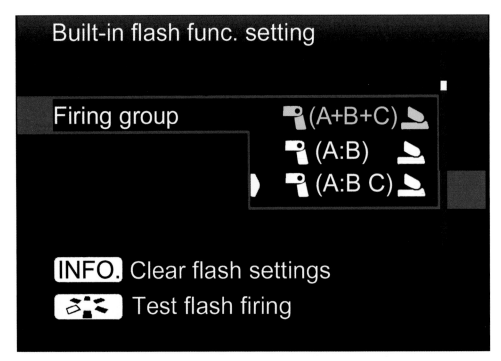

Figure 11.11
Setting the firing group controls.

SETTING SLAVE/GROUP ID WITH THE 580EX II

1. Press the Zoom button for two seconds or longer until the display blinks.

2. Rotate the control dial until the Slave indicator blinks.

3. Press the control dial button to confirm Slave operation.

4. To change from Group A to another group, press the Zoom button until the Group A indicator blinks.

5. Rotate the control dial until the A indicator is replaced by the B or C indicators.

6. Press the control dial button to confirm the group ID.

Group Configurations

As noted previously, you can choose any of three different group configurations, with one or more than one flash allocated to each group. Here is what each group allocation does.

- **A+B+C.** This is the configuration to use when you want to illuminate a large area. All the Speedlites in each of up to three groups will fire simultaneously and at the same power level. The EOS 7D will meter the exposure from the preflash and adjust the output of all the units to provide the optimal exposure.

- **A:B.** You can allocate one or more external slaves to Groups A or B, and then adjust the power ratio between the groups to achieve the lighting effect you want. In this configuration, all the slaves in Group A function as a single unit, and all those in Group B function as a single unit. Use the A:B fire ratio entry in the Built-in flash func. setting screen to adjust the power ratios between the two groups. (See Figure 11.12.) Note that the possible settings include 8:1 to 1:1 (with Group A equal to, or more powerful than Group B), or 1:1 to 1:8 (in which Group B will be set to a higher power level relative to Group A). You can bump up/down the output of all the flash units in Groups A and B by using the Flash exp. comp setting, shown in Figure 11.13.

Figure 11.12
Setting the firing group controls.

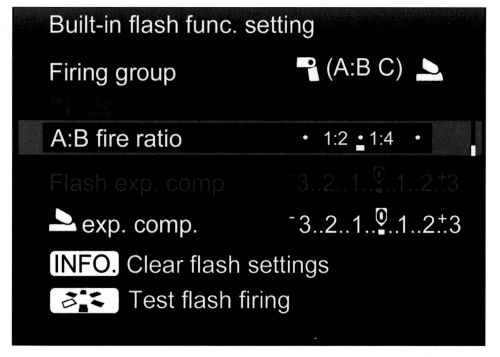

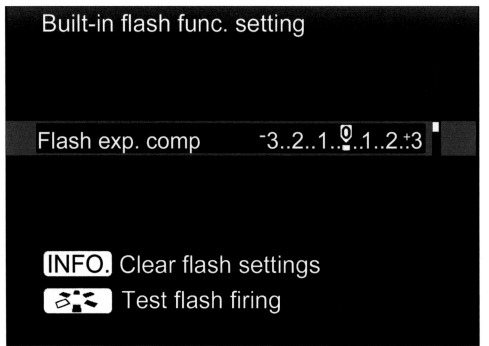

Figure 11.13
Use Flash exposure compensation to adjust the output of Group A and B strobes.

- **A:B C.** In this configuration, you can control the power levels of A:B relative to one another, as described previously. However, a third collection of slave units, Group C, is added to the mix. You can adjust the relative output of Group C, compared to Groups A and B, using the Group C exp. comp. entry, shown in Figure 11.14. A similar exposure compensation setting (A,B exp. comp.) is available to add/subtract from the output of all the units in Groups A and B.

FLASH EXPOSURE COMPENSATION

Remember that when you set the exposure compensation to anything but 0, you're telling the flash to fire at a different output than the E-TTL would normally choose. You can select anywhere from three f-stops worth of compensation over or under the normal output in 1/3 f-stop increments. This is different from setting a power ratio, which affects the light output of the different flash units in relation to one another, but still operating under the control of Canon's E-TTL exposure technology.

It's possible to set exposure compensation for one flash group versus another, for all flash groups, or for the camera's ambient light (non-flash) exposure.

Figure 11.14
If you've acti-
vated Group C,
exposure com-
pensation is
available for
that group, too.

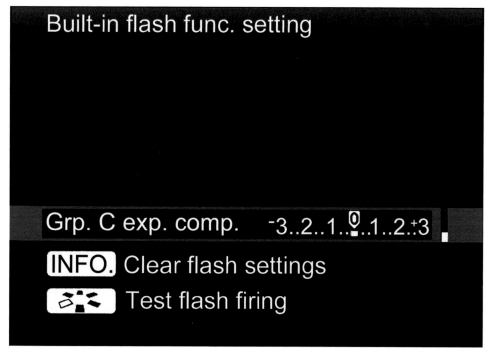

Figure 11.14
If you've activated Group C, exposure compensation is available for that group, too.

Choosing a Channel

Canon's wireless flash system can work on any of four channels, so if more than one photographer is using the Canon system, each can set his gear to a different channel so they don't accidentally trigger each other's strobes. You need to be sure all of your gear is set to the same channel.

The ability to operate flash units on one of four channels isn't really important unless you're shooting in an environment where other photographers are also using the Canon wireless flash system. If the system only offered one channel, then each photographer's wireless flash controller would be firing every Canon flash set for wireless operation. By having four channels available, the photographers can coordinate their use to avoid that problem. Such situations are common at sporting events and other activities that draw a lot of shooters.

It's always a good idea to double-check your flash units before you set them up to make sure they're all set to the same channel, and this should also be one of your first troubleshooting questions if a flash doesn't fire the first time you try to use it wirelessly.

You do this as follows:

1. **Set flash units to the channel you want to use for all your groups.** Each flash unit may use its own procedure for setting that strobe's channel. Consult your Speedlite's manual for instructions. With the 580EX II, press the Zoom button repeatedly until the CH. Indicator blinks, then rotate the control dial to select Channel 1,2,3, or 4. Press the control dial center button to confirm.

2. **Navigate to the 7D's channel selection option.** In the Built-in flash func. settings screen, use the Quick Control Dial to scroll down to the Channel setting and push the SET button.

3. **Select the channel your flashes are set to.** You can then use the Quick Control Dial to advance the channel number from 1 to 4 or back down again (you have to reverse the Quick Control Dial direction to get back to one; you can't just keep advancing it to get there—it doesn't "wrap around).

4. **Double-check to make sure your flash units are set to the appropriate channel.** Your wireless flash units must be set to the same channel as the 7D's wireless flash controller; otherwise, the Speedlites won't fire.

Using Wireless Flash Creatively

Getting the flash off the camera is fundamental to improving the quality of your lighting. Wireless flash lets you control the light's direction and allows you to use a number of light sources to create more interesting and attractive images.

These next sections look at some ways of using wireless flash to improve your photography. They break down into tips and tricks based on the number of flash units used to create an image. Keep in mind, even just one small flash unit, used creatively, can lead to a significant improvement in your photos, especially when you can use your external flash off camera and you're not tied down to the accessory shoe.

REMINDER

Keep in mind that when the Canon Speedlite 580EXII is ready to fire as a slave, the AF-assist beam will blink at one-second intervals. The unit will *not* go into a sleep mode while it is waiting to be used as a slave, but the camera will shut off at the interval you've specified in the menus.

Single-Flash Unit Ideas

As you've seen, using a Canon Speedlite wirelessly is simple with the 7D. Most Canon flash units come with a handy table stand accessory that allows you to set up the flash as a freestanding light. Just configure the strobe for wireless connectivity to the camera, as described previously in this chapter, and then position it wherever you want. So long as the strobe and the camera can see each other (the wireless signal from the 7D can even be bounced off of walls to connect with the flash) they will communicate with each other.

Some handy uses for a single off-camera flash include moving it closer to the subject to increase its effectiveness (remember the inverse square law), placing it off to the side of the subject to show detail (or positioned alongside a reflective surface such as a white wall or reflector to provide main light and fill), or raised up high and angled to one side to get rid of harsh shadows.

While the number of possibilities is endless, here are some examples of things that can be done with a single off-camera flash. Some of these are done with just a basic flash unit, while others rely on light modifiers to create unusual effects.

Single Flash Unit and Sunlight

When shooting outdoors you can often combine sunlight and an off-camera flash to create a more pleasing looking portrait. Position your subject so the sun is at a 45-degree angle to her and your off camera flash is lighting her from the parallel 45-degree angle. You can either go with equal exposures (for flat portrait lighting) or expose the flashlit side brighter or darker than the sun's exposure for a more stylistic type of lighting.

You can improve the quality of the light by firing the flash unit into a soft box or umbrella as in this photograph of Porsche Brosseau (shown in Figure 11.15). Placing the soft box and flash closer to the subject would soften the light even more (the larger the light source in relation to the subject, the softer the light) and make the flash unit's effective output even greater.

Single Flash Unit with a Reflector

This is similar to the sun and flash combo shot, but this approach relies on the off-camera flash as the main light and uses reflected ("bounced") light from either a white wall or a reflector of some kind. Here the flash will be the stronger light source, and the distance the reflector is positioned from the light will determine the lighting ratio between the two light sources (flash and reflector). Generally, you want to have the reflector pretty close to the subject to keep the lighting ratio manageable. If it's too far away, one side of the face will end up in deep shadow.

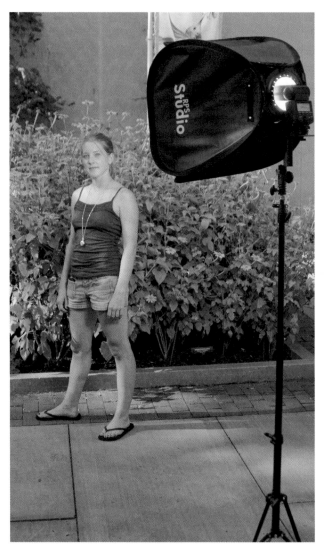

Figure 11.15
A Canon 580EX II Speedlite was mounted on a light stand and fired through a soft box to one side, while the sun illuminated Porsche Brosseau from the other.

Side Lighting for Effect

Lighting from the side is useful for showing texture and detail as the light fills in shadows on one side and emphasizes them on the other. It's also a more dramatic style of light, particularly if the light is restricted by a grid, snoot, or barn doors attachment as this photo of Lisa shows (see Figure 11.16).

This is a very moody and dramatic style of lighting. Depending on how you modify the light it can produce a very dramatic effect (by restricting the light with a snoot, barn doors, or grids) or by allowing the light to spread a bit by firing the flash directly from the side. You can even try bouncing it off a wall from the side to spread the light a bit more. Each technique can produce a compelling image.

Figure 11.16
A gridded
Canon 580EX
II mounted on
a light stand
provided all the
illumination
for Lisa Simon
in this portrait.
The black
backdrop
helped empha-
size the mystery
to this image.

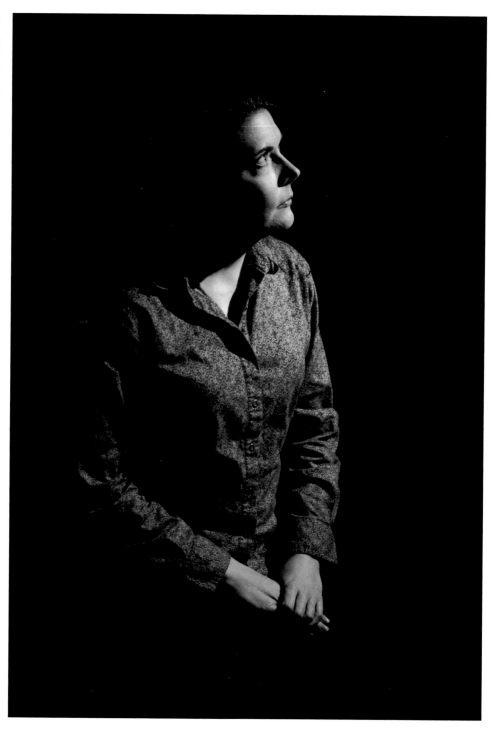

Shooting Through Blinds

You can fire a flash unit through a set of window blinds to mimic the effect of sunlight streaming through a window. I even keep a set of blinds in my studio for this effect. Position the blinds and a flash unit on a light stand both angled to the side of your subject and fire the flash unit through the blinds.

There are even some interesting variations you can try with this idea. One is to attach a 1/4 or 1/2 yellow or orange gel to the flash head to add some color to the light. This will mimic the effect of early or late daylight streaming through the blinds. Another option is to add a second light or reflector to fill in some of the shadows. (See Figures 11.17 and 11.18.)

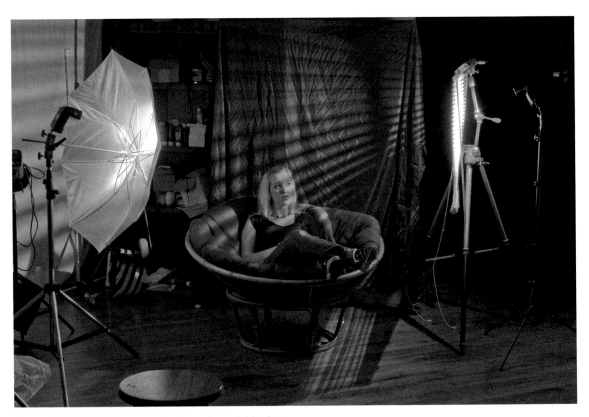

Figure 11.17 Lighting setup for shoot through blinds image.

Figure 11.18
A Canon 580EX II was mounted on a light stand and fired through a set of blinds to create the shadow pattern on Lindsey Miller.

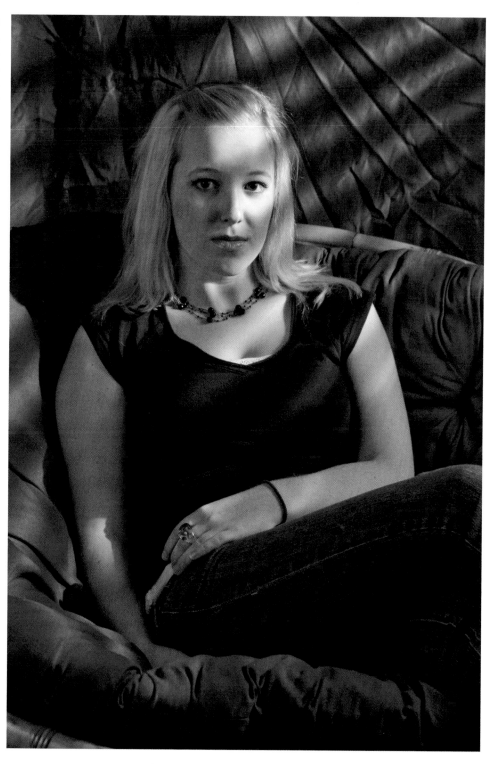

Adding a Gel for a Special Effect

Gels are colored filters for your flash. Put one of these over the flash head (either via Gaffer's tape or a gel holder) and color the light from the flash. You can use a red, yellow, or orange gel to create a late day type of light. Or, you can use funkier colors to go for something on the wild side.

You can also put a gel on a background flash and use it to turn a white background into a background of a different color. (See Figure 11.19.)

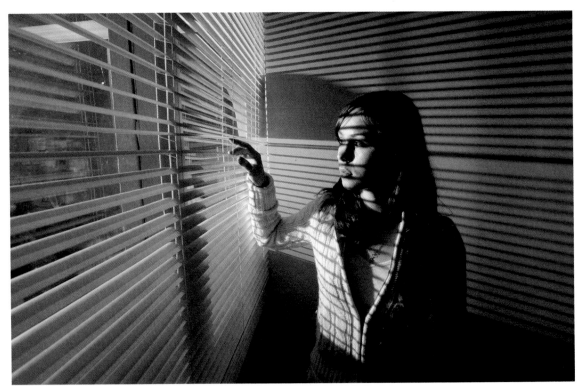

Figure 11.19 A yellow gel was taped to the flash head to produce the yellow light on Callie Harlan.

Raising Your Flash Up High Via Monopod or Light Stand

Mounting your flash on a monopod, using one of the many available flash shoe/tripod adapters, gives you the option of positioning your light farther from your camera and allows you to direct its light where you need it (you may have to hold the camera with just one hand or talk someone else into holding the monopod flash combo for you). While it's common to raise it up to get rid of shadows, you can also position it to light from the side. If you're using a monopod with built-in legs (such as the Trek Tech Go Pro) you now have a freestanding light stand too. Or, if you have a portable light stand, you can do the same thing. (See Figure 11.20.)

Figure 11.20
Lisa holds a monopod mounted flash unit.

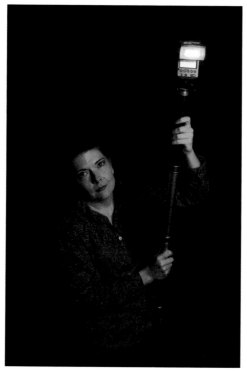

Two-Light Setups

When you can bring in a second off-camera flash your possibilities can get even more interesting. Whether you're trying for portrait style lighting or creating moody, stylistic lighting, bringing in that second flash can add a lot of depth to your photography. The second flash is also a boon for macro, close-up, and detail work.

At a bare minimum, two flash units enable you to create a basic portrait lighting kit that gives you great control over how you light your subject. It's also perfect for macro photography.

"Old" Hollywood Glamour Lighting Revisited

While the single flash does a nice job for a tight shot, bringing in a second flash from the side to throw some light on the legs and body makes this shot even more glamorous. Set the power ratio for 2:1 so you don't lose the spotlight effect from the main light.

Macro Lighting

A pair of wireless flash units is perfect for macro and close-up photography. Position the lights at 45-degree angles to the surface of the subject and get nice, even lighting that shows detail beautifully.

Lighting Family Get-Togethers

Sometimes you're just trying to get photos in a crowded home during the holidays or at some other family gathering and just don't have time to set up and rearrange lights. In cases such as this, one of the easiest things to do is just rig a couple of flash units on light stands and point them straight up at a white ceiling or into a corner. Put the lights at opposite diagonals if you can and you can expect to get soft, even lighting for most of the shots you take. Keep in mind that you're going to have to be careful to keep the light stands and flash units out of your photos.

If you have to fire the flash units into a colored surface, make sure you set a custom white balance for the resulting light. This will correct for the colorcast that would otherwise result from the light from the flash units picking up the color of the wall or ceiling.

Outdoor Lighting for Cleaner Images

This shot of Amanda cooling off (Figure 11.21) was made with a pair of Speedlites fired wirelessly at equal power. Each was positioned at a 45-degree angle to the model. While it might seem like an outdoor shoot on a bright sunny day would be the last time you need to use flash, overhead sun produces very contrasty light filled with harsh shadows. The wireless flash units provided clean, even lighting on Amanda and helped freeze the water splashing on her.

Three-Light Setups

If you have three external strobes at your disposal, you can put together even more complex lighting effects. As described earlier in this chapter, you can set up these multiple Speedlites into individual groups, so you can control each of them individually, making adjustments to their power ratios as required. Here are some of the things you can do.

Special Effects Macro Lighting

For a special effects shot, position one of your flashes under an upside-down plastic salad bowl, put a small bowl of ice atop the salad bowl, and a shrimp or some other object on the ice. Then position another flash to light the subject. The result is shrimp on glowing ice. Gel the underneath flash to give the ice a colored glow (Figure 11.22).

Figure 11.21
Amanda cools off while a pair of Canon wireless flash units provide light to clean up any shadows from the midday sun.

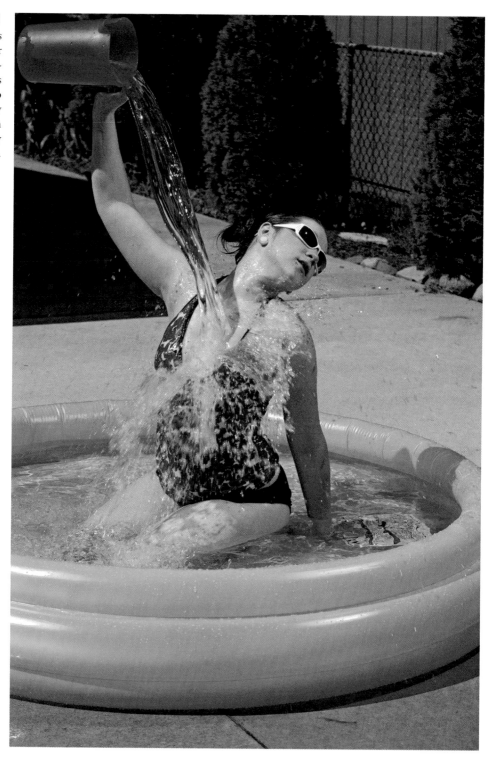

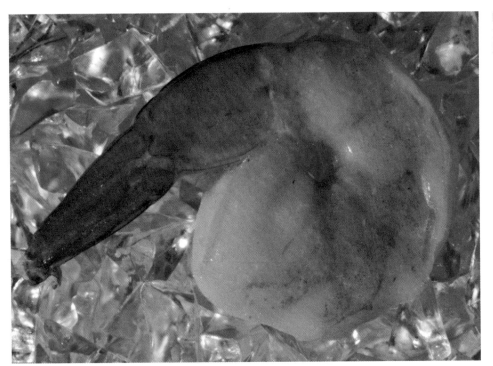

Figure 11.22
Backlit macro lighting.

With one flash positioned on the table to fire upward, a plastic container was turned upside down and placed over the flash unit. A small bowl filled with crushed ice was positioned on top of it and the product was placed on the ice. Two more flash units were then used to light the subject, each positioned at a 45-degree angle. The two main lights were set to Group A, while the light on the table was set to Group B. A 2:1 lighting ratio was used.

Studio Portraiture with Off-Camera Wireless Shoe Mount Flash Units

Combine multiple flash units, light modifiers, and light stands and you can manage a pretty nice portable portrait studio. For the shot of Karina, a Canon 580EX II was fired through a shoot-through umbrella to the camera's right, while a 550EX was fired into a reflective umbrella to the camera's left. If you look closely at the bottom of the stool she's sitting on, you can see the legs of another light stand. There was a 420EX flash unit mounted on that light stand to provide some separation between the model Karina Croskey and the backdrop (Figures 11.23 and 11.24).

Figure 11.23
Lighting setup for a wireless flash portrait studio.

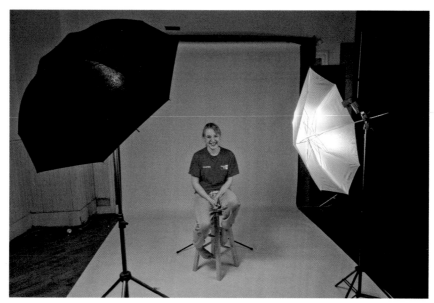

Figure 11.24
Resulting portrait.

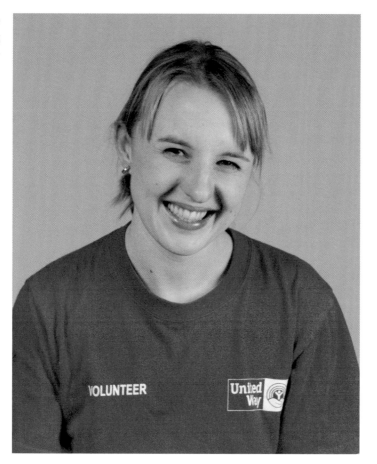

Part IV

Enhancing Your Experience

What do you do after the shutter clicks and your image has been captured in electrons for posterity? This final part of the book will help you get more from your Canon EOS 7D as you download, edit, and print the pictures you've taken, and take the steps necessary to keep your camera humming like the finely-tuned (non-oiled) machine that it really is.

Chapter 12 details some of your options for downloading and editing your photographs. I'll provide quick introductions to the software bundled with your camera, and describe some of the other applications available to convert RAW files and fine-tune images. The chapter is not a software how-to—this book is virtually 100 percent devoted to photographic shooting techniques. (I want to help you *avoid* having to patch up your pictures in Photoshop where possible, by capturing them correctly in the camera.) The chapter also explains the printing options built into the 7D, for those times when you want a quick snapshot from your personal printer or nearby kiosk or minilab.

Chapter 13 tells you everything you need to know about upgrading your camera's firmware, protecting your LCD and Compact Flash card data, and, when necessary, cleaning your sensor manually.

12

Downloading, Editing, and Printing Your Images

Taking the picture is only half the work and, in some cases, only half the fun. After you've captured some great images and have them safely stored on your Canon EOS 7D's memory card, you'll need to transfer them from your camera and memory card to your computer, where they can be organized, fine-tuned in an image editor, and prepared for web display, printing, or some other final destination.

Fortunately, there are lots of software utilities and applications to help you do all these things. This chapter will introduce you to a few of them.

Printing

You can print your images directly from some of the software applications and utilities described later in this chapter, but your EOS 7D can also be used to print from the camera, and to set up print "orders." These next sections will explain your options.

Direct Printing from the Camera

You can print photos stored on your camera's memory card directly to a PictBridge-compatible printer using the cable supplied with the 7D. Just follow these steps to get started:

1. **Set up your printer.** Follow the instructions for your PictBridge-compatible printer to load it with paper, and prepare it for printing.

2. **Connect the camera to the printer.** With the 7D and printer both powered down, open the port cover on the left side of the camera (closest to the back of the camera when it's held in shooting position), and plug the Interface Cable IFC-200U into the A/V Out/Digital port. Connect the other end to the USB input port of your printer.

3. **Turn printer and camera on.** Flip the switch on the 7D, and power up your printer using its power switch.

4. **Press the Playback button on the camera.** Navigate to the image on your memory card that you want to print using the Quick Control Dial.

5. **Select options.** The image, overlaid with the current status for options like those shown in Figure 12.1, will appear when the camera and printer are connected with a cable. (The options will vary, depending on what printer you have.) I'll describe the options next.

The EOS 7D offers a surprising number of options when direct printing from your camera. You can choose effects, print date and time on your hardcopies, select the number of copies to be output, trim the image, and select paper settings—from your camera! While you can print using the current values as shown in the status screen, to adjust the settings, follow these steps, briefly summarized here:

- **Access the print options screen.** Press SET when the screen shown in Figure 12.1 is shown on your LCD.

- **Rotate the Quick Control Dial.** Highlight the options shown at left in Figure 12.2 in any order, and press SET to adjust that option. Within each option, use the SET button to confirm your entry, or the MENU button to back out of the option's screen.

- **Printing effects.** Rotate the QCD and choose Off (no effects), On (the printer's automatic corrections will be applied), Default (values stored in your printer, and which will vary depending on your printer), Vivid (higher saturation in blues and greens), or NR (noise reduction is applied). Three B/W choices are also available, for B/W (true blacks), B/W Cool tone (bluish blacks), and B/W Warm tone (yellowish blacks). Natural and Natural M choices are also available to provide true colors. If the INFO. icon appears, you can press it to make some adjustments to the printing effect, including image brightening, levels, and red-eye correction.

- **Date/File number imprint.** You can set this On or Off

- **Copies.** Select 1 to 99 copies of the selected image.

- **Trimming.** Use this to crop your image. Your image appears on a trimming screen. Press the Zoom in and Zoom out buttons to magnify or reduce the size of the cropping frame. Use the multi-controller to move the cropping frame around within

Figure 12.1
You can print directly from the EOS 7D.

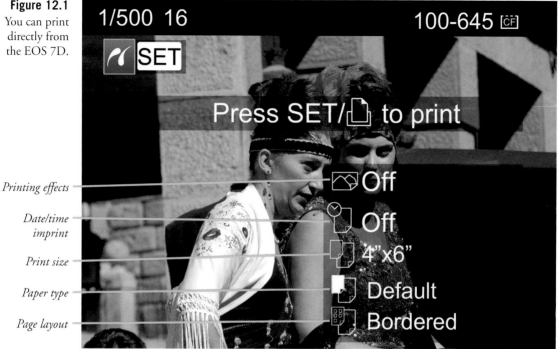

Printing effects

Date/time imprint

Print size

Paper type

Page layout

Figure 12.2
Choose the number of copies, crop the image, and apply other settings and preferences.

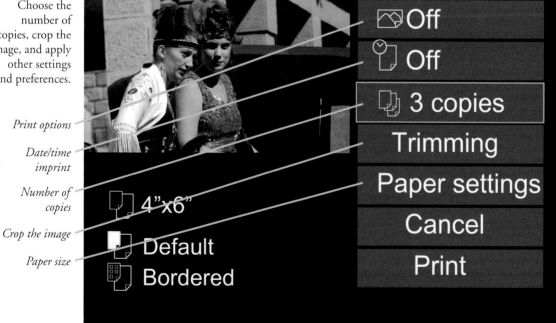

Print options

Date/time imprint

Number of copies

Crop the image

Paper size

the image. Rotate the Quick Control Dial to rotate the image. Press the INFO. button to toggle the cropping frame between horizontal and vertical orientations. When you've defined the crop for the image, press the SET button to apply your trimming to the image.

- **Paper settings.** Choose the paper size, type, and layout. Use the QCD to select your paper size, with choices from credit card size through 8.5 × 11 inches. Press SET to confirm, and the screen changes to a Paper type selection. After choosing Paper type, press SET once more and choose a layout, from Borderless, Bordered, 2-up, 4-up, 9-up, 16-up, and 20-up (multiple copies of the image on a single sheet). When using Letter size (8.5 × 11-inch) paper, you can also elect to print 20-up and 35-up thumbnails of images you've chosen using the DPOF options described later in this chapter. The 20-up version will also include shooting information, such as camera and lens used, shooting mode, shutter speed, aperture, and other data. Another press of the SET button confirms Paper type and returns to the settings screen.

- **Cancel.** Returns to the status screen (seen in Figure 12.1).

- **Print.** Starts the printing process with the selected options. The camera warns you not to disconnect the cable during printing. To print another photo using the same settings, just select it, highlight Print and press the SET button.

Direct Print Order Format (DPOF) Printing

If you don't want to print directly from the camera, you can set some of the same options from the Playback 1 menu's Print order entry, and designate single or multiple images on your memory card for printing. Once marked for DPOF printing, you can print the selected images, or take your memory card to a digital lab or kiosk, which is equipped to read the print order and make the copies you've specified. (You can't "order" prints of RAW images or movies.)

To create a DPOF print order, just follow these steps:

1. **Access Print order screen.** In the Playback 1 menu, navigate to Print order. (See Figure 12.3.) Press SET.

2. **Access Set up.** The Print order screen will appear. (See Figure 12.4.) Rotate the Quick Control Dial to highlight Set up. Press SET.

3. **Select Print type.** Choose Print type (Standard, Index/Thumbnails print, or Both), and specify whether Date or File number imprinting should be turned on or off. (You can turn one or the other on, but not both Date and File number imprinting.) Press MENU to return to the Print order screen.

Figure 12.3
Print orders can be assembled from the Playback 1 menu.

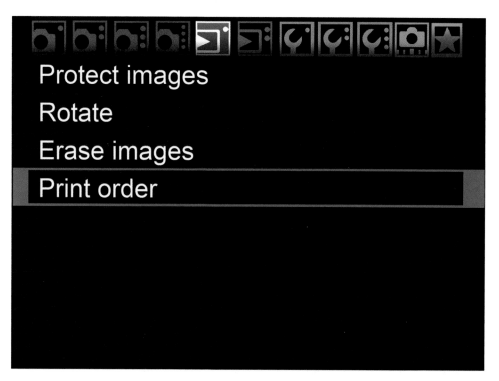

Figure 12.4
Select the images to be printed individually, by folder, or all the images on your memory card.

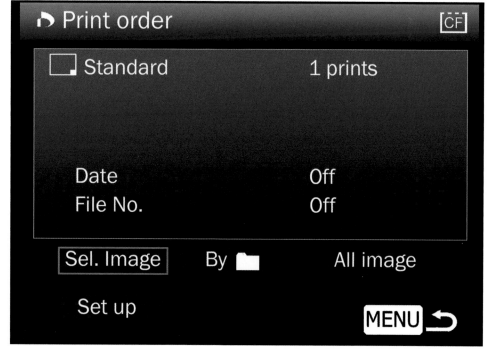

4. **Choose selection method.** Highlight either Sel. image (choose individual images), By folder (to select/deselect all images in a folder), or All image (to mark/unmark all the images on your memory card). Press SET.

5. **Select individual images.** With Sel. image, rotate the QCD to view the images, and press SET to mark or unmark an image for printing. If you'd rather view thumbnails of images, press the Thumbnail/Zoom in button. Press the Magnify/Zoom out button to return to single-image view.

6. **Choose number of prints.** Once an image is selected, rotate the Quick Control Dial to specify 1 to 99 prints for that image. (For Index prints, you can only specify whether the selected image is included in the index print, not the number of copies.) Press SET to confirm. You can then rotate the QCD to select additional images. Press MENU when finished selecting to return to the Print order screen.

7. **Output your hardcopies.** If the camera is linked to a PictBridge-compatible printer, an additional option appears on the Print order screen, Print. You can select that, optionally adjust Paper settings as described in the previous section, and start the printing process. Alternately, you can exit the Print order screen, remove the memory card, and insert it in the memory card slot of a compatible printer, retailer kiosk, or digital minilab.

Using the Supplied Software

Your Canon EOS 7D came with software programs on CD for both Windows PCs and Macs. Pop the CD into your computer and it will self-install a selection of these useful applications and utilities. Manuals for all these programs are included on CD, too, but here's a summary of what you get on the EOS Digital Solutions disk:

EOS Utility

Both Windows and Mac versions are provided for this useful program. It serves as command center for several useful functions, all available from the main control panel, shown in Figure 12.5. Using the Control Camera panel, you can jump to modules that download images to either Digital Photo Professional or ZoomBrowser EX, change camera settings when your 7D is linked to your computer with the USB cable, shoot remotely with a Live View image previewed on your computer screen, and monitor folders for new images.

The most-used of these options will probably be the download utility shown in Figure 12.6. But many will appreciate the camera settings/remote shooting module that allows you to link your computer with the 7D and use a dialog box (see Figure 12.7) to change camera settings and to control the camera for remote shooting. You can have access to many of the 7D's menus right from the software. The Settings feature is especially useful for changing Picture Styles quickly, while you'll find the remote shooting capabilities useful when you want to program a delay before the camera takes a picture, or do some interval (time-lapse) shooting. The updated version of the utility supports the 7D's Live View and Dust Delete Data functions. It includes many preferences you can use to tailor its operation (see Figure 12.8).

Figure 12.5
The EOS Utility's main screen is your command center for a variety of functions.

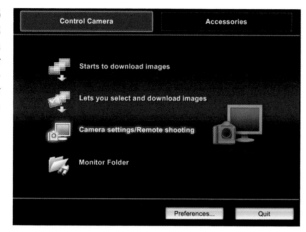

Figure 12.6
The download utility allows transfer of photos from your camera or memory card to Digital Photo Professional or ZoomBrowser EX.

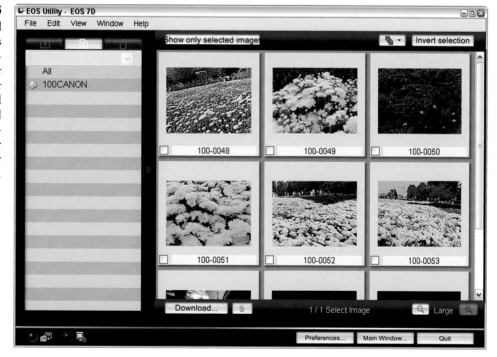

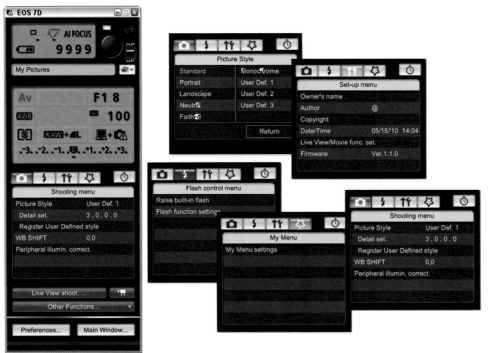

Figure 12.7
The EOS Utility gives you direct control of camera settings for remote shooting.

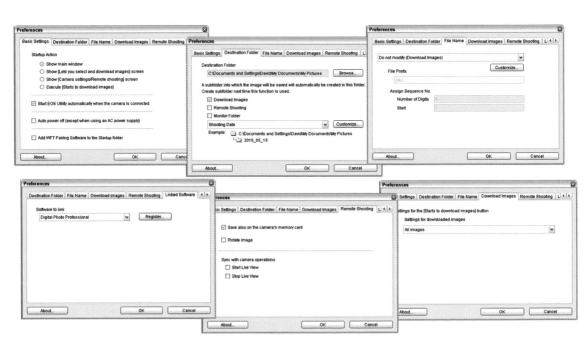

Figure 12.8 The EOS Utility six tabs' worth of preferences for modifying how it behaves.

The Accessories panel includes modules for working with the optional WFT-E3/E3A/B/C/D wireless communications link (for saving your pictures directly to external media over a WiFi network). If you're using the OSK-E3 Data Security Kit, you can access the Original Data Security (ODS) Administrator tool and Utility, which are used to register and manage OS card verification information for image encryption and decryption, management of authorized users and cameras, verified card duplication, and other functions. There is also a link to the Picture Style Editor.

Digital Photo Professional

While far from a Photoshop replacement, Digital Photo Professional is a useful image-editing program that helps you organize, trim, correct, and print images. You can make RAW adjustments, correct tonal curves, color tone, color saturation, sharpness, as well as brightness and contrast. Especially handy are the "recipes" that can be developed and saved so that a given set of corrections can be kept separate from the file itself, and, if desired, applied to other images (see Figure 12.9).

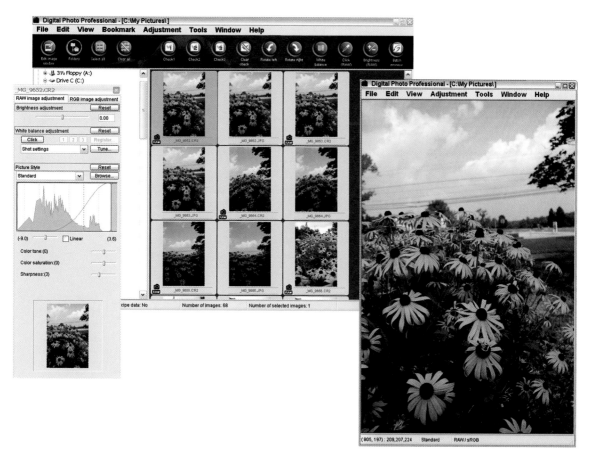

Figure 12.9 Digital Photo Professional will never replace Photoshop, but it has some basic image-editing features.

Picture Style Editor

As discussed in Chapter 4, the Picture Style Editor, shown in Figure 12.10, allows you to create your own custom Picture Styles, or edit existing styles, including the Standard, Landscape, Faithful, and other predefined settings already present in your 7D. You can change sharpness, contrast, color saturation, and color tone—and a lot more—and then save the modifications as a PF2 file that can be uploaded to the camera, or used by Digital Photo Professional (described later in this chapter) to modify a RAW image as it is imported.

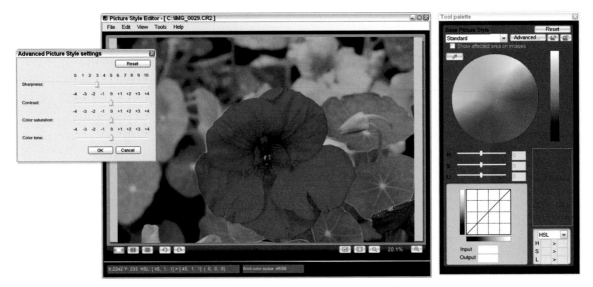

Figure 12.10 The Picture Style Editor lets you create your own Picture Styles for use by the 7D or Digital Photo Professional when importing image files.

You can define your own color response using a color picker in a sample RAW photograph to choose a specific hue, which you can then modify using hue/saturation/luminance adjustments. The range of adjacent colors affected by your new settings can also be specified. Before/after views let you compare the Picture Style settings you've entered with standard settings using a sample image you upload.

ZoomBrowser/ImageBrowser

This is an image viewing and editing application for Windows PCs (the equivalent program for Macs is called ImageBrowser and performs the same functions). You can organize, sort, classify, and rename files, and convert JPEG files in batches. This utility is especially useful for printing index sheets of groups of images (see Figure 12.11). It can also prepare images for e-mailing. It works with RAW Image Task for converting CR2 files to some other format for editing.

The simple image-editing facilities of ZoomBrowser/ImageBrowser allow red-eye correction, brightness/contrast and color correction, manipulating sharpness, trimming photos, and a few other functions. For more complex editing, you can transfer images directly from this application to Photoshop or another image editor.

Figure 12.11
ZoomBrowser allows organizing your images and performing simple fixes.

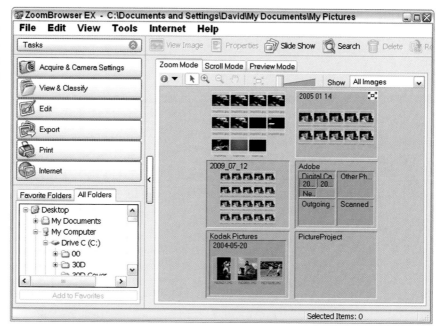

PhotoStitch

This Windows/Mac utility, available free from Canon, allows you to take several JPEG images and combine them to create a panorama in a single new file. You can choose the images to be merged in ZoomBrowser and then transfer them to PhotoStitch, or operate the utility as a standalone module and select the images using the standard File > Open commands (see Figure 12.12).

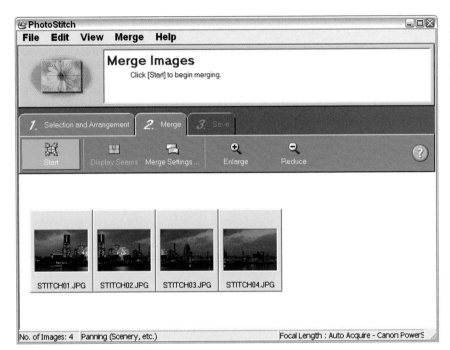

Figure 12.12
Panoramas are easy to create with PhotoStitch.

Transferring Your Photos

While it's rewarding to capture some great images and have them ensconced in your camera, eventually you'll be transferring them to your laptop or PC, whether you're using a Windows or Macintosh machine. You have three options for image transfer: direct transfer over a USB cable, automated transfer using a card reader and transfer software such as the EOS Utility or Adobe Photoshop Elements Photo Downloader, or manual transfer using drag and drop from a memory card inserted in a card reader.

Using a Card Reader and Software

You can also use a memory card reader and software to transfer photos and automate the process using the EOS Utility, Photoshop Elements' Photo Downloader, or the downloading program supplied with some other third-party applications. This method is more frugal in its use of your 7D's battery and can be faster if you have a speedy USB 2.0 or FireWire card reader attached to an appropriate port.

The installed software automatically remains in memory as you work, and it recognizes when a memory card is inserted in your card reader; you don't have to launch it yourself. With Photoshop Elements's Photo Downloader, you can click Get Photos to begin the transfer of all images immediately (see Figure 12.13) or choose Advanced Dialog to produce a dialog box that allows you to select which images to download from the memory card by marking their thumbnails with a check. You can select the photos you want to transfer, plus options such as Automatically Fix Red Eyes. Start the download, and a confirmation dialog box like the one in Figure 12.14 shows the progress.

Figure 12.13
Photoshop Elements Organizer allows you to download all images, or select the photos you want to copy to your computer and apply some options such as new filenames or red-eye fixes automatically.

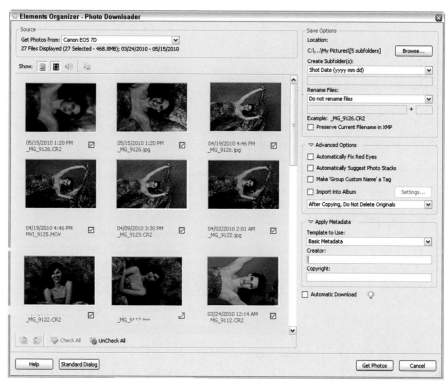

Figure 12.14
The downloader's confirmation dialog box shows the progress as images are transferred.

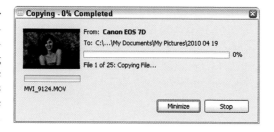

Dragging and Dropping

The final way to move photos from your memory card to your computer is the old-fashioned way: manually dragging and dropping the files from one window on your computer to another. The procedure works pretty much the same whether you're using a Mac or a PC.

1. Remove the memory card from the 7D and insert it in your memory card reader.

2. Using Windows Explorer, My Computer, or your Mac desktop, open the icon representing the memory card, which appears on your desktop as just another disk drive. (You can also link your camera directly to your computer with a USB cable, and it will appear as a disk drive, too.)

3. Open a second window representing the folder on your computer that you want to use as the destination for the files you are copying or moving.

4. Drag and drop the files from the memory card window to the folder on your computer. You can select individual files, press Ctrl/Command+A to select all the files, or Ctrl/Command+click to select multiple files.

Editing Your Photos

Image manipulation tasks fall into several categories. You might want to fine-tune your images, retouch them, change color balance, composite several images together, and perform other tasks we know as image editing, with a program like Adobe Photoshop, Photoshop Elements, or Corel Photo Paint.

You might want to play with the settings in RAW files, too, as you import them from their CR2 state into an image editor. There are specialized tools expressly for tweaking RAW files, ranging from Canon's own Digital Photo Professional to Adobe Camera Raw, and PhaseOne's Capture One Pro (C1 Pro). A third type of manipulation is the specialized task of noise reduction, which can be performed within Photoshop, Adobe Camera Raw, or tools like Bibble Professional. There are also specialized tools just for noise reduction, such as Noise Ninja (also included with Bibble) and Neat Image.

Each of these utilities and applications deserves a chapter of its own, so I'm simply going to enumerate some of the most popular image-editing and RAW conversion programs here and tell you a little about what they do.

Image Editors

Image editors are general-purpose photo-editing applications that can do color correction, tonal modifications, retouching, combining of several images into one, and usually include tools for working with RAW files and reducing noise. So, you'll find programs like those listed here good for all-around image manipulation. The leading programs are as follows:

Adobe Photoshop/Photoshop Elements. Photoshop is the serious photographer's number one choice for image editing, and Elements is an excellent option for those who need most of Photoshop's power, but not all of its professional-level features. Both editors use the latest version of Adobe's Camera Raw plug-in, which makes it easy to adjust things like color space profiles, color depth (either 8 bits or 16 bits per color channel), image resolution, white balance, exposure, shadows, brightness, sharpness, luminance, and noise reduction. One plus with the Adobe products is that they are available in identical versions for both Windows and Macs (eventually!).

Corel Photo Paint. This is the image-editing program that is included in the popular CorelDRAW Graphics suite. Although a Mac version was available in the past, this is primarily a Windows application today. It's a full-featured photo retouching and image-editing program with selection, retouching, and painting tools for manual image manipulations, and it also includes convenient automated commands for a few common tasks, such as red-eye removal. Photo Paint accepts Photoshop plug-ins to expand its assortment of filters and special effects.

Corel Paint Shop Pro. This is a general-purpose Windows-only image editor that has gained a reputation as the "poor man's Photoshop" for providing a substantial portion of Photoshop's capabilities at a fraction of the cost. It includes a nifty set of wizard-like commands that automate common tasks, such as removing red eye and scratches, as well as filters and effects, which can be expanded with other Photoshop plug-ins.

Corel Painter. Here's another image-editing program from Corel for both Mac and Windows. This one's strength is in mimicking natural media, such as charcoal, pastels, and various kinds of paint. Painter includes a basic assortment of tools that you can use to edit existing images, but the program is really designed for artists to use in creating original illustrations. As a photographer, you might prefer another image editor, but if you like to paint on top of your photographic images, nothing else really does the job of Painter.

Corel PhotoImpact. Corel finally brought one of the last remaining non-Adobe image editors into its fold when it acquired Ulead PhotoImpact. This is a general-purpose photo-editing program for Windows with a huge assortment of brushes for painting, retouching, and cloning, in addition to the usual selection, cropping, and fill tools. If you frequently find yourself performing the same image manipulations on a number of files, you'll appreciate PhotoImpact's batch operations. Using this feature, you can select multiple image files and then apply any one of a long list of filters, enhancements, or auto-process commands to all the selected files.

RAW Utilities

Your software choices for manipulating RAW files are broader than you might think. Camera vendors always supply a utility to read their cameras' own RAW files, but sometimes, particularly with those point-and-shoot cameras that can produce RAW files, the options are fairly limited. Other vendors, such as Nikon (with its Nikon Capture), offer RAW file handling that is much more flexible and powerful.

Because in the past digital camera vendors offered RAW converters that weren't very good (Canon's File View Utility comes to mind), there is a lively market for third-party RAW utilities available at extra cost. However, the EOS Utility and Digital Photo Professional do a good job and may be all that you need.

The third-party solutions are usually available as standalone applications (often for both Windows and Macintosh platforms), as Photoshop-compatible plug-ins, or both. Because the RAW plug-ins displace Photoshop's own RAW converter, I tend to prefer to use most RAW utilities in standalone mode. That way, if I choose to open a file directly in Photoshop, it automatically opens using Photoshop's fast and easy-to-use Adobe Camera Raw (ACR) plug-in. If I have more time or need the capabilities of another converter, I can load that, open the file, and make my corrections there. Most are able to transfer the processed file directly to Photoshop even if you aren't using plug-in mode.

This section provides a quick overview of the range of RAW file handlers, so you can get a better idea of the kinds of information available with particular applications. I'm going to include both high-end and low-end RAW browsers so you can see just what is available.

Digital Photo Professional

Digital Photo Professional, introduced earlier in this chapter, is preferred by many for Canon dSLR cameras like the 7D. DPP offers much higher-speed processing of RAW images than was available with the late, not lamented, sluggardly File Viewer Utility (as much as six times faster). Canon says this utility rivals third-party standalone and plug-in RAW converters in speed and features. It supports both Canon's original CRW format and the newer CR2 RAW format used by the 7D, along with TIFF, Exif TIFF, and JPEG.

You can save settings that include multiple adjustments and apply them to other images, and use the clever comparison mode to compare your original and edited versions of an image either side by side or within a single split image. The utility allows easy adjustment of color channels, tone curves, exposure compensation, white balance, dynamic range, brightness, contrast, color saturation, ICC Profile embedding, and assignment of monitor profiles. A new feature is the ability to continue editing images while batches of previously adjusted RAW files are rendered and saved in the background.

IrfanView

At the low (free) end of the price scale is IrfanView, a Windows freeware program you can download at www.irfanview.com. It can read many common RAW photo formats. It's a quick way to view RAW files (just drag and drop to the IrfanView window) and make fast changes to the unprocessed file. You can crop, rotate, or correct your image, and do some cool things like swap the colors around (red for blue, blue for green, and so forth) to create false color pictures.

The price is right, and IrfanView has some valuable capabilities. Check out www.irfanview.com.

Phase One Capture One Pro (C1 Pro)

If there is a Cadillac of RAW converters for Nikon and Canon digital SLR cameras, C1 Pro has to be it. This premium-priced program does everything, does it well, and does it quickly. If you can't justify the price tag of this professional-level software, there are "lite" versions for serious amateurs and cash-challenged professionals called Capture and Capture One 5, which cost as little as $129.

Aimed at photographers with high-volume needs (that would include school and portrait photographers, as well as busy commercial photographers), C1 Pro is available for both Windows and Mac OS X, and supports a broad range of Canon digital cameras. Phase One is a leading supplier of megabucks digital camera backs for medium and larger format cameras, so they really understand the needs of photographers.

The latest features include individual noise reduction controls for each image, automatic levels adjustment, a "quick develop" option that allows speedy conversion from RAW to TIFF or JPEG formats, dual-image side-by-side views for comparison purposes, and helpful grids and guides that can be superimposed over an image. Photographers concerned about copyright protection will appreciate the ability to add watermarks to the output images. See www.phaseone.com.

Bibble Pro

One of my personal favorites among third-party RAW converters is Bibble Pro. It supports one of the broadest ranges of RAW file formats available (which can be handy if you find yourself with the need to convert a file from a friend or colleague's non-Canon camera). The utility supports lots of different platforms, too. It's available for Windows, Mac OS X, and, believe it or not, Linux.

Bibble works fast because it offers instantaneous previews and real-time feedback as changes are made. That's important when you have to convert many images in a short time. Bibble's batch-processing capabilities also let you convert large numbers of files using settings you specify without further intervention.

Its customizable interface lets you organize and edit images quickly and then output them in a variety of formats, including 16-bit TIFF and PNG. You can even create a web gallery from within Bibble. I often find myself disliking the generic filenames applied to digital images by cameras, so I really like Bibble's ability to rename batches of files using new names that you specify.

Bibble is fully color managed, which means it can support all the popular color spaces (Adobe sRGB and so forth) and use custom profiles generated by third-party color-management software. There are two editions of Bibble, a Pro version and a Lite version. Because the Pro version is reasonably priced at $129, I don't really see the need to save $60 with the Lite edition, which lacks the top-line's options for tethered shooting, embedding IPTC-compatible captions in images, and can also be used as a Photoshop plug-in (if you prefer not to work with the application in its standalone mode). Bibble Pro now incorporates Noise Ninja technology, a state of the art noise reduction module, so you can get double-duty from this valuable application. See www.bibblelabs.com.

BreezeBrowser

BreezeBrowser was long the RAW converter of choice for Canon dSLR owners who run Windows and who were dissatisfied with Canon's lame antique File Viewer Utility. It works quickly and has lots of options for converting CRW and CR2 files to other formats. You can choose to show highlights that will be blown out in your finished photo as flashing areas (so they can be more easily identified and corrected), use histograms to correct tones, add color profiles, auto rotate images, and adjust all those raw image parameters, such as white balance, color space, saturation, contrast, sharpening, color tone, EV compensation, and other settings.

You can also control noise reduction (choosing from low, normal, or high reduction), evaluate your changes in the live preview, and then save the file as a compressed JPEG or as either an 8-bit or 16-bit TIFF file. BreezeBrowser can also create HTML web galleries directly from your selection of images. See www.breezesys.com.

Adobe Photoshop

Adobe Photoshop includes a built-in RAW plug-in that is compatible with the proprietary formats of a growing number of digital cameras, both new and old. This plug-in also works with Photoshop Elements. Note that it's always advisable to visit the Adobe downloads site from time to time, as new versions of Adobe Camera Raw are provided, with support for newer cameras and, sometimes, additional features.

While you can use Adobe Camera Raw to open JPEG files, some adjustments are disabled. It works best with RAW files. To open a RAW image in Photoshop, just follow these steps (Elements users can use much the same workflow, although fewer settings are available):

1. Transfer the RAW images from your camera to your computer's hard drive.

2. In Photoshop, choose Open from the File menu, or use Bridge.

3. Select a RAW image file. The Adobe Camera Raw plug-in will pop up, showing a preview of the image, like the one shown in Figure 12.15.

Figure 12.15
The basic ACR dialog box looks like this when processing a single image.

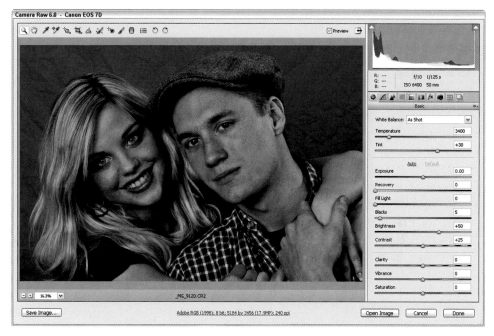

4. If you like, use one of the tools found in the toolbar at the top left of the dialog box. From left to right, they are as follows:

   ■ **Zoom.** Operates just like the Zoom tool in Photoshop.

   ■ **Hand.** Use like the Hand tool in Photoshop.

   ■ **White Balance.** Click an area in the image that should be neutral gray or white to set the white balance quickly.

   ■ **Color Sampler.** Use to determine the RGB values of areas you click with this eyedropper.

- **Crop.** Pre-crops the image so that only the portion you specify is imported into Photoshop. This option saves time when you want to work on a section of a large image, and you don't need the entire file.

- **Straighten.** Drag in the preview image to define what should be a horizontal or vertical line, and ACR will realign the image to straighten it.

- **Retouch.** Used to heal or clone areas you define.

- **Red-Eye Removal.** Quickly zap red pupils in your human subjects.

- **ACR Preferences.** Produces a dialog box of Adobe Camera Raw preferences.

- **Rotate Counterclockwise.** Rotates counterclockwise in 90-degree increments with a click.

- **Rotate Clockwise.** Rotates clockwise in 90-degree increments with a click.

5. Using the Basic tab, you can have ACR show you red and blue highlights in the preview that indicate shadow areas that are clipped (too dark to show detail) and light areas that are blown out (too bright). Click the triangles in the upper-left corner of the histogram display (shadow clipping) and upper-right corner (highlight clipping) to toggle these indicators on or off.

6. Also in the Basic tab you can choose white balance, either from the drop-down list or by setting a color temperature and green/magenta color bias (tint) using the sliders.

7. Other sliders are available to control exposure, recovery, fill light, blacks, brightness, contrast, vibrance, and saturation. A checkbox can be marked to convert the image to grayscale.

8. Make other adjustments (described in more detail below).

9. ACR makes automatic adjustments for you. You can click Default and make the changes for yourself, or click the Auto link (located just above the Exposure slider) to reapply the automatic adjustments after you've made your own modifications.

10. If you've marked more than one image to be opened, the additional images appear in a "filmstrip" at the left side of the screen. You can click on each thumbnail in the filmstrip in turn and apply different settings to each.

11. Click Open image/Open image(s) into Photoshop using the settings you've made, or click Save image at the bottom left to save the settings you've made without opening the file.

The Basic tab is displayed by default when the ACR dialog box opens, and it includes most of the sliders and controls you'll need to fine-tune your image as you import it into Photoshop. These include:

- **White Balance.** Leave it As Shot or change to a value such as Daylight, Cloudy, Shade, Tungsten, Fluorescent, or Flash. If you like, you can set a custom white balance using the Temperature and Tint sliders.

- **Exposure.** This slider adjusts the overall brightness and darkness of the image.

- **Recovery.** Restores detail in the red, green, and blue color channels.

- **Fill Light.** Reconstructs detail in shadows.

- **Blacks.** Increases the number of tones represented as black in the final image, emphasizing tones in the shadow areas of the image.

- **Brightness.** This slider adjusts the brightness and darkness of an image.

- **Contrast.** Manipulates the contrast of the midtones of your image.

- **Convert to Grayscale.** Mark this box to convert the image to black and white.

- **Vibrance.** Prevents over-saturation when enriching the colors of an image.

- **Saturation.** Manipulates the richness of all colors equally, from zero saturation (gray/black, no color) at the −100 setting to double the usual saturation at the +100 setting.

Additional controls are available on the Tone Curve, Detail, HSL/Grayscale, Split Toning, Lens Corrections, Camera Calibration, FX, Presets, and Snapshots tabs, shown in Figure 12.16. The Tone Curve tab can change the tonal values of your image. The Detail tab lets you adjust sharpness, luminance smoothing, and apply color noise reduction. The HSL/Grayscale tab offers controls for adjusting hue, saturation, and lightness and converting an image to black and white. Split Toning helps you colorize an image with sepia or cyanotype (blue) shades. The Lens Corrections tab has sliders to adjust for chromatic aberrations and vignetting. The Camera Calibration tab provides a way for calibrating the color corrections made in the Camera Raw plug-in.

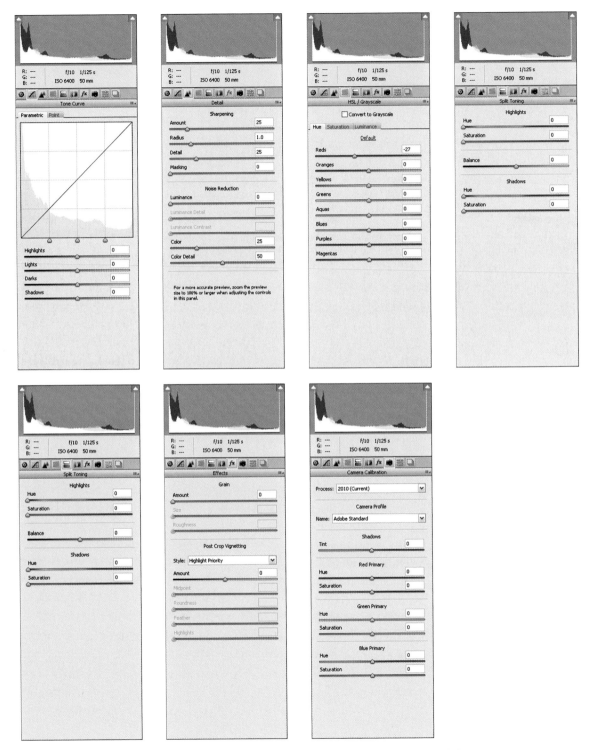

Figure 12.16 More controls are available within the additional tabbed dialog boxes in Adobe Camera Raw.

13

Canon EOS 7D: Troubleshooting and Prevention

One of the nice things about modern electronic cameras like the Canon EOS 7D is that they have fewer mechanical moving parts to fail, so they are less likely to "wear out." No film transport mechanism, no wind lever or motor drive, no complicated mechanical linkages from camera to lens to physically stop down the lens aperture. Instead, tiny, reliable motors are built into each lens (and you lose the use of only that lens should something fail), and one of the few major moving parts in the camera itself is a light-weight mirror (its small size one of the advantages of the 7D's 1.6X crop factor) that flips up and down with each shot.

Of course, the camera also has a moving shutter that can fail, but the shutter is built rugged enough that you can expect it to last 100,000 shutter cycles or more. Unless you're shooting sports in continuous mode day in and day out, the shutter on your 7D is likely to last as long as you expect to use the camera.

The only other things on the camera that move are switches, dials, buttons, the flip-up electronic flash, and the door that slides open to allow you to remove and insert the Compact Flash card. Unless you're extraordinarily clumsy or unlucky and manage to bend the internal pins in the CF card slot, or give your built-in flash a good whack while it is in use, there's not a lot that can go wrong mechanically with your EOS 7D.

On the other hand, one of the chief drawbacks of modern electronic cameras is that they are modern *electronic* cameras. Your 7D is fully dependent on two different batteries. Without them, the camera can't be used. There are numerous other electrical and electronic connections in the camera (many connected to those mechanical switches and dials), and components like the color LCD and top-panel status LCD that can potentially fail or suffer damage. The camera also relies on its "operating system," or *firmware,* which can be plagued by bugs that cause unexpected behavior. Luckily, electronic components are generally more reliable and trouble-free, especially when compared to their mechanical counterparts from the pre-electronic film camera days. (Film cameras of the last 10 to 20 years have had almost as many electronic features as digital cameras, but, believe it or not, there were whole generations of film cameras that had *no* electronics or batteries.)

Digital cameras have problems unique to their breed, too; the most troublesome being the need to clean the sensor of dust and grime periodically. This chapter will show you how to diagnose problems, fix some common ills, and, importantly, learn how to avoid them in the future.

Updating Your Firmware

As I said, the firmware in your EOS 7D is the camera's operating system, which handles everything from menu display (including fonts, colors, and the actual entries themselves), what languages are available, and even support for specific devices and features. Upgrading the firmware to a new version makes it possible to add new features while fixing some of the bugs that sneak in.

Official Firmware

Official firmware for your 7D is given a version number that you can view by turning the power on, pressing the MENU button, and scrolling to Firmware Ver. x.x.x in the Set-up 3 menu. As I write this, the current version is 1.2.1. The first number in the string represents the major release number, while the second and third represent less significant upgrades and minor tweaks, respectively. Theoretically, a camera should have a firmware version number of 1.0.0 when it is introduced, but vendors have been known to do some minor fixes during testing and unveil a camera with a 1.0.1 firmware designation. If a given model is available long enough, it can evolve into significant upgrades, such as 2.0.3.

Oddly enough, sometimes an update is so minor that it doesn't earn an upgraded number. When Canon introduced firmware version 1.0.4 for a predecessor of the 7D, it discovered that some of the characters for Simplified Chinese and Traditional Chinese languages caused problems when displayed on the LCD monitor, and issued a *new*

Version 1.0.4. It recommended installing this fixed firmware for anyone experiencing the problem, even if the user had already upgraded to Version 1.0.4.

Firmware upgrades are used most frequently to fix bugs in the software, and much less frequently to add or enhance features. For example, previous firmware upgrades for Canon cameras have mended things like incorrect color temperature reporting when using specific Canon Speedlites, or problems communicating with Compact Flash cards under certain conditions. The exact changes made to the firmware are generally spelled out in the firmware release announcement. You can examine the remedies provided and decide if a given firmware patch is important to you. If not, you can usually safely wait a while before going through the bother of upgrading your firmware—at least long enough for the early adopters to report whether the bug fixes have introduced new bugs of their own. Each new firmware release incorporates the changes from previous releases, so if you skip a minor upgrade you should have no problems.

Upgrading Your Firmware

If you're computer savvy, you might wonder how your EOS 7D is able to overwrite its own operating system—that is, how can the existing firmware be used to load the new version on top of itself? It's a little like lifting yourself by reaching down and pulling up on your bootstraps. Not ironically, that's almost exactly what happens: At your command (when you start the upgrade process), the 7D shifts into a special mode in which it is no longer operating from its firmware but, rather, from a small piece of software called a *bootstrap loader*, a separate, protected software program that functions only at startup or when upgrading firmware. The loader's function is to look for firmware to launch or, when directed, to copy new firmware from a Compact Flash card or your computer to the internal memory space where the old firmware is located. Once the new firmware has replaced the old, you can turn your camera off and then on again, and the updated operating system will be loaded.

Because the loader software is small in size and limited in function, there are some restrictions on what it can do. For example, the loader software isn't set up to go hunting through your Compact Flash card for the firmware file. It looks only in the top or root directory of your card, so that's where you must copy the firmware you download.

> **WARNING**
>
> Use a fully charged battery or Canon's optional ACK-E6 AC adapter kit to ensure that you'll have enough power to operate the camera for the entire upgrade. Moreover, you should not turn off the camera while your old firmware is being overwritten. Don't open the Compact Flash card door or do anything else that might disrupt operation of the 7D while the firmware is being installed.

Once you've determined that a new firmware update is available for your camera and that you want to install it, just follow these steps. (If you chicken out, any Canon service center can install the firmware upgrade for you.)

1. Download the firmware from Canon (you'll find it in the Downloads section of the Support portion of Canon's website) and place it on your computer's hard drive. The firmware is contained in a self-extracting file for either Windows or Mac OS. It will have a name such as 7d000121.fir.

2. In your camera, format a Compact Flash card . Choose Format from the Set-up menu, and initialize the card (make sure you don't have images you want to keep before you do this!).

3. You can copy the upgrade software to the card either using a CF card reader or by connecting the camera to your computer with a USB cable and using the EOS Utility application furnished with your camera (and described in the next section).

4. Insert the CF card in the camera and then turn the camera on. With the 7D set to any mode other than Creative Auto or Full Auto, press MENU and scroll to Firmware Ver. x.x.x in the Set-up 3 menu (see Figure 13.1) and press the SET button.

5. You'll see the current firmware version, and an option to update, as shown in Figure 13.2. Choose OK and press the SET button to begin loading the update program.

6. A confirmation screen will appear (see Figure 13.3). Select OK and press SET to continue. As the Firmware Update Program loads, you'll see the screen shown in Figure 13.4.

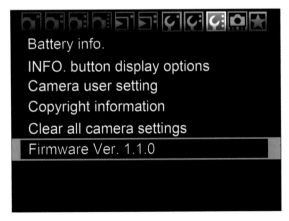

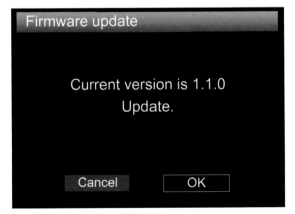

Figure 13.1 Determine the current version number.

Figure 13.2

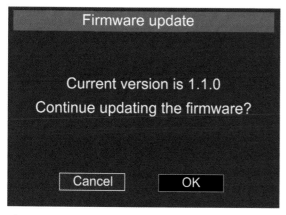

Figure 13.3

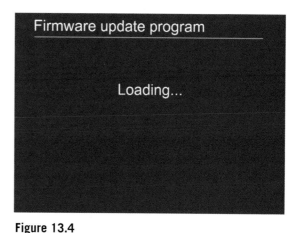

Figure 13.4

7. Next, you'll get the opportunity to confirm that the version you're upgrading to is the one you want, as you can see in Figure 13.5. You can press the MENU button to cancel. (Yes, I know there are a lot of confirmation screens; Canon wants to make sure you don't upgrade your firmware by accident, or, possibly, intentionally.)

8. Finally, the very last confirmation screen (See Figure 13.6). Select OK, and press SET, and, I promise, the actual firmware update will really begin.

9. While the firmware updates, you'll be warned not to turn off the power switch or touch any of the 7D's buttons. (See Figure 13.7.)

10. When the update complete screen appears (Figure 13.8), you can turn off the EOS 7D, remove the AC adapter, if used, and replace or recharge the battery. Then turn the camera on to boot up your camera with the new firmware update.

11. Be sure to reformat the card before returning it to regular use to remove the firmware software.

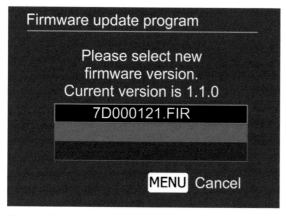

Figure 13.5

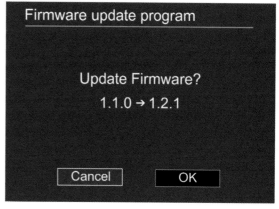

Figure 13.6

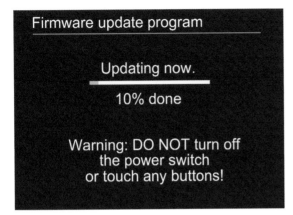

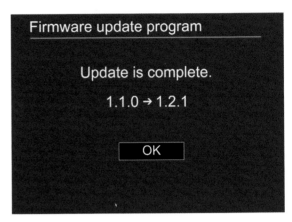

Figure 13.7   **Figure 13.8**

Using Direct Camera USB Link to Copy the Software

The procedure is slightly different (and a little more automated) if you choose to transfer the firmware software to the camera through a USB linkup. Follow these instructions to get started:

1. Connect the camera (with a freshly charged battery or attached to AC Adapter) to the computer using the USB cable and turn it on.

2. Load the EOS Utility.

3. Click the Camera/Settings/Remote Shooting button.

4. Select the firmware update option. When the Update Firmware window appears at the bottom of the EOS Utility, choose OK.

5. Click Yes in the confirmation screen.

6. Follow the instructions in the dialog boxes that pop up next by pressing the SET button on the camera.

Protecting Your LCD

The color LCD on the back of your EOS 7D almost seems like a target for banging, scratching, and other abuse. Fortunately, it's quite rugged, and a few errant knocks are unlikely to shatter the protective cover over the LCD, and scratches won't easily mar its surface. However, if you want to be on the safe side, there are a number of protective products you can purchase to keep your LCD safe—and, in some cases, make it a little easier to view.

Here's a quick overview of your options.

■ **Plastic overlays.** The simplest solution (although not always the cheapest) is to apply a plastic overlay sheet or "skin" cut to fit your LCD. These adhere either by static electricity or through a light adhesive coating that's even less clingy than stick-it notes. You can cut down overlays made for PDAs (although these can be pricey at up to $19.95 for a set of several sheets), or purchase overlays sold specifically for digital cameras. Vendors such as Hoodman (www.hoodmanusa.com) and Belkin (www.belkin.com) offer overlays of this type. These products will do a good job of shielding your 7D's LCD screen from scratches and minor impacts, but will not offer much protection from a good whack.

■ **Acrylic shields.** These scratch-resistant acrylic panels, laser cut to fit your camera perfectly, are my choice as the best protection solution, and what I use on my own 7D. At about $6 each, they also happen to be the least expensive option as well. I get mine, shown in Figure 13.9, from a company called 'da Products (www.daproducts.com). They attach using strips of sticky adhesive that hold the panel flush and tight, but which allow the acrylic to be pried off and the adhesive removed easily if you want to remove or replace the shield. They don't attenuate your view of the LCD and are non-reflective enough for use under a variety of lighting conditions. A company called GGS makes some nice glass protectors; they're available from eBay, Amazon.com, and other online vendors.

Figure 13.9

A tough acrylic shield, here shown with a piece of plastic containing a set of peel-off sticky strips to help it adhere to the camera, can protect your LCD from scratches.

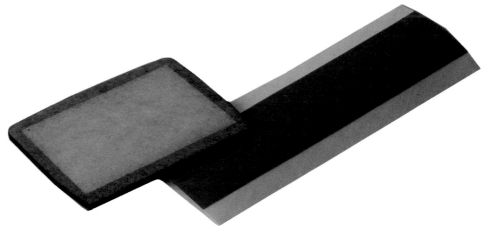

- **Flip-up hoods.** These protectors slip on using the flanges around your 7D's eye-piece, and provide a cover that completely shields the LCD, but unfolds to provide a three-sided hood that allows viewing the LCD while minimizing the extraneous light falling on it and reducing contrast. They're sold for about $40 by Hoodman. If you want to completely protect your LCD from hard knocks and need to view the screen outdoors in bright sunlight, there is nothing better. However, I have a couple problems with these devices. First, with the cover closed, you can't peek down after taking a shot to see what your image looks like during picture review. You must open the cap each time you want to look at the LCD. Moreover, with the hood unfolded, it's difficult to look through the viewfinder: Don't count on being able to use the viewfinder *and* the LCD at the same time with one of these hoods in place.

- **Magnifiers.** If you look hard enough, you should be able to find an LCD magnifier that fits over the monitor panel and provides a 2X magnification. These often strap on clumsily, and serve better as a way to get an enlarged view of the LCD than as protection. Hoodman and other suppliers offer these specialized devices.

Troubleshooting Memory Cards

Sometimes good memory cards go bad. Sometimes good photographers can treat their memory cards badly. It's possible that a memory card that works fine in one camera won't be recognized when inserted into another. In the worst case, you can have a card full of important photos and find that the card seems to be corrupted and you can't access any of them. Don't panic! If these scenarios sound horrific to you, there are lots of things you can do to prevent them from happening, and a variety of remedies available if they do occur. You'll want to take some time—before disaster strikes—to consider your options.

All Your Eggs in One Basket?

The debate about whether it's better to use one large memory card or several smaller ones has been going on since even before there were memory cards. I can remember when computer users wondered whether it was smarter to install a pair of 200MB (not *gigabyte*) hard drives in their computer, or if they should go for one of those new-fangled 500MB models. By the same token, a few years ago the user groups were full of proponents who insisted that you ought to use 128MB Compact Flash cards rather than the huge 512MB versions. Today, most of the arguments involve 8GB cards versus 16GB cards, and I expect that as prices for 32GB Compact Flash cards continue to drop, they'll find their way into the debate as well. Size is especially important when you're using a camera like the 7D that captures 18-megapixel images.

Why all the fuss? Are 16GB memory cards more likely to fail than 8GB cards? Are you risking all your photos if you trust your images to a larger card? Isn't it better to use several smaller cards, so that if one fails you lose only half as many photos? Or, isn't it wiser to put all your photos onto one larger card, because the more cards you use, the better your odds of misplacing or damaging one and losing at least some pictures?

In the end, the "eggs in one basket" argument boils down to statistics, and how you happen to use your 7D. The rationales can go both ways. If you have multiple smaller cards, you do increase your chances of something happening to one of them, so, arguably, you might be boosting the odds of losing some pictures. If all your images are important, the fact that you've lost 100 rather than 200 pictures isn't very comforting.

Also consider that the eggs/basket scenario assumes that the cards that are lost or damaged are always full. It's actually likely that your 16GB card might suffer a mishap when it's less than half-full (indeed, it's more likely that a large card won't be completely filled before it's offloaded to a computer), so you really might not lose any more shots with a single 16GB card than with multiple 8GB cards.

If you shoot photojournalist-type pictures, you probably change memory cards when they're less than completely full in order to avoid the need to do so at a crucial moment. (When I shoot sports, my cards rarely reach 80 to 90 percent of capacity before I change them.) Using multiple smaller cards means you have to change them that more often, which can be a real pain when you're taking a lot of photos. As an example, if you use tiny 2GB memory cards with an EOS 7D and shoot RAW+JPEG FINE, you may get only 68 pictures on the card. That's not even twice the capacity of a 36-exposure roll of film (remember those?). In my book, I prefer keeping all my eggs in one basket, and then making very sure that nothing happens to that basket.

There are only two really good reasons to justify limiting yourself to smaller memory cards when larger ones can be purchased at the same cost per-gigabyte. One of them is when every single picture is precious to you and the loss of any of them would be a disaster. If you're a wedding photographer, for example, and unlikely to be able to restage the nuptials if a memory card goes bad, you'll probably want to shoot no more pictures than you can afford to lose on a single card, and have an assistant ready to copy each card removed from the camera onto a backup hard drive or DVD onsite.

To be even safer, you'd want to alternate cameras or have a second photographer at least partially duplicating your coverage so your shots are distributed over several memory cards simultaneously. (Strictly speaking, the safest route of all is to spend some significant bucks on Canon's Wireless File Transmitter WFT-E3/WFT-E3A/B/C/D, and beam the images to a computer as you shoot them.

If none of these options are available to you, consider *interleaving* your shots. Say you don't shoot weddings, but you do go on vacation from time to time. Take 50 or so pictures on one card, or whatever number of images might fill about 25 percent of its capacity. Then, replace it with a different card and shoot about 25 percent of that card's available space. Repeat these steps with diligence (you'd have to be determined to go through this inconvenience), and, if you use four or more memory cards, you'll find your pictures from each location scattered among the different Compact Flash cards. If you lose or damage one, you'll still have *some* pictures from all the various stops on your trip on the other cards. That's more work than I like to do (I usually tote around a portable hard disk and copy the files to the drive as I go), but it's an option.

What Can Go Wrong?

There are lots of things that can go wrong with your memory card, but the ones that aren't caused by human stupidity are statistically very rare. Yes, a Compact Flash card's internal bit bin or controller can suddenly fail due to a manufacturing error or some inexplicable event caused by old age. However, if your CF card works for the first week or two that you own it, it should work forever. There's really not a lot that can wear out.

The typical Compact Flash card is rated for a Mean Time Between Failures of 1,000,000 hours of use. That's constant use 24/7 for more than 100 years! According to the manufacturers, they are good for 10,000 insertions in your camera, and should be able to retain their data (and that's without an external power source) for something on the order of 11 years. Of course, with the millions of Compact Flash cards in use, there are bound to be a few lemons here or there.

Given the reliability of solid-state memory, compared to magnetic memory, though, it's more likely that your Compact Flash problems will stem from something that you do. Although they're not as tiny as the SD and xD cards a few other digital SLRs use, CF cards are still small and easy to misplace if you're not careful. For that reason, it's a good idea to keep them in their original cases or a "card safe" offered by Gepe (www.gepecard-safe.com), Pelican (www.pelican.com), and others. Always placing your memory card in a case can provide protection from the second-most common mishap that befalls Compact Flash cards: the common household laundry. If you slip a memory card in a pocket, rather than a case or your camera bag, often enough, sooner or later it's going to end up in the washing machine and probably the clothes dryer, too. There are plenty of reports of relieved digital camera owners who've laundered their memory cards and found they still worked fine, but it's not uncommon for such mistreatment to do some damage.

Memory cards can also be stomped on, accidentally bent, dropped into the ocean, chewed by pets, and otherwise rendered unusable in myriad ways. It's also possible to force a card into your 7D's Compact Flash card slot incorrectly if you're diligent enough, doing little damage to the card itself, but bending the connector pins in the camera, eliminating its ability to read or write to any memory card. Or, if the card is formatted in your computer with a memory card reader, your 7D may fail to recognize it.

Occasionally, I've found that a memory card used in one camera would fail if used in a different camera (until I reformatted it in Windows, and then again in the camera). Every once in awhile, a card goes completely bad and—seemingly—can't be salvaged.

Another way to lose images is to do commonplace things with your Compact Flash card at an inopportune time. If you remove the card from the 7D while the camera is writing images to the card, you'll lose any photos in the buffer and may damage the file structure of the card, making it difficult or impossible to retrieve the other pictures you've taken. The same thing can happen if you remove the Compact Flash card from your computer's card reader while the computer is writing to the card (say, to erase files you've already moved to your computer). You can avoid this by *not* using your computer to erase files on a Compact Flash card but, instead, always reformatting the card in your 7D before you use it again.

What Can You Do?

Pay attention: If you're having problems, the *first* thing you should do is *stop* using that memory card. Don't take any more pictures. Don't do anything with the card until you've figured out what's wrong. Your second line of defense (your first line is to be sufficiently careful with your cards that you avoid problems in the first place) is to *do no harm* that hasn't already been done. Read the rest of this section and then, if necessary, decide on a course of action (such as using a data recovery service or software described later) before you risk damaging the data on your card further.

Now that you've calmed down, the first thing to check is whether you've actually inserted a card in the camera. If you've set the camera in the Shooting menu so that Shoot w/o card has been turned on, it's entirely possible (although not particularly plausible) that you've been snapping away with no memory card to store the pictures to, which can lead to massive disappointment later on. Of course, the No CF card message appears on the LCD when the camera is powered up, and it is superimposed on the review image after every shot, but maybe you're inattentive, aren't using picture review, or have purchased one of those LCD fold-up hoods mentioned earlier in this chapter. You can avoid all this by turning the Shoot w/o card feature off and leaving it off.

Things get more exciting when the card itself is put in jeopardy. If you lose a card, there's not a lot you can do other than take a picture of a similar card and print up some Have You Seen This Lost Flash Memory? flyers to post on utility poles all around town.

If all you care about is reusing the card, and have resigned yourself to losing the pictures, try reformatting the card in your camera. You may find that reformatting removes the corrupted data and restores your card to health. Sometimes I've had success reformatting a card in my computer using a memory card reader (this is normally a no-no because your operating system doesn't understand the needs of your 7D), and *then* reformatting again in the camera.

If your Compact Flash card is not behaving properly, and you *do* want to recover your images, things get a little more complicated. If your pictures are very valuable, either to you or to others (for example, a wedding), you can always turn to professional data recovery firms. Be prepared to pay hundreds of dollars to get your pictures back, but these pros often do an amazing job. You wouldn't want them working on your memory card on behalf of the police if you'd tried to erase some incriminating pictures. There are many firms of this type, and I've never used them myself, so I can't offer a recommendation. Use a Google search to turn up a ton of them. I use a software program called RescuePro, which came free with one of my SanDisk memory cards.

THE ULTIMATE IRONY

I recently purchased an 8GB Kingston memory card that was furnished with some nifty OnTrack data recovery software. The first thing I did was format the card to make sure it was OK. Then I hunted around for the free software, only to discover it was preloaded onto the memory card. I was supposed to copy the software to my computer before using the memory card for the first time.

Fortunately, I had the OnTrack software that would reverse my dumb move, so I could retrieve the software. No, wait. I *didn't* have the software I needed to recover the software I erased. I'd reformatted it to oblivion. Chalk this one up as either the ultimate irony or Stupid Photographer Trick #523.

A more reasonable approach is to try special data recovery software you can install on your computer and use to attempt to resurrect your "lost" images yourself. They may not actually be gone completely. Perhaps your CF card's "table of contents" is jumbled, or only a few pictures are damaged in such a way that your camera and computer can't read some or any of the pictures on the card. Some of the available software was written specifically to reconstruct lost pictures, while other utilities are more general-purpose applications that can be used with any media, including floppy disks and hard disk drives. They have names like OnTrack, Photo Rescue 2, Digital Image Recovery, MediaRecover, Image Recall, and the aptly named Recover My Photos.

DIMINISHING RETURNS

Usually, once you've recovered any images on a Compact Flash card, reformatted it, and returned it to service, it will function reliably for the rest of its useful life. However, if you find a particular card going bad more than once, you'll almost certainly want to stop using it forever. See if you can get it replaced by the manufacturer, if you can, but, in the case of CF card failures, the third time is never the charm.

You'll find a comprehensive list and links, as well as some picture-recovery tips at www.ultimateslr.com/memory-card-recovery.php.

Replacing Your Clock Battery

In addition to the large rechargeable lithium ion battery that provides most of the power for your Canon EOS 7D, a second battery nestles in the same compartment to provide enough power to retain your current settings and preferences, as well as the local date and time. This coin-sized *clock* battery is a long-lived C1616 3-volt lithium manganese dioxide cell, located in a slide-out carrier near the hinge of the battery door.

You may never notice this battery at all, as it may last several years without needing replacement. Your first clue will be when you switch on your 7D and a message on your LCD asks you to input the date and time. That's your cue to trot down to the electronics store and buy a new one.

To install it, remove the main camera battery, then just slide out the plastic carrier and remove the old clock battery. There is a pair of plastic tabs holding it in tight, and you may have to pry one up to free the dead cell. Then slide the new one in and return the carrier to your camera. When you turn the power on, you'll need to enter the current date and time. Don't forget to choose OK when finished; if you simply exit the settings screen by pressing the MENU button, your time setting will not be entered. You'll also have to re-enter other camera and user settings that the EOS 7D normally "remembers."

Cleaning Your Sensor

There's no avoiding dust. No matter how careful you are, some of it is going to settle on your camera and on the mounts of your lenses, eventually making its way inside your camera to settle in the mirror chamber. As you take photos, the mirror flipping up and down causes the dust to become airborne and eventually make its way past the shutter curtain to come to rest on the anti-aliasing filter atop your sensor. There, dust and particles can show up in every single picture you take at a small enough aperture to bring the foreign matter into sharp focus. No matter how careful you are and how cleanly you work, eventually you will get some of this dust on your camera's sensor. Some say that CMOS sensors, like the one found in the EOS 7D, "attract" less dust than CCD sensors found in cameras from other vendors. But even the cleanest-working photographers using Canon cameras are far from immune.

Fortunately, one of the EOS 7D's most useful new features is the automatic sensor cleaning system that reduces or eliminates the need to clean your camera's sensor manually. Canon has applied anti-static coatings to the sensor and other portions of the camera body interior to counter charge build-ups that attract dust. A separate filter over the sensor vibrates ultrasonically each time the 7D is powered on or off, shaking loose any dust.

Although the automatic sensor cleaning feature operates when you power the camera up or turn it off, you can activate it at any time. Choose Sensor cleaning from the Set-Up 2 menu, and select Clean now. If you'd rather turn the feature on or off, choose Auto cleaning instead, and then choose either Enable or Disable with the Quick Control Dial. Press SET, then press the MENU button to return to the Set-up 2 menu (see Figure 13.10).

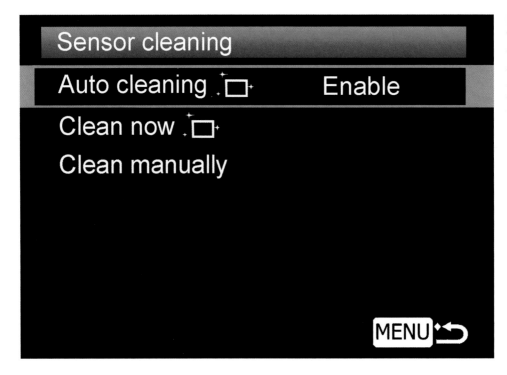

Figure 13.10
You can acti-vate automatic sensor cleaning immediately or enable/disable the feature.

If some dust does collect on your sensor, you can often map it out of your images (making it invisible) using software techniques with the Dust Delete Data feature in the Shooting 3 menu. Operation of this feature is described in Chapter 7. Of course, even with the EOS 7D's automatic sensor cleaning/dust resistance features, you may still be required to manually clean your sensor from time to time. This section explains the phenomenon and provides some tips on minimizing dust and eliminating it when it begins to affect your shots. I also cover this subject in my book, *Digital SLR Pro Secrets*, with complete instructions for constructing your own sensor cleaning tools. However, I'll provide a condensed version here of some of the information in that book, because sensor dust and sensor cleaning are two of the most contentious subjects Canon EOS 7D owners have to deal with.

Dust the FAQs, Ma'am

Here are some of the most frequently asked questions about sensor dust issues.

Q. I see tiny specks in my viewfinder. Do I have dust on my sensor?

A. If you see sharp, well-defined specks, they are clinging to the underside of your focus screen and not on your sensor. They have absolutely no effect on your photographs, and are merely annoying or distracting.

Q. I can see dust on my mirror. How can I remove it?

A. Like focus-screen dust, any artifacts that have settled on your mirror won't affect your photos. You can often remove dust on the mirror or focus screen with a bulb air blower, which will loosen it and whisk it away. Stubborn dust on the focus screen can sometimes be gently flicked away with a soft brush designed for cleaning lenses. I don't recommend brushing the mirror or touching it in any way. The mirror is a special front-surface-silvered optical device (unlike conventional mirrors, which are silvered on the back side of a piece of glass or plastic) and can be easily scratched. If you can't blow mirror dust off, it's best to just forget about it. You can't see it in the viewfinder, anyway.

Q. I see a bright spot in the same place in all of my photos. Is that sensor dust?

A. You've probably got either a "hot" pixel or one that is permanently "stuck" due to a defect in the sensor. A hot pixel is one that shows up as a bright spot only during long exposures as the sensor warms. A pixel stuck in the "on" position always appears in the image. Both show up as bright red, green, or blue pixels, usually surrounded by a small cluster of other improperly illuminated pixels, caused by the camera's interpolating the hot or stuck pixel into its surroundings, as shown in Figure 13.11. A stuck pixel can also be permanently dark. Either kind is likely to show up when they contrast with plain, evenly colored areas of your image.

Figure 13.11
A stuck pixel is surrounded by improperly interpolated pixels created by the 7D's demosaicing algorithm.

Finding one or two hot or stuck pixels in your sensor is unfortunately fairly common. They can be "removed" by telling the 7D to ignore them through a simple process called *pixel mapping*. If the bad pixels become bothersome, Canon can remap your sensor's pixels with a quick trip to a service center.

Bad pixels can also show up on your camera's color LCD panel, but, unless they are abundant, the wisest course is to just ignore them.

Q. I see an irregular out-of-focus blob in the same place in my photos. Is that sensor dust?

A. Yes. Sensor contaminants can take the form of tiny spots, larger blobs, or even curvy lines if they are caused by minuscule fibers that have settled on the sensor. They'll appear out of focus because they aren't actually on the sensor surface but, rather, a fraction of a millimeter above it on the filter that covers the sensor. The smaller the f/stop used, the more in-focus the dust becomes. At large apertures, it may not be visible at all.

Q. I never see any dust on my sensor. What's all the fuss about?

A. Those who never have dust problems with their EOS 7D fall into one of four categories: those for whom the camera's automatic dust removal features are working well; those who seldom change their lenses and have clean working habits that minimize the amount of dust that invades their cameras in the first place; those who simply don't notice the dust (often because they don't shoot many macro photos or other pictures using the small f/stops that makes dust evident in their images); and those who are very, very lucky.

Identifying and Dealing with Dust

Sensor dust is less of a problem than it might be because it shows up only under certain circumstances. Indeed, you might have dust on your sensor right now and not be aware if it. The dust doesn't actually settle on the sensor itself, but, rather, on a protective filter a very tiny distance above the sensor, subjecting it to the phenomenon of *depth-of-focus*. Depth-of-focus is the distance the focal plane can be moved and still render an object in sharp focus. At f/2.8 to f/5.6 or even smaller, sensor dust, particularly if small, is likely to be outside the range of depth-of-focus and blur into an unnoticeable dot.

However, if you're shooting at f/16 to f/22 or smaller, those dust motes suddenly pop into focus. Forget about trying to spot them by peering directly at your sensor with the shutter open and the lens removed. The period at the end of this sentence, about .33mm in diameter, could block a group of pixels measuring 40×40 pixels (160 pixels in all!). Dust spots that are even smaller than that can easily show up in your images if you're shooting large, empty areas that are light colored. Dust motes are most likely to show up in the sky, as in Figure 13.12, or in white backgrounds of your seamless product shots and are less likely to be a problem in images that contain lots of dark areas and detail.

Figure 13.12
Only the dust spots in the sky are apparent in this shot.

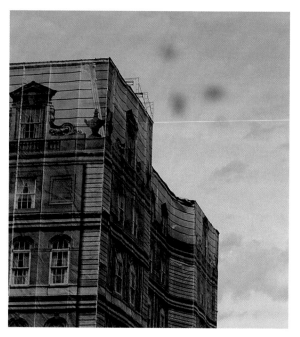

To see if you have dust on your sensor, take a few test shots of a plain, blank surface (such as a piece of paper or a cloudless sky) at small f/stops, such as f/22, and a few wide open. Open Photoshop, copy several shots into a single document in separate layers, then flip back and forth between layers to see if any spots you see are present in all layers. You may have to boost contrast and sharpness to make the dust easier to spot.

Avoiding Dust

Of course, the easiest way to protect your sensor from dust is to prevent it from settling on the sensor in the first place. Some Canon lenses come with rubberized seals around the lens mounts that help keep dust from infiltrating, but you'll find that dust will still find a way to get inside. Here are my tips for eliminating the problem before it begins.

- **Clean environment.** Avoid working in dusty areas if you can do so. Hah! Serious photographers will take this one with a grain of salt, because it usually makes sense to go where the pictures are. Only a few of us are so paranoid about sensor dust (considering that it is so easily removed) that we'll avoid moderately grimy locations just to protect something that is, when you get down to it, just a tool. If you find a great picture opportunity at a raging fire, during a sandstorm, or while surrounded by dust clouds, you might hesitate to take the picture, but, with a little caution (don't remove your lens in these situations, and clean the camera afterwards!) you can still shoot. However, it still makes sense to store your camera in a clean environment. One place cameras and lenses pick up a lot of dust is inside a camera bag. Clean your bag from time to time, and you can avoid problems.

■ **Clean lenses.** There are a few paranoid types that avoid swapping lenses in order to minimize the chance of dust getting inside their cameras. It makes more sense just to use a blower or brush to dust off the rear lens mount of the replacement lens first, so you won't be introducing dust into your camera simply by attaching a new, dusty lens. Do this before you remove the lens from your camera, and then avoid stirring up dust before making the exchange.

■ **Work fast.** Minimize the time your camera is lens-less and exposed to dust. That means having your replacement lens ready and dusted off, and a place to set down the old lens as soon as it is removed, so you can quickly attach the new lens.

■ **Let gravity help you.** Face the camera downward when the lens is detached so any dust in the mirror box will tend to fall away from the sensor. Turn your back to any breezes, indoor forced air vents, fans, or other sources of dust to minimize infiltration.

■ **Protect the lens you just removed.** Once you've attached the new lens, quickly put the end cap on the one you just removed to reduce the dust that might fall on it.

■ **Clean out the vestibule.** From time to time, remove the lens while in a relatively dust-free environment and use a blower bulb like the pair shown in Figure 13.9 (*not* compressed air or a vacuum hose) to clean out the mirror box area. A blower bulb is generally safer than a can of compressed air, or a strong positive/negative airflow, which can tend to drive dust further into nooks and crannies.

■ **Be prepared.** If you're embarking on an important shooting session, it's a good idea to clean your sensor *now*, rather than come home with hundreds or thousands of images with dust spots caused by flecks that were sitting on your sensor before you even started. Before I left on my recent trip to Spain, I put both cameras I was taking through a rigid cleaning regimen, figuring they could remain dust-free for a measly 10 days. I even left my bulky blower bulb at home. It was a big mistake, but my intentions were good.

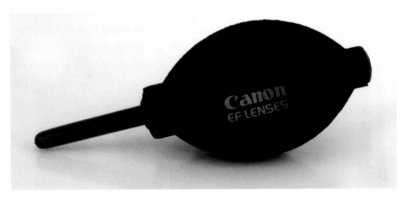

Figure 13.13
Use a robust air bulb for cleaning your sensor.

■ **Clone out existing spots in your image editor.** Photoshop and other editors have a clone tool or healing brush you can use to copy pixels from surrounding areas over the dust spot or dead pixel. This process can be tedious, especially if you have lots of dust spots and/or lots of images to be corrected. The advantage is that this sort of manual fix-it probably will do the least damage to the rest of your photo. Only the cloned pixels will be affected.

■ **Use filtration in your image editor.** A semi-smart filter like Photoshop's Dust & Scratches filter can remove dust and other artifacts by selectively blurring areas that the plug-in decides represent dust spots. This method can work well if you have many dust spots, because you won't need to patch them manually. However, any automated method like this has the possibility of blurring areas of your image that you didn't intend to soften.

Sensor Cleaning

Those new to the concept of sensor dust actually hesitate before deciding to clean their camera themselves. Isn't it a better idea to pack up your 7D and send it to a Canon service center so their crack technical staff can do the job for you? Or, at the very least, shouldn't you let the friendly folks at your local camera store do it?

Of course, if you choose to let someone else clean your sensor, they will be using methods that are more or less identical to the techniques you would use yourself. None of these techniques are difficult, and the only difference between their cleaning and your cleaning is that they might have done it dozens or hundreds of times. If you're careful, you can do just as good a job.

Of course vendors like Canon won't tell you this, but it's not because they don't trust you. It's not that difficult for a real goofball to mess up his camera by hurrying or taking a shortcut. Perhaps the person uses the "Bulb" method of holding the shutter open and a finger slips, allowing the shutter curtain to close on top of a sensor cleaning brush. Or, someone tries to clean the sensor using masking tape, and ends up with goo all over its surface. If Canon recommended *any* method that's mildly risky, someone would do it wrong, and then the company would face lawsuits from those who'd contend they did it exactly in the way the vendor suggested, so the ruined camera is not their fault. If you visit Canon's website, you'll find this recommendation: "If the image sensor needs cleaning, we recommend having it cleaned at a Canon service center, as it is a very delicate component."

You can see that vendors like Canon tend to be conservative in their recommendations, and, in doing so, make it seem as if sensor cleaning is more daunting and dangerous than it really is. Some vendors recommend only dust-off cleaning, through the use of reasonably gentle blasts of air, while condemning more serious scrubbing with swabs and cleaning fluids. However, these cleaning kits for the exact types of cleaning they recommended against are for sale in Japan only, where, apparently, your average photographer is more dexterous than those of us in the rest of the world. These kits are similar to those used by official repair staff to clean your sensor if you decide to send your camera in for a dust-up.

As I noted, sensors can be affected by dust particles that are much smaller than you might be able to spot visually on the surface of your lens. The filters that cover sensors tend to be fairly hard compared to optical glass. Cleaning the 22.3mm × 14.9mm sensor in your Canon 7D within the tight confines of the mirror box can call for a steady hand and careful touch. If your sensor's filter becomes scratched through inept cleaning, you can't simply remove it yourself and replace it with a new one.

There are four basic kinds of cleaning processes that can be used to remove dusty and sticky stuff that settles on your dSLR's sensor. All of these must be performed with the shutter locked open. I'll describe these methods and provide instructions for locking the shutter later in this section.

- **Air cleaning.** This process involves squirting blasts of air inside your camera with the shutter locked open. This works well for dust that's not clinging stubbornly to your sensor.

- **Brushing.** A soft, very fine brush is passed across the surface of the sensor's filter, dislodging mildly persistent dust particles and sweeping them off the imager.

- **Liquid cleaning.** A soft swab dipped in a cleaning solution such as ethanol is used to wipe the sensor filter, removing more obstinate particles.

- **Tape cleaning.** There are some who get good results by applying a special form of tape to the surface of their sensor. When the tape is peeled off, all the dust goes with it. Supposedly. I'd be remiss if I didn't point out right now that this form of cleaning is somewhat controversial; the other three methods are much more widely accepted. Now that Canon has equipped the front-sensor filter with a special anti-dust coating, I wouldn't chance damaging that coating by using any kind of adhesive tape.

Placing the Shutter in the Locked and Fully Upright Position for Landing

Make sure you're using a fully charged battery or the optional AC Adapter Kit ACK-E6.

1. Remove the lens from the camera and then turn the camera on.

2. Set the EOS 7D to any one of the non-fully automatic modes . The shutter cannot be locked open in Full Auto or Creative Auto.

3. You'll find the Clean manually menu choice in the Set-up 2 menu under Sensor cleaning (see Figure 13.10, shown earlier). Press the SET button.

4. Select OK and press SET again. The mirror will flip up and the shutter will open (see Figure 13.14).

5. Use one of the methods described below to remove dust and grime from your sensor. Be careful not to accidentally switch the power off or open the Compact Flash card or battery compartment doors as you work. If that happens, the shutter may be damaged if it closes onto your cleaning tool.

6. When you're finished, turn the power off, replace your lens, and switch your camera back on.

Figure 13.14
With the shutter open and the mirror locked up, you can commence cleaning the exposed sensor.

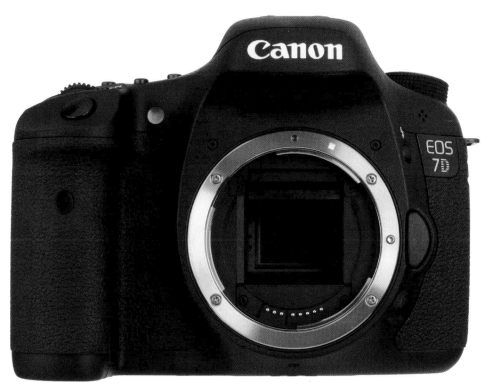

Air Cleaning

Your first attempts at cleaning your sensor should always involve gentle blasts of air. Many times, you'll be able to dislodge dust spots, which will fall off the sensor and, with luck, out of the mirror box. Attempt one of the other methods only when you've already tried air cleaning and it didn't remove all the dust.

Here are some tips for doing air cleaning:

- **Use a clean, powerful air bulb.** Your best bet is bulb cleaners designed for the job, like the Giottos Rocket. Smaller bulbs, like those air bulbs with a brush attached sometimes sold for lens cleaning or weak nasal aspirators, may not provide sufficient air or a strong enough blast to do much good.

- **Hold the EOS 7D upside down.** Then look up into the mirror box as you squirt your air blasts, increasing the odds that gravity will help pull the expelled dust downward, away from the sensor. You may have to use some imagination in positioning yourself. (See Figure 13.15.)

- **Never use air canisters.** The propellant inside these cans can permanently coat your sensor if you tilt the can while spraying. It's not worth taking a chance.

- **Avoid air compressors.** Super-strong blasts of air are likely to force dust under the sensor filter.

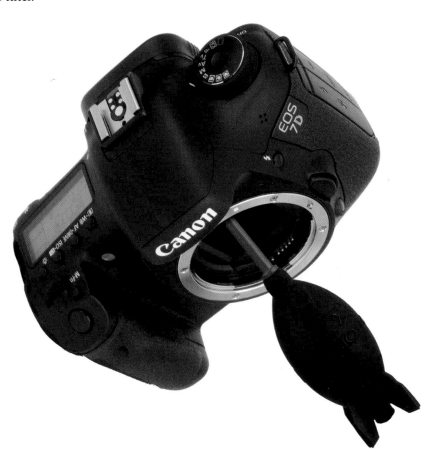

Figure 13.15
Hold the camera upside down when cleaning to allow dust to fall out.

Brush Cleaning

If your dust is a little more stubborn and can't be dislodged by air alone, you may want to try a brush, charged with static electricity, that can pick off dust spots by electrical attraction. One good, but expensive, option is the Sensor Brush sold at www.visible-dust.com. A cheaper version can be purchased at www.copperhillimages.com. You need a 16mm version, like the one shown in Figure 13.16, that can be stroked across the short dimension of your 7D's sensor.

Figure 13.16
A proper brush, preferably with a grounding strap to eliminate static electricity, is required for dusting off your sensor.

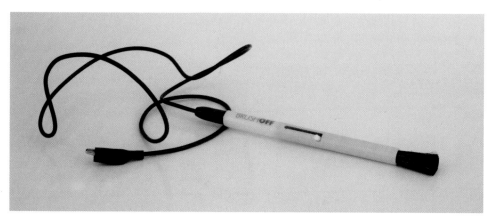

Ordinary artist's brushes are much too coarse and stiff and have fibers that are tangled or can come loose and settle on your sensor. A good sensor brush's fibers are resilient and described as "thinner than a human hair." Moreover, the brush has a wooden handle that reduces the risk of static sparks. Check out my *Digital SLR Pro Secrets* book if you want to make a sensor brush (or sensor swabs) yourself.

Brush cleaning is done with a dry brush by gently swiping the surface of the sensor filter with the tip. The dust particles are attracted to the brush particles and cling to them. You should clean the brush with compressed air before and after each use, and store it in an appropriate air-tight container between applications to keep it clean and dust-free. Although these special brushes are expensive, one should last you a long time.

Liquid Cleaning

Unfortunately, you'll often encounter really stubborn dust spots that can't be removed with a blast of air or flick of a brush. These spots may be combined with some grease or a liquid that causes them to stick to the sensor filter's surface. In such cases, liquid cleaning with a swab may be necessary. During my first clumsy attempts to clean my own sensor, I accidentally got my blower bulb tip too close to the sensor, and some sort of deposit from the tip of the bulb ended up on the sensor. I panicked until I discovered that liquid cleaning did a good job of removing whatever it was that took up residence on my sensor.

You can make your own swabs out of pieces of plastic (some use fast food restaurant knives, with the tip cut at an angle to the proper size) covered with a soft cloth or Pec-Pad, as shown in Figures 13.17 and 13.18. However, if you've got the bucks to spend, you can't go wrong with good-quality commercial sensor cleaning swabs, such as those sold by Photographic Solutions, Inc. (www.photosol.com/swabproduct.htm).

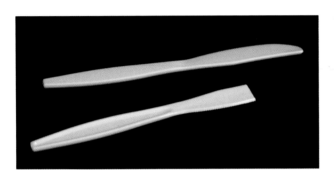

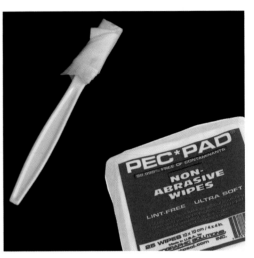

Figure 13.17 You can make your own sensor swab from a plastic knife that's been truncated.

Figure 13.18 Carefully wrap a Pec-Pad around the swab.

You want a sturdy swab that won't bend or break so you can apply gentle pressure to the swab as you wipe the sensor surface. Use the swab with methanol (as pure as you can get it, particularly medical grade; other ingredients can leave a residue), or the Eclipse solution also sold by Photographic Solutions. Eclipse is actually quite a bit purer than even medical-grade methanol. A couple drops of solution should be enough, unless you have a spot that's extremely difficult to remove. In that case, you may need to use extra solution on the swab to help "soak" the dirt off.

Once you overcome your nervousness at touching your 7D's sensor, the process is easy. You'll wipe continuously with the swab in one direction, then flip it over and wipe in the other direction. You need to completely wipe the entire surface; otherwise, you may end up depositing the dust you collect at the far end of your stroke. Wipe; don't rub.

If you want a close-up look at your sensor to make sure the dust has been removed, you can pay $50-$100 for a special sensor "microscope" with an illuminator. (See Figure 13.19.) Or, you can do like I do and work with a plain old Carson MiniBrite PO-25 illuminated 3X magnifier, as seen in Figure 13.20. (Older packaging and ads may call this a 2X magnifier, but it's actually a 3X unit.) It has a built-in LED and, held a few inches from the lens mount with the lens removed from your 7D, provides a sharp, close-up view of the sensor, with enough contrast to reveal any dust that remains.

Figure 13.19
This SensorKlear magnifier provides a view of your sensor as you work.

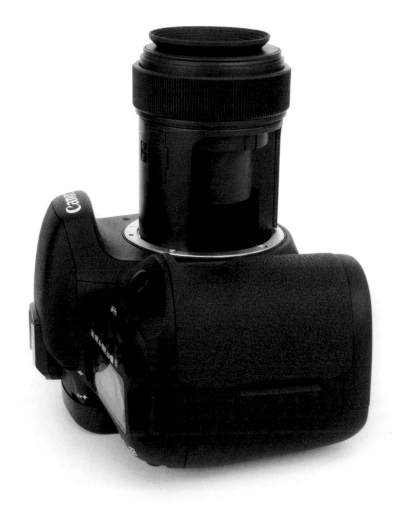

Figure 13.20
An illuminated magnifier like this Carson MiniBrite PO-25 can be used as a 'scope to view your sensor.

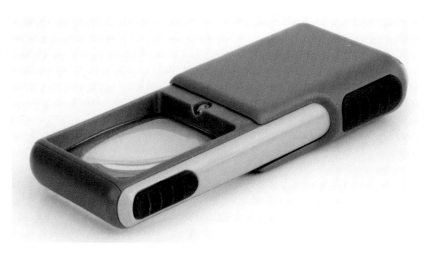

Tape Cleaning

There are people who absolutely swear by the tape method of sensor cleaning. The concept seems totally wacky, and I have never tried it personally, so I can't say with certainty that it either does or does not work. In the interest of completeness, I'm including it here. I can't give you a recommendation, so if you have problems, please don't blame me. The EOS 7D is still too new to have generated any reports of users accidentally damaging the anti-dust coating on the sensor filter using this method.

Tape cleaning works by applying a layer of Scotch Brand Magic Tape to the sensor. This is a minimally sticky tape that some of the tape cleaning proponents claim contains no adhesive. I did check this out with 3M, and can say that Magic Tape certainly *does* contain an adhesive. The question is whether the adhesive comes off when you peel back the tape, taking any dust spots on your sensor with it. The folks who love this method claim there is no residue. There have been reports from those who don't like the method that residue is left behind. This is all anecdotal evidence, so you're pretty much on your own in making the decision whether to try out the tape cleaning method.

Glossary

Here are some terms you might encounter while reading this book or working with your Canon EOS 7D.

additive primary colors The red, green, and blue hues that are used alone or in combinations to create all other colors that you capture with a digital camera, view on a computer monitor, or work with in an image-editing program, such as Photoshop. *See also* CMYK color model.

Adobe RGB One of two color space choices offered by the Canon EOS 7D. Adobe RGB is an expanded color space useful for commercial and professional printing, and it can reproduce a larger number of colors. Canon recommends against using this color space if your images will be displayed primarily on your computer screen or output by your personal printer. *See also* sRGB.

AEB Automatic exposure bracketing takes a series of pictures at different exposure increments to improve the chances of producing one picture that is perfectly exposed.

ambient lighting Diffuse, non-directional lighting that doesn't appear to come from a specific source but, rather, bounces off walls, ceilings, and other objects in the scene when a picture is taken.

analog/digital converter The electronics built into a camera that convert the analog information captured by the 7D's sensor into digital bits that can be stored as an image bitmap.

angle of view The area of a scene that a lens can capture, determined by the focal length of the lens. Lenses with a shorter focal length have a wider angle of view than lenses with a longer focal length.

anti-alias A process that smoothes the look of rough edges in images (called *jaggies* or *staircasing*) by adding partially transparent pixels along the boundaries of diagonal lines that are merged into a smoother line by our eyes. *See also* jaggies.

aperture value (aperture-priority) A camera setting that allows you to specify the lens opening or f/stop that you want to use, with the camera selecting the required shutter speed automatically based on its light meter reading. This setting is represented by the abbreviation Av on the 7D's Mode Dial. *See also* shutter value.

artifact A type of noise in an image, or an unintentional image component produced in error by a digital camera during processing, usually caused by the JPEG compression process in digital cameras.

aspect ratio The proportions of an image as printed, displayed on a monitor, or captured by a digital camera.

autofocus A camera setting that allows the Canon EOS 7D to choose the correct focus distance for you, based on the contrast of an image (the image will be at maximum contrast when in sharp focus). The camera can be set for One-Shot (generically known as *single autofocus*, in which the lens is not focused until the shutter release is partially depressed), AI Servo (known as *continuous autofocus,* in which the lens refocuses constantly as you frame and reframe the image), or AI AF, which allows the camera to switch back and forth between One-Shot and AI Servo based on subject movement. You can choose the focus point or zone used to calculate autofocus, or allow the camera to select the point for you.

backlighting A lighting effect produced when the main light source is located behind the subject. Backlighting can be used to create a silhouette effect, or to illuminate translucent objects. *See also* front lighting and sidelighting.

barrel distortion A lens defect that causes straight lines at the top or side edges of an image to bow outward into a barrel shape. *See also* pincushion distortion.

blooming An image distortion caused when a photosite in an image sensor has absorbed all the photons it can handle so that additional photons reaching that pixel overflow to affect surrounding pixels, producing unwanted brightness and overexposure around the edges of objects.

blur To soften an image or part of an image by throwing it out of focus, or by allowing it to become soft due to subject or camera motion. Blur can also be applied in an image-editing program.

bokeh A term derived from the Japanese word for blur, which describes the aesthetic qualities of the out-of-focus parts of an image. Some lenses produce "good" bokeh and others offer "bad" bokeh. Some lenses produce uniformly illuminated out-of-focus discs. Others produce a disc that has a bright edge and a dark center, producing a "doughnut" effect, which is the worst from a bokeh standpoint. Lenses that generate a bright center that fades to a darker edge are favored, because their bokeh allows the circle of confusion to blend more smoothly with the surroundings. The bokeh characteristics of a lens are most important when you're using selective focus (say, when shooting a portrait) to deemphasize the background, or when shallow depth-of-field is a given because you're working with a macro lens, a long telephoto, or a wide-open aperture. *See also* circle of confusion.

bounce lighting Light bounced off a reflector, including ceiling and walls, to provide a soft, natural-looking light.

bracketing Taking a series of photographs of the same subject at different settings, including exposure and white balance, to help ensure that one setting will be the correct one. The Canon EOS 7D allows you to choose the order in which bracketed settings are applied, or bracket sequence.

buffer The digital camera's internal memory where an image is stored immediately after it is taken until it can be written to the camera's non-volatile (semi-permanent) memory or a memory card.

burst mode The digital camera's equivalent of the film camera's motor drive, used to take multiple shots within a short period of time, with each shot stored in a memory buffer temporarily before writing it to the media.

calibration A process used to correct for the differences in the output of a printer or monitor when compared to the original image. Once you've calibrated your scanner, monitor, and/or your image editor, the images you see on the screen more closely represent what you'll get from your printer, even though calibration is never perfect.

Camera Raw A plug-in included with Photoshop and Photoshop Elements that can manipulate the unprocessed images captured by digital cameras, such as the Canon EOS 7D's CR2 files. The latest versions of this module can also work with JPEG and TIFF images.

camera shake Movement of the camera, aggravated by slower shutter speeds, which produces a blurred image. You can minimize camera shake by using a lens with built-in image stabilization.

CCD *See* charge-coupled device (CCD).

center-weighted meter A light-measuring device that emphasizes the area in the middle of the frame when calculating the correct exposure for an image. *See also* spot meter.

charge-coupled device (CCD) A type of solid-state sensor that captures the image used in scanners and digital cameras. *See also* complementary metal-oxide semiconductor (CMOS).

chromatic aberration An image defect, often seen as green or purple fringing around the edges of an object, caused by a lens failing to focus all colors of a light source at the same point. *See also* fringing.

circle of confusion A term applied to the fuzzy discs produced when a point of light is out of focus. The circle of confusion is not a fixed size. The viewing distance and amount of enlargement of the image determine whether we see a particular spot on the image as a point or as a disc. *See also* bokeh.

close-up lens A lens add-on that allows you to take pictures at a distance that is less than the closest-focusing distance of the lens alone.

CMOS *See* complementary metal-oxide semiconductor (CMOS).

CMYK color model A way of defining all possible colors in percentages of cyan, magenta, yellow, and frequently, black. (K represents black, to differentiate it from blue in the RGB color model.) Black is added to improve rendition of shadow detail. CMYK is commonly used for printing (both on press and with your inkjet or laser color printer).

color correction Changing the relative amounts of color in an image to produce a desired effect, typically a more accurate representation of those colors. Color correction can fix faulty color balance in the original image, or compensate for the deficiencies of the inks used to reproduce the image.

complementary metal-oxide semiconductor (CMOS) A method for manufacturing a type of solid-state sensor that captures an image; used in scanners and digital cameras such as the EOS 7D and other cameras from Canon.

compression Reducing the size of a file by encoding using fewer bits of information to represent the original. Some compression schemes, such as JPEG, operate by discarding some image information, while others, such as RAW, preserve all the detail in the original, discarding only redundant data.

continuous autofocus An automatic focusing setting (AI Servo) in which the camera constantly refocuses the image as you frame the picture. This setting is often the best choice for moving subjects. *See also* single autofocus.

contrast The range between the lightest and darkest tones in an image. A high-contrast image is one in which the shades fall at the extremes of the range between white and black. In a low-contrast image, the tones are closer together.

Custom Functions (C.Fn) A group of settings you can make to specify how the EOS 7D behaves, such as the function of certain controls, electronic flash features, and other customizable attributes.

dedicated flash An electronic flash unit, such as the Canon 580EX II Speedlite, designed to work with the automatic exposure features of a specific camera.

depth-of-field A distance range in a photograph in which all included portions of an image are at least acceptably sharp. With the Canon EOS 7D, you can see the available depth-of-field at the taking aperture by pressing the Depth-of-field preview button, or estimate the range by viewing the depth-of-field scale found on many lenses.

diaphragm An adjustable component, similar to the iris in the human eye, that can open and close to provide specific-sized lens openings, or f/stops, and thus control the amount of light reaching the sensor or film.

diffuse lighting Soft, low-contrast lighting.

digital processing chip A solid-state device found in digital cameras (such as the EOS 7D's twin DIGIC 4 modules) that's in charge of applying the image algorithms to the raw picture data prior to storage on the memory card.

diopter A value used to represent the magnification power of a lens, calculated as the reciprocal of a lens's focal length (in meters). Diopters are most often used to represent the optical correction used in a viewfinder to adjust for limitations of the photographer's eyesight, and to describe the magnification of a close-up lens attachment.

equivalent focal length A digital camera's focal length translated into the corresponding values for a 35mm film camera. This value can be calculated for lenses used with the Canon EOS 7D by multiplying by 1.6.

evaluative metering One system of exposure calculation used by the EOS 7D that looks at many different segments of an image to determine the brightest and darkest portions.

exchangeable image file format (Exif) Developed to standardize the exchange of image data between hardware devices and software. A variation on JPEG, Exif is used by most digital cameras, and includes information such as the date and time a photo was taken, the camera settings, resolution, amount of compression, and other data.

Exif *See* exchangeable image file format (Exif).

exposure The amount of light allowed to reach the film or sensor, determined by the intensity of the light, the amount admitted by the iris of the lens, the length of time determined by the shutter speed, and the ISO sensitivity setting for the sensor.

exposure values (EV) EV settings are a way of adding or decreasing exposure without the need to reference f/stops or shutter speeds. For example, if you tell your camera to add +1EV, it will provide twice as much exposure by using a larger f/stop, slower shutter speed, or both.

fill lighting In photography, lighting is used to illuminate shadows. Reflectors or additional incandescent lighting or electronic flash can be used to brighten shadows. One common technique for outdoors is to use the camera's flash as a fill.

filter In photography, a device that fits over the lens, changing the light in some way. In image editing, a feature that changes the pixels in an image to produce blurring, sharpening, and other special effects. Photoshop includes several interesting filter effects, including Lens Blur and Photo Filters.

flash sync The timing mechanism that ensures that an internal or external electronic flash fires at the correct time during the exposure cycle. A digital SLR's flash sync speed is the highest shutter speed or range of speeds that can be used with flash, ordinarily 30 seconds to 1/250th of a second with the Canon EOS 7D. *See also* front-curtain sync and rear-curtain sync.

focal length The distance between the film and the optical center of the lens when the lens is focused on infinity, usually measured in millimeters.

focal plane An imaginary line, perpendicular to the optical access, that passes through the focal point forming a plane of sharp focus when the lens is set at infinity. A focal plane indicator is etched into the Canon EOS 7D at the right side of the pentaprism.

focus tracking The ability of the automatic focus feature of a camera to change focus as the distance between the subject and the camera changes. One type of focus tracking is *predictive,* in which the mechanism anticipates the motion of the object being focused on, and adjusts the focus to suit.

format To erase a memory card and prepare it to accept files.

fringing A chromatic aberration that produces fringes of color around the edges of subjects, caused by a lens's inability to focus the various wavelengths of light onto the same spot. Purple fringing is especially troublesome with backlit images.

front-curtain sync (first-curtain sync) The default kind of electronic flash synchronization technique, originally associated with focal plane shutters, which consists of a traveling set of curtains, including a *front curtain* (1st curtain in the 7D's menus), which opens to reveal the film or sensor, and a *rear curtain* (2nd curtain in the 7D's menus), which follows at a distance determined by shutter speed to conceal the film or sensor at the conclusion of the exposure. For a flash picture to be taken, the entire sensor must be exposed at one time to the brief flash exposure, so the image is exposed after the front curtain has reached the other side of the focal plane, but before the rear curtain begins to move. Front-curtain sync causes the flash to fire at the beginning of this period when the shutter is completely open, in the instant that the first curtain of the focal plane shutter finishes its movement across the film or sensor plane. With slow shutter speeds, this feature can create a blur effect from the ambient light, showing as patterns that follow a moving subject, with the subject shown sharply frozen at the beginning of the blur trail. *See also* rear-curtain sync.

front lighting Illumination that comes from the direction of the camera. *See also* back-lighting and sidelighting.

f/stop The relative size of the lens aperture, which helps determine both exposure and depth-of-field. The larger the f/stop number, the smaller the f/stop itself.

graduated filter A lens attachment with variable density or color from one edge to another. A graduated neutral-density filter, for example, can be oriented so the neutral-density portion is concentrated at the top of the lens's view with the less dense or clear portion at the bottom, thus reducing the amount of light from a very bright sky while not interfering with the exposure of the landscape in the foreground. Graduated filters can also be split into several color sections to provide a color gradient between portions of the image.

gray card A piece of cardboard or other material with a standardized 18-percent reflectance. Gray cards can be used as a reference for determining correct exposure or for setting white balance.

HDMI (High Definition Multimedia Interface) An interface for transmitting audio and video information between a source, such as a digital camera or television tuner, to an output device, such as a high definition television (HDTV) monitor.

high contrast A wide range of density in a print, negative, or other image.

High dynamic range (HDR) imaging A technique for expanding the tonal range of an image by combining several bracketed exposures, which, together, contain detail in both the darkest shadows and brightest highlights of an image.

highlights The brightest parts of an image containing detail.

histogram A kind of chart showing the relationship of tones in an image using a series of 256 vertical bars, one for each brightness level. A histogram chart, such as the one the Canon EOS 7D can display during picture review, typically looks like a curve with one or more slopes and peaks, depending on how many highlight, midtone, and shadow tones are present in the image. The 7D can also display separate histograms for the red, green, and blue channels of an image.

hot shoe A mount on top of a camera used to hold an electronic flash, while providing an electrical connection between the flash and the camera.

hyperfocal distance A point of focus where everything from half that distance to infinity appears to be acceptably sharp. For example, if your lens has a hyperfocal distance of four feet, everything from two feet to infinity would be sharp. The hyperfocal distance varies by the lens and the aperture in use. If you know you'll be making a grab shot without warning, sometimes it is useful to turn off your camera's automatic focus, and set the lens to infinity, or, better yet, the hyperfocal distance. Then, you can snap off a quick picture without having to wait for the lag that occurs with most digital cameras as their autofocus locks in.

image rotation A feature that senses whether a picture was taken in horizontal or vertical orientation. That information is embedded in the picture file so that the camera and compatible software applications can automatically display the image in the correct orientation.

image stabilization A technology that compensates for camera shake, usually by adjusting the position of the camera sensor (with some vendors) or, in the case of Canon, lens elements that shift in response to movements of the camera.

incident light Light measured as it falls on a surface, as opposed to light reflected from that surface.

International Organization for Standardization (ISO) A governing body that provides standards used to represent film speed, or the equivalent sensitivity of a digital camera's sensor. Digital camera sensitivity is expressed in ISO settings.

interpolation A technique digital cameras, scanners, and image editors use to create new pixels required whenever you resize or change the resolution of an image based on the values of surrounding pixels. Devices such as scanners and digital cameras can use interpolation to create pixels in addition to those actually captured, thereby increasing the apparent resolution or color information in an image.

ISO *See* International Organization for Standardization (ISO).

jaggies Staircasing effect of lines, most easily seen at large magnifications, that are not perfectly horizontal or vertical, caused by pixels that are too large to represent the line accurately. *See also* anti-alias.

JPEG Short for Joint Photographic Experts Group. A file "lossy" format that supports 24-bit color and reduces file sizes by selectively discarding image data. Digital cameras generally use JPEG compression to pack more images onto memory cards. You can select how much compression is used (and, therefore, how much information is thrown away) by selecting from among the Standard, Fine, Super Fine, or other quality settings offered by your camera. *See also* RAW.

Kelvin (K) A unit of measure based on the absolute temperature scale in which absolute zero is zero; it's used to describe the color of continuous-spectrum light sources and applied when setting white balance. For example, daylight has a color temperature of about 5,500K, and a tungsten lamp has a temperature of about 3,400K.

lag time The interval between when the shutter is pressed and when the picture is actually taken. During that span, the camera may be automatically focusing and calculating exposure. With digital SLRs like the Canon EOS 7D, lag time is generally very short; with non-dSLRs, the elapsed time easily can be one second or more.

latitude The range of camera exposure that produces acceptable images with a particular digital sensor or film.

lens flare A feature of conventional photography that is both a bane and a creative outlet. It is an effect produced by the reflection of light internally among elements of an optical lens. Bright light sources within or just outside the field of view cause lens flare. Flare can be reduced by the use of coatings on the lens elements or with the use of lens hoods. Photographers sometimes use the effect as a creative technique, and Photoshop includes a filter that lets you add lens flare at your whim.

lighting ratio The proportional relationship between the amount of light falling on the subject from the main light and other lights, expressed in a ratio, such as 3:1.

Live View The ability of some Canon cameras, including the 7D, to provide a real-time preview image, as seen by the sensor, on the rear-panel color LCD, achieved by flipping up the mirror and opening the shutter.

lossless compression An image-compression scheme that preserves all image detail. When the image is decompressed, it is identical to the original version.

lossy compression An image-compression scheme, such as JPEG, that creates smaller files by discarding image information, which can affect image quality.

macro lens A lens that provides continuous focusing from infinity to extreme close-ups, often to a reproduction ratio of 1:2 (half life-size) or 1:1 (life-size).

maximum burst The number of frames that can be exposed at the current settings until the buffer fills. See also *burst mode.*

midtones Parts of an image with tones of an intermediate value, usually in the 25 to 75 percent brightness range. Many image-editing features allow you to manipulate mid-tones independently from the highlights and shadows.

mirror lock-up The ability of the 7D to flip up its mirror to reduce vibration prior to taking the photo and to allow access to the sensor for cleaning.

neutral color A color in which red, green, and blue are present in equal amounts, producing a gray.

neutral-density filter A gray camera filter that reduces the amount of light entering the camera without affecting the colors.

noise In an image, pixels with randomly distributed color values. Noise in digital photographs tends to be the product of low-light conditions and long exposures, particularly when you've set your camera to an ISO rating higher than about ISO 1600.

noise reduction A technology used to cut down on the amount of random information in a digital picture, usually caused by long exposures at increased sensitivity ratings. In the Canon EOS 7D, noise reduction is automatically applied for long exposures, and it involves the camera automatically taking a second blank/dark exposure at the same settings that contain only noise, and then using the blank photo's information to cancel out the noise in the original picture. Although the process is very quick, it does double the amount of time required to take the photo. Noise reduction can be switched off if you'd rather not use it.

normal lens A lens that makes the image in a photograph appear in a perspective that is like that of the original scene, typically with a field of view of roughly 45 degrees.

overexposure A condition in which too much light reaches the film or sensor, producing a dense negative or a very bright/light print, slide, or digital image.

pincushion distortion A type of lens distortion in which lines at the top and side edges of an image are bent inward, producing an effect that looks like a pincushion. *See also* barrel distortion.

polarizing filter A filter that forces light, which normally vibrates in all directions, to vibrate only in a single plane, reducing or removing the specular reflections from the surface of objects. Such filters tend to increase the contrast between colors and make blue skies more dramatic, most strongly when the sun is located at a 90-degree angle from the direction the camera is pointed.

RAW An image file format, such as the CR2 format in the Canon EOS 7D, which includes all the unprocessed information captured by the camera after conversion to digital form. RAW files are very large compared to JPEG files and must be processed by a special program such as Canon Digital Photo Pro or Adobe's Camera Raw filter after being downloaded from the camera.

rear-curtain sync (second-curtain sync) An optional kind of electronic flash synchronization technique, originally associated with focal plane shutters, which consists of a traveling set of curtains, including a *front (first) curtain* (which opens to reveal the film or sensor) and a *rear (second) curtain* (which follows at a distance determined by shutter speed to conceal the film or sensor at the conclusion of the exposure). For a flash picture to be taken, the entire sensor must be exposed at one time to the brief flash exposure, so the image is exposed after the front curtain has reached the other side of the focal plane, but before the rear curtain begins to move. Rear-curtain sync causes the flash to fire at the end of the exposure, a fraction of an instant before the second or rear curtain of the focal plane shutter begins to move. With slow shutter speeds, this feature can create a blur effect from the ambient light, showing as patterns that follow a moving subject with the subject shown sharply frozen at the end of the blur trail. If you were shooting a photo of The Flash, the superhero would appear sharp, with a ghostly trail behind him. *See also* front-curtain sync (first-curtain sync).

red-eye An effect from flash photography that appears to make a person's eyes glow red, or an animal's yellow or green. It's caused by light bouncing from the retina of the eye and is most pronounced in dim illumination (when the irises are wide open) and when the electronic flash is close to the lens and, therefore, prone to reflect directly back. Image editors can fix red-eye through cloning other pixels over the offending red or orange ones. The 7D has a red-eye reduction mode that provides a burst of light that causes the irises to close down (if the subject is looking at the camera), reducing the effect.

RGB color A color model that represents the three colors—red, green, and blue—used by devices such as scanners or monitors to reproduce color. Photoshop works in RGB mode by default, and even displays CMYK images by converting them to RGB.

saturation The purity of color; the amount by which a pure color is diluted with white or gray.

selective focus Choosing a lens opening that produces a shallow depth-of-field. Usually this is used to isolate a subject in portraits, close-ups, and other types of images, by causing most other elements in the scene to be blurred.

self-timer A mechanism that delays the opening of the shutter for some seconds after the release has been operated.

sensitivity A measure of the degree of response of a film or sensor to light, measured using the ISO setting.

shadow The darkest part of an image, represented on a digital image by pixels with low numeric values.

sharpening Increasing the apparent sharpness of an image by boosting the contrast between adjacent pixels that form an edge.

shutter In a conventional film camera, the shutter is a mechanism consisting of blades, a curtain, a plate, or some other movable cover that controls the time during which light reaches the film. Digital cameras may use actual mechanical shutters for the slower shutter speeds (less than 1/200th second) and an electronic shutter for higher speeds.

shutter preferred (shutter-priority) An exposure mode, represented by the letters Tv (Time Value) on the 7D's Mode Dial, in which you set the shutter speed and the camera determines the appropriate f/stop. *See also* aperture value.

sidelighting Applying illumination from the left or right sides of the camera. *See also* backlighting and front lighting.

single autofocus The autofocus mode in which the camera locks focus once when the shutter button is pressed halfway, and retains that focus point until the picture is taken or the button is released.

slave unit An accessory flash unit that supplements the main flash, usually triggered electronically when the slave senses the light output by the main unit, through radio waves, or through a pre-burst emitted by the camera's main flash unit.

slow sync An electronic flash synchronizing method that uses a slow shutter speed so that ambient light is recorded by the camera in addition to the electronic flash illumination. This allows the background to receive more exposure for a more realistic effect.

specular highlight Bright spots in an image caused by reflection of light sources, often from shiny surfaces.

spot meter An exposure system that concentrates on a small area in the image, represented by the circle in the center of the EOS 7D's viewfinder. *See also* center-weighted meter.

sRGB One of two color space choices available with the Canon EOS 7D. The sRGB setting is recommended for images that will be output locally on the user's own printer, as this color space matches that of the typical inkjet printer and a properly calibrated monitor fairly closely. *See also* Adobe RGB.

subtractive primary colors Cyan, magenta, and yellow, which are the printing inks that theoretically absorb all color and produce black. In practice, however, they generate a muddy brown, so black is added to preserve detail (especially in shadows). The combination of the three colors and black is referred to as CMYK. (K represents black, to differentiate it from blue in the RGB model.)

time exposure A picture taken by leaving the shutter open for a long period, usually more than one second. The camera is generally locked down with a tripod to prevent blur during the long exposure.

through-the-lens (TTL) A system of providing viewing and exposure calculation through the actual lens taking the picture.

tungsten light Light from ordinary room lamps and ceiling fixtures, as opposed to fluorescent illumination.

underexposure A condition in which too little light reaches the film or sensor, producing a thin negative, a dark slide, a muddy-looking print, or a dark digital image.

unsharp masking The process for increasing the contrast between adjacent pixels in an image, increasing sharpness, especially around edges.

vignetting Dark corners of an image, often produced by using a lens hood that is too small for the field of view, a lens that does not completely fill the image frame, or generated artificially using image-editing techniques.

white balance The adjustment of a digital camera to the color temperature of the light source. Interior illumination is relatively red; outdoor light is relatively blue. Digital cameras like the EOS 7D set correct white balance automatically or let you do it through menus. Image editors can often do some color correction of images that were exposed using the wrong white balance setting, especially when working with RAW files that contain the information originally captured by the camera before white balance was applied.

wireless flash Electronic flash controlled by electronic communications from the camera, a "master" flash, or a special flash transmitter, through a preflash signal, so that no physical connection between the camera and external flash units is required.

Index